Common Sense

Common Sense

A POLITICAL HISTORY

Sophia Rosenfeld

Harvard University Press

Cambridge, Massachusetts · London, England

2011

Library of Congress Cataloging-in-Publication Data

Rosenfeld, Sophia A.
Common sense : a political history / Sophia Rosenfeld.
p.   cm.
Includes bibliographical references and index.
ISBN 978-0-674-05781-4 (alk. paper)
1. Political science—History—18th century.   2. Paine, Thomas, 1737–1809. Common
sense.   3. United States—Politics and government—1775–1783.   4. France—Politics
and government—1789–1799.   5. Democracy—United States.   I. Title.
JA83.R724 2011
320.01'1—dc22   2010038504

Contents

Introduction   1

1. The Ghost of Common Sense
   London, 1688–1739   17

2. Everyman's Perception of the World
   Aberdeen, 1758–1770   56

3. The Radical Uses of *Bon Sens*
   Amsterdam, 1760–1775   90

4. Building a Common Sense Republic
   Philadelphia, 1776   136

5. Making War on Revolutionary Reason
   Paris, 1790–1792   181

6. Königsberg to New York
   The Fate of Common Sense in the Modern World   221

Notes   259

Acknowledgments   321

Index   325

Common Sense

Introduction

The familiar, precisely because it is familiar,
is for that very reason unknown.
G. W. F. Hegel, *Phenomenology of Spirit*

HOT THINGS CAN BURN YOU. Two plus two make four. Seeing is believing. Blue is different from black. A leopard cannot change its spots. If I am writing these words, I exist.

There are many reasons not to write a book about common sense, especially if you happen to be a historian. For one, common sense is, by definition, ahistorical terrain. In modern parlance, we sometimes use common sense to mean the basic human faculty that lets us make elemental judgments about everyday matters based on everyday, real-world experience (e.g., If you used your common sense, you would know the principles stated above!). Other times we mean the widely shared and seemingly self-evident conclusions drawn from this faculty, the truisms about which all sensible people agree without argument or even discussion, including principles of amount, difference, prudence, cause and effect. Either way, common sense is supposed to define that which is the common property of all humans regardless of the variance of time or space.[1]

If that is not problem enough, the tenets of common sense are ostensibly so banal, so taken for granted, that they generally go without saying. On the rare occasions when they are explicitly stated as such, it is, normally, only to counter perceived violations. The rest of the time, the speaker feels compelled to employ a preceding "of course" as a signal that he or she is stating the obvious and offering up a cliché rather than treating the interlocutor as childish or insane. Otherwise these presuppositions simply inhere in the ordinary words we use, forming the tacit backdrop to all our more conscious activities and thoughts and supporting us through daily life.[2] For historians, this makes for an amorphous subject indeed.

Moreover, when historians do consider common sense, they generally do so from a position of hostility; it is what social scientists see as their professional obligation to work against.[3] Philosophers may spend their days pondering its epistemological validity. But those who study the past typically interest themselves in common sense with the goal of undermining the authority of what passes for it today in the particular society in which they live and write. Do you think it is common sense that a family is made up of two parents of opposite sexes and their direct offspring? Historians looking backward, like anthropologists looking in other places, can show you that there is nothing natural or inevitable here, only culture that familiarity and indoctrination have rendered falsely commonsensical in feel. This is the message several decades' worth of readers have taken from Clifford Geertz's great essay "Common Sense as a Cultural System."[4]

There *is* a good reason, however, why historians might well want to pause and reflect on the history of common sense itself, including its evolving content, meanings, uses, and effects. That reason is the centrality of the very idea of common sense to modern political life and, especially, to democracy.

Consider for a moment Thomas Paine's eighteenth-century boast that common sense is firmly on the side of the people and thus opposed to the rulership of kings. We have no reason, even now, to accept this pairing of common sense and republican governance as anything more than wishful thinking or a rhetorical masterstroke on the part of Paine. For most of history, and indeed even in North America in early 1776, the opposite was surely the case; the direct rule of the people was deemed an obvious recipe for disorder, instability, and worse. It is worth noticing, though, that ever since the appearance of *Common Sense,* Paine's famous call to arms of that fateful year, Americans in particular, but ultimately exponents of democracy everywhere, have paid enormous lip service to the epistemological value of the collective, everyday, instinctive judgments of ordinary people. This is particularly true when it comes to matters of public life. Not only has the superiority of the many to the few become one of those basic, unchallengeable assumptions that, following the lead of political philosopher John Rawls, could now be said to constitute "democratic common sense."[5] Trust in common sense—meaning both the shared faculty of discernment and those few fundamental, inviolable principles with which everyone is acquainted and everyone agrees—has, in the context of contemporary democratic politics, itself become commonsensical. Politics has been recast (no matter the growing complexity of the world we inhabit) as the domain of simple, quotidian determinations and basic moral precepts, of truths that should be self-evident to all.

A few modern political philosophers, including Hannah Arendt, have gone even farther in contemplating this pairing and argued that common sense is the lifeblood of democracy. In the more than 200 years since Paine's little pamphlet came off the Philadelphia presses, the idea of common sense has repeatedly jumpstarted the participation of ordinary citizens, that is, those with no specialized knowledge or expertise, in the business of making political judgments. In turn, Arendt has proposed, the common sense produced by ordinary people engaging in unfettered discussion and debate should be thought of as constituting the shared ground on which a rich, communal political life—or real democracy—becomes possible.[6] For Arendt, writing in the wake of World War II but with the revolutionary era firmly in her thoughts, democracy is largely a result of habits of mind. And common sense becomes both the groundwork and the goal of any successful democratic regime.

Arendt thus leads us back to a basic historical question, albeit one framed in light of the present: How did this come to be? How—and with what lingering consequences—did common sense develop its special relationship in modern times with the kind of popular rule that we call democracy?

The answer requires stepping back, at least initially, well before the era of Paine. Both those basic assumptions that collectively go by the name of common sense and the very idea of common sense (or, allowing for limited conceptual variation and translation, good sense, common reason, *sensus communis, le sens commun, le bon sens, il senso comune, il buon senso, gemeiner Verstand,* and *gesunder Menschenverstand,* among other terms) have long and complex pasts, despite definitional claims to the contrary. This is a history that, in modern times, stretches across both sides of the northern Atlantic world. It is also a history that is closely bound up with the rise of new conceptions of popular sovereignty between the Glorious Revolution of the late seventeenth century and the French Revolution of the late eighteenth—or what is sometimes called, following Paine's own coinage, the "Age of Revolutions."[7]

In the course of those hundred or so years, the appeal to the "oracle" of common sense became, as Immanuel Kant was to complain less than a decade after the first printing of Paine's famous pamphlet, "one of the subtle discoveries of modern times, by means of which the most superficial ranter can safely enter the lists with the most thorough thinker and hold his own."[8] What Kant does not mention is that the story of the transformation of what was once a technical term of Aristotelian science into a democratizing rhetorical trope, or way of legitimizing the airing of nonexpert opinion in the public sphere, was itself made possible by a series of prior developments. It also produced rather extraordinary effects.

During the seventeenth century and for reasons that we will soon encounter, the idea gradually took hold in northern Europe that certain basic, largely unquestioned notions were common (in the sense of shared or jointly held) to common (in the sense of ordinary) people simply because of their common (again, shared) natures and, especially, experiences. That included observation of the world around them and communication with one another.[9] What is more, these elemental and universal judgments, even if arrived at without prior formal training and unprovable to the standards of science, offered an unusually high level of certainty or truth-value. They were maximally plausible without any further evidence or even discussion being required. Common sense was thus ripe for revalorization by the start of the eighteenth century as a new "epistemic authority" with the potential to go head to head with considerably more established forms of authority, including history, law, custom, faith, logic, and reason, especially when it came to matters of social or moral life.[10] This process occurred first in philosophy (much to Kant's dismay), where readers were encouraged to join a new alliance against the conspiracy by which ostensibly authoritative thinkers of the past had imposed their fantastical and misguided views on the world. (Think of the great English philosopher George Berkeley famously "siding with the mob" at the very start of the century.) Very soon thereafter, the appeal extended into the political sphere. There common sense provided a platform for a challenge to the existing political order in terms of people and ideas alike. It also led to a reformulation of the very domain labeled "politics." Indeed, in the context of profound challenges to traditional notions of both representation and regulation, this new way of thinking about thinking would cease to be simply one idea circulating among many and would become absorbed into the realm we still call common sense.

This is a largely unfamiliar story. In the standard liberal account, the triumph of "Reason," born of the Reformation and then the Scientific Revolution and heavily nurtured in the eighteenth century, plays the crucial role in the invention of the modern rights-bearing individual and the liberal constitutionalism on which democratic politics was eventually constructed. This explanation is itself a creation of the posthumously named Age of Enlightenment and has endured ever since, appropriating new ingredients (natural rights theory; resistance arguments aimed at sovereign authority; and the rise of capitalism, empire, and a new, educated middle class eager to see its needs reflected in "public opinion") in its wake. Even postmodernists tell the same tale and simply invert the moral, making the individual endowed with instrumental reason the source of the twentieth century's greatest tragedies rather than triumphs.

Yet democracy as it came into being in the late eighteenth century and exists to this day is actually a strange hybrid, combining a literal reading of the old idea of popular sovereignty, or the rule of "the people," with constitutionalism and representative government. The concept of a collective common sense—sometimes in alliance with the idea of the rational individual, sometimes in conflict—played a vital, if often tacit, role in the construction of democracy's popular, as opposed to constitutional, face. In this regard, common sense seems much like sympathy and natural sentiment, those now widely discussed eighteenth-century emotional inventions that were also seen as important sources of social bonds and communally produced truth in the Age of Revolutions. One might even be tempted to think of the role of common sense in similarly communitarian terms, especially given the emphasis on social cohesion that links the two. But what the concept of common sense in its modern form enabled is actually less a particular vision of how political order should be constituted than a new political style and a new approach to what politics is. The idea of common sense provided an epistemological foundation and justification for the populism that remains one of democracy's pillars (if we are to subscribe to Arendt's view), but also one of democracy's primary and perennial threats.[11]

What is populism? Political theorists do not agree on any one definition. Most often they describe it as a form of persuasion, available to any part of the modern political spectrum, which depends upon an appeal on behalf of those who feel left out of the political process for a more active public role for those same people.[12] Typically that means the mass of ordinary folks (the illusory "people" or "silent majority")[13] who believe that those who rule do not or cannot adequately represent their interests. One argument in defense of this position can be called historical or even nostalgic in form: that "the people" have in recent times been denied a power that they once freely and rightfully possessed. The other, though, is epistemological in that it depends on a particular understanding of human cognitive and moral capabilities. Here the standard claim is that "the people," when not being misled by false authorities, are in possession of a kind of infallible, instinctive sense of what is right and true, born of or nurtured by day-to-day experience in the world, that necessarily trumps the "expert" judgments and knowledge of a minority of establishment insiders. The latter category—the peddlers of dangerous nonsense—has by now expanded to include, varyingly, intellectuals, scientists, financiers, lawyers, journalists, power brokers, politicians, and other overeducated, elite pretenders, as well as foreigners and outliers of different kinds. Yet the point has remained the same. Not only do ordinary people (in the aggregate) know better, but politics itself will become simpler, clearer, and ultimately less contentious once all the complex speculation and obfuscating jargon associated with an exclusive political class are finally pushed aside and the *real* people are finally able to see it and tell it like it is.

In its best-known forms, this is a style of politics with its roots in the late nineteenth century, especially in the American Midwest and South. Michael Kazin, for example, while insisting on the tenacity of the populist idiom in U.S. history, opens his wise and witty *The Populist Persuasion: An American History* with the rise in the 1890s of the oxymoronicly titled People's Party of the Great Plains and Old Confederacy.[14] However, one of the arguments of the present book is that at least a century before anyone called him- or herself a populist, this plainspoken, angry, and ostensibly grassroots mode of persuasion was already taking form around the abstract notion of common sense. This happened in multiple Enlightenment outposts, among radicals and conservatives alike, and with mixed but lasting results for the practice of democratic politics.

In the course of the eighteenth century, faith in the collective, quotidian insight of "the people" (and not simply the rational capacity of the individual) emerged hand in hand with the idea of self-rule. Then, in Philadelphia in 1776, common sense buttressed the first modern experiments in generating widespread popular participation in governance. It remains a central element of the democratic creed. But precisely because the rule of the people is such a vague formulation and so difficult at times to reconcile with democracy's other, constitutional face—in America as well as elsewhere—common sense has, over time, become as much an antagonist to democracy's modern, establishment permutations as a form of support. Its other roots lie in the international Counter-Revolution provoked by events in France after 1789. And ever since, common sense has also served to underwrite challenges to established forms of legitimate rule, including democracies, in the name of the special kind of intuition belonging to the people. This, then, is meant to be a book about a slippery subject: the long, complex marriage between the populist (and now largely taken for granted) appeal to the people's common sense and the political form we call democracy.

Methodologically, this provides an intriguing challenge. Can one write the intellectual history of a fundamentally anti-intellectual construct that signifies an assortment of pre-rational, tacit suppositions? Some help in this endeavor can certainly come from the history of concepts, or *Begriffsgeschichte,* the branch of intellectual history concerned with tracing the sources and evolution of the mental and linguistic apparatuses used for classifying and categorizing our thoughts.[15] The revelation of lost distinctions, forgotten connections, and unfamiliar or contested uses of abstract terms, whether by ordinary people or philosophers, can be helpful in making sense of the roots of political innovation in the past. It can also aid in thinking about the limitations of our contemporary political vocabulary or considering how those same concepts might be used in the future. For this reason, we begin with an account of ancient Greek and Roman conceptions of what we now label common sense, keeping an eye on both discontinuities in signification and the lasting residue of antiquated meanings, especially in the realm of metaphors. However, in our larger endeavor we need also to look for aid to the social history of ideas (the area of history focused on the social context in which ideas take root); the social history of knowledge (the historical field concerned with the changing structures within which what counts as knowledge are produced, disseminated, and adapted to new uses); and, particularly, the history of what French historians call *les usages commun:* the evolving, everyday perceptions, beliefs, and social practices of whole social bodies in the past.[16] After all, concepts themselves take form and gain authority not only in texts but also in social life. Our ambition is ultimately to explore the relationship between, on the one hand, the development of the kind of articulate idea— common sense—that is the normal bread and butter of intellectual history and, on the other, the history of a set of beliefs that rarely gets articulated, despite its importance to religion, ethics, politics, and daily life, precisely because history has relegated it to this very same, naturalizing rubric. This is, in other words, intended to be a story about the discursive construction of the social (insofar as common sense is an imaginary common realm born directly out of daily interaction with the world and its inhabitants and specially oriented toward social life).

It is also designed as a story about the social construction of the discursive and conceptual.

The solution employed here is thus closest to what historians of science call "historical epistemology." Typically this method involves revealing the seemingly timeless organizing concepts of modern science and knowledge production—categories like truth or objectivity—not only as historical constructs but also as products of practices and values that now seem far removed from the domain we have set apart as "science." These include standards of beauty, manners, and morals, economic competition, the search for social status, institutional pressures, religious practices and ideals, and gender norms, as well as genres, discourses, and disciplines.[17] However, the focus of this study is ultimately on the links between what has long been considered most unchanging and invisible in the historical record—common sense as a way of knowing—and what is seemingly least—political life.[18] And as it turns out, the epistemological, emotional, and evidentiary foundations of politics are not always consonant with those of the natural, physical, or even social sciences. Even though the new science and common sense were close allies for most of the eighteenth century, sharing roots in a Protestant emphasis on direct, experiential knowledge, simplicity, and the value of "ordinary life,"[19] their proponents eventually parted ways, producing a schism whose implications have lasted to the present. Science increasingly became the domain of specialists for whom experience, without controlled experimentation backed up by technical training, was insufficient as a foundation for arriving at truths.[20] Political reasoning took a different turn. It is in tracing the ways by which an anti-expert ethos attached itself particularly to the realm of politics that a cultural and intellectual history of populism finally becomes possible.

Three large historical shifts that took varied forms in different locations across the Northern and Western hemispheres provide the framework for this story. And as befits a study of what the ancient Greeks called *endoxic* or commonplace knowledge,[21] these broad themes help bring to light the extraordinary paradoxes that run through the history of common sense and, indeed, of populism as a style of politics based on this imagined authority.

The first of these major developments is the phenomenal growth of cities, most of them clustered near the edges of the northern Atlantic or in some way connected to transoceanic commerce. London, Paris, Aberdeen, Philadelphia, Edinburgh, Amsterdam, Geneva, the Hague: these urban centers should be understood to be places of local knowledge, marked by a variety of particular and distinctive mores, religious cultures, legal regimes, political systems, businesses, institutions, class formations, languages, and even public spaces, from universities to printing shops to restaurants, in which ideas could take shape. They were also all, to different degrees depending on location and size, places of movement and exchange, borrowing, appropriation, and diffusion. Early modern cities on both sides of the Atlantic and Channel existed in a symbiotic relationship with smaller towns and the surrounding countryside, which they depended upon for food and labor. They also functioned in an increasingly international arena. Those cities whose fortunes were linked to the Atlantic in the eighteenth century were centers of communication as well as capital, places where terms, ideas, gossip, information, goods (including manuscripts, books, pamphlets, and journals), and people were frequent transplants from elsewhere. Tom Paine, with his wanderings between London, Philadelphia, and Paris, is simply a case in point. Even those who themselves never strayed far from their birthplaces, from slave laborers born in the New World to philosophers in Prussian university towns, were implicated in a global system of trade, an increasingly borderless Republic of Letters, interimperial conflict, or all of the above. This tension between stasis and flux, the local and the global, is critical to our story. Common sense, with its culturally specific inflections and universalizing pretensions, came into being as part and parcel of urban life across the eighteenth-century Atlantic world.[22]

The second critical substory here is the growth, within these cities big and small, Catholic, Protestant, and multireligious, of a new social type: the person who would set about to establish himself (and soon herself), whether through plays, novels, essays, newspaper articles, prints, pamphlets, philosophical tracts, lectures, or street corner harangues, as an independent spokesperson for the truth. *Gens de lettres* (men of letters) did not represent a particular social class or institutional type in the eighteenth century. We will meet representatives ranging from debauched libertines on the run from their noble families like the Marquis D'Argens, to impoverished country parsons-turned-moralizing professors like James Beattie, to the cantankerous artisan and radical pamphleteer Tom Paine himself. Their ranks increasingly expanded in the course of the century to encompass women, too; we will also encounter the French revolutionary playwright Olympe de Gouges, the English counter-revolutionary Hannah More, and the imagined female characters Mothers Gérard and Duchesne, though assumptions about the relationship between women and common sense were always complex. A good number of these figures had deep roots in Protestant culture, with its long tradition of valuing the quotidian over the exceptional and unmediated experience over higher reflection, whether as a vocation or in pursuit of salvation and truth in daily life. But by the eighteenth century, advocates of common sense could come to their positions from within orthodox Catholicism or from within a range of heterodoxies, from deism to full-blown atheism, too. The success of these figures in economic terms varied as well. A few even found themselves, as circumstances changed within their own lives, alternately holding formal positions in churches, universities, or governments, currying favor with private patrons, living off family income, and trying to survive by their pens alone.

What eighteenth-century *gens de lettres,* whether male or female, typically shared by virtue of the job they set out to do, was a need to articulate their own function in terms that were at once social and epistemological. Most had little obvious regard for common people, especially those who clearly did not belong to the literate public behind that other new (and extremely well-documented) enlightened social force, public opinion.[23] Even at the height of the American and French Revolutions, and even among those who would ultimately prove to be instrumental to its modern apotheosis, few expressed anything but horror at the notion of "democracy" insofar as it collapsed the distinction between themselves and the rabble. But against a backdrop of a crisis of authority that began with the Reformation and continued in the context of the new science, writers also tended increasingly in the eighteenth century to try to make a name for themselves as challengers to those with greater social status or intellectual heft, whether in the realm of philosophy, religion, or government. And in this pursuit, they increasingly found themselves pinning their own legitimacy to another abstract authority—"the people"—and making claims in defense of its nonintellectual and even anti-intellectual relationship to the world and, later, in its name. Ordinary people, male and female, were, of course, already active participants in the political landscape of urban Europe well before these enlightened *gens de lettres* deigned to celebrate commoners' capacity for practical and moral judgment. Popular collective action, including petitioning, food riots, tax protests, and rebellions, must be seen as a fundamental component of early modern political culture, a repeated challenge to rulers' exclusive claims to political sovereignty. But eighteenth-century social tensions—among people we might now call intellectuals; the authorities that they hoped both to emulate and to supersede; and the common folk that they often spoke for but usually despised and hardly knew—are fundamental to understanding the emergence of a politics dependent upon the idea of common sense. As they worked out their own precarious social positions, these spokesmen and women directly (if often inadvertently) paved the way for the transformation of ordinary people into active political participants, most prominently in the form of voters. They also helped initiate a transformation in politics itself: from what was perceived to be an esoteric and difficult science mastered only through long study into something that could be sold as the perfect match for ordinary people's basic perceptual and intellectual capacities and practicality.

Third, and perhaps most important, as befits a subject in the history of the conceptualization, production, and circulation of knowledge, this is a story about the relationship between censorship and what we call today "freedom of expression." The history of common sense is deeply intertwined with the history of experiments in the modification and lifting of formal regulations on thought, speech, and print that is so central to the liberal narrative of the eighteenth century on both sides of the Atlantic. The critical moments in this liberal account include the lapsing of the Licensing Act in England in the 1690s, one of the world's first great examples of the deregulation of the press; the carving out of small spaces of de facto toleration for heterodox ideas in certain continental Protestant cities, such as Amsterdam; the explicit enshrinement of free speech rights in the original American state constitutions and then the First Amendment to the American Constitution; and, finally, the similar establishment of free expression as a human right in the French Declaration of the Rights of Man of 1789 (which, though it ended in the restoration of draconian censorship laws under Napoleon, set the standard for the rest of Europe's democratic movements in the following century). But the history of common sense is also wrapped up in a contemporaneous story about the continued appeal of various and less explicit forms of censorship as a means to political stability, social harmony, and the efficacious determination of truth.

At moments when the formal law deeply circumscribed the realm of acceptable public pronouncement, including regulating and policing the printing and book trades, a claim to speak from common sense could—as in continental Europe for most of the eighteenth century—work as a way to challenge existing authority; it became a means to legitimize the articulation of political or religious dissent. However, in places where freedom of conscience combined with the deregulation of ideas had produced a dizzying and dismaying proliferation of diverse opinions and, indeed, something like a "knowledge explosion" comparable to the information overload of our Internet-driven world today, the appeal to common sense could work quite the opposite way. It frequently became a mechanism for trying informally, and without advocating a return to more heavy-handed kinds of regulation, to impose a minimal level of conformity (also known as self-censorship) necessary, it was thought, for the existence of secure communities and a secure, delimited realm of truth. For something to be pegged as absurd, incongruous, or nonsensical was, ideally, to disqualify it from serious consideration. But conversely, for something to be read as common sense was to produce, from the ground up, a foundation for subsequent knowledge and a shared sense of the common good, a counterweight to a dangerous relativism or skepticism. And it was to do so without imposing an orthodoxy from on high (though, as we will see, oaths of loyalty to new political bodies often temporarily complicated matters). No wonder the cultivation of common sense came to seem a political panacea, a way not only to construct an effective form of governance in the name of the people but, later, to ensure the peaceful survival of popular rule.

In recent years, a subset of legal scholars has admiringly drawn attention to the function of just such informal sets of rules, or what they call "social norms," in the present world. In many parts of our society, they claim, internalized norms work in lieu of formal law as effective forms of constraint, especially insofar as compliance brings a payoff in terms of economic well-being, status, or not calling attention to oneself, and violations or deviations produce social penalties. Such norms should be preserved and encouraged, these scholars argue, because these informal laws make it possible for the government to do less and, indeed, are often more efficient than state coercion in the controlling of behavior or the creation of social solidarity.[24] The cultivation of something like national common sense, especially through early schooling, would seem to fit this mold. But as the sociologist Pierre Bourdieu has reminded us, in the absence of regulative censorship, common sense can and has become a kind of structural or constitutive censorship. It has turned into an unspectacular instrument of domination that works constantly and silently not only to keep individuals in line but also to exclude outlying voices as either criminal or crazy and to limit the parameters of public debate.[25] The end result is a kind of conformity that can best be described as a depoliticization of the public realm, the replacement of legitimate intellectual strife with knee-jerk consensus.[26] Or so its chief advocates, from the great early newspapermen Joseph Addison and Richard Steele in early eighteenth-century London to the unemployed refractory priests who composed cheap royalist propaganda during the first years of the French Revolution in Paris, hoped. Ultimately the story of the changing laws concerned with the regulation of dissent is critical to the writing of any history of common sense, from its origins to its consequences.

In light of these larger historical phenomena, what quickly becomes clear is that nothing about common sense is, or has been, exactly what it seems at first glance. Common sense may (still) conjure up something universal, permanent, unassailable, nonideological, and rooted in the ordinary experience of everyone, a kind of infallible wisdom of the heartland. That is, of course, how it is used today by politicians, pundits, and advertisers alike, who typically set it in opposition to complexity, expertise, inside knowledge, urbanity, jargon, conflict, partisanship, and debate. But examined historically, it becomes apparent not only that common sense's tenets are culturally and temporally variable in content. What gets counted as common sense is also never really fully consensual even in its time.

After all, common sense tends to be defined and reinforced—despite its rhetorical associations with "savages," "natural men," laborers, farmers, and others untainted by politics or fancy educations—by elites clustered in cities and with access to print, a kind of mediation it should hardly require. It also works in practice to create new forms of exclusion just as much as interclass solidarity or identity. For common sense almost always exists in contrast to other views perceived as superstitious, marginal, or deluded, on the one hand, or overly abstract, specialized, or dogmatic, on the other. Indeed, the tenets of common sense themselves often point in conflicting directions and reinforce conflicting views. (Consider the multiple, opposing conclusions that might be effectively drawn from the banality "A leopard cannot change its spots" with which we began.) This is why we cannot be surprised that common sense is typically evoked and held up as authoritative only at moments of crisis in other forms of legitimacy. Revolutions, which, by definition, result in divided loyalties and the upending of the rules to multiple domains at once, are a case in point. Otherwise common sense does not need to call attention to itself.[27]

What this means, then, is that claims about common sense are, in public life, almost always polemical: statements about consensus and certainty used to particular, partisan, and destabilizing effect. Rather than end conflicts, the evocation of common sense just as often brings about new ones, becoming—regardless of its advocates' fervent claims of universality and moderation—a pivot around which even violent disagreements can turn. Common sense, as a presumed form of knowledge, cannot be divorced from power or protest. Why does this matter? It matters because the same tensions or paradoxes are at the heart of the populist response to the unfulfilled promise of democracy even today.

In the end, this study should be approached as an exercise in philosophical history.[28] That means the goal is to discover not only what happened in the past but also whether Arendt was right. Is it really common sense, born of the quotidian experiences and social interactions of ordinary people, that both makes democracy possible and sustains it? And if so, at what price? The pages that follow are intended as one historian's answer.

CHAPTER 1

The Ghost of Common Sense

London, 1688–1739

And all henceforth, who murder Common-Sense,
Learn from these Scenes that tho' Success you boast,
You shall at last be haunted with her Ghost.

Henry Fielding, *Pasquin*

OUR STORY BEGINS with a disappearance of sorts. In 1736, in a popular farce entitled *Pasquin,* the great English playwright Henry Fielding announced the untimely end of one Queen Common Sense, the erstwhile ruler of the world. Her murder, as Fielding explained it, was the product of a conspiracy that went to the very heart of modern life: she had been done in by the combined forces of religion, medicine, and law. But in Fielding's telling, this disappearance came with a twist. For common sense promised to haunt the future. In her new, apparitional form, she would—like many of the great forces of history—be invisible to the naked eye, at least on a regular basis.[1] Yet she would also be impossible to ignore. It is with this death and ghostly reappearance in early eighteenth-century London, in the wake of the particular kind of liberalism produced by the English Revolution of 1688, that the modern history of common sense takes off.

For ironically, at just the moment of her presumed demise, common sense assumed the multiple and resolutely political faces that she has continued to wear to this day. At the start of the new century, she became, in refined London circles, an extralegal means of defining the boundaries of acceptable discourse and behavior and a potential foundation for a new kind of self-regulating community. Very soon after, she was transformed into an ideological weapon that helped fuel an extra-parliamentary political culture built around permanent opposition and dissent. Finally, despite all the strategic tears over her disappearance, she became the ingrained and seemingly commonsensical authority figure that we still today hardly think about except to agree, de facto, that she, or it, is a force for the good. The apotheosis of the ghost of common sense, in the age of Fielding, marks a first and important chapter in the story of what made possible a series of revolutions across the eighteenth-century Atlantic world and then the rise of modern democratic regimes in all their contradictions.

To begin, one could, of course, back up much further than the Augustan Age and travel much farther afield than London. Common sense is a very old term. In a formulation that proved to have extraordinary staying power, Aristotle suggested as early as the fourth century B.C. that not only does every human come endowed with the five basic senses with which we are familiar: vision, hearing, taste, smell, and touch. The human subject also possesses a kind of central or "common" sense *(koinè aisthèsis),* at the point of intersection of all the rest, that has the primary function of comparing and coordinating the impressions received by each of them—and thus of allowing certain minimal judgments about sense objects to occur independent of reason. As Aristotle explained it in the third book of *De Anima,* this faculty was responsible for several discrete mental tasks. It gave humans the ability to perceive "common sensibles": motion, rest, number, figure, size, and other qualities typically perceived by more than one sense at once. It made humans aware that they were engaged in the act of perception itself. And most important for our purposes, this super sense performed the dual job of determining the unity of sense objects and of discriminating between them. In other words, it was the common sense that allowed humans to figure out that what is simultaneously sweet and white is sugar but also that sweet and white are different kinds of sensible qualities and sugar is ultimately different from salt.[2]

This understanding of humans' mental capacity persisted in psychology, medicine, and aesthetics through the medieval and early modern eras, in Arabic, Hebrew, Latin, and eventually French and English texts alike, though with certain important modifications. In the wake of the eleventh-century Persian philosopher Avicenna's commentary on Aristotle's *De Anima*, the common sense was recast as the chief of the "internal senses," the fundamental link between sensations, on the one hand, and reason and cognition, on the other. This tradition continued in Scholastic thought, not least in the works of Thomas Aquinas, where Aristotle and Avicenna were harmonized with the Church Fathers and the notion of multiple "internal senses," beginning with the common sense, continued to hold sway. As late as the seventeenth century, the *sensus communis* was still understood by many commentators to be a cognitive faculty vital to the most basic and prosaic of human tasks: the discernment of the character of objects, individuals, and circumstances and of the basic differences among them.[3]

Across the centuries, this faculty also migrated in terms of where it made its home. It traveled from the heart, where Aristotle had originally envisioned it, to the brain, with ever more attention paid to locating its exact position within.[4] Already for Avicenna, the common sense, as the first of the internal senses, was understood to reside in the front of the first cerebral ventricle, in close proximity to its working partner, imagination. Subsequent investigators from Leonardo da Vinci to the seventeenth-century English physician Thomas Willis, who placed the common sense in the corpus striatum at the seat of the reception of sensation, continually fine-tuned those claims in an ongoing early modern effort to understand better how humans' cognitive and perceptual capabilities fit together.

Thus, by the end of the sixteenth century and the start of the seventeenth, the common sense or *sensus communis* had become so recognizable as both a physiological and psychological construct that it could be readily adapted to an allegorical reading—and a political one at that. Certainly this was the case for post-Reformation anatomists such as André du Laurens (also known as Laurentius), ordinary professor of medicine in Montpellier and court physician to Henri IV, and Helkiah Crooke, an English popularizer who synthesized many of the leading post-Vesalian anatomical studies of the previous century upon an Aristotelian foundation and held the title of surgeon to James I. The human body was best understood by both as a "little worlde," a simulacrum of the larger world or geocosm in an extended microcosm-macrocosm analogy. And for these anatomists, not to mention a host of literary figures in search of arresting metaphors in the early seventeenth century, the common sense was nothing less than the "judge and censor" within the human mind.[5]

We cannot be entirely surprised at this essentially legalistic imagining of the work of the *sensus communis*. After all, the organic and profoundly hierarchical political theory of the late sixteenth and seventeenth centuries relied heavily on bodily metaphors.[6] The king or sovereign was understood to rule over the body politic in a mutually dependent relationship, much as the head, the most exalted part of man and the seat of the soul, ruled over the physical body with which it functioned in concert. An effective state necessarily mirrored the image of man. In the same way, anatomists and medical theorists, borrowing from Plato's *Republic* as much as from Aristotelian natural philosophy, explained the operation of the brain—an increasing object of scientific scrutiny starting in the sixteenth century—by imagining it as a commonwealth, kingdom, palace, or city. In this political space, each faculty could be shown to serve a different administrative function, including the surveillance, censorship, and dissemination of information.[7] In Bartolommeo Del Bene's early seventeenth-century *City of Truth* (*Civitas Veri*), for example, the five external senses constitute the gates to the city, but it is the three internal senses that provide access to the temples dedicated to the intellectual virtues at the city's core.[8] And in Crooke's own allegorical account, the brain is a "royall Court" endowed with "guard[s] of outward Sences," "Councellors of state and all their aequipage," and even "spies." The common sense, as the court's "censor," becomes the "privy-chamber of the soule," gathering data from its externally focused informers (the senses), sorting it, and making policy determinations at the behest of the sovereign prince.[9] The mind, in all its particulars, performed in much the same way in the early modern period as an ideal polity or monarchical state. At least at the level of the imaginary, politics and psychology thoroughly bolstered one another.

But this still essentially ancient conception of human psychology was to meet its demise over the next century or so, just as our story is really beginning. René Descartes is generally credited with making obsolete the notion that there was an actual faculty within the human brain that functioned as the *sensus communis*.[10] The French philosopher did not fully reject the idea of the inner senses, which he appropriated from the Scholastics. But he distanced himself from the Aristotelian conception of a common sense faculty, abandoning it entirely by the time of his *Passions of the Soul* (1649). His mechanistic account of the body and brain, and his desire to root knowledge firmly in cognition rather than sensation, rendered unnecessary the common sense as a specific, locatable mental faculty. Gradually other seventeenth- and eighteenth-century philosophers, directly or indirectly, followed suit, inspired by advancements in anatomical rendering, too. John Locke abandoned the idea of a common sense faculty whose job was to compare and to synthesize impressions from several senses, even as he maintained the idea of "common sensibles." George Berkeley gave up on both. Medical doctors and specialists in the human body eventually did as well, though we should not exaggerate the speed or completeness of this project. Franz Josef Gall, the inventor of phrenology, was, for example, still invested in the search for the specific locations of each of the internal senses, including the common sense, as late as the end of the eighteenth century. What happened instead can be described as a series of gradual shifts in the meaning and then the utility of this ancient term against the background of its slow scientific demise.

Two developments in particular set common sense on a new post-Aristotelian course—and give us reason to speak of something as initially unconvincing as the beginning of the modern history of common sense in the London of Queen Anne. Both hark back to an ancient conversation about common sense as a form of discernment and, ultimately, censorship. And both point the way to the rise and much lamented death of a different queen whom we have already met. That, of course, is Queen Common Sense.

One of these shifts is definitional. Over the course of the early modern period, the two words that made up *sensus communis* or *sens commun* or *common sense* came to be used in less technical senses right alongside Aristotelian ones. Locke employed the term "common sense" and Descartes *le bon sens* (literally, good sense, a close kin of *le sens commun*) with the aim of signifying not a specific faculty but rather the rudimentary ability to form clear perceptions, make elementary judgments, and engage in simple reasoning about everyday, practical matters without falling into bald-faced contradictions and inconsistencies. It was assumed that such skills were—or should be—within the capacity of all humans, with the exception of the insane and the truly thick. In early modern Europe, to address oneself to common sense was a shorthand way to appeal to the plain wisdom of ordinary people, not a very high threshold but a real and increasingly important one nevertheless. Protestantism, with its emphasis on the moral worth of everyday, profane concerns and its refusal to identify any privileged locus of the sacred, certainly contributed to this new valuation. "By a man of *common sense*," summarized one helpful early eighteenth-century English commentator in a decidedly commonsensical manner, "we mean one who knows, as we say, *white from black,* and *chalk from cheese; that two and two make four; and that a mountain is bigger than a mole hill.*"[11] Distinctions among ordinary words and things, elementary facts about arithmetic, basic knowledge about how familiar objects work, the primary tenets of prudence: these became the special domain of that mental process that we still call common sense.

And once common sense ceased to belong, as a technical term, to the cutting edge of either psychology or anatomy and instead became a name for a less rigorously defined cognitive capacity, its meaning also began to expand. More precisely, its connotations became as much social as epistemological. The watered-down Aristotelian notion of a common sense faculty merged (albeit precariously) with the old Roman conception of *sensus communis:* the shared, though generally tacit, values and beliefs of a community. This had been the meaning of the term for the Stoics, and it had endured in the work of Cicero, who used the term to signify the notions all men held in common, as well as in the writings of Horace and Quintillian.[12] Indeed, this notion too had Greek roots, as evocations of *loci communes*, or commonly held beliefs, had long been central to the ancient rhetorician's craft. At the start of the eighteenth century, with the revival of interest in all of these sources, common sense came also to mean, in English, those plain, self-evident truths or conventional wisdom that one needed no sophistication to grasp and no proof to accept precisely because they accorded so well with the basic (common sense) intellectual capacities and experiences of the whole social body.[13] To possess good or common sense was, conversely, to readily accept these "general notions" or commonplaces about quantities or space or time or other observed phenomena as simply how things were. In this way, common sense also became a key component of intersubjectivity.

The aesthete and invalid Whig essayist Anthony Ashley Cooper, the third Earl of Shaftesbury, then took this definition one step further in a meandering and influential philosophical tract entitled *Sensus Communis: An Essay on the Freedom of Wit and Humour*, first published in 1709. Augustan commentators tended to agree that common sense was a distinctive form of knowledge in that it depended upon free and open conversation, the informal sharing of knowledge derived initially from sense experience.[14] In this faith, they reflected the new world of cultivated, urban sociability in which they lived. But Shaftesbury memorably insisted that definitive judgments and basic agreements about matters of both ethics and taste were also made possible by an innate "sense of the publick weal and of the common interest," a trait most often found among men of "thorough good breeding" (such as himself), though sometimes intuitively in the "common honest man."[15] Shaftesbury called this instinct, after the Roman fashion, *sensus communis*, too.[16] In an era in which all sorts of old certainties seemed to Shaftesbury to have been thrown into question, not least by Thomas Hobbes's nominalism in the moral realm, common sense was offered up as an independent, disinterested, and sure epistemic authority related to questions of beauty, harmony, goodness, truth, and other communal value judgments. Indeed, at the start of the eighteenth century, Shaftesbury envisioned this sense as both a potential source of social cohesion and a foundation for a secure, participatory moral and political order.

Shifting definitions are thus only one part of the story. A second development that was to affect the early history of modern common sense took place simultaneously. That was a profound change in the context in which common sense was to resonate as an idea. Before a more social and protean conception of common sense could be turned into a slogan, a pen name, a fashionable literary character, or any other kind of authority capable of holding its own against (and sometimes even trumping) history, custom, reason, religion, or great books of the past, it had to become the solution to a problem. And it was only in the new public spaces of the great city of London, and in the wake of the Glorious Revolution and its reaffirmation of Protestantism and English liberty, that just such a problem emerged to which common sense would soon seem to be the answer. That was how to hold a heterogeneous society together with a minimum of force. By the time of the purported death of Queen Common Sense in the London of the 1730s, an earlier history of common sense had indeed been superseded. But the traces of an ancient prehistory, in which common sense, sovereignty, and censorship were intimately bound together, remained everywhere in evidence, and common sense had already acquired a new political function tailored to its new circumstances.

Only rarely does anyone talk, or even think, about common sense when all is in order. Why dwell on the obvious? Common sense generally only comes out of the shadows and draws attention to itself at moments of perceived crisis or collapsing consensus. Early eighteenth-century London was no exception.

In many ways, the start of the new century was an auspicious time in England's capital. London's political class congratulated itself that the revolution that brought William and Mary to the throne had been so brief and uneventful that it had hardly been a revolution at all. Certainly the success of the new regime only added luster to the image of England's leading urban center, which was well on its way toward becoming the first modern metropolis, a "wonder city" of government, manufacturing, commerce, and public culture.[17] Its size, noise, and energy (not to mention filth) fascinated foreigners and Englishmen alike.

But how to maintain that prosperity? How to avoid the return of conflict? London also remained, circa 1700, a city scarred by enmity. A century of religious war and political revolution had left behind a legacy of mistrust: of old centers of expertise, whether judicial or theological, and of old methods of truth finding and decision -making. Authority was hard to reestablish. And famously, the first decades of the new century were fraught with anxiety about divergent opinions and, consequently, about factionalism or "party-spirit" leading to renewed civil strife. This was the fear, despite the fact that all Englishmen wanted was to overcome their ideological divisions and, consequently, enjoy some hard-won social and political stability.[18] The problem was not new to the reign of Queen Anne. Widespread desire for some kind of compromise was already pronounced at the conclusion of the Civil War in the middle of the seventeenth century; Charles II was, after all, welcomed back to England in 1660 specifically for "the moderating of Extremities, the Reconciling of Differences, and the satisfying of all Interests."[19] It was simply that this fundamental Whig ambition became more marked (and possibly even more elusive) after the Revolution of 1688, the Toleration Act of 1689, and, most especially, the lapsing of the Licensing Act in 1695.

It was the latter that established freedom of expression as henceforth a, if not the, essential element of English "liberty." Following on the heels of the official acceptance of diversity of creed within English Protestantism, the lapsing of the Licensing Act brought an end to the need for pre-publication approval of printed texts and opened up the possibility of active participation in public discussion to an ever greater number of subjects. The idea was that this change in law would promote internal peace as well as profits.[20] Yet rather than resulting in a new consensus or even social and religious harmony, it seemed, in the short run, to produce the opposite: an explosion of conflicting opinions and rival assertions, many of them hostile or downright wrongheaded and dishonest (at least in the eyes of their opponents). Definitive answers became that much more difficult to find, leading to new fears that the search might be abandoned entirely. And if that were not bad enough, in the aftermath of all of this liberal legislation, a bitter and threatening sectarianism dominated London's public life, from the coffee houses one frequented to the hospitals in which one died.[21]

Beginning with the reign of Queen Anne and continuing after her death in 1714, when George I assumed the throne, the city's Whig spokesmen and publicists thus became consumed with the question of how to produce order out of what one historian calls "the babble, diversity, and liberty of the new discursive world of the Town."[22] Thinkers struggled not only to discover what, both internal and external to the mind, accounted for the wide variety of clashing opinions on matters of importance that came to the fore as a result of new freedoms. They also sought out a means to achieve basic social and intellectual cooperation and to sow the seeds of a common culture—without resorting ever again to those artificial and tyrannical sources of unanimity that were absolutism and a related censorship apparatus. For the English upper and middle classes, one of the great challenges of the postrevolutionary era was to discover new, extralegal ways to mitigate the most extreme forms of pluralism, that is, to distinguish understanding from misunderstanding and to promote a low-level kind of consensus about basic ideas, all within the context of religious toleration and the legal deregulation of speech and print.

One key solution was politeness. An upper-class gentility that prized emotional restraint and avoidance of extremes or individualistic zeal of any kind could be instrumental in forging a community of the fundamentally like-minded. Real conversation depended, as Shaftesbury pointed out repeatedly, upon toleration and freedom from external constraints, upon the ability to question, to ridicule, to debate. But politeness potentially helped to reconcile, or at least paper over, the differences among truth claims and the competitiveness upon which modern politics, urban social life, and commercial culture, as opposed to court culture, seemed to thrive. Together with good taste, the politeness prized by early eighteenth-century English elites suggested one path toward public virtue and concern with the general good—and away from constant ideologically driven strife.[23]

A related proposal, insofar as it could be seen either as a desirable outgrowth of polite sociability or the groundwork for its operation, involved the cultivation of common sense, within individuals and within the community as a whole. Common sense promised to provide a minimal form of authority on which a common identity could be founded.

Conversely, the maintenance of a community built around certain widely accepted, plainly stated core assumptions suggested another potential antidote to excessive individualism, political animosity, and factionalism. The essayist Joseph Addison was only partly joking when he noted that he yearned for the day when associations of men took this, instead of sectarian pursuits, to be their goal. In the pages of the *Spectator*, Addison let himself imagine a "neutral body" that would be open to all people unwilling to call themselves Whig or Tory and disinterested in passion, speculation, or private interest, the typical sources of what he called "that furious Party spirit." The criterion for belonging would simply be adherence to a set of basic mathematical axioms and linguistic distinctions upon which all honest men should have no trouble agreeing. One would have to swear that "two plus two make four," that "six is less than seven in all Times and all Places," and that "ten will not be more three years hence than it is at present." It would also be essential that "we shall upon all Occasions oppose such persons that upon any Day of the Year shall call black white, or white black, with the utmost Peril of our Lives and Fortunes."[24] Provided men were to stick to these common sense observations, the seeds of civil war might be extinguished and a sufficiently unified body politic finally reestablished.

Unfortunately, the current climate of division and animosity led in the opposite direction. It was, in Addison's commonplace formulation, "fatal both to Mens [*sic*] Morals and their Understandings." Moreover, it "destroys even Common Sense," by which he meant the ability to make sound judgments or to agree on basic truths down to the very names of things.[25] At almost the same moment, Shaftesbury made the same claim: faction was simply "the abuse or irregularity of that social love or common affection [*sensus communis*] which is natural to mankind."[26] And when necessary, Addison had a seemingly endless stream of anecdotes that he could marshal to demonstrate that a mean-spirited factionalism, often rooted in divergent speculative claims, had resulted in all sorts of nonsense and absurdities, not least petty fights over choices of words. But the revival of common sense struck Addison, like many of his contemporaries, as also a potential political cure, a minimum standard for social and ideological cohesion and even constraint in the context of the risky experiment with pluralism that was early eighteenth-century English liberalism.

In fact, the promise of a mythical common sense lay only partly in the formal political realm. The factionalism characteristic of early eighteenth-century political culture was still intimately related to religious disagreement, and religious sectarianism seemed to many commentators to stem directly from a similar kind of zeal and epistemological dogmatism to that which Addison disparaged on the political front.[27] The source of the problem was the insistence on the certainty and exclusive truth of one's own position, whether one spoke from the vantage point of the radical doubt and moral relativism of the skeptic, on the one hand, or the nonconformity of the enthusiast or religious individualist endowed with private revelations, on the other. Here, too, Shaftesbury evoked a common sense instinct as a way to check such antagonistic views in the context of legally protected liberty of thought and expression. If, in politics, common sense found its antonym in "party spirit" and "interest," in religion the pejorative "enthusiasm" played this role beginning in the previous century and continuing well into the new one.

As early as the mid-seventeenth century, the Cambridge Platonist Benjamin Whichcote (whose sermons Shaftesbury had published at the beginning of his career) had defined enthusiasm as, literally, "speaking without sense."[28] Thereafter the great Latitudinarian Anglican divines of the later seventeenth century, including Edward Stillingfleet and John Tillotson, had together developed a kind of common sense Protestantism as both a reaction to and a bulwark against extreme positions of all kinds, from the excessive rationality of deists, Hobbists, Spinozists, or other devotees of post-Cartesian philosophy to the excessive irrationality of all kinds of radical dissenters and fideists, including, above all, Catholics.[29] These moderate clerics had appealed to reasonable and mannerly English men and women in a precise and often prosaic language with few metaphors or learned citations and little emotional expression. This, of course, was a variant of the anti-Ciceronian and anti-Scholastic "plain style" made famous by the experimental philosophers of the Royal Society. It was also fully in keeping with a long Protestant tradition of valuing simplicity and direct observation over elaborateness and higher reflection.[30] And following an age of bloody disputes associated with the triumph of various enthusiasms, these divines chose to employ this stripped-down, everyday idiom in favor of a reasonable Christianity, consistent if not with the absolute, infallible truth of any one authority (pure reason, personal revelation, or the pope himself), then with moral certainty or the "mitigated skepticism" of what could not help but strike a reasonable person as self-evident.[31] This, claimed Stillingfleet, was as much certainty as most people required in their everyday lives.[32] It should certainly be enough, according to these clerics, to persuade the public of the existence of a benevolent God and the basic truth of Christianity. Rejecting the need for speculation and interpretation whenever possible, the Latitudinarians offered a plain, direct doctrine that was intended to be entirely congruent with the practical good sense and established values of its audience. The benefits for its genteel adherents would be evident in terms of health, material well-being, reputation, and social relations: the business of daily life. As Tillotson, the archbishop of Canterbury in the reign of William III, had memorably put it, "the laws of God are reasonable, that is suited to our nature and advantageous to our interest."[33] Furthermore, when it came to the teachings of Christianity, "God hath shewn us what is good by the general Vote and Consent of Mankind."[34] The sermons of Tillotson and Stillingfleet overflowed with the kinds of statements that encouraged social cohesion and spiritual unity precisely because they could be so readily met with agreement. (This is a trick that politicians like to employ to this day.)

A common sense approach to matters of theology continued, especially among Low Churchmen, well into the new century. The stock sermons of the Augustan church routinely borrowed their style and themes from Tillotson, and Tillotson's "His Commandments Are Not Grievous" easily obtained the title of most popular sermon of the eighteenth century.[35] But this attachment to what was just as often called common reason or reasonableness (as opposed to pure reason or rationality, which tended to shade into either skepticism or Scholasticism) was gradually adopted by other Protestant denominations between the seventeenth and eighteenth centuries. It was also secularized. In the course of the first half of the 1700s, common sense came to provide a solid, if modest, epistemic and stylistic foundation for a wide variety of disciplines, including law, philosophy, history, natural science, and literature. For the members of polite society, especially in London, it seemed an antidote not only to what were increasingly contemptuously described as popular superstitions and common prejudices, the results of irrational beliefs and enthusiasms. Advocates touted common sense as a bulwark against *all* grand schemes and unnecessarily speculative, esoteric, or passionate enterprises, including highly learned ones, since they, too, were likely to lead people down the path to error, sectarianism, and, finally, strife. This censorious attitude applied particularly to the disputatious and word-bound culture of Scholasticism, the perennial target of natural philosophers from Francis Bacon onward. In the early eighteenth century, Whigs and Tories alike pontificated against what Nicholas Armhurst described as the "syllogistical hocus-pocus," "learned gibberish," and "ethico-logico-physio-metaphysio-theological drama" still taught at the great universities and called for plain speech and a less erudite common sense to take their place.[36] In the decades that immediately followed the revolutionary settlement, the ordinary sense of the ordinary man in ordinary circumstances was envisioned as a respectable, trustworthy, and superior standard for judgment in such seemingly disparate arenas as religion, ethics, aesthetic taste, justice, and politics.[37] It was also envisioned as a tool in the creation of a noncombative common culture. The key to the general promotion of sound thinking, according to the philosopher George Berkeley (whose anti-skeptical but immaterialist philosophy seemed to many of his contemporaries actually to fly in the face of common sense), was "to be eternally banishing Metaphisics [*sic*], etc. and recalling Men to common Sense."[38] Or, as the closing lines of a more popular early eighteenth-century pamphlet on methods of avoiding arguments urged its readers to make their motto, "Exert with Diligence and Fortitude the Common Use of Common Sense."[39]

The burgeoning London periodical press assumed the lion's share of this responsibility. More precisely, the publicists of the Whig establishment in England's intellectual and political capital took on a twofold task at the start of the eighteenth century: to define what counted as common sense (along with good taste) in terms of style, method, and content and then to communicate this version of common sense to a substantial "sensible," literate, urban public. The aim was to construct the audience and then the standards of gentlemanliness and moderate reasonableness that the term seemed to suggest were already, naturally, in existence and already universally acknowledged.

The project began with the rise of the serial publication in the second half of the seventeenth century. But the phenomenally successful early Augustan periodical, the *Spectator* (1711–1712), soon set the standard. Addison and Richard Steele, the paper's editors, repeatedly celebrated good sense as commensurate with good breeding and men of sense for their capacity for friendship and conversation. Readers could turn to the journal to discover where good or plain or common sense—defined variably as "right reason, and what all men should consent to" or as the "capacity of judging right"—could be found.[40] They could also learn where it was in short supply. The list of those who frequently violated its dictates included women; contemporary playwrights; humorists; those of no fortune (the poor); those possessing too much (ostentatious, libertine aristocrats); pedantic scholars who argued against their own sense experience; and zealots of all kinds, whether Catholics or skeptical atheists. These precepts were conveyed in a casual, anti-academic style in which the imaginary editor, Mr. Spectator, called upon his readers' common sense and engaged them in a simulated epistolary conversation, deferring to their collective judgments as well as passing on his own in their name. In this, the *Spectator*'s editors seem to have borrowed a page from Shaftesbury, who made similar use of the form and quotidian style of letters, dialogues, and conversations, eschewing the more figurative, showy language then associated with the wordsmith, the pedant, or, just as often, the Frenchman. Their common aim was to suggest engagement in a community endeavor. But for the editors of the *Spectator*, the goal was also to incubate a specific value within the journal's wide audience. Readers, Addison pronounced, "can improve their Stock of Sense" by reading better books and engaging in conversation with men of judgment.[41] It was only a matter of willpower and of exposure to the right influences. With wit and morality bolstering one another, the *Spectator* was explicitly calculated "to diffuse good Sense through the Bulk of a People."[42]

Yet it is important to emphasize that by "a People" Addison and Steele did not really mean all people, and by "common sense" the two editors did not have in mind the truly common. Certainly the *Spectator* contains appreciations of the basic values of the unlearned and of the songs and fables that convey these values. Such examples helped the editors to make the case for the fundamental sameness of human nature everywhere: "it is impossible that any thing should be universally tasted and approved by a Multitude, tho' they are only the Rabble of a Nation, which hath not in it some peculiar Aptness to please and gratify the Mind of Man."[43] But it is also clear that neither the source nor the audience for the *Spectator*'s common sense extended to all classes of people. Women, like aristocrats, were expected to have less of it, though they might well benefit from the paper's lessons. The rural and urban poor were expected to have little and were clearly outside the journal's intended readership. When common sense was touted in this paper, it was not meant to be taken as a celebration either of commoner culture or of the common understanding, with its implications of prejudice, superstition, ignorance, and credulity.[44] Much the same held true for theories of political representation in this era, where "the people" and "the public" remained largely a rhetorical abstraction, and actual common people were considered cognitively and morally ill equipped to participate directly in political decision making.[45] As Samuel Johnson pointed out slightly later, in this discussion it remained essential to distinguish between opinions that were true because they were widely acknowledged (which he called "cant") and opinions that were widely acknowledged because they were true (which he called "true sense").[46] Even if it were not as dependent on learning and leisure as formal reasoning, common sense, like taste, was fashioned in the early eighteenth century as a virtue of the relatively cultivated and the at least moderately well-off.

Addison and Steele, like Shaftesbury, saw themselves forming the taste, manners, and beliefs of an increasingly cohesive, if expanded, elite. This elite was synonymous with the paper's gentlemen and gentlewomen readers, or what one literary critic calls more fully "a polite public of reasonable, decent, tasteful, virtuous people of the combined middling and upper classes."[47] Through language, rather than law or more formal codes of exclusion and coercion, the *Spectator* assumed the task of establishing the cognitive authority of this segment of the population and making its values, culture, and consumption habits, again as defined by the editors, as normative as was possible. Simultaneously the journal worked to delegitimize other stances and beliefs, including key elements of both folk culture and contemporary philosophy as not only unlearned, superstitious, or antiquated but nonsensical and outside the boundaries of real-world common sense. It was not always easy, of course, to decide what observations fell on which side of the fence. But common sense, as portrayed in the *Spectator,* helped to establish these distinctions as to what was acceptable or unacceptable in language and understanding and to promote a kind of self-censoring within the "polite" classes, even as it suggested a truly inclusive culture. If the old notion of common sense had been as "censor and judge" in the individual mind, here it became generalized and collectivized as a means of cultural regulation. It became a form of what sociologists would eventually describe as the structural censorship characteristic of all societies that pride themselves on their formal deregulation of speech.[48]

Other journals, like the Whiggish biweekly *The Free Thinker* (1718–1721), followed suit, building on a successful formula in promising to treat all matters in accordance with "the plain Notions of *Common Sense*" in an effort to delineate a reasonable culture to which elites could reflexively subscribe.[49] In effect, print culture as a whole was given this normative role in Augustan London. Theorists of literature and the arts insisted that poetry and plays and other cultural products had less a duty to advance new things than, didactically, "to represent the common Sense of Mankind in more strong, more beautiful, or more uncommon Lights."[50] Common sense provided a foundation for taste, a set of critical rules against which violations, such as excessive imagination or innovation or obscurity, could be measured and judged and with which conformity could be praised.[51] Even guides to conduct or "how to" books took up a similar aim. That was to illustrate and inculcate this same "good sense"—frequently described as the most important form of wisdom—among readers who, tautologically, already considered themselves not "Blockheads, Mechanicks, and Perverse Tempers" but rather "men [or women] of sense."[52]

Common sense thus soon joined the panoply of values, including virtue, sociability, patriotism, and moderation, that suggested both national distinctiveness and national pride in the wake of the Glorious Revolution. Already by the beginning of the 1720s, good old English or British common sense had become a recognizable idea, an entity to which writers and publicists could eagerly appeal.[53] Soon it became identifiable as one of the key traits that distinguished the English from what they took to be the impractical, verbose, obfuscating, deceitful, and all-around pretentious French. As such, it helped foster a growing allegiance to an exalted conception of the specialness of the English nation.

Common sense was understood to be a special ally of liberty, of course. That was one way it manifested its Englishness. But common sense could also be imaginatively tied to that other special (and semantically linked) national achievement, the common law. The distinctiveness of the common law, according to a host of great seventeenth- and eighteenth-century commentators, lay in its foundations: the ancient, unwritten customs, or collective experience and wisdom, of the English people. These social origins meant not only that English common law, in contradistinction to more formal kinds of law, was unusually suited to efficacious, just, and reasonable decision making about human affairs. They also meant that the common law—even though best interpreted, it was agreed, by expert jurists trained in its dictates and the application of legal reason—helped indirectly to produce and to reinforce a sense of participatory community.[54] Much the same could be said about common sense. In its widespread cultivation, one could point simultaneously to the historical greatness of the English people, with their traditional commitment to the establishment of peaceable, consensual social norms, and to the leading role of the English nation in the modern-day advancement of reason and civilization. It was, in the eyes of its propagators, a dazzling combination.

The culture of common sense was, at its roots, a Latitudinarian and Whig creation, a historically specific reaction against perceived excesses of all kinds rooted in the religious, intellectual, and political culture of the late seventeenth century. The playwright and Whig apologist

Thomas Shadwell, who replaced the Catholic John Dryden as poet lau-
reate in 1689 after years of banishment from London's stages, self-
servingly insisted that it was only with the ascent of William and Mary
that "a Liberty of speaking Common Sence [*sic*], which tho' not long
since forbidden, is now grown current."[55] Yet by the beginning of the
reign of George I, a taste for common sense had become generalized in
urban England to the extent that embracing a practically minded epistemology, rooted in certain basic shared assumptions derived from ordinary experience, had become the common sense of the combined middle
and upper classes of the day.[56] This is how it was to be celebrated for
the rest of the century. As one London paper put it a decade later,
"Happiness in life depends more upon it than upon any other Sense
whatsoever."[57] No wonder the anonymous author of a fiendishly clever
1769 novel called *The Life and Adventures of Common Sense* insisted that
the eponymous main character (Common Sense), after centuries of frus-
trating and peripatetic work trying to cure the delusions of popes, em-
perors, and kings, had finally, in the Protestant England of Georges I and
II, and especially among "the middling People," found a satisfying
home.[58] Thanks to foreign and native observers alike, this myth of the
English—and, eventually, British—as plain in style, wise in a prosaic sort
of way, and devoted to their common sense, feet-on-the-ground perspective, as well as to their liberty, endured into the twentieth century. When
the great historian G. M. Trevelyan famously declared just before World
War II that the Glorious Revolution might better be known as "the Sensible Revolution" for the role it had played in fostering this characteristic
trait, he was only giving credence to a Whiggish cliché established in the
wake of 1688.[59] And that cliché would prove to have lasting value for a
political vision in which the "sense" of the people could be said to be at
the root of all good laws, and good laws could be defined as those that
appeared self-evident to all people endowed with the capacity for common sense.

The making of common sense into an epistemological ideal suitable to
govern a stable, practically minded yet civil libertarian society is, however, only part of the story of the birth of modern common sense as a

political instrument. The rest has to do with the partisan and often acrimonious contest over its appropriate referents and legitimate spokesmen that soon followed. So attractive was common sense as an ally in a political sphere that increasingly stretched well beyond the doors of Parliament and into London's taverns, theaters, printers' offices, markets, and other public spaces that it rather quickly became something worth fighting over.

Now it is sometimes said that concepts can be deemed a success precisely when they begin to provoke opposing definitions and to generate unintended uses.[60] Moreover, certain terms—art and fascism are classic examples—serve an important function not despite but precisely because of their being contested; they become pivots for important arguments.[61] But common sense is, in this regard, an odd case. For we are dealing with a term that, by definition, signifies a realm closed to variant interpretations and beyond debate. And once a claim to common sense became a rhetorical weapon in the arsenal of multiple, conflicting constituencies, all of whom insisted that they were representing only what was obvious and common to all mankind, it not only fostered a new form of political deception. It seems also to have exacerbated the difficulties involved in arriving at just such a consensual or "common" sense in practice. Paradoxically, the growing popularity of common sense as both an idea and a slogan produced a competition to define and embody it, which, in turn, ultimately helped legitimate disagreement, dissent, and even full-blown, extra-parliamentary opposition as established elements of modern political culture. This twist in the story is all the more remarkable in that it occurred at a moment that is generally thought to mark the final demise of the explosive ideological squabbles associated with the previous century's wars of religion and the emergence of extraordinary social and political stability and even consensus. During the few decades stretching from the late 1710s to the conclusion of the 1730s, or the middle of the reign of the first two Georges, common sense went from being a means to stem the tide of conflict to a spur to new forms of it.

The so-called Bangorian controversy of 1716–1718 constituted the first serious crisis in the idea of a single Whig-derived common sense. The bishop of Bangor, Benjamin Hoadly, was already a controversial figure, despised by Tory sympathizers and by High Churchmen for his politics and his theology respectively, when he published a particularly strongly worded refutation of conservative Anglican thought in the spring of 1716. Entitled *A Preservative against the Principles and Practices of the Nonjurors Both in Church and State* and subtitled *Or, an Appeal to the Consciences and Common Sense of the Christian Laity,* this pamphlet set in motion a controversy that was only exacerbated the following year by Hoadly's contentious sermon "The Nature of the Kingdom or Church of Christ." Central to the debate Hoadly provoked was the question of the source of truth, both at the level of institutions and at the level of human psychology. Among the many controversial positions that the notorious bishop staked out, none was more provocative than his suggestion that the essence of Christianity lay in the unrestricted rights of individual conscience or, to put it differently, that the judgments of the individual mind superseded the authority of that church's divinely ordained clergy. The politically protected bishop, with his Latitudinarian and Lockean leanings, seemed to be arguing a radical line directly contrary to Anglican orthodoxy. But Hoadly insisted in *A Preservative* that he had built his case upon the most secure, elemental, and unambiguous of foundations: "some few Common Uncontested Principles of Civil Government" and "the plain and express Declarations of the Gospel itself." He also appealed directly to the common sense of the laity, rather than other clerics, in his own defense, promising his audience to "lend you to such Principles and Maxims, as will be found True in themselves; and easily applied to every Difficulty upon these Subjects, which is now, or may be, from time to time, thrown your way."[62]

His appeals and subsequent clarifications notwithstanding, Hoadly unleashed a firestorm of opposition in the form of literally hundreds of pamphlets, sermons, and even poems. Self-declared "laymen of conscience and common sense," as well as High Churchmen all across Britain, responded that they were anything but in agreement about where common sense lay when it came to the nature of the authority of the church over its members.[63] The notion of common sense offered an epistemological prop to both sides in the controversy. Its use by writers as opposed as William Law and Thomas Pyle suggests that its authority in matters of religion was now beyond challenge; for Protestants, common sense was "what the Laity may justly pretend to," and "heresy" was equally possible against this human attribute as it was against God, religion, and "the Nature of Things."[64] But the nature of what common sense dictated, like the boundaries between orthodoxy and heterodoxy, proved much harder to determine insofar as its tenets (much like the old *loci communes* of ancient debate) pointed in multiple directions. In effect, the Bangorian controversy, as it came to be known, laid bare early in the reign of George I a set of religious and political problems that would continue to plague all subsequent societies that chose to adopt the idea of common sense as an objective, communally approved epistemological authority. How were its contours to be effectively determined? Who within the body politic could rightfully speak on its behalf? Finally, what should be done when divergent versions of common sense presented themselves as equally legitimate?

These questions remained unsettled in the 1720s. The real test for the idea of a single English common sense as the foundation for modern social and political life did not come until the mid-1730s, when the focus of public strife in London had largely shifted from religion to ministerial corruption. This was the decade that saw the resurgence of the so-called Country Opposition, that much-analyzed loose alliance of discontented Whigs and conservative, Tory-sympathizing country gentry, whose ranks included many of the great writers and intellects of the age.[65] Central to the strategy of these diverse opponents of the present regime was the appropriation of "common sense," along with "patriotism," "public spirit," "liberty," and a small number of other exalted slogans of the dominant, post-1688 political culture, to new effect. Opposition propagandists hoped to use these high-minded and already widely accepted terms to craft an alternative "country" or "patriot" ideology that would unite this unstable coalition of disaffected parties as the true protectors of the revolutionary settlement and defenders of the common good. The leaders of this opposition movement also sought in the notion of common sense a way to legitimize their merciless criticism of George II's de facto prime minister, Sir Robert Walpole, and of the corruption of the present government, or "Robinocracy," as anything but a clash of differing opinions or demonstration of true political dissent.

References to common sense, and particularly to its current scarcity, began making appearances in Opposition essays and verse early in the new century. John Gay, for example, in a 1728 poem dedicated "to the modern politician," cheerfully denounced the current age as one where "corruption sways mankind . . . int'rest too perverts the mind . . . [and] bribes have blinded common sense, foil'd reason, truth, and eloquence."[66] It was, however, a hit London play of 1736, which the French *philosophe* Claude Adrien Helvétius remembered years later as a meditation about the nature of *le bon sens,* that cemented the connection between the politics of the Opposition and this particular term.[67] That year, the witty and well-connected young novelist and playwright Henry Fielding (who had begun his literary career writing flattering verses in praise of George II) dazzled local audiences with a new farce full of topical references. Called *Pasquin,* this parodic entertainment was composed in haste and acted by what appears to have been a barely competent cast assembled for the purpose at the Haymarket Theatre. Nevertheless, it became London's most successful theatrical performance of the decade—and a key moment in the history of common sense.

Pasquin dramatizes the rehearsals of two different plays-within-a-play. The first, billed as a comedy, pokes fun at the corruption of contemporary elections, where bribery ran rampant. The second, ostensibly a tragedy and entitled "The Life and Death of Common Sense," portrays the invasion and triumph of a foreign force named Queen Ignorance, who, with her local acolytes—Law, Physick, and Firebrand, the priest—sets out to and succeeds in murdering Queen Common Sense.

Neither rehearsal's contents were as pointed and overtly partisan as much of Fielding's subsequent writing for the stage or the anonymous essays that he was producing simultaneously for the leading Opposition journal, the *Craftsman.* On the surface, the play offended all parties with equal verve; the actor reciting the prologue to *Pasquin* declared the author willing "without Fear and Favor . . . [to] maul" Whig and Tory, Court and Country alike.[68] But both the large targets and numerous small innuendos in this satire made Fielding's ultimately partisan intentions clear. Corruption in all forms, and especially that of elections, was already a standard Opposition theme at the time of *Pasquin*'s arrival on the stage. Furthermore, the allegorical battle between Queen Common Sense and Queen Ignorance could only have been seen as an ironic take on Alexander Pope's famous earlier depiction, in the *First Dunciad* (1728), of the decline of British morals and the progress of a different personified moral force, the Goddess Dulness, in Walpole's England. After barbed attacks on all sorts of contemporary targets, not least within the theater, Fielding's play ends with the queen's invocation of a "topsy turvey" world to come, where "the powers of Common-Sense are all destroy'd" and "Physick shall kill, and Law enslave the World."[69] And in case the implications of such lines were not entirely clear, Fielding resorted here, as in many of his works, to external commentators to do the job. Fictitious playwrights, prompters, critics, and generic men of good sense watch the plays-within-a-play and, in the tradition of the cynic Lucian, frequently question the customs on view so as to expose whatever in them runs counter to true common sense.[70]

Indeed, the political potential of *Pasquin* and, by extension, the idea of common sense as a vehicle of the Opposition were made manifest by Fielding himself in numerous sly ways. Consider the playbill that helped advertise the play on the occasion of a benefit performance in April 1736: "N. B. As Mr. Fustian [a character in the play] is the first Poet that ever cared to own, that he brought Ignorance upon the Stage, he hopes all her Friends will excuse his calling in particular upon them, and favour him with their Company along with the Friends of Common Sense, which he hopes will be the Foundation of a Coalition of Parties."[71] It is in the same spirit that the ghost of Queen Common Sense promises in the closing scene of the play that she will continue into the distant future to "haunt" those responsible for her murder, that is, the triumphant army of ignorance headed by experts in religion, medicine, and law and their deluded followers.

Taking these hints literally, two of Fielding's close friends, the twenty-seven-year-old "Boy Patriot" George Lyttelton and the renowned statesman and recently established Opposition leader Philip Stanhope, Lord Chesterfield, decided in the early months of 1737 to launch (and bankroll) a new political journal that would adopt this cause. They would break through old divides in order to line up diverse parties behind them. And they would fight the chief emblems of the reign of ignorance. First they sought the editorial assistance of the well-known Irish Catholic journalist Charles Molloy. Then, permanently inflating the value of an old, ostensibly antipolitical word, they named this newspaper directly after Fielding's example: *Common Sense.*[72]

Ideologically, *Common Sense: or, the Englishman's Journal,* betrayed none of the subtleties or indirection of Fielding's *Pasquin.* The weekly paper aimed to pick up precisely where the *Craftsman* and the *Weekly Journal* left off. Alongside discussion of manners and taste in the style of Addison and Steele, *Common Sense* became a humorous vehicle for the propagation of the new doctrine of the Opposition. In the late 1730s, the most obvious source of this platform was certainly Lord Bolingbroke, whose *Dissertation upon Parties,* first printed serially in the *Craftsman* in 1734–1735, introduced most of the key themes that *Common Sense* and other Opposition journals would develop in the later part of the decade. These included the limited prerogative of the crown, the danger of party labels, and the need for moral regeneration—not least the subordination of private interest to concern with the common good and the nation—in a time of rampant corruption.[73] But we should not overlook the important influence of Lyttelton himself, whose immensely popular *Letters from a Persian in England, to His Friend at Ispahan* of 1735 borrowed Montesquieu's trope of the rational foreign observer considering the absurdities of contemporary European ways as a means to advance the moral themes of Bolingbroke. Lyttelton combined the language of patriotism with his own Whiggish brand of anticlericalism.[74] In eleven witty letters, Lyttelton extended the famous story of the Troglodytes to allegorize the demise of practicality, public-mindedness, simplicity, and easy comprehensibility in all domains of English life, from religion to philosophy to politics to law to language itself. The situation had become so desperate in recent times, according to Lyttelton, that the justice system had spawned multiple incompatible layers of courts, and now very few Englishmen had either the stamina or the funds to make it to the last stage in the process, namely, the court of "common sense."[75]

This image played a larger role in *Common Sense* than simply providing the terms for a title. In some issues of this paper, common sense was incarnated as a literary character, similar to Fielding's queen or, earlier, Mr. Spectator, who commented on the issues of the day in a manner consistent with his main personality trait. At other times common sense was imagined as a commodity, one more bit player in an expanding commercial culture offered for purchase on "very cheap and easy Terms."[76] Most often, though, common sense functioned metaphorically in this journal as a special tribunal run by a hypothetical jury of everyone in the nation. In this independent and impartial court, the conduct and opinions of any or all people, whether kings, cobblers, authors, or ladies (though expectations for women were again low), could be held up and measured. All departures from the norm—as defined by the editors—could then be pointed out as injustices, or follies, or evils, or falsehoods, or even sins.[77] Here in the pages of this newspaper, one would find the final court of appeals that, according to Lyttelton in his *Letters from a Persian*, had almost ceased to exist in English society. His collaborator, Chesterfield, explained in the first issue: "the Design of my Paper, is to take in all Subjects whatsoever, and try them by the Standard of Common Sense. I shall erect a Kind of Tribunal, for the 'Crimina lesi Sensus Communis,' or the Pleas of Common Sense. . . . The Cause of Common Sense shall be pleaded in Common Sense."[78]

Chesterfield insisted upon the deep English roots of this quasi-legal tradition: "Our constitution is founded upon common sense itself, and every Deviation from one is a Violation of the other."[79] Common law, too, that ancient body of legal ideas, was frequently mentioned as a close relation of common sense; both, after all, required the populace to regulate its behavior through constant submission to tacit, uncontestable rules. But, like Fielding, Chesterfield despaired that this ancient standard called common sense had, along with "common honesty," been largely abandoned in the present. Articulating what was to become a constant theme of Opposition writing into the 1740s, the editors never failed to remind their readers that common sense had "for some years, been under a Sort of Proscription from Courts and Ministerial Employments," not to mention foreign policy.[80] In other words, the old, idealized isomorphism between politics and cognitive processes had ceased to exist. Or, as Chesterfield put it in his introductory essay, the authority evoked in the title of his journal had "met with great discouragement in the noble science of politics; our chief professors having thought themselves much above those obvious rules that had been followed by our ancestors and that lay open to vulgar understandings."[81] With this paper, he continued in his mock-serious tone, it was hoped that the "fashion" for common sense, at least among the political classes, could become common again.

Whether or not *Common Sense* brought about any kind of widespread cognitive or social changes in the England where it circulated, this London journal was, at least for a few years, a commercial and political success. The employment of common sense—defined facetiously in the first issue as "that Rule by which Men judge of other Peoples [*sic*] Actions, than direct their own; the plain Result of right Reason admitted by all, and practiced by few" and, later, by the "vulgar Expression of knowing what's what"—was, from a rhetorical point of view, a stroke of genius.[82] The trick lay in its two faces.

On the one hand, the trope of the common sense tribunal served as a highly effective vehicle for attacking Walpole and his associates, including the king, in the increasingly nasty skirmish between Court and Country that took place in the late 1730s. After the controversy had simmered down in the middle of that decade over whether a general excise tax on wine and tobacco constituted a threat to British liberty, the issue of Spanish depredations, or privateering on open seas, took its symbolic place. Soon the adequacy (or inadequacy) of Britain's negotiations with Spain and what they spelled for British freedom and British commerce became the key issue dividing the Opposition from the Whig establishment. *Common Sense,* among other journals, took the lead both in inflaming public opinion in support of war with Spain and in using the issue to further the attack on Walpole. It was an effort that lasted until his resignation four years later. What is important to notice from our perspective is that *Common Sense* assigned to its much-vaunted guiding principle an almost entirely subversive role, using it humorously to undermine both ministerial and clerical authority at every turn. The most notorious example was the allegorical satire known as "The Dream of the Golden Rump" in which Walpole, in the guise of a magician, subjects

George II to a highly undignified procedure.[83] But in almost every issue, common sense functioned as a means to place the Court and its supporters outside the legitimate and commonly accepted boundaries of social, political, and moral life, to reduce them, in short, to the nonsensical in the eyes of a broad, literate public.

That this technique was effective can be demonstrated by the degree of government hostility the journal provoked. The impact of the newspaper's use of common sense as a political weapon can also be measured by its many Opposition imitators, who seized upon the form's commercial as well as polemical potential. When Fielding (an occasional anonymous contributor to his friends' publication) began to edit his own paper, the *Champion*, in 1739, his fictional alter ego, the wonderfully named Captain Hercules Vinegar, also fashioned himself a satirical guardian of common sense and once again made use of the court model to try cases that fell outside of the established "law," including vanity, folly, and abuses of the English language.[84] Ballads, almanacs, and satirical prints borrowing themes from *Common Sense,* including the story of the Golden Rump, followed suit. By the end of the decade, the Opposition had made considerable headway in attaching the value of common sense to one highly partisan side in a whole series of interrelated oppositions. Common sense seemed increasingly to belong (despite the location of its editors) to the country rather than the morally depraved city; to "real" drama rather than the commercial theater of puppet shows and pantomimes; and, above all, to the Patriot platform and the Opposition rather than the corrupt court culture surrounding Walpole, George II, and their minions.

But on the other hand, the success of the common sense tribunal as an organ of pointed political critique lay in its architects' insistence that it was something else entirely. Shaftesbury had controversially proposed in both his famous *Letter on Enthusiasm* and its companion essay, *Sensus Communis,* that irony and ridicule should be encouraged in the context of free speech for the important role they could play in remedying vice and disarming "superstition and melancholy delusion," that is, in exposing the gap between what accords with the *sensus communis* and what actually exists.[85] Many Augustan commentators took this to mean that ridicule, rather than being simply a means to generate laughter at another's expense, was a technique for arriving at truth. What made it effective was the shared human capacity to see what was readily apparent once rhetorical smokescreens and faulty reasoning were brushed aside.[86] Thus the editors of *Common Sense*, at the same time as they were using satire, parody, scandalous allegation, and other forms of humor and raillery to further their own partisan cause, could convincingly declare themselves champions of a disinterested common sense, that old scourge of faction, party, or private enthusiasm. Moreover, they could celebrate their frequent recourse to scurrility as but a means to achieve principled, nonpartisan, even antipolitical aims. The real purpose of their journal, the editors explained in the opening issue, was to "rebuke Vice, correct Errors, reform Abuses and shame Folly and Prejudice, without Regard to any Thing but Common Sense, which . . . implies common Decency too."[87] In the context of Bolingbroke's insistence that the choice before the British people was not between two parties (Whig versus Tory) but, rather, between liberty and slavery, to have said otherwise would have discredited the paper's creators from the start. In the hands of the Opposition, common sense could be touted as simply a tool of moral and cultural regulation. It became a means of exposing the foibles, pretensions, and mystifications of the few and of restoring already-accepted and sensible community norms in a world without either effective governance or a formal censorship apparatus.

Furthermore, the authority of common sense had the advantage of being, at least at the level of rhetoric, connected to ordinary people outside government circles, which is to say, the journal's readers. Arguing from, or appealing to, common sense signaled to the desired audience that the humble, unpretentious writer of the words in question aspired to no glory for himself. He was only doing his duty, speaking in the name of an undefined people and appealing to that same people's instinctive good sense on their or the nation's behalf. The historian C. John Sommerville describes a critical tension in the early English newspaper trade (and in commercial media ever since) between being socially divisive enough to strengthen readers' self-identification by contrast with other groups within the nation and being socially inclusive enough to generate sufficient sales.[88] And even though *Common Sense* was quite clearly aimed specifically at the gentry and "honest well meaning People of a middle Rank," and even though the paper was in the business of supplying these particular classes with opinions, the central value announced in the journal's title aided its authors' efforts to suggest the contrary.[89] That is, the claim that they were really articulating the otherwise inaudible "sense of the people" as a whole or even the mythic vox populi.[90]

Indeed, the cynical and nascent "protesting" populism of the journal not only helped the Opposition to make a case against the ministerial party's comparative disregard for the public welfare.[91] It also led the paper's editors to portray the extra-parliamentary nation as an alternative source of legitimacy, with a right to challenge the actions of its representatives, as long as it did so in support of the moral and commonsensical, which was to say Opposition, cause. Combing through *Common Sense,* one is struck by occasionally radical claims as to the authority of the public and its sense in the political arena. Significantly, the question of expanding the franchise or democratization does not emerge. The point is primarily one of principle. One contributor asks rhetorically: "If the electors of England should declare to you [the Parliament], you shall not make laws for us, we will do it ourselves: will any man say they may not do it?"[92] On another occasion a quote appears from the Leveler Richard Overton's century-old *A Remonstrance of Many Thousand Citizens* to the effect that "We [the people] are principals, and you [the men of Parliament] our agents."[93] The message here is that the people, rather than having abrogated all their power to their representatives, retained the ability to make judgments and even occasionally to act upon them when their collective common sense was, by those elected to represent them, sufficiently affronted. In fact, with its firm roots in the real, commonsensical world, the judgment of ordinary men and even women was often superior to that of their social and intellectual betters. Here was an old theme in the literature celebrating common sense—the defense of the common people, based on their natural instinct for knowing and saying what's what—turned toward newly political and, indeed, populist ends.[94] As the editor of *Common Sense* put it in one of many discussions of British policy toward Spain, using a classic "common sense" example, "a Parliament may vote, that black is white. It may be so; but black will be black still, in Spite of all the Votes in the World. . . . [The great Assembly of the Nation] will not give a Sanction to Madness and Folly."[95]

And while this paper (like all its competitors) was busy attempting to politicize the consciousness of its London readers for financial and political gain, it could also use the notion of common sense to claim to be engaged in the project of restraining all kinds of political power. The editors could argue that they were protecting the public, through instruction, against government actions, or inactions, that were not in the collective interest.[96] *Common Sense* went so far as to take on the mantle of guardian of British liberty, trumpeting its freedom to proselytize in the name of common sense as a means to guard against all other forms of oppression, whether institutional or moral.

The problem with this extravagant polemic was that it left the ministerial forces in a bind. Despite the government's ostensible commitment to freedom of expression, Walpole paid journalists and bankrolled leading newspapers to counter what he saw as seditious and even treasonous propaganda. He also pushed the Theatrical Licensing Act of 1737 through Parliament, in part in response to the success of *Pasquin* (which, of course, only increased the sense of the potency of Fielding's critique). But liberty of the press had become sacrosanct to the British public by the first half of the eighteenth century. Furthermore, Opposition papers, including *Common Sense,* were already eager to exploit any hint that the court, in its lack of commitment to liberty, was interested in extending the licensing system or otherwise suppressing its foes simply for speaking too freely. In between its attacks on everything from the comportment of pretentious wives to the follies of Methodism, there was always space in *Common Sense* for an eloquent defense of freedom of expression and religion. Thus, beyond attempting to hinder distribution networks and putting other kinds of financial pressure on the journals of the Opposition, Walpole and his minions were left trying to ward off the effects of offensive words by putting forth alternative ones. Common sense proved a special challenge.

As in so many such fights in earlier decades, the Whig establishment set about responding in its own pamphlets, essays, verses, and newspapers, some established solely for the purpose of counteracting *Common*

Sense and most heavily subsidized by the government. Apologists for the ministerial party sputtered with indignation in short-lived publications such as the *Nonsense of Common Sense*, as well as in the pages of the key government journals. Other London newspapers duly reported on this war over the appropriation and possession of common sense, more than happy to sell papers by stirring up or stoking controversies of this sort. The highly popular *Gentleman's Magazine*, in particular, chronicled all developments in the battle to stake a legitimate claim to the concept while simultaneously engaging in a particularly heated, satirical campaign of its own in a three-way fight against *London Magazine* and *Common Sense*. London in the 1730s was, in retrospect, full of such trumped-up struggles over publications, authorship, and control of terms.

But in this instance, the frustration of the pro-ministerial writers is especially palpable. At least at the level of language, the Opposition, and particularly *Common Sense* with its trademark rallying cry, seemed in the late 1730s to be winning the battle. Walpole's supporters clearly felt robbed. As a commentator in the *Gentleman's Magazine* put it in 1739, the upstart journal was to be dreaded precisely for its title, "behind which he [the author] has the Art of sheltering himself in perfect Security. He defeats his Enemies by calling them *Enemies of Common Sense*, and silences the strongest Objections and the clearest Reasonings, by assuring his Readers that *they are contrary to Common Sense*. I must confess . . . that I remember but two Instances of a Genius able to use a few Syllables to such great and so various Purposes."[97]

No one writing on behalf of Walpole and the ministerial cause was about to declare common sense unimportant; part of the anger of the Court Whigs certainly stemmed from the fact that they, too, accepted the idea of common sense both as a method of ascertaining truth that involved stripping things down to their most basic, self-evident parts, much like what contemporary scientists called "analysis," and as an autonomous, legitimate epistemic authority. Additionally, no one wanted to debunk the idea that there was indeed a single English common sense that had only to be correctly identified as such and acted upon. True plurality was not an option. In the end, all commentators—no matter how partisan—were invested in maintaining a pose of neutrality or impartiality, of exclusive interest in truth and moral virtue and public-mindedness (in contrast to the self-interest of their opponents).[98] This was especially true of female polemicists, who ran an even greater risk of looking eager for personal gain or glory. Yet all pro-ministerial writers, male or female, had still to find a way to combat the version of common sense promulgated by the cleverly named *Common Sense.* The problem had a practical dimension. It also had a metaphysical one, since it required grappling with some of the most perplexing questions left over from the religious and scientific battles of the past century, including how to account for variance and multiplicity of interpretations and how to arrive at clear, plain, incontrovertible truth even when subjects exceeded rational demonstration.

One basic strategy of counterattack was established early on in the skirmish by Lord Hervey, one of Walpole's closest allies and most eloquent defenders, in his anonymous *A Letter to the Author of Common-Sense,* published in the spring of 1737. That was to approach the problem at the level of meaning—or, more precisely, sense. Hervey's starting tack was to unmask common sense, as used by Lyttelton and Chesterfield and their associates, as an example of what Locke had famously called in his *Essay on Human Understanding* an "abuse of words." With the stated aim "to shew the Publick how little your paper [*Common Sense*] deserv'd its Title," Hervey downplayed questions of policy and content and instead went after the newspaper's "dogmatical Manner" and faulty and deceitful use of terms, not least that of common sense itself.[99] Hervey's next step was then, like most of his allies in this partisan fight, to apply a dose of what one present-day political philosopher calls "language medicine."[100] Hervey tried to shift the balance of power by rectifying the meaning of the words in question or, as we might say now, by realigning signs and their referents. The phrase "common sense," it was agreed, needed first to be given back its former or "true" signification, its common sense. It had to be shown, one critic observed, that the phrase "what says Common Sense?" refers not to "the impudent impotent Libel, that so improperly, and immodestly, assumes that Name, but real Common Sense."[101] The remedy, then, depended on describing what had passed temporarily as common sense as its antithesis, relabeling, in

Hervey's words, "your poor sickly Common-Sense" as first "Common-Place" and, finally, "Uncommon Nonsense."[102] When, six months later, another prominent supporter of Walpole (and Fielding's second cousin), Lady Mary Wortley Montagu, began her own occasional essay journal solely to combat the writing of Lyttelton, Chesterfield, and their colleagues, she echoed this point, calling her journal the *Nonsense of Common Sense* to show up all the "vulgar Errors" that now went under the exalted name of "common sense" and to restore to "these poor words" the meanings they had had just the previous Christmas.[103]

This approach had been tried before. Responses to the Opposition were, in the early and mid-1730s, full of charges of the "Misrepresentation of Persons and Things" and expositions of the effects of such abuses on confusing public debate.[104] Readers were warned that disloyal writers were using patriotism to mean opposition and opposition to mean faction or party or self-interest, regularly turning the established significations of words topsy-turvy and against inherited sense. Commentators often fixed on the abuse of words as a way to explain both accidental and deliberate variance—and to discredit all alternatives to the status quo. The message here was that the fight in question could not be a rational disagreement between two equally well-meaning parties. It could not simply be a matter of politics. Rather, it was a misunderstanding or misconstruction stemming from the imprecise and malleable nature of words or the deluded or dishonest use of them.[105] Ultimately, then, this was a problem that had to be combated on exactly that level so as to restore a unitary sense of common sense.

For many commentators, including Lady Montagu, the problem was not, however, exclusively one of language and sense. The reason for the mistaken conception of common sense at the core of the newspaper *Common Sense* lay with the spokesmen themselves—or the social context in which such sense had become common. Lady Montagu took the approach that the Opposition's error in explaining common sense derived also from the segment of the population whose sense was being described. Perhaps, she suggested, the problems of language in *Common Sense* simply stemmed from the fact that the editors meant "Sense of the common People," as "they [the editors] appear possessed of the way of Thinking that used to be peculiar to the lowest of that Class." That, as well as the "Inspiration of Gin," would explain the indecency and scurrility of the paper's wit or what was sometimes called its "low" style.[106] The vulgarity of all that was truly common was a frequent theme among pro-ministry respondents, such as Thomas Newcomb, who announced in his own attack on *Common Sense* simply that "what'er is common we despise."[107]

Other commentators, though, took the opposite approach in sociological terms. The danger lay not in the editors' populism or appeal to a "Mob Sense"; it was their desire to speak only for themselves and their private interests and passions. Writing as Marforio (Pasquin's traditional counterpart), another anonymous pamphleteer argued that it was a mistake to see Opposition journals, such as *Common Sense*, as speaking "the Sense, not only of the Heads of the Party, but of the People in general," as was frequently claimed. On the contrary, "no Man can be so weak as to think that a People of Good Sense, such as the English are, will ever be laughed into an Opposition to the Government."[108] Usually the authors of *Common Sense* were exposed in the pro-ministerial press as spokesmen for special interests or for factions that were only hiding behind the idea of common sense because it connoted impartial wisdom and popular sentiment. A contributor to the government's chief organ, the *Daily Gazetteer,* insisted that the editor of *Common Sense* was nothing more than an "Imposter that had set himself up as an Advocate for the People" or demagogue. In fact, he and his colleagues, the *Daily Gazetteer*'s columnist continued, were a dangerous mixture of "Libertines, Atheists, Scotch Presbyterian Jacobites, Romish Priests and Irish Papists" in desperate need of exposure and censure.[109] Others claimed that the editors had even more petty drives; they were simply angry because they were not "in Place," and this had led them to try to unsettle the regime with the backing of "disappointed Jacobites, mingled with wild Republicans."[110] Most also blamed base concerns, the fact that the marketplace required down-on-their-luck authors to prostitute themselves by writing trash. As if being an emissary of the pope were not enough, the *Daily Gazetteer* continued with further guesses as to the true identity of its journalistic opponents: "Fellows that have beggar'd themselves with their Debaucheries in their Youth, and are obliged to turn Hackney Writers to support themselves in their Age."[111] Even Lady Montagu decried the fact that there was no money to be made on a "moral Paper," that there existed at present what would later be called a kind of censorship of the market.[112] And if malice and greed and other passions and interests were not sufficient to generate mistaken ideas, the journalist's last resort was to cry madness, that is, the inability on the part of Opposition writers to determine wherein true common sense lay.[113]

Clearly these writers hoped that exposure of deceitful language and deceptive motives—the failure of sense and then of true commonality—would stem the popular advance of the Opposition. In case this tactic proved insufficient, pro-ministerial hacks also peddled apocalyptic forecasts of the political and moral outcome should the dissidents' distorted vision of common sense prevail. But in truth none of these counterarguments found much traction at the end of the 1730s. Disagreements about how common sense should be determined perpetuated divisiveness, to the benefit of a coalition of protesters that, on the surface, was only for liberty, unity, and the common good. When a two-volume collection of the first issues of *Common Sense* was printed in 1738, the printer smugly congratulated the people of England on the fact that "all the Wit and Good Sense should have appeared on the Side of Liberty" despite the fact that government writers had tried their best "to be arch and merry on the Side of Corruption."[114] Even if the Opposition saw few concrete victories in Parliament during these years, that historically related abstraction, public opinion, seemed increasingly to be moving to its side, especially in the case of policy toward Spain. For a jingoistic and "patriotic" press successfully inflamed readers to see the situation in life-or-death terms—to the extent that public protest eventually played a critical role in forcing war with Spain in October 1739, which, in turn, helped precipitate the fall of Walpole only a few years later.[115] Common sense had, by the end of the 1730s, become an important weapon in the development of an increasingly established, extra-parliamentary protesting political culture.

The problem was so acute that an anonymous pro-ministerial author felt compelled to publish, in the heat of the battle over Spanish depredations, a full-blown philosophical discourse entitled *Common Sense: Its*

Nature and Use, with the Manner of Bringing All Disputable Cases in Common Life, to a Trial and Final Determination by It, with a post-script that read almost as an afterthought: *Applied to the Spanish Affair.* The point of this tract was not only to unmask (one more time) the appeal to common sense put forth by the newspaper of that name as a deception and an affront to readers' understanding, particularly where Spanish policy was concerned. It was also—more unusually—to explore "what Common Sense really is" so that those ignorantly and innocently led astray could begin to make "common use" of it.[116]

The author of this obscure pamphlet went on to offer one of the era's most extensive definitions of this exalted principle. As he explained it:

> [Common sense] is not only that by which we keep ourselves from falling into Fire and Water, and chuse [*sic*] a Piece of Bread to eat, rather than a Piece of Wood; but I also mean that general Perception or Sensation of Things which is common to all Men. That is the Perception of the Distinction between Wood and Bread, which makes it appear to one Man as it does to another, and here only it is that we can come at a true View of any Case. Particular Men may be biass'd or blinded by Interest, Passions, Appetites, or Humours, which often are opposite, and contradictory, and may be as various as there are Men, or Sets of Men, debating the Matter; but when the Case is refer'd to this *General* or *Common Sense* of the whole World, the Partialities of particular Mens [*sic*] Interests and Humours are not at all in the Question.[117]

The message, following closely on the moral lessons of the *Spectator* a few decades earlier, amounted to the claim that a failure to listen to and to heed common sense judgments lay at the heart of most mistakes in human understanding. All men possessed this kind of basic sense; it was what potentially linked them together and allowed them to "see Things in the same Manner." They had only to learn to ignore their passions and interests, and remain unaffected by deceivers throwing dust in their eyes and telling them two different things were the same, in order for common sense to triumph and problems in multiple realms to be effectively solved.

But then, finally, the author of this tract articulated his own, obviously partial and partisan, version of the "Sentence of universal Common Sense" regarding the highly contested Spanish affair. And an Opposition critic soon responded with a common sense motto of his own: "if a Man does not wear a Lyon's skin, every Ass will piss upon him."[118] How could they have done otherwise? Common sense had become, at once, an eighteenth-century cultural ideal dependent upon the idea of natural, broad-based agreement about certain fundamental truths and a commonplace polemical tool in a bitterly fought struggle over the future of politics.

In sum, between 1690 and the end of the 1730s, an odd kind of transformation had occurred with an ancient psychological category at its center. The process had begun in reaction to a perceived crisis of legitimacy in both epistemology and public life. Within a ruling class anxious for security and calm, and yet also determined to insulate individuals from the pressure to conform ideologically lest such a move threaten the peace further, the notion of common sense had come to seem a baseline upon which a nonconflictual but also noncoercive social and moral order could be erected. Common sense would limit hostility born of divergent opinions simply by furnishing consensual parameters for debate. Sure enough, something like a tacit general agreement about the value of common sense and its particular suitability to ethical and political questions helped provide a foundation for the astonishing Whig oligarchy and elite social solidarity that grew up in the first few decades of the eighteenth century.

But so successful was this rhetorical invention called "common sense" in the London of the early 1700s that it simultaneously created just the opposite of what it promised: a mechanism for producing and even intensifying ideological strife within the context of this increasingly stable political order. Because it sounded objective and indisputable; because it drew on the power of the community as a whole; and, above all, because it had already become a widely accepted epistemic and moral authority with deep connections to Protestant culture and an assumed suitability to questions of public life, common sense turned out to be a formidable weapon of protest and dissent and a key element in the de facto creation of legitimate opposition. It effectively disguised the contest between multiple points of view that it actually helped to stoke. Moreover, public arguments over the ownership and nature of common sense, at the same time as they reinforced its standing as an indisputable establishment value, set the stage for a series of claims that would eventually undermine other establishment values—in London and elsewhere. These claims included the position that the vox populi (even as defined by elites without any direct input from the lower classes) could be an alternative source of legitimacy and the position that there is sometimes good sense in challenging the way things currently are. The concept of common sense would ultimately prove vital both to the so-called redemptive face of democratic politics, in which popular sovereignty is imagined as a means to justice, peace, and settled truth, and to the so-called pragmatic face, in which protest and disagreement become an accepted part of public life.[119] It would also transform the subject matter and methods of politics to match its newly exalted status.

This, however, is to get ahead of our story. For first, stealthily and well before any of the formal features of modern democracy came into being, the value of that spectral presence we still call common sense had to insinuate itself into thinking about the sources of public order, thinking about governance, and thinking about thought itself. Moreover, the gap between its narrow social base in practice and its ostensible universality as a concept had to be brought to light. This is what happened in London during the span of Fielding's own brief life. Faith in the rightness of common sense has been firmly a part of Western common sense ever since—and to this day, we rarely notice the multiple, contradictory purposes to which this familiar abstraction lends its authority.

CHAPTER 2

Everyman's Perception of the World

Aberdeen, 1758–1770

The rudest of the vulgar know most perfectly what they mean,
when they say, Three months ago I was at such a town, and have
ever since been at home.

James Beattie, *An Essay on the Nature and Immutability of Truth*

A MERE THIRTY-FOUR YEARS after Henry Fielding insisted that
Queen Common Sense was already dead, an obscure Scottish university professor and former schoolteacher named James Beattie took on a job few would want. He set out from a remote corner of Scotland not simply to revive her sphere of influence but also to establish a list of the basic principles to which all must subscribe without giving them another thought. What were these principles? From the vantage point of twenty-first-century philosophy, the list is rather a hodgepodge: I exist. I am the same being today that I was yesterday—or even twenty years ago. Things equal to one and the same thing are equal to one another. Ingratitude ought to be blamed and punished. The three angles of a triangle are equal to two right angles. A whole is greater than a part. Every effect has a cause. The senses can be believed. The ground on which I stand is hard, material, solid, and has a real, separate, independent existence. The sun will rise tomorrow. I have a soul distinct from my body. Virtue and vice are different. So are heat and cold, red and white, an ox and an ass. Truth exists. There is a God.

How can we know that these propositions are not simply the result of our imaginations working overtime? Beattie insisted the proof of the validity of such convictions lay in the fact that the mind immediately assents to them without requiring any demonstration. Though we cannot prove them, we feel we have no choice but to believe them. But in case readers were not so easily persuaded, Beattie had a second argument. To form the contrary opinion, to deny such axioms, pulled one into the realm of the absurd. So, largely for rhetorical effect, he compiled in the course of his grandiosely entitled opus, *An Essay on the Nature and Immutability of Truth, in Opposition to Sophistry and Scepticism* (1770), a second, contrasting, list. He laid out a countercanon of the ridiculous. Could anything be more contrary to common sense, he asked, than to be convinced that 1 and 2 are equal to 6, a part is greater than a whole, a circle could be a triangle, or that it may be possible for the same thing, at the same time, to be and not to be? Could anyone reasonably believe to see with the soles of his feet? Or be convinced that one and the same body may be in 10,000 different places at the same time? Or speak and act in the evening as if one thought that one had become a different person since morning? Or, finally, deny the existence of God?

Such were the parameters of common sense in the small Scottish city of Aberdeen in the late 1760s. For Beattie and his contemporaries, these distinctions were self-evident (though the fact of needing to spell them out and defend their authority tells us that, in Beattie's estimation at least, they were not as certain as they should be). London may have been the site of the modern apotheosis of Queen Common Sense, that allegorical figure who had, in better days, ostensibly governed the world. But the hope that her ghost—so global in its connotations and potential applications—might be persuaded to return to her throne for the benefit of all humanity did not confine itself to London's city limits. Rather, like many other successful buzzwords of its era, common sense followed the geographical progression of books, letters, and personal conversations across the many urban centers of the eighteenth-century trans-European and, increasingly, transatlantic Republic of Letters.

Some responsibility belongs, surely, to the third Earl of Shaftesbury. Shaftesbury singlehandedly, in the early years of the eighteenth century, gave the old idea of *sensus communis* a transnational reach in practical as well as conceptual terms. Poor health and regular political upheaval

together forced the great earl to venture repeatedly during his short life
outside the confines of England. Considerable wealth made such pere-
grinations feasible. Thus this consummate early eighteenth-century cosmopolitan found himself carting about his favorite ideas just as one might
favorite possessions, adding to them and swapping them as he proceeded.
For everywhere he went, common sense (or one of its many variants)
could be presented, albeit in different forms, as one potential solution to
a different crisis in health: the unsure status of both virtue and truth in
the modern age.

As a young man, Shaftesbury spent several years on the Grand Tour,
traveling first through France and the Italian peninsula, then, out of
political exigency, all the way east to Laibach (now Ljubljana), Vienna,
Prague, and Berlin. In 1698–1699 and again in 1703–1704, before he made
his reputation as a moralist, the aristocratic Whig made his home, at first
incognito, in Rotterdam, the city of Pierre Bayle and an outpost of both
Huguenot and free thought. The differences in opinion and style between Bayle and Shaftesbury are easy to list. But on Bayle's death in 1706,
the deist Shaftesbury left a tribute to Bayle in which, rather than decry
the older man's purported skepticism, Shaftesbury extolled "the Test of
his Piercing Reason" for its impact on Shaftesbury's own thinking and
as a model for philosophy more generally. One can see in this friendship
between the exiled Frenchman and the peripatetic Englishman, perhaps, the roots of some of Shaftesbury's antipathy to orthodoxies and
commitment to the idea of freedom of expression, including engagement
in ridicule, as a means to expose errors and cant wherever they might
reside.[1]

Then, in 1711, after the publication of Shaftesbury's main works and
an extended stay back in England, failing health associated with severe
asthma sent the great earl in the other direction: to torrid Naples and the
Mediterranean coast. There he became a member of the circle who gathered around Giuseppe Valletta, owner of the city's greatest library, and
most likely became acquainted with the humanist rhetorician Giambattista Vico, an encounter about which Vico scholars have continued to
speculate, in part because of the parallels between the two men's work.[2]
Vico famously insisted in his *New Science*, the first edition of which

appeared in 1725, that the *sensus communis,* which he defined as "judgment without reflection, shared by an entire class, an entire people, an
entire nation, or the entire human race," constituted nothing less than
"what is certain in the natural law of the *gentes* [early nations]."[3] For
Vico, as for Shaftesbury, this common sense was a kind of social glue,
holding together the very first societies well prior to the development of
any political order. One is left to wonder about the parallels between the
two men's thinking in terms of their anti-Cartesianism but also their
commitment to the social dimension of truth. What is sure is that just
before his death in 1713, Shaftesbury employed local Neapolitan drafts-
men to make emblematic prints for the second edition of his *Character-
istiks,* including the emblem for common sense.[4]

It was, however, a decidedly less cosmopolitan place, a distant corner
of northeast Scotland which Shaftesbury surely never visited in sickness
or in health, that most fully took up the banner of common sense as a
cause. There, decades after Shaftesbury's own death, in the diminutive,
misty city of Aberdeen on the coast of the North Sea, a small, homoge-
neous group of pious professional men endeavored to retrofit common
sense as the centerpiece of an anti-skeptical philosophical method attached to a moral campaign. These were Presbyterian ministers and
university professors, men much less wealthy, worldly, or well connected
than Shaftesbury and deeply rooted in local, Scottish institutions. But
they were also expansive and up-to-date readers, active participants in a
much broader, multidirectional Republic of Letters. By midcentury,
they had consumed with great interest and enthusiasm the writings
not only of the great English scientists of the preceding hundred years
but also the works of the author of *Sensus Communis* and his most famous literary contemporaries, the Augustan stylists Addison, Steele,
and Pope. Moreover, they had read Shaftesbury's ancient predecessors,
from the Stoics to Cicero. And they also knew well his recent successors, including Francis Hutcheson, Lord Kames, and local hero George
Turnbull, all of whom owed a debt to Shaftesbury as they postulated
the existence of an innate "moral sense," or instinct for virtue, that
naturally led mankind to act benevolently and to consider the common
good.[5]

From these multiple sources, as well as their deep Presbyterian faith, the leading intellectuals of northeast Scotland formed their basic ideas about the world they inhabited. They formed their first line of defense, too. For at the same time, these learned Aberdonians had also familiarized themselves with the radical new philosophical ideas that had flowed over the last century and a half from Amsterdam and Paris (Descartes and Voltaire), London (Locke and Berkeley), and, finally, closer to home, comparatively cosmopolitan Edinburgh (David Hume). What struck them in their reading was a sense of dissonance: between, on the one hand, philosophies that seemed (despite their author's intentions in some cases) to throw all ideas into doubt and, on the other, the pastoral, Christian world that they saw around them on Scotland's remote northern coast and that they imagined preserving for the benefit of their charges.

The conflict seemed to demand a response. This coterie of moral educators, including the canon-making James Beattie, toiled collectively over several decades in the middle of the eighteenth century to find an effective, "scientific" way to refute what they took to be a worrisome trend toward relativism and doubt. For these provincial academics, this was, at its core, a problem belonging to the specialized world of philosophy. For most, though, including Beattie, the real danger of a skeptical approach to truth stemmed from its suitability to, and indeed successful invasion of, the larger culture of Britain's urban commercial centers, including the great Scottish city of Edinburgh, where it brought the threat of irreligion and community dissolution in its wake. New notions of toleration, combined with a relatively free commercial press—the lasting products of a postrevolutionary settlement that had been expanded to cover the whole of the British Isles—had produced a desirable proliferation of knowledge. But from what might be called a communitarian perspective, this pluralism threatened (as it had earlier in London) to undermine any sense of secure truths or even the idea that humans had a capacity to determine such truths in everyday life, providing dangerously fertile ground for the flourishing of a philosophy rooted in individual doubt.[6] Somehow this impulse needed to be checked, these Scottish clerics and academics reasoned, but without turning away from the

methods of Newton and without reversing the tide toward open, unfettered intellectual exchange or compromising a now deeply held British
commitment to the protection of confessional differences. In the idea of
common sense—an outgrowth of the moral sense theory that began with
Shaftesbury and his *sensus communis* in the first half of the century—
they found the very modern ally that they needed.

Much as in London some decades earlier, the appeal to an abstraction
called "common sense" became, in midcentury Aberdeen, a mainstay of
a polemical campaign, this time directed against moral *and* epistemological skepticism. Within a lightly and informally regulated marketplace of ideas that stretched, legally and illegally, across multiple urban
centers within the Republic of Letters, it represented a highly useful
rhetorical weapon. But at the same time, common sense, in the hands of
Aberdeen's leading intellectuals, also took on new significance to human
psychology: as an authoritative "power" located within the human brain
and the source of convictions that, when acknowledged, could make
many basic beliefs simply beyond challenge. And in this double form,
the old and seemingly modest idea of common sense offered to become
both an informal source of ideational regulation—a way to create lines of
intellectual inclusion and exclusion essential for the reinforcement of
community—and the foundation for a moral renaissance. For Beattie
and his colleagues, a plainspoken defense of the basic capacity of humans to have and to know common sense suggested a particularly efficacious way to naturalize and thus to preserve the Christian beliefs that
they cherished both as explanations of how the world worked and as
mechanisms for keeping their own ethical universe intact. Beattie hoped
that this notion could be employed, within the still-novel context of
"free speech," to head off the social dissolution and moral rot emanating
from Edinburgh and cities beyond.

What Beattie could not have anticipated, though, were all the side effects of common sense's continued success. One of the main results of
calling upon common sense as "sovereign authority," as Beattie's colleague Thomas Reid put it in 1764, was to help propel the entrance of a
largely unintended democratic ethos into the realm of public judgment.[7]
For in the service of this essentially conservative moral project, Beattie

and his contemporaries not only found themselves having to disparage the claims of certain kinds of men of learning or other elites who would typically have passed for intellectual authorities, further extending the leveling impulse of Protestantism, with its refusal to identify special loci of sacredness. They also ended up elevating the instinctive, collective, quotidian beliefs of "common" men to a new high, rejecting the attribution of superior judgment to any one class, sex, race, or religion. The common sense defense of common sense became, in the hands of a small group of mid-eighteenth-century professional men in Aberdeen, the foundation for a decidedly populist epistemology, rooted in the wisdom of the ordinary and the aggregate. When it came time to find truth in the realm of common life, they argued, there was no better starting point than what everybody already agreed to be true; the "unlearned" person was actually less likely to be misled than the overeducated person, and the collective sentiment trumped the individual or the isolated genius every time. In this line of argument, the Aberdonians far surpassed their more worldly and politically engaged London predecessors, including the deeply elitist (and deist) Shaftesbury.

Furthermore, the defense of this distinctive epistemology produced in eighteenth-century Aberdeen the phenomenon of a new and lasting social type: the educated avatar of common sense who has no choice but to define himself (and only considerably later, herself) as a spokesman for the truths already established by masses of ordinary people. This was the individual who found himself in the uncomfortable position of climbing the social ranks as the public harbinger of ideas that should, in theory, require neither the learned nor the clever to promote them. As John Coates has dryly noted in a study of Cambridge philosophers between World Wars I and II, "There remains something odd about a specialist in common sense."[8] But the invention of the popular guru with claims to common sense on his side was to have important, if unplanned, historical consequences. For it was he who would lay the foundations for a new model of politics that emphasized the inherent, infallible capacity for judgment of "the people" (which, at least initially, meant white, property-owning, English-speaking men) when it came to public matters and, conversely, the suitability of political questions to simple, quotidian, determinations of goodness and truth. And it was he who would set the intellectual stage for demagoguery and democracy alike.

How (and why) did this happen first on the edges of the North Sea? The Treaty of Union of 1707 brought Scotland firmly into the new state of Britain. It also helped produce a series of outposts of a trans-European Enlightenment in Scotland's main university towns. The centerpiece of the Scottish Enlightenment was, of course, Edinburgh, celebrated ever since as the home of David Hume. But Glasgow boasted its own intellectual celebrities, learned societies, and literary culture. Aberdeen, to the north and east, also soon acquired many of the ideas and social patterns that made it a recognizably enlightened city, including a fascination with the new science still associated with Bacon and Newton. By the middle of the eighteenth century, the sense of belonging to a nation in the grips of change permeated all of Scotland's urban centers.

Nevertheless, historians of the Scottish Enlightenment have generally taken pains to emphasize what made Aberdeen distinctive, a world apart even from other Scottish university towns in the second half of the eighteenth century. For all the commonalities among the nation's urban centers in terms of religion, language, law, and social structure, each also maintained a strong sense of regional identity tied largely to its particular geographical situation and the background of its literati. This was especially true of Aberdeen. Without the flourishing commercial sector of large English towns or Edinburgh or even Glasgow to the south and without any direct links to imperial concerns or far-off national political institutions, Aberdeen was, in both economic and political terms, a parochial place in the mid-eighteenth century. Certainly it was the antithesis of London. Neither capitalist ventures nor new political schemes held much attraction following the end of the Jacobite threat circa 1745; relief from poverty still seemed to most Aberdonian elites most likely to come from agricultural reform and increased piety. Socially Aberdeen remained insular as well, with a population of approximately 22,000 at midcentury that made it more comparable in size at that moment to the distant British colonial city of Philadelphia (though Philadelphia was to grow at a considerably faster rate in the years to come) than to Edinburgh.[9] These circumstances meant that, in one sense, Aberdeen remained more conservative, more tied to traditional ways of doing and thinking than its neighbors to the south, especially in the moral realm. Aberdeen was, however, by 1750, blessedly free from many of the anxieties and squabbles of the era, whether economic, political, or religious, which also left it relatively intellectually unencumbered. This apartness was coupled with a strong commitment among its elites to freedom of inquiry and minimal state regulation of ideas as one of the hallmarks of "modern" British law. And in terms of religion, a long tradition of independence, including openness to Episcopalianism and to intellectual currents flowing once from the Baltic, France, and the Low Countries and, increasingly, from England and the extended British Empire, should make one hesitant about imagining this provincial capital and port city as simply a backwater.

Indeed, this very particular combination of relative isolation and intellectual tolerance, not to mention piety, made a special mark on those mid-eighteenth-century Aberdonian institutions whose key purpose was the definition and diffusion of truth. Foremost among these was the Presbyterian Church. As the result of seventeenth-century compromises, Presbyterianism in the northeast of Scotland had incorporated an unusual number of the hallmarks of Low Church Episcopalianism. Local ministers, disdainful of Protestant enthusiasm and of Catholic superstition alike, frequently borrowed themes and even sermons from the English Latitudinarians before them, crafting a kind of moderate, pragmatic Presbyterianism in which virtuous living and toleration of doctrinal differences were prized above Calvinist dogma, including the idea of the original depravity of man. And while the Kirk remained the key institution of authority in the North East, clerical elites themselves were often in the forefront in the eighteenth century in promoting interest in the new science and in related forms of "improvement" with a decidedly forward-looking cast. As many local ministers saw it, one of their primary jobs was to use the methods of advanced science to fight against an invidious skepticism and to bring new certainty to the beliefs and especially moral values of Christianity.[10]

A similar mission, born of parochialism and a commitment to unfettered inquiry alike, characterized the two universities of eighteenth-century Aberdeen: Marischal College and King's College. Like many other British universities, Marischal (though not King's) saw its teaching practices evolve in the 1750s as regenting, or teaching across fields, disappeared and an era of academic specialization began. Both Aberdeen universities also experienced the overhauling of their curriculums at midcentury, as leading professors, continuing an effort begun by George Turnbull at Marischal in the 1720s, led a concerted effort to move the arts away from the vestiges of Scholasticism. Faculty like Turnbull had championed the empirical, inductive methods of the new science as a means to truth and had urged attention to the laws governing the human mind as well as the material world. But as befits these universities' function as largely a training ground for Protestant ministers and teachers, it was still widely agreed at midcentury that the principles of Newton were ultimately to be used to support the values of the church and of the northeast establishment more generally. The same went for the anti-dogmatic moral sense philosophy of Shaftesbury and Hutcheson. Science (including pneumatology, or the empirical investigation of the human mind), religion, and practical morality were to be taught as means of illuminating and buttressing one another.[11]

Above all, though, it was the newest institution devoted to justifying and certifying the pillars of knowledge, the Philosophical Society of Aberdeen, formed in 1758, that characterized the Aberdeen Enlightenment—and played a central role in the history of common sense. Known colloquially as the Wise Club for its concentration of very smart men, this "philosophical society" was one of the many, many such voluntary social-intellectual bodies so constituted in eighteenth-century Europe and its empires. This one, like its counterparts in London, Lyon, Berlin, Philadelphia, and Cap François (Saint-Domingue), among other urban centers, had its roots in the perceived benefits of sociability, along with free inquiry, in the pursuit of truths of different sorts. Men of varied professional interests agreed to meet at regular intervals, in some places in the company of women (as in the Parisian salons) and in other places entirely apart (as in Aberdeen), for polite, convivial conversation

and orderly debate about a wide range of topical questions, from education to agriculture. The idea was that all this talk would lead to self-
improvement on the part of members and, more importantly, to progress
or reform in the world at large. Central to the very idea of these clubs was
a by-then commonplace communitarian epistemology: that sharing
knowledge and reasoning in common would ultimately benefit the common good, producing intellectual, moral, medical, and even economic
betterment on a collective as well as individual scale. Here was a social
experiment that depended equally upon the optimistic view of human
nature propagated by the new science and by certain strains of Protestantism; the example of earlier statist efforts to control the production of
knowledge through the establishment of official academies; and the parallel rise of informal public gathering places, such as coffeehouses and
salons, as aspects of the culture of an emergent, expanding, urban "middle" order. In the British context, this ideal had been given new life in
the Augustan period by journals like the *Spectator,* where Addison had
promised to bring "Philosophy out of Closets and Libraries, Schools
and Colleges," and by popular essay collections like that of Shaftesbury,
who had imagined a salutary *sensus communis* arising from unimpeded
conversation in just this mold.[12] Scottish cities, without their own political institutions to provide a focal point for public debate after the start of
the eighteenth century, fell particularly hard for this vision.

But this Aberdonian club—or "epistemological community" in Peter
Burke's phrase—adopted a very particular mission even in comparison
to other eighteenth-century Scottish learned societies.[13] Perhaps this
was the result of its relative isolation in geographic as well as political
terms; it operated almost entirely free of government oversight. Perhaps
it was the common professional and social horizons of the sixteen men
who were members at one time or another between 1758 and 1773, all of
whom came from the region, were connected to one another through
family relations, friendship, institutional affiliation, or patronage, and
made their livings as ministers or professors or both.[14] This homogene-
ity must surely have produced a certain kind of intellectual conformity,
or at least common sense of purpose, that ultimately made neither the
idea of a common sense capacity nor the existence of a single set of com-

mon sense principles seem too elusive an idea. For what distinguished the Wise Club was its members' eagerness to use their fashionable association to produce a slate of arguments *against* the most fashionable philosophy of their day—and to do so by returning to the most basic of philosophical questions: how do we know anything? Thus while also taking up typical "improving" topics of the moment, from the effectiveness of lime as a fertilizer to the "origins of the blacks," the founding members of the Wise Club kept coming back to problems of evidence and proof.[15] They also, in accordance with their founding rules, made it a priority to examine "False Schemes of Philosophy and false Methods of Philosophizing," meaning the Humean skepticism that made it seem as if there were no grounds on which to accept one thing as true rather than another, especially in the context of freedom of expression.[16] This was, of course, a question of epistemology at heart. But it, too, was motivated by a sense of social and moral duty on the part of a society of Christian educators. For the men of the Wise Club saw themselves grappling with nothing less than a crisis in authority that began at the level of the human mind and spread outward from there.[17]

But how did they envision waging this battle? One way was to agree in advance on a single, collective working method or set of ground rules for arriving at consensual truths. This intimate group of colleagues and friends declared from the start that they would derive the knowledge they hoped to share only from observation, experimentation, and the methods of natural philosophy associated with Bacon, Locke, and Newton. Accordingly, the men of the Wise Club also promised to place limits on how questions might be framed and even on what might be open to investigation; all that was outside the capacity of human minds to determine definitively was to be avoided. Moreover, according to the original club bylaws, there would be none of the witty banter, taste for paradox, word games, fruitless speculation, or logical quibbling that the founding members took to be hallmarks of metaphysics, whether in its now-disdained Scholastic form or in its modern, skeptical, incarnation. Words themselves would not be open to discussion (though philosophy of language, understood as a social artifact, was to be a central concern). Also, certain subject matters were to be avoided if they could lead one in morally compromising directions. The idea, as David Skene explained in his first discourse read at the club, was simple: "A man who values his happiness and wants to enjoy Life with relish, however fond of coming at Truth, must be afraid of venturing upon a Subject where there is a chance of making discoveries at the expense of his most darling views."[18] Only in recognizing self-imposed boundaries to their intellectual activities, club members agreed, would they have a chance of arriving at philosophically and morally valid truth to which they could all assent.

The second goal was then to use this model method, with its emphasis on empiricism and free inquiry within a circumscribed domain, to explore "the anatomy of the human mind," as Reid was to call it.[19] For what the members of the Wise Club ultimately sought was a counter-epistemology to that of dangerous modern skeptics such as Hume. In truth, they were not actually interested in refuting the great philosopher of Edinburgh as much as entering into dialogue with him (and secondarily, with Locke and his *Essay on Human Understanding*); all of the Wise Club members, with the possible exception of Beattie, were great admirers of Hume's intellect. But they also believed it imperative to vindicate religious and moral principles from the implications of Humean skepticism—an idea fully consonant with the curricular emphases of the Aberdeen colleges of the 1750s and 1760s and the teachings of the Presbyterian church. By reopening the question of the workings of the human mind, they hoped to discover nothing less than grounds for validating what one believes, indeed seems to know in some instinctive way, as the truth, and for reaffirming (middle-class, Christian) community norms in the process.

The solution, they came to agree, lay in the development of an actual philosophy of common sense. Precise definitions varied from member to member. But over the first decade and a half of the Wise Club's existence, the authority of common sense, or the self-evident, became an Aberdonian leitmotif. It provided the starting point for their own collective intellectual labors as they met on the second and fourth Wednesday nights of each month. It constituted a standard of judgment, a court of final appeal for the detection of errors, as they constructed their widely circulated critiques of "false schemes of philosophy" anchored by abuses

of words and violations of common sense. Finally, it became the centerpiece of their own philosophy of mind, a resounding rejoinder to other
philosophers about what can be believed and why, and a foundation—
alongside conscience—for the establishment of true and secure knowledge, including of God's purpose. This was the message that the professors and ministers of the Wise Club tried over several decades to instill
in university students, congregants, and readers alike. The idea, rooted
in a surprising optimism about human nature given the Calvinist roots
of Scottish culture, was that by reaching these multiple audiences with
this message, the path would be set for broad-based moral reform to
follow.

Certainly these men, with their many correspondents across Britain,
were well aware that "common sense," like "club" for that matter, was a
fashionable phrase and a potentially fighting one at that. The professional class in Aberdeen was made up at midcentury of many eager students of the style of London's polite literary culture, especially when it
came to periodicals. *The Spectator,* with its constant moralizing tributes
to good and common sense, was well known (Beattie reported it to be an
enduring inspiration). So were its Georgian successors, many of which—
including Lyttelton and Chesterfield's *Common Sense*—came out in reprint in Edinburgh shortly after their London publication date. Indeed,
closer to home, the appeal to common sense had, by the time of the formation of the Wise Club, become a commonplace of pamphleteering in
Edinburgh and Dublin, too, much as it had long been in the southern
half of Great Britain. At midcentury, that ambiguous and multivalent
pairing of the words "common" and "sense" was still being used in defense
of a range of different religious positions.[20] Either by itself or in conjunction with a second, more conventional authority—reason, experience,
revelation, Scripture, the Constitution—it was also frequently called
upon by Scottish and Irish writers to support any number of divergent
opinions about issues of municipal and national politics. These included
the promotion of woolen manufacturing, an end to patronage, and the
definition of representation, to name but a few.[21] And in the ongoing
struggle to lay waste to the enemy position by defining one's own as indisputable and impervious to challenge, there was always the possibility

of revising the "the spirit of common sense" toward aesthetic ends. In mid-eighteenth-century Edinburgh, the evocation of the ghost of common sense still offered an effective way to attack what an author deemed a wretched night at the theater.[22]

But the members of the Wise Club, and especially founding member Thomas Reid, had bigger and more serious ambitions. In fact, Reid's interest in reform beginning with common sense predated the founding of the Wise Club. Trained at Marischal under Turnbull in the 1720s, when a vague notion of common sense was already in vogue as a counterweight to moral skepticism, Reid had begun making rhetorical use of this concept as early as the 1750s, when he was named a regent at King's and had had to find some way to deal with Hume in his third-year lecture courses devoted to the philosophy of the human mind.[23] Already in his first discourse presented to the Philosophical Society in June 1758, Reid had accused Hume of "shock[ing] the common sense of mankind" through the abuse of words and had personified this notion if not precisely as a queen than at least as a female "adversary . . . who never fails at last to triumph over those who wage war with her."[24] Soon he was at work building on Shaftesbury and Hutcheson's moral sense theory, as interpreted by Turnbull and then Lord Kames, expanding its purview to cover determinations of truth and falsehood as well as good and evil and giving it an explicitly Christian purpose in the bargain. Under the guise of "common" sense, what had been understood to be a matter of feeling evolved toward a form of objective judgment. But in the context of the Wise Club, spelling out exactly what common sense was and how it functioned was a group effort, beginning from the first discussions of evidence in 1759.[25] Reid clearly envisioned the club as a springboard for his own thinking as he considered how best to respond to Hume's skepticism and to the theory of ideas that he took to be its source. Other members followed suit, even as their worries and explanations took subtly different forms. Soon a series of remarkable publications issuing from the best presses of Edinburgh, London, and, later, Continental publishing centers—in effect, the chief seats of all this fashionable and dangerous thinking—spread the vigorously oppositional arguments of Reid and company well beyond their small circle of "middling" provincial scholars meeting twice monthly in Aberdeen.[26]

Suspicion of metaphysical speculation, coupled with an appeal to common sense as an antidote, characterized several of the first books to spring from the Wise Club. These included Alexander Gerard's *Essay on Taste* of 1759 and especially George Campbell's 1762 *Dissertation on Miracles,* which began life as an anti-Humean sermon sponsored by the Synod of Aberdeen and was transformed into a treatise on evidence in the context of the club.[27] It was, however, Reid's 1764 *An Inquiry into the Human Mind, on the Principles of Common Sense,* a work that had its origins in discussions and papers presented at Wise Club meetings, which became the defining philosophical text of the movement, or what later became known as the Common Sense School.[28]

Hume provided Reid, like Campbell, with a starting point. And Reid found much to admire in Hume's reasoning abilities and philosophical rigor. Hume was, however, unusual in the Scottish context for eschewing moderate Presbyterianism as a baseline for his ideas. Moreover, from Reid's perspective, Hume's epistemological skepticism—his seeming rejection of the independent existence of external reality and, even more, his argument that ideas can feel certain or be widely accepted without necessarily being true—posed a serious threat to basic beliefs and to the category of belief itself.[29] For Reid, this kind of doubt constituted every bit as large a threat as the explicitly moral skepticism that had so troubled Shaftesbury. Indeed for Reid, the two kinds of skepticism were intimately linked. The Humean approach left open the possibility that one could make a case for anything at all. And in the context of postrevolutionary British liberalism, where ideas were expected to compete for popular attention without the steadying hand of clerical or state regulation, the public would have no grounds upon which to determine why one idea, or approach to ideas, might be more legitimate than another. What was needed, in Reid's estimation, was not simply one more refutation of the link between skepticism and irreligion in the moralizing manner of a sermon. It was a new philosophy of mind, an alternative both to Cartesian rationalism (according to which all truths can be arrived at through rational demonstration) and to the empiricism of Locke and Berkeley (by which everything we know comes via the senses). Starting from Newton's *regulae philosophandi,* themselves "maxims of common sense . . . practiced everyday in common life," Reid set out in his *Inquiry* to offer a theory of immediate perception that, he hoped, would do away once and for all with the notion that we can have direct knowledge only of the contents of the mind (i.e., ideas), not external objects themselves, and with the notion that credibility is unrelated to truth. Crucial to the solution was a commitment to something he called common sense.[30]

What is common sense, according to Reid? It is most definitely not a special sense, as in the Aristotelian tradition. Sometimes Reid suggested that it is a mental capacity essential to social life; in a later work, he called it "that degree of judgment which is common to men with whom we can converse and transact business."[31] Here it means something very close to good sense, the common intelligence of all functioning people. More often it is an amorphous set of basic judgments or propositions, evident in the common language in which it is entrenched, to which all sane adult people, anywhere, anytime, must subscribe.[32] Reid included under this rubric not only first principles of reasoning or axioms, a traditional line of thought; much more innovatively, he also included all the things we take for granted in going about our everyday lives.[33] According to Reid's own definition in his *Inquiry:* "there are certain principles . . . which the constitution of our nature leads us to believe, and which we are under a necessity to take for granted in the common concerns of life, without being able to give a reason for them." These he labeled "the principles of common sense." Then, for emphasis, he added, "what is manifestly contrary to them, is what we call absurd."[34] Yet Reid's common sense still turns out to be a rather odd beast. Its tenets do not admit of direct proof. They actually thwart and exceed all efforts at demonstration, which means there is no point in arguing about them even when we are conscious of holding them (which is not all the time). Nevertheless we know them to be true on several grounds. They feel obvious or self-evident to us. They also cannot be denied; to do so would be not only to propagate a falsehood but also to lead others to conclude we are engaged in "lunacy" and belong in a "mad-house." And even when we try on an individual basis to doubt them, we quickly find we have no choice but to accept them just like everyone else in order to go about leading our lives. (As Reid later pointed out sardonically, "I never heard that any sceptic run his head against a post, or stepped into a kennel, because he did not

believe his eyes."[35]) In the end, we are required to accept these principles, in this form and without additional proof, because of the very
way God constituted us.

Reid conceded in the *Inquiry* that it is not always easy to figure out
which notions count (he did not make his own list of common sense
principles for another two decades). Commonness was not evidence
enough in and of itself. Still, the purview he gave to these beliefs is enormous. In Reid's telling, the principles of common sense are universal in
two important ways. Everything we know about the world, from advanced
science to how to survive on a day-to-day level, depends upon our ante-
cedent acceptance of these principles, which are "older, and of more authority, than Philosophy: she rests upon them as her basis, not they upon
her."[36] They are also integral to the belief system of everyone—with the
exception of the infantile, the mentally defective, and the deranged—all
over the world and at all moments.[37]

Yet therein lay the problem. In the fashionable intellectual environs of
London and Edinburgh, these principles were not nowadays actually
always recognized as such. Instead they were routinely flouted, especially by self-involved philosophers who set themselves above the fray
and looked down on their fellow men. How else could one explain challenges to the existence of the material world (in the case of Berkeley) or
even the existence of the self (in the case of Hume)? That—according to
James Beattie, a former scholarship student who rose through Aberdonian society to become professor of moral philosophy at Marischal in
1760 and, thanks to the patronage of his former teacher Alexander Gerard, a member of the Wise Club the following year—was the great danger of the age. No one writes about common sense who is not convinced
that it is under assault or fast disappearing. Dismayed that Reid's defense
of common sense was destined only to be read by other philosophers and
eager to make a name for himself as a thinker, the considerably less original and more overheated Beattie spent the second half of the 1760s consumed with a single project. That was to popularize Reid's approach
and to make it the foundation for an anti-relativist Christian moral project at whose need Reid had already hinted in the introduction to the *Inquiry*. By 1765, the more scholarly and well-born Reid had relocated

with his wife and nine children to Glasgow. There, thanks to good patronage and a growing reputation as a philosopher, he was to assume the university chair held previously by Adam Smith and, before that, Hutcheson. Beattie, in contrast, continued doggedly to pursue his mission from his lifelong and more remote home base of Marischal College and the Wise Club of Aberdeen, in close collaboration with his small band of fellow teachers and ministers. Finally, his *Essay on the Nature and Immutability of Truth,* a common sense approach to common sense, complete with the lists with which we began this chapter, appeared from an Edinburgh press in 1770. The result was a real success in commercial terms: the most commonly pitched and, soon, most commonly read (though certainly not the most profound) book on common sense in the first seven decades of the eighteenth century. No one professed to be more surprised than Beattie, who became the apostle for a soon-to-be transatlantic movement whereby social and ethical reform was to begin with the reassertion of the normative value of ordinary people's ordinary way of perceiving the world about them.[38]

Several features distinguished Beattie's *Essay* from its predecessors, including Reid's *Inquiry.* First, in an effort to reach new readers, including "those who may not have leisure, or subtlety, or metaphysical knowledge, sufficient to qualify them for a logical confutation of all its [skepticism's] premises," Beattie simplified Reid's argument.[39] Then he gave these lay readers enhanced "criteria" for knowing what is erroneous and what is true. According to Beattie, there exist certain kinds of problems, such as mathematical ones, where a distinct faculty called reason is required to determine an answer for sure. But there are many other questions we encounter in going about our lives for which a special and prior human capacity—common sense, or "that power by which we perceive self-evident truth"—provides all the proof we need.[40] Unsatisfied with previous definitions, Beattie explained common sense more fully as

that power of the mind which perceives truth, or commands belief, not by progressive argumentation, but by an instantaneous and instinctive impulse; derived neither from education nor from habit, but from nature; acting independently on our will, whenever its object is presented, according to an established law, and therefore not improperly called *Sense;* and acting in a similar manner upon all, or at least upon a great majority of mankind, and therefore properly called *Common Sense.*[41]

In the domain of common sense, we know something is true not because it corresponds to external reality but because it is what "we feel we must believe."[42] Here we are very close to the Protestant notion of faith; "the pious man," Beattie clarifies, knows by "evidence too sublime for their [skeptics'] comprehension" that the greatest pleasure in life comes from contemplation of divine nature.[43] Moreover, he notes, God would not deceive us; in a being God has made, irresistible beliefs can only be true (a principle that runs the risk of being tautological insofar as God is used to establish the existence of common sense, and common sense, in turn, offers proof of the existence of God).

The message that his readers—ordinary, "middling" people, un-trained in philosophy—were expected to take away is that they can trust what they perceive. The eyes do not lie, and resulting beliefs about ob-jects are not merely the result of convention. Readers can also trust what they say to reflect these perceptions accurately and to be understood as such by others: "Every body who uses the English language, calls snow white, and grass green; and it would be in the highest degree absurd to suppose, that what they call the sensation of whiteness, is not the same sensation which I call by that name." In Beattie's terms, even "the rudest of the vulgar know most perfectly what they mean" when they make de-clarative statements about what transpires in their own lives.[44] What Beattie hoped to convey was that the remedy for irreligion and skeptical talk was not more rational debate, which led only to the absurdity of try-ing to demonstrate the indemonstrable and further skepticism when this effort failed. It was the unquestioned acceptance of what always has and still does feel objectively true to all.

Beattie, too, had no easy answer for how to distinguish common sense "convictions," as he called them, from prejudices. Yet he was confident enough to try to lay out a long list of basic beliefs across all domains, from prudence to physics to religion, that we have no reason to doubt.

And as befitted a man who first made his name as a poet, Beattie chose to do so "warmly," as he euphemistically put it, but also with "great plainness of speech," plenty of examples drawn from recognizable real-life experience, and a fair amount of ridicule toward the arguments of his enemies, a tried-and-true technique from Shaftesbury onward for suggesting that some positions are simply beyond logical refutation and should be dismissed as mere nonsense.[45] As Dugald Stewart, another of Reid's disciples, later pointed out, the principle appeal of Beattie's book lay in "the variety and felicity of illustration with which the Author has contrived to enliven and adorn a subject so little attractive in itself to the generality of readers."[46]

Beattie's main innovation, though, was to enlist directly the epistemology that took root in the Wise Club and reached all the way back to Shaftesbury in what he imagined to be a public service project. In place of Reid's careful, judicious disagreements with his philosophical contemporaries, Beattie waged a full-scale attack on the "modern skeptics," chief among them Hume, whom he accused of being Scholastics in new clothing, men whose taste was less for uncovering truth than for paradox, relativism, wrangling, and wordplay. Beattie then spun out an alarming tale of the potential dangers of this metaphysical style and dogma taking root beyond the rarified world of philosophy, claiming it could lead only to atheism, licentiousness, and moral ruin—unless it were reined in by common sense. For in fact, Beattie was not only worried about Hume (despite his virulent efforts to discredit his Edinburgh counterpart by accusing him of misleading his readers through the twisting of words). The Aberdonian professor was equally exercised by a fashionable skepticism that he perceived as endemic to everyday life in an increasingly secular, individualized, mobile, and commercial world overrun with information and opinions—or what one historian succinctly calls "the culture of the metropolis"—in the middle of the eighteenth century.[47] There Hume and his admirers were symptoms as much as sources. For Beattie, like many of his interlocutors, repeatedly sounded the alarm that a taste for doubting was becoming "the spirit of the age."[48] His frequent correspondent, the physician John Gregory, reporting from Edinburgh in the latter half of the 1760s, concurred, seemingly traumatized by the moral culture of the big city after years in Aberdeen and in the company of his Wise Club companions.[49] In Beattie's long-distance estimation, the consequences could only be dire for "private happiness" and "public good" alike.[50]

At the personal level, Beattie warned, one doubt led inexorably to another, gradually undermining all of an individual's beliefs and convictions until the words *God* and *religion* and *immortality* were no more than "empty sounds."[51] Then the effects would turn psychological, as even the "happiest moments of human life," those spent contemplating creation and adoring its author, became embittered.[52] Soon conduct would begin to suffer, too; the nihilistic individual, upon finding himself left with nothing but his own anxieties, would be rendered unfit for "action" and "useless" as well as "wretched."[53] Where common sense linked one to a community, skepticism, in Beattie's assessment, was a product of the individualism characteristic of modern urban culture run amok.

Indeed, it was at the level of civil society, Beattie suggested, that skepticism had its most devastating effects. It cut off whole groups of people, not least the poor and desperate, from the source of consolation that is religion. It also sundered them from the sense of community that arises around shared beliefs and duties. In the end, skepticism led to general confusion, ignorance, and, potentially, the end of social order itself. As Reid had warned in the dedication to his *Inquiry,* if all belief were laid aside, "piety, patriotism, friendship, paternal affection, and private virtue, would appear as ridiculous as knight-errantry."[54] What Beattie (along with the moderate Presbyterian minister James Oswald, author of a similarly morally inclined treatise called *An Appeal to Common Sense in Behalf of Religion* at almost the same moment) saw in Reid's epistemology was a curative, a modern and advanced means to attempt to preserve the traditional Christian morality and communal ethos of their own world.[55]

It all came down to a question of balance. For the leading citizens of Aberdeen at the midcentury mark, any plausible explanation of the world needed now to be rooted in the methods of science. There was no turning the clock back. But such methods could be dangerous when applied without careful attention to where they might lead, especially when it came to moral questions. A scientifically grounded notion of common sense could, Beattie determined, be used to establish self-preserving and socially beneficial limits to what might reasonably be asked and also to what might reasonably be demonstrated, limits that protected and supported faith. As he explained, if it were better for human reasoning "not [to] wander into forbidden paths, or attempt to penetrate inaccessible regions . . . it is the authority of common sense that fixeth this boundary."[56] Furthermore, because common sense, like common language, offered a shared foundation for knowing—that is, for distinguishing truth from untruth, good from bad, beauty from ugliness—it also helped preserve the community as a moral entity. And it did so without compromising freedom of speech or of writing and without requiring any unwanted interference of "civil power" in the progress of rational inquiry, as Beattie continually took pains to point out.[57] In Beattie's *Essay*, an epistemology founded upon common sense could attach itself to advanced science and to the liberal, anti-dogmatic cultural ethos of post-Restoration Britain, while also anchoring a practical ethics designed to bolster prevailing local institutions and Christianity itself. Indeed, despite his own professed commitment to moderation and the plain language of common sense, Beattie went out of his way to emphasize that what he was engaged in on behalf of common sense was nothing less than "warfare," a battle in the open market of ideas over the moral future of Great Britain, his nation, and his own, much narrower, lived world. Beattie hoped to be the first soldier for common sense.

The problems began with the waging of this war. The more hyperbolic and heated Beattie's claims for common sense as the critical step on the path to true wisdom became, the more the tensions in his argument came to the fore—tensions that would prove to have large and unanticipated political consequences later in the century. For while his moral vision, with its emphasis on deference, hierarchy, and duty, pointed in one direction, his anti-authoritarian and largely antihierarchical politics of knowledge, inherited in good part from Reid, suggested another direction entirely.

Hints of this proto-political conflict were there from the start. Skepticism about the superiority of "experts" and elites, whether in terms of virtue or knowledge, was very much part of the culture of the Wise Club from its origins, despite its conservative moral stance. In one club meeting of 1767, David Skene answered the question "If Mankind are considered in respect of Rank or Fortune, in what Class may We expect to find the Virtuous Principle most Prevalent?" with a tribute to those in the middle, such as the professional men who surrounded him, though he took pains to clarify that virtue was in the breast of every man. The difference stemmed from circumstances. Those of "lowest fortune," he insisted, were hindered by "a Confined Education, Illiberal Sentiments and bad example," not to mention a misapprehension about the purpose of the law. But he had even less good to say about those of the highest rank, whom he castigated more fully as a result of their situation. They were victims of vanity, temptation, and habits of indulgence that rendered them impatient under restraint and distant from compassion.[58] Such class-based moral condemnations were standard fare in polite British discourse for most of the eighteenth century. What was more unusual was that *les grands,* whether distinguished by wealth or learning or social position, came in for similar treatment from the men of the Wise Club when it came to their claims to a prerogative on truth.

In the writings of Reid and even more in those of Beattie, the argument for common sense judgment as the foundation for knowledge produced not only a critique of elites for their distance from the daily life of the ordinary man. It also generated a logic of social leveling rooted in epistemological egalitarianism. For Reid, as one twenty-first-century commentator puts it, "the philosopher has no option but to join with the rest of humanity in conducting his thinking within the confines of common sense. He cannot lift himself above the herd."[59] What this means is that he must both live and reason like everyone else, including the vulgar or common, if he is to find his way to truth.

If the philosopher does not recognize this fact or chooses to ignore it, the "plain man" will, in Reid's words, justifiably find the philosopher to be "merry." Or the plain man will conclude, in fine populist form, that "too much learning is apt to make men mad; and that the man who seriously entertains this belief, though in other respects he may be a very good man, as a man may be who believes that he is made of glass; yet surely he hath a soft place in his understanding, and hath been hurt by much thinking."[60] Inversely, the philosopher who separates himself from others and disdains the sentiments of his fellow men out of vanity and misplaced pity for the "credulity of the vulgar," who believe there is "a sun, moon, and stars . . . country, friends, and relations," will soon find that the joke is on him.[61] As Reid concluded in his later *Essays on the Intellectual Powers of Man,* when it comes to judgments about first principles, whether of science, ethics, or everyday life, "the philosopher . . . has no prerogative above the illiterate, or even above the savage. . . . The learned and the unlearned, the philosopher and the day-labourer, are upon a level, and will Pass the same judgment" (though he qualified this claim with the vital clause "when they are not misled by some bias, or taught to renounce their understanding from some mistaken religious principle," most likely to avoid potentially radical implications).[62] For common sense, a gift from the author of nature, requires no training, skills, or special cultivation. It is, in the view of these moderate Presbyterian thinkers, potentially the equal inheritance of every class and even every sex, religion, or race. It is the outliers, those who refuse to get with the program out of perversity, madness, or self-regard, who are to be shunned as dangerous.

Beattie agreed: all of his sensible "middling" readers of the sort praised by Skene should not only be able to recognize "the evidences" of human nature and moral subjects as well as self-proclaimed authorities; they should be actively offended by the idea that God would reveal himself to mankind "in such a manner that none but the learned and contemplative can understand him."[63] Beattie (at least on the page) had nothing but scorn for those whose elevated or privileged status led them to think they were more perceptive than others, since even "the vulgar" would spot the philosopher for a fool if skepticism carried the day.[64] Reid similarly laid the blame in his later work squarely at the puffed-up philosopher's door, chiding him for the undeserved sense of superiority that made him "unwilling to give the name of judgment to that wherein the most ignorant and unimproved of the species are his equals," meaning in judgments grounded in sense perception, memory, or consciousness.[65] The message of these Protestant thinkers was clear—and flattering to ordinary, lay readers. They were not only capable of ascertaining truth themselves; they were already in the business of doing so. It was philosophers who should be listening to and learning from an amorphous body of ordinary folk as protection against falling into error or doubt.

From this principle, then, came the seeds of a political argument. Reid and Beattie concurred that what has the acceptance of the "generality of mankind" and the "consent of ages and nations, of the learned and unlearned" has "authority" over individual determinations in the conduct of human life.[66] Or as David Skene put it in a variant of the traditional argument from universal consent or the *consensus gentium,* "a thing is only right when a man feels it to be at all times and . . . finds the feelings of the rest of mankind correspond."[67] Reid realized that this collective rather than individualist standard for truth posed the uncomfortable question "Is truth to be determined by most votes?"[68] And he clarified in his later work that in matters beyond common understanding, the many must be led by the few (i.e., experts) and yield to their authority. But in that murky but vast, quotidian terrain that he considered the realm of common sense, he insisted that "the few must yield to the many, when local and temporary prejudices"—or what we might call custom—"are removed."[69] In daily life, the commonly held belief, the belief that transcends local culture and history and belongs to all men by nature of their very God-given constitution, necessarily garners the status of law, just as common sense trumps philosophy, every time.

Here the men of the Wise Club might seem to have been positioning themselves in the realist tradition of Berkeley, who had half a century earlier defended the ordinary perceptual capacities of ordinary people and their trust in their senses, claiming repeatedly that he "side[d] in all things with the Mob" or "with the Vulgar against the Learned" in the defense of common sense.[70] Bishop Berkeley was, however, one of Reid and Beattie's chief targets precisely because of his insistence on the immateriality of everything we perceive around us—houses, butterflies, teacups—that is, his claim that they are merely collections of ideas that God produces in our minds. The Common Sense philosophy of Aberdeen began from the premise that the existence of the material world was itself common sense precisely because this conviction, like a host of others derived from sense experience, seemed so apparent to the vast majority of people everywhere. Common language provided yet more empirical evidence insofar as it constituted the collective voice of the people. What the Wise Club members unwittingly established on the backs of an earlier generation of "moral sense" philosophers who had already made repeated examples out of the hypothetical "honest Farmer"[71] was a solid epistemological foundation for a style of political agitation whereby the supposed instinct for both truth and morality of an unspecified, indivisible, classless "people" trumps that of outliers of all kinds, including specialists and established elites.

The implications of this position could, of course, have remained abstract or even inconsequential for Beattie. There is also no reason to think of populism as incompatible with a conservative moral outlook—then or now. Except that, as his book caught on, especially among British elites eager to read a modern defense of Christianity and the established order, this ambitious and insecure provincial intellectual from modest roots soon found himself caught in a morass that he had helped to create. That was how to define his own role as an intellectual leader and "authority" at the same time as he spoke for and to the people's common sense—a problem that would be critical for all would-be populist spokesmen henceforth. Aberdeen was not, from any perspective, a major metropolis in the 1760s and 1770s. The *Essay on the Nature and Immutability of Truth* was not, despite its grandiose title, a great book. But Beattie, in his quest to become a missionary for common sense, provides us with a lived example of the brewing tension in even minor mid-eighteenth-century urban centers between the stirrings of individualism (in the form of a focus on personal expression, initiative, merit, opportunity, social mobility, and financial reward) and the desire to reassert community, commonality, and duty or obligation to others. Beattie was clearly pulled in both directions.

From a combination of the extensive notes kept during the Wise Club years, Beattie's meticulous list making and diary keeping, and his voluminous correspondence (around two thousand letters between the philosopher and his friends and business acquaintances across a large, British urban network are still extant), one can clearly follow the development of Beattie's ideas as he worked them out in the course of the 1760s. We learn of his first unhappy and uncomprehending reads of the modern moral philosophers. Then there is the impact of Reid's *Inquiry* on his thinking and his growing confidence in his own anti-skeptical instincts, a shift doubly evident in his teaching, which combined psychology with practical ethics, jurisprudence, and other related subjects,[72] and in his eagerness to ponder questions of human nature in his interventions in the Wise Club. By the end of 1765, Beattie had proposed that his colleagues take up the question "What is the difference between Common Sense, and reason?"[73] Shortly afterward he told various correspondents that he was working on an "Essay on the Fundamental Principles of Evidence," then "An Essay on Reason and Common Sense," and a year and a half later, a more expansive, three-part "Essay on the Immutability of Truth, Intellectual, Moral, and Critical."[74] Simultaneously, Beattie's growing obsession with the dangers of skepticism led him to compose a satirical allegory called "The Castle of Skepticism," which suggests nothing so much as Bartolommeo Del Bene's "soul as city" under siege. Hume (again) appears as the prince of this shady realm, and "pilgrims" must check their common sense at special extramural temples devoted to affection, ignorance, self-conceit, fashion, licentiousness, ambition, avarice, and hypothesis before they are allowed to proceed any farther toward the castle's core.[75] Egged on by colleagues near and far, Beattie seems to have became more and more convinced that it was his great mission in life to "undeceive" those around him and to impart the lesson, before it was too late, that there is indeed "a Standard of Truth in the human mind."[76]

One can also trace the difficult personal path that Beattie—a man plagued by a tragic family life, poor health (about which he complained incessantly to anyone who would listen), and little income—tried to walk as the century's first evangelist for common sense as well as a modern man of letters.[77] Initially, in the late 1760s, he worked hard to promote what he, rather disingenuously, insisted was a piece of writing that would likely have no popularity in a licentious age, with its "profligacy and want of principles."[78] He repeatedly despaired of even finding a willing publisher, though he never ceased to seek one out. Then after 1770, with claims of surprise at being proved wrong about the interest generated by his book and strong disavowals of any personal motives, he tried even harder to reap the benefits, especially as his *Essay* won him prestigious admirers and friends far outside his previously cloistered experience in Aberdeen. Yet the combination of his personal predicament and his epistemological populism, with its communal vision of both knowledge production and ethics, forced him to reject the well-trodden paths toward success as a philosopher or writer in late eighteenth-century Britain and to seek a new way to present himself.

Beattie's letters make clear that the provincial professor was eager for social, professional, and, above all, financial advancement from the start. As the son of a shopkeeper and tenant farmer with a mentally ill wife and multiple children to support on only a meager university salary and his students' subscription fees, neither fortune nor fame was within easy reach. It was Beattie's ambition, along with a gift for cultivating patrons, that seems to have propelled him forward from his very earliest days as a student at Marischal and then schoolmaster in the nearby village of Fordoun. His correspondence indicates that he took an active interest in every detail of publishing his *Essay*, from the size of the volume and the quality of the paper to the methods of publicity on the part of the bookseller. His goal was always to reach audiences in Edinburgh, London, and, through translation, across the European continent.[79] His letters also show that he used every contact and every possible review or appraisal (including the negative ones) to his advantage. He hounded his better-connected, wealthier friends, old and new, male and female, for invitations, introductions, publicity, and various forms of financial aid. He repeated one individual's praise or good deeds on his behalf to another and begged still others for news concerning his burgeoning reputation, writing despairingly, "I much long to hear, what people are saying of me."[80] And he made periodic trips to Edinburgh and especially to London to take advantage of the offers of prominent friends to introduce him to an ever-wider circle of people who might be in a position to aid him in the long run.[81] That Beattie succeeded in this quest is evident not only from the multiple editions of his work that poured off the London and Edinburgh presses in the early and mid-1770s, including a luxury subscription edition arranged by the London Bluestocking Mrs. Montagu.[82] Beattie himself gradually came into possession of an honorary degree from Oxford, a pension from King George III, and a portrait by the great painter Sir Joshua Reynolds showing the philosopher from Aberdeen vanquishing the great infidels of the age, including Voltaire, Hume, and Gibbon, by means of common sense.[83] In one regard, Beattie's constant military metaphors proved apt: "The Triumph of Truth," as the picture was called, signaled a victory for the forces of common sense.

Yet Beattie, who kept his painting behind a green velvet curtain in his home so that it would be both private and the dramatic focus of his residence, was also fully aware from the beginning of the pitfalls attendant upon the common sense reformer making too much of his own genius or originality. Much like modern charismatic leaders of the populist variety, he seems to have sensed that, given his philosophical claims, he would be judged by his character and self-professed motivations more than by his special insights or special authority rooted in his training or position. For his moral conservatism was also, even more than for the professor-cleric Reid, dependent upon his epistemological populism. The suggestion was that, in the end, he was only articulating and defending the viewpoint of all ordinary, ethical men going about their daily lives—in contradistinction to the vainglorious and self-motivated Hume. Which meant that even as Beattie became unexpectedly famous, the kind of person who had been invited to an audience with King George III and his wife, Queen Charlotte, he could not afford to play the role of the great philosopher in any traditional sense.

Beattie's letters are rife with the anxiety that this challenge produced: that he would disappoint or, even more, that he would to be taken for an illiberal bigot or for venal. Consider this tortured message, written in 1770, at the height of his fame, to his constant correspondent William Forbes, while in discussion of a second edition of *An Essay on the Nature and Immutability of Truth:* "nothing would hurt me more, than to think that any of my friends should suspect me of having too strong an attachment to *filthy lucre;* and yet it is well known, that 50 guineas to a man in my way neither is, nor ought to be, an object of indifference."[84] Beattie's solution was a kind of compensatory modesty derived from a Christian language of public service and duty that would endure into the nineteenth century even as competition and personal ambition became increasingly the norm. In Beattie's case, this meant he felt obligated to play up his own humility, indeed, his claim to be interested only in the public good and the fate of humanity, at the same time as he worked hard to cultivate his own success, especially among people of rank and connection. And rather than admit of his triumph (since common sense always needs an adversary), he paid more and more heed to what he took to be "his enemies," understood to be a cabal or "party" organized around Hume but gradually expanded to include critics like Joseph Priestley and French thinkers, too.[85] Eventually Beattie declined all sorts of positions that became possible through British social connections, worried that acceptance of a "living" in the Church of England would only make him look insincere or that a professorship in Edinburgh would throw him at the mercy of his "powerful enemies."[86] He was eager, too, not to risk his status as, in the words of one Scottish reviewer, "a good citizen" as well as an agreeable writer.[87] So he stayed put in Aberdeen long after some of his closest colleagues had, like Reid, departed for bigger cities. There he lived for the rest of his years with a wife suffering (ironically) from increasing madness, or want of common sense,[88] legions of adolescent male students, his prized painting, and his many complaints. He could not afford Shaftesbury's solution to ill health or hard times, which was to travel to far-off climes. Instead he continued to write longingly to his London friends in search of news of the world that he wanted but whose realization would put him out of work. Living on the fringes of the urban Republic of Letters, Beattie found the support mechanisms—a professorship, a literary club, a post office—that made it possible for him to join an international literary culture of patrons, publishers, writers, booksellers, and readers. But only on the outskirts, he convinced himself, was he also able to remain a staunch critic of the excesses and elitism of the big-city version of that culture and an interpreter and conduit for what ordinary people, in more ordinary places, intuitively know.

In truth, there was nothing overtly democratic or even explicitly political about this stance on the part of Beattie or most of the Wise Club's philosophically inclined members (though both Beattie and Reid were eventually to support the early stages of the French Revolution and, in

Reid's case, the American Revolution, too). Not surprisingly, given their distance from any governmental bodies, the Wise Club members did not put much faith in political solutions to the problems of the day. Nor did they typically imagine beneficial outcomes stemming from either increased commercial exchange or, with the exception of William Ogilvie, economic redistribution schemes.[89] Beattie's energies, in particular, were overwhelmingly directed toward supplying comfort, as opposed to recipes for political or economic change or empowerment, to those unhappy in their social situations. The Wise Club members' day-to-day intellectual life was also largely confined to men of their own religion and class, even if some, like Beattie, had come from more humble rural origins and were all too willing to let aristocratic English women take the lead in their social and financial advancement.[90] In his teaching, too, the Anglophilic Beattie functioned largely as an apologist for the status quo, a great defender of the essential rightness of the British constitution, British social hierarchy, and loyalty to church and king.[91] Even Beattie's most notable ethical stances, such as his repeated public denunciations of the slavery of African peoples, should be seen as consonant with his conservative Christian outlook and his position on the outside of the new world of imperial business, not as an example of radical, grassroots political agitation. Beattie was convinced that commerce, greed, and impiety throughout the British Empire had gotten in the way of the instinctive, common sense outrage that all persons should feel when confronted with an institution that confused men with property and failed to recognize the humanness and basic liberty of all.[92]

What draws our attention to Beattie now, and more generally to all the Presbyterian ministers and professors who gathered for the duration of the 1760s in the meeting rooms of Aberdeen's Wise Club, is the distinctive role accorded to common sense within their unremarkable Protestant moral vision. Beattie and company crafted something much more substantial out of this old trope than either the cultural ideal or the practical tool of partisan persuasion that it had been for London's great Augustan writers. In the service of both anti-skepticism and a commitment to free inquiry, the men of the Wise Club not only made common sense into a new kind of "epistemic authority" to be distinguished from reason in its immediateness and communal connotations. They also made it into a potential social agent and source of principles by which the collective people (provided they saw the world in a similar manner to these middle-class, professional men of Aberdeen) might be able to rule themselves.

First, the so-called Common Sense philosophers used the idea of a universal instinct for truth to collapse the difference between philosophers as intellectual authority figures and "the people" as a whole. That is, they denied that philosophers had any special purchase on the truth, even if philosophers were cleverer than most when it came to words. And they gave new validity to the judgments of the everyman, the ordinary guy whose perceptions of the world are unclouded by fancy dialectics or jargon. Second, Beattie and his colleagues insisted that the sense of the collective people, derived from this universal instinct for basic truth, could serve a double purpose: it could be a means to shore up a community and its institutions in light of the threat of intellectual and moral atomization, and it could be a foundation for sure knowledge in every domain. Finally, the main figures in the Wise Club of the 1760s and early 1770s offered their disciples an idiom for giving voice to their (preexisting) anger and resentment at those few obstinate individuals or groups who stood in the way of this ambition.

We need not swallow entirely the scathing indictment of Immanuel Kant that all this "convenient" talk of common sense was simply a perverse and philistine form of anti-intellectualism, an endorsement of "the opinion of the multitude, of whose applause the philosopher is ashamed, while the popular charlatan glories and boasts in it."[93] Kant, as we will see later, had his reasons for despising this whole trajectory in the history of common sense. The same goes for the excited pronouncement of the scientist and dissenter Joseph Priestley that it was essential to "stop this sudden torrent of nonsense and abuse that is pouring down upon us from the North" before it led to new forms of dogmatism, intolerance, and what we would now call demagoguery.[94] Were such ideas to prevail, Priestley prophesied that "politicians also, possessing of this advantage, may venture once more to thunder out upon us their exploded doctrines of passive obedience and non-resistance." For, he continued in a sarcastic vein, "having now nothing to fear from the powers of reason," they would be empowered to "giv[e] out their own mandates as the decisions of this new tribunal."[95]

Surely this is not what Reid or Beattie or even Oswald had in mind. Reid, in particular, emphasized repeatedly that he was concerned only with those notions that humans held in common as a result of their common constitution. He also clarified that he in no way meant either to suggest an endorsement of vulgar opinion as truth or to give an individual, claiming popular will, license to short-circuit public debate and impose his subjective judgments on the multitude. Yet neither can we say that Priestley and Kant were entirely wrong in their different assessments of the claims for common sense issuing from Aberdeen in the middle of the eighteenth century. What both foresaw were the serious implications of common sense philosophy in terms of how, and on whose behalf, political claims might be issued in the future. With this rewriting of the scope of common sense—which was soon to make Aberdeen as much an exporter of new ideas as an importer[96]—came several essential pieces of the mental infrastructure necessary for the development of a politics in the popular, democratic mode, as well as for eventual popular challenges to that same order.

CHAPTER 3

The Radical Uses of *Bon Sens*

Amsterdam, 1760–1775

Good sense seems to be the lot of the Dutch.
Marquis d'Argens, *Lettres juives*

IN 1773, AN EIGHT-VOLUME, multiauthor, French-language *Portable Library of Good Sense (La Bibliothèque du bon sens portatif)* rolled off the press under a London imprint.[1] The collection never had much commercial success. Today these volumes of "sensible" writings are extremely rare and survive in only a small handful of scholarly libraries. (The one copy in the French National Library disappeared sometime before 1914.)

Yet everything about the title of this collection suggests that it had the makings of a popular series in its moment. In the great age of dictionaries, encyclopedias, and compilations, the term *bibliothèque* indicated a comprehensive library's worth of offerings on a given subject. *Portatif* or "portable" too had functioned as a commonplace publishing term since the end of the seventeenth century. Voltaire's great *Portable Philosophical Dictionary (Dictionnaire philosophique portatif)* of 1768 is only the most famous example. Whether the subject was fine arts, artillery, theology, or weather, the designation "portable" signaled a book's limited impact on the pocketbook, its suitability for regular consultation, and its potential ease of use, as if the reader might just grab a copy and head out into the world with it in hand.[2]

Then there is the fact that, like many other philosophical works of this era, this *Portable Library of Good Sense* drew on the appeal of that most fashionable, if abstract, of concepts: *le bon sens*. Le bon sens (literally, good sense) did not, in the mid-eighteenth century, possess the full range of meanings that were then associated with the English cognate "common sense." The French term failed to convey the collective, intersubjective dimension of "common sense" or the more rare French term *le sens commun*. From Descartes' famous opening to his *Discourse on Method* onward, *le bon sens* was understood as the "power of judging rightly" common to all humans, cultivated or not. But, as Descartes ironically acknowledged, most people (their self-perceptions to the contrary) did not make regular use of this capacity, "for it is not enough to have a good mind; the main thing is to use it well."[3] Or as Pierre Richelet more bluntly summarized it half a century later, "many people think they have it who do not."[4] Moreover, good sense did not, unlike common sense, refer secondarily to the collective wisdom or widely shared assumptions that stemmed from the generalized employment of this power.

Nevertheless, in French-language contexts, *le bon sens* and the related term, *le sens commun*, were often used interchangeably by the late seventeenth century, and the primary significations of *le bon sens* and the English term "common sense" coincided closely in the following century.[5] That is, *le bon sens* was widely defined as the faculty of basic reasoning, ordinary discernment, and, as Montesquieu put it, "the precise comparison of things" that allowed for the establishment of certain basic conceptual truths known to and accepted by all.[6] Over the course of its first two hundred years of existence, the dictionary of the Académie Française, following what it called "the common language," continually noted the existence of the *homme de bon sens*, meaning one who uses his faculty of understanding things and judging them in accordance with right reason.[7] Conversely, it was understood that when rules were established on the basis of good sense, they were so apparent that there was no need to prove the truth of them to any sensible person. As the Abbé Galiani announced in 1770, "Good sense is the only sovereign court that is never in recess."[8] Though often reportedly "shocked," "insulted," "violated," "outraged," "abused," "offended," or "repulsed," *le bon sens* offered a potentially infallible, constant, and unimpeachable standard by which to operate in daily life as well as philosophy.

Indeed, by the middle of the second half of that century, the moment at which the *Portable Library of Good Sense* appeared, the popularity of the idea of *le bon sens* across Francophone Europe stemmed in good measure from its ordinariness and even banality. Labeling this era "the Age of Reason" can be as misleading as it is helpful. Reason was, certainly, widely touted in France and across the European continent as a catch-all solution to myriad woes. But there existed more than one kind of reason, and during the years of the so-called High Enlightenment, the very basic, low-level, quotidian form of reason associated with "good sense" often found itself pitted against the system-building, Scholastic logic of theology or Cartesianism, as well as against pedantry of all kinds. What made *le bon sens* distinct as a positive subset of the larger category "reason" for many mid- and late eighteenth-century Francophone writers was that it was understood to be premised neither upon scholarly erudition nor upon contemplative leisure time given over to complex thinking. Rather, it depended solely upon the experiences and observations common to everyday life. Consequently, good sense came to be considered an ordinary attribute of an ordinary man or (sometimes) woman. Even Jean-Jacques Rousseau, that great defender of gender difference, claimed that regardless of jokes to the contrary, "good sense belongs equally to the two sexes."[9] And as Bernard de Fontenelle noted ironically at the end of the seventeenth century, much to the astonishment of Europeans, it turned out that "people coming from the ends of the earth, of sallow complexion [and] living entirely differently from us" and even "our own shepherds" have the common sense that comes with just going about their business as humans.[10] This is what made *le bon sens,* in the words of the great *Encyclopédie* of Diderot and D'Alembert, so essential to putting one "in the state to cope with the ordinary business of society" or dealing with everyday practical matters.[11]

For the greatest of the French *philosophes* were also very clear that good sense should not be confused with the genius characteristic of the exceptional individual. As Diderot explained in another context, with common sense one has just about everything necessary to be "a good father, a good husband, a good merchant, [and] a good man," not to mention "a bad orator, a bad poet, a bad musician, a bad painter, a bad sculptor, [and] a dull lover."[12] The Abbé de Condillac made the same point. *Le bon sens,* as opposed to *l'esprit* or real intelligence, did not allow a man either to grasp the complexities of mathematics or to imagine new things. But it did grant him the opportunity to see what was what when it came to the wide variety of concrete things "that pass by one's eyes every day," the obvious precondition for both real knowledge and good taste.[13] That was what made good sense Emile's greatest trait, in Rousseau's estimation.[14] Good sense was both potentially available to all and the key to living successfully with others.

Let us return, then, to these volumes of 1773. At that moment, a *Portable Library of Good Sense*—even with the weighty subtitle "Collection of Works on Different Matters Important to Salvation"—held out the promise that, within, cumbersome logic, wild speculation, and ponderous prose had been jettisoned in favor of a strong dose of commonly accepted, practical wisdom. The starting point was to be ordinary, worldly perceptions familiar to ordinary people. The language of communication was to be plain, even down-to-earth. The results would be destined for and within the cognitive reach of ordinary readers, even if focused on the most abstract, vexing, and potentially contentious of issues. What the reader would be left with was a recognizable and unassailable view of the world. In this, the unnamed publisher's venture would have conformed to a decidedly eighteenth-century trend. The small group of Scottish intellectuals that included Beattie and Reid had spent the previous two decades using the idea of an innate common sense to mitigate the effects of a currently fashionable skepticism, as well as to defend the existence of God. Just the year before the appearance of this *Library,* the Baron d'Holbach, one of the prime (though unnamed) voices in this new collection of 1773, had anonymously published his own popular account of his chief ideas with the similarly simple title *Good Sense (Le Bon Sens).* This, in turn, followed on the heels of such recent tomes as *The New Philosophy of Good Sense (La Nouvelle philosophie du bon sens,* published in Vienna in 1771) and *Appeal to Good Sense (Appel au bon sens,* first published with a different title in Rome in 1769). Our 1773 collection has to be seen as one more attempt to capitalize on this trans-European current of thought and to reach an audience of individuals who would be glad if these volumes were easy to grasp in both a physical and an abstract sense.

But here is where the story grows interesting. Appearances, including title pages, can, after all, be deceiving. (Think of the commonplace French adage "Grosse teste, peu de sens," or "Fat head, little sense," meaning beware of extrapolating anything about the interior from the superficial qualities of the exterior.)[15] When the Baron d'Holbach, a fabulously wealthy amateur philosopher known on the continental side of the Channel mainly for his lavish dinner parties, adopted the term *le bon sens,* he may well have been picking up on a trend. Yet he in no way can be said to have been following the Scottish example or even that of other recent continental accounts of good sense. On the contrary, both d'Holbach's *Good Sense* and the heterogeneous texts by the Baron and others that appeared within the *Portable Library of Good Sense* were written with the goal of turning the world of appearances, including what seemed to constitute common sense, on its head.

Little, it turns out, about either of these works was what it seemed. Or to put it differently, everything was in play. The authors' names listed in the individual volumes of the *Portable Library* constituted the simplest form of deception. Most were deliberately misattributed. The collection began with a text by the French atheist grammarian César Chesneau Du Marsais that had circulated for years in manuscript (here disguised as an essay by the long dead Seigneur de Saint-Évremond). It then soldiered onward, via numerous anonymous and pseudonymous offerings by Voltaire and d'Holbach, to the posthumous meditations of Théodore Louis Lau, an obscure German critic of organized religion who insisted churches were nothing more than a form of social control.[16] These were the writings of peripatetic cosmopolitans, some dead and some still alive, most on the outs with church, state, and family alike and all used to being only one step ahead of the law as they propagated ideas that ran diametrically opposed to the reigning truths of the day. In contrast to our well-situated Scottish professors and clerics, these men placed very little stock in institutions. And whether they were on the way up or (more often) down the social ladder, disguises and subterfuge of various kinds were part of their existence. D'Holbach's *Good Sense* had made its way across Europe the previous year with no author's name attached. *The Portable Library of Good Sense,* a publisher's compilation built out of overstock, had no discernable editorial roots at all.

Furthermore, in neither instance was the place of publication London, as stated on the title page. Nor was it Paris, as the French titles might suggest. Rather, it was Amsterdam, home of Marc-Michel Rey, the entrepreneurial publisher of a decade of d'Holbach's clandestine writings, and a hotbed of multilingual, seditious, materialist book production and distribution that fed the underground of much of Europe and even its overseas colonies in the eighteenth century. In the 1770s, Dutch cities offered one of the most tolerant publishing environments in continental Europe, as we will see. But even in Amsterdam, the biggest and richest city in the powerful province of Holland, it was as dangerous for publishers as for authors to attach their names to texts that ran directly counter to prevailing moral, religious, or political norms. In the case of this *Portable Library of Good Sense,* it did not help that the contents were also likely pirated.[17] Secrecy and outright deception applied to the geography of imprints as well.

Most significantly, d'Holbach and other radical, primarily French-speaking writers who made polyglot Amsterdam their material base in the second half of the eighteenth century used the term *le bon sens* neither as an indicator of epistemological modesty nor as a sign of their investment in a status quo built on consensual truths. Rather, they turned this notion into an ideological weapon in an effort to dismantle the good sense associated with conventional wisdom, beliefs, behavior, and ultimately even language—and to promote a new good sense that led directly to an atheism that few even in d'Holbach's circle of devoted friends and disciples were willing to accept. If, in eighteenth-century Britain, common sense promised to fulfill a regulatory function, maintaining community norms in the absence of an elaborate apparatus of censorship laws, in continental Europe its cognate, good sense, promised to do the opposite. It would aid in undermining social and religious orthodoxies in violation of the formal laws governing ideas. Whereas, in the British context, common sense was meant to encourage taking things as they generally seemed, on the continent its French counterpart stood for the human potential to see beneath misleading facades and to expose *le non-sense* (itself an eighteenth-century neologism meaning "absurdity") in an effort at subversion. And while d'Holbach, in particular, may well have been eager to construct his argument in an accessible vein and market it as such, both his *Good Sense* and the collective *Portable Library of Good Sense* were essentially calls to arms against all assumptions that could be deemed popular or common in any sociological sense. Good or common sense was here part of a concerted international project, centered in the great commercial capitals of the Dutch Republic, to promote just what Beattie and company had most feared: seditious laughter, from outside established institutions, at the expense of the Christian religion, its clergy, its churches, and its moral values. Moreover, the method associated with this term was increasingly made available, through example, to any able-minded individual or social group interested in challenging recognized authorities and their verities. In its radical anti-establishment incarnation, the *bon sens* of the urban Francophone underground in the Dutch Netherlands also had a fundamental role to play in the making of the populist idiom that would be so essential to the first modern experiments with democratic governance, as well as the reaction against them, that began in the Age of Revolutions.

What had happened? First we must look backward. D'Holbach and his contemporaries who belonged to Marc-Michel Rey's Dutch publishing network in the 1760s and 1770s had, in effect, developed their take on the fashionable notion of good or common sense out of a long, socially elevated, and primarily French intellectual tradition—that is, if radical transgressiveness can be described as a tradition. This approach to the world drew its power from challenging, if not exploiting, a fine but vital line. That was the usually tacit distinction between what the members of a society unquestioningly accept as how things are and what those same people consider impossible to take seriously and, consequently, either dangerous or merely crazy. In other words, it was a tradition of setting good (as in simple, reasonable, and universal) against common (as in widespread and customary) sense.

On the one hand, France in the last decades of the Old Regime was still a place in which custom, derived from common usage and unwritten convention, held considerable sway as a source of precepts by which ordinary people could live in harmony with others. Here we are not only talking about manners or fashions or hairstyles, where the use of expressions like "tyranny" and "punishment" was largely metaphoric. The *consensus gentium,* which depended upon the tacit agreement of an ill-defined "people," was, as Vico was to recognize, an essential source of inviolable rules in almost every domain in early modern European life. Custom determined vital aspects of early modern economic life, from wages and conditions of employment to the settlement of debts. It helped keep social hierarchies in place. It governed religious practice. And even in the age of absolutism, when the monarchy and the church had ostensibly jointly assumed absolute responsibility for articulating the locus of truth and maintaining a single *doxa* (a task which included preventing false or competing ideas from getting a hearing through an elaborate policing and censorship system), custom could hardly be discounted as a restraint on the authority of the state.

Two examples will make clear the degree to which custom could, in early modern France as elsewhere in continental Europe, be formally binding. One is the civil law of the Old Regime, which is best understood as a form of unwritten or customary law, much like English common law. Roman jurisprudence had held that most customary practices had at their source deep-rooted local knowledge (what Baldus called "the experience of things"), combined with "natural reason" or a kind of basic common sense.[18] But it was unspoken yet general agreement, confirmed through long-standing, normative practice within a large social group, that gave these customs legal force and a status equivalent (in Roman vulgar law and in French civil law) to written law. A very similar model was, in seventeenth-century France, extended to language, the collection of words and expressions used to articulate what is true and what is just. Writing in 1647, the grammarian Claude Favre de Vaugelas insisted that usage was the "master of languages" and that it was "good usage," apart from any considerations of artificial reason or logic, that should be taken as authoritative.[19] The state-sponsored Académie Française followed this line of thought from its mid-seventeenth-century inception onward. Its forty august members took as their purpose the granting of established linguistic customs, determined and sustained by "the tacit consent of men," the quality of inviolable national laws.[20]

Of course, the very act of documenting and codifying the common language meant that well before the onset of the eighteenth century, standards of language usage, like common law, were actually now, in practice, being explicitly defined by "experts" (though the term was yet to exist) in court circles. In the course of the early modern period, state-sponsored authorities with specialized training and knowledge largely took over the task of articulating, defining, codifying, and controlling, whether the subject was language or civil law or statecraft more generally.[21] Collectively the popular classes and even the upper classes played less and less of a role in the process. Moreover, the "usage" that mattered was, at least in France, to be that of an extremely restricted, if variable, domain: "the soundest [*la plus saine*] part of the Court" and "the soundest [*la plus saine*] part of the Authors of our time," according to Vaugelas.[22] Though the official dictionary would take common usage as its foundation, for subsequent conversation or writing to be correct, it would now have to conform to a dictionary (the linguistic equivalent of a law code) written by appointees of the state. But the fiction of an original commonality—indeed of the superiority of the collective people over individuals, and of custom over reason, as sometimes expressed in the old Christian saying *Vox populi vox Dei*—endured. The power of custom in early modern France became, in fact, one of the clichés of modern French history, sustained and frequently overdrawn both by its advocates and by an equally long-lasting enlightened, and then revolutionary, mythology that turned it into a target.

For on the other hand (and here is where we see the roots of a subversive *bon sens*), wherever one looks in the history of seventeenth- and eighteenth-century France, one also sees suspicion of the attitudes of others. And, ultimately, one sees very little faith in either the existence of common sentiments or their value. Take, for example, proverbs. Anonymous, formulaic words to live by, proverbs would seem to be the very stuff of common sense, an anthropologist's or historian's treasure trove for all they potentially reveal about widely held, time-tested attitudes about space, time, health, family, sex, and other universal obsessions as they played out in a given society in a given moment in time. French culture of the Old Regime was rife with proverbs of all sorts, understood as the source of a practical code of basic conduct and decision making applicable across various social divides. Some of these sayings still strike us as obvious, which is to say valid: "Good fruits come from good harvests." Others reinforce the strangeness of a past in which it was widely agreed that "Good blood cannot lie."[23] And many of them concern the tight relations between the possession of good sense and acceptance of the existence of God. As one old proverb went, "As long as a man has good sense, he must confess that there is a God."[24] No doubt, the repetition of such sayings, as much as their content, helped reinforce local social norms and foster a kind of shared wisdom and communal sensibility.[25] And yet when it came to good or common sense (a frequent proverbial theme), what many traditional French-language proverbs emphasize is all the places it is not to be found. The rich and mighty, it turns out, do not have much. Savants, with their heads in the clouds, do not either. The same goes for the young, the crazy, and women (which may tell us more about how these sayings got formed and transmitted than about anything else).

In fact, the charge of lacking *le bon sens* was reciprocal in social terms in early modern France. The maxims of literary elites were also marked by a strong cynicism by the late seventeenth century about the existence of anything like a widely agreed-upon set of dictates commensurate with good sense. La Rochefoucauld's well-known maxim "Nous ne trouvons guère de gens de bon sens, que ceux qui sont de notre avis" (literally, "we never find anyone to have good sense except those who agree with us") may be foremost a denunciation of the human tendency toward self-love and vanity.[26] It is also an argument against the existence of any concrete set of interior convictions that do not fall into the trap of being subjective opinions. For alongside official French and, more generally, European reverence for a shared, customary realm, one finds in elite French thought a long strand of distrust of all that is popular, habitual, a product of supposed "universal consent," or a matter of "common" sense, especially in the search for certain truth. This skepticism extended equally to the opinions of the very learned (including theologians, doctors, and savants) *and* to those of a deluded populace.

In the first half of the seventeenth century, the most famous of these challenges issued from the pen of Descartes. In the celebrated opening of his *Discourse on Method* (1637), just after linking the concept of *le bon sens* (here synonymous with basic reason and judgment) to the unique human capacity to distinguish the true from the false, Descartes made the radical gesture of removing himself from all social contact and then systematically negating the epistemological value of all of the key sources of his education. In pursuit of truth, he claimed to have determined the need to turn his back on all the unworldly opinions contained in books: "those reasonings that a man of letters makes in his private room, which touch on speculations producing no effect, and which for him have no other consequence except perhaps that the more they are removed from common sense, he will derive all the more vanity from them." Yet Descartes also purported to have found no answers in observing the customs of other men, many of which "although they seemed very extravagant and ridiculous to us, did not cease being commonly accepted and approved by other great peoples."[27] Even those beliefs and social practices that met with universal consent often turned out to be a tissue of "prejudices" and errors that needed to be eliminated in the quest for truth. For the Descartes of the *Discourse on Method,* anything that inhibited hearing the internal voice of basic reason, including anything derived from custom, had to be forsaken in the quest for certain knowledge.

But Descartes was, in effect, responding to (and actually hoping to stem) an already established and much more thoroughgoing wave of skepticism about the foundations of knowledge and about human nature. Even earlier, at the dawn of the seventeenth century, the neo-Stoic Pierre Charron had denounced custom, or *coutume,* as nothing more than the effect of habit and unreason spread person to person like an infectious disease. Rather than treat widespread tacit approval of existing norms as a form of proof of their validity, the author behind *Of Wisdom* (1601) counseled, anyone seeking wisdom should run the other way. To find truth, a man needed to put himself on guard against his own pathetic passions and presumptions and then to flee from "the contagion of the world," by which he meant all that is approved by the multitude, all that passes for popular, whatever it is that everyone says, does, and believes. The only answer, according to Charron, was uncertainty or doubt.[28]

This was an argument that the next generation of well-born French libertines and skeptics was to build upon directly—and toward extraordinarily elitist ends. One might say that popular belief garnered low approval ratings in the seventeenth century among all kinds of humanists. A century of religious struggles, the unsettling revelations produced by the new science, the discovery of other parts of the world and the diverse religious practices and beliefs that they displayed: all of these factors added to the growing sense that variety—not to mention error rooted in pretension, deception, self-love, and greed—were common to every realm of thought. Certainly most seventeenth-century thinkers continued to insist that there were some things beyond questioning, at least among what one commentator, Charles Sorel, called "reasonable and educated people." Sorel had ready examples: Animals do not talk or reason. It is unjust to hurt one's kin. The good are worthy of praise. God exists. To argue otherwise, this commentator continued, was to violate "true common sense" and to open oneself up to ridicule.[29] Except that, for the men of this new generation of erudite, aristocratic skeptics, like François de La Mothe le Vayer, tutor in his later years to the young Louis XIV, "there were no opinions more assuredly false than the most universally believed."[30] Even the most banal of unquestioned commonplaces generally turned out to be wrong. And when, in 1648, just a few years after the appearance of Descartes' *Discourse,* La Mothe le Vayer published a small treatise with the title *Opuscule or Small Skeptical Treatise on the Common Expression "To not have any Common Sense,"* much of its purpose was to demonstrate that there simply was no such thing as common sense. What went by that name, according to La Mothe le Vayer, was generally neither common nor sensible given both the multitude of forms of expression in the world and the strange process by which all other opinions, save the one that accidentally landed the label "common," were repeatedly written off by consensus as madness. If one really sought to avoid error, one had, La Mothe le Vayer exhorted, to turn one's back on all commonly held and vulgar opinions, of "the stupid multitude adorned in silk as well as those in fustian" and of those "who frequent gilded offices as well as fairs."[31] The only hope was to restrict one's knowledge to simple logical truths, or *le bon sens,* understood as the antithesis of subjective opinions.

But where Cartesians believed the dictates of this basic good sense could ultimately lead one back to certain answers on subjects ranging from the nature of God to happiness in this life,[32] skeptics had something else in mind. La Mothe le Vayer and his small coterie placed no hope in ever arriving at any unshakable moral, political, or metaphysical truths or any new dogma of any kind (though La Mothe le Vayer never explicitly professed atheism). For true skeptics, the only purpose of the philosopher was to demystify habits and beliefs that too great familiarity had erroneously imposed as common sense truths. The philosopher's job was to hold up *paradox,* or propositions contrary to received opinion, to the *doxa.*[33] The goal was to produce derisive laughter and ultimately, among "superior minds" who held themselves apart from both the masses and those who ran the world, moral relativism and doubt. And this is where good sense promised to be so useful. *Le bon sens,* understood as the most minimal level of reason and discernment, could be used to cut through contradictions, to expose hypocrisies and pretensions, and to weed out falsehood. It could also be used to shatter logical absurdities and linguistic *galimatias* (a favorite word in this discourse),[34] whether of peasants and the unlearned or of philosophers, doctors, government ministers, theologians, and the overly learned.[35] Drawing on this faculty was an efficacious and thorough means to work directly against the bias toward the authority of tradition and popular consensus associated with all kinds of customary knowledge, especially when it came to matters of religion, morals, or sex. Indeed, it was a means to destroy, in the name of pluralism and toleration, not to mention humor, the notion that any such consensual knowledge could ever be found.

These early skeptics were in agreement with Reid and Beattie on one count: the skeptic's *bon sens* could not lead one to happiness. In La Mothe le Vayer's telling, this was because the resulting truth had the potential to incite public hatred and make its mouthpiece an outcast. (Those already living in deserts or in solitude were exceptions, he noted dryly.) But it would, La Mothe le Vayer pointed out in an earlier essay, produce a kind of personal liberation for the select individual.[36] It was a position that was, at once, highly dependent upon social distinction and epistemologically radical in the extreme, not least in the suggestion that all humans really had in common was a kind of underutilized radar detector for the erroneous when it came to their own collective wisdom. Here, at the seventeenth-century French court, we find the very obverse of the kind of reasoning that formed the backdrop to the Common Sense philosophy of the Scots 150 years later.

It was not, however, in aristocratic circles in France that this radical conception of good sense entered the eighteenth century and flourished as a tool of subversion, challenging the locus of authority and ultimately transforming the relationship between "experts" and ordinary people in the process. It was as an import. *Le bon sens* found its prime home in the late seventeenth and eighteenth centuries among a heterogeneous collection of marginal men of letters clustered in a string of cities in the small, densely populated, and remarkably commercial state hovering competitively on France's northeast corner: the Dutch Republic. For many travelers and refugees, urban life in the Netherlands held little obvious appeal; Amsterdam was reportedly smelly, unrefined, money centered, and constantly wet.[37] But it was the Dutch Republic, not the France of clerical and royal authority, noted the exiled freethinker and libertine, the Marquis d'Argens, in his rollicking, youthful memoirs, which uniquely warranted the title "the land of good sense and liberty."[38]

The Dutch Republic, with its comparatively minimal levels of press censorship and its decentralized political culture, had a reputation as one of the most tolerant places in Europe as early as the mid-seventeenth century. In contrast to France, religious plurality was a fact of life; despite the fact that the Dutch Reformed Church remained established, Jews, Catholics, and Protestants of all kinds, as well as freethinkers and other religious radicals, could survive without persecution. Plus this tiny nation had by this date already become one of the communication centers of Europe, publishing and distributing books, periodicals, and pamphlets in multiple languages to an extent that far surpassed its size. Laws against seditious or immoral publications remained in place, but regulation of the market was largely left up to consumers and their taste. When those books published were good or entertaining, the Marquis d'Argens pointed out later, the Dutch read them. When they did not have much value, readers left them alone. Faith in market forces as the prime regulator of ideas was, for d'Argens, the key reason—along with the acceptance of religious difference and a commitment to the welfare and tranquility of civil society—that the Dutch Republic deserved to be considered the world capital of good sense.[39]

What d'Argens did not spell out is that these qualities had long made Dutch cities into places of refuge for those fleeing other European locales and that these same qualities had been enhanced and extended (to the horror of many foreign commentators) by the arrival of various waves of émigrés. After 1685, French Protestant refugees, many of them highly learned to begin with, having previously made a living in France as scholars, teachers, pastors, and other kinds of *érudits*, formed one of the largest such groups. In exile, many soon joined indigenous Dutch men of letters in the publishing or journalistic world, creating new media and new markets simultaneously, most of them in French. (We cannot be surprised that the first French-language translation of Shaftesbury's essay on the concept of the *sensus communis* and the first French-language imitations of the *Spectator*, including one with the title *Le Censeur*, issued from Dutch presses at the start of the eighteenth century.)[40]

At the same time, Huguenot refugees contributed mightily to making the Dutch Republic, still fundamentally a Calvinist nation despite its tolerant legal structure, a hotbed of religious radicalism and impiety. By the end of the seventeenth century, the commercial and political hubs of the Republic—Amsterdam, Rotterdam, Leiden, The Hague—had become centers for the production of a new, international heterodox culture with strong echoes of a native Spinozism (also known as pantheism), as well as French skepticism and rationalism, English deism, and the new science associated with Newton.[41] In individuals, this could take many forms, from simple anticlericalism to radical deism or full-blown atheism.

What linked these currents was not just hostility to the contemporary Catholic Church but a more general anti-authoritarian, which is to say anti-French but also anticustomary, stance when it came to religion, politics, and morality. It was also the promotion of the individual's good sense—or natural light *(lumière naturelle)* or right reason *(droite raison)*, as it was also known—as a critical tool in this campaign against all forms of received wisdom or authority.

Take the example of the emblematic late seventeenth-century emigré Pierre Bayle, himself an admirer of Charron and La Mothe le Vayer. Outwardly Bayle, a prominent figure in Protestant Rotterdam, continued to uphold the principle tenets of Calvinism and to insist upon the existence of God. He also, like La Mothe le Vayer, remained a staunch supporter of *raison d'état* and a strong monarchy precisely because he saw "the people" as a fanatical force and a threat to public order. But in his *Philosophical Commentary on These Words of Jesus Christ, Compel Them to Come In* of 1686, he took it as his overriding purpose (despite some disclaimers to the contrary) to turn natural reason toward Christian ideals and moral principles with the goal of exposing what is "manifestly opposed to good sense, to natural light, to the general principles of reason, in a word, to the primitive and original rule for discerning truth from falsehood, the good from the bad," which is to say what is "absurd" in all forms of dogma, whether scholarly or products of common consent.[42] For Bayle, no text, no claim related to human existence, was too sacred or too well established to be off limits for scrutiny. Even for theologians, Bayle argued, "reason speaking by the axioms of natural light" must be "the supreme tribunal that judges, as the last resort and without appeal, all that is proposed to us."[43] It was the only way to real truth.

Yet the importance to this story of the main cities of the Netherlands, and ultimately of Amsterdam in particular, lies not only in a few great, original Huguenot thinkers like Bayle. By the start of the eighteenth century, the Dutch Republic formed a central point for a loose web of producers and consumers of all kinds of dissenting or impious polemics, in manuscript as well as print, that extended outward to most of the major cities in northern Europe, Catholic as well as Protestant. And this clandestine intellectual world was soon to absorb a new group of men in flight, many of whom were only too happy to pick up where Bayle left off: wielding *le bon sens* as a sword, in a variety of more popular forums, in an effort to undermine what ordinary people believed about the world, how they arrived at and defended those beliefs, and even the language they used to express those notions. Here we are no longer talking primarily about Huguenots but rather about a heterogeneous collection of renegade former French Catholics, men who chafed at the dominant rules governing behavior as well as self-expression in the land of absolutism and, generally, had the education and sense of adventure (or, in many cases, desperation) to do something about it.

In the first decades of the eighteenth century, Holland's literary advocates of *le bon sens* were more likely than not defrocked monks, debauched aristocrats, military adventurers, or debt-ridden itinerant playboys with *lettres de cachet* hanging over their heads.[44] These were French nationals who had led such unconventional lives that they eventually wound up—often after travels that had taken them as far afield as Canada or Constantinople—seeking refuge in the cities of the Dutch Republic. For in The Hague or Amsterdam, they saw the possibility of remaking themselves as *broodschrivers,* or writers for hire, in the world of underground book production. It was a position that left many of these men feeling bitter and hostile toward the dominant culture of their places of origin. But their exile seems also to have accorded them a sense of apartness or, at least, marginality that had its uses from the perspective of social criticism. And while some developed, at least outwardly, lasting ties to the official Dutch Protestant church, when it came time to put pen to paper many made it their business to thwart the status quo—that is, to challenge the religious, moral, and sexual *doxa* of Dutch culture as well as a despised France—in the philosophical positions they espoused, too. It is hard to say when this was a matter of personal inclination (like displaced peoples everywhere, most were virulently opposed to the reign they left behind), a case of principle, an attempt to earn enough for dinner, or some combination thereof. None of these men can be called revolutionaries. Their goal, as they tried to circumvent the book police across northern Europe, not to mention the Papal Index, was typically amused astonishment on the part of their readers. But ultimately these émigrés hoped to convince some of their readers that moral and intellectual authority lay in none of the places that they might ordinarily look.

The project began, as for Beattie, in recasting the function of the author. He was to be less the possessor of specialized knowledge than simply an emissary of good, practical sense. However, rather than position him on the side of the people as they are (in the manner of the Scottish Common Sense philosophers), the idea was to remake him as a mouthpiece for the people as they once were in some distant and more primitive past. The new author found an alter ego in the imagined role of the noble savage: a generic everyman uncorrupted by the artificial ways of civilization (read, Europe) and endowed only with the basic mental tools with which all humans are born for making sense of the world around them. When placed in dialogue or correspondence with representatives of the dominant culture and recognizable authority figures, the savage, looking in from outside, had a double job. He was, in all his naïveté, to say the otherwise unsayable and expose the hypocrisy of the majority culture. And he was (in contrast to earlier forms of dialogue) to unsettle any easy assurances about where the dividing line between good and bad, true and false, actually lay.[45]

The writings produced in The Hague at the start of the new century by Louis-Armand de Lom d'Arce, Baron de Lahontan, provide us with a particularly good, and early, example of how this might be done, though variants of this technique can be found throughout eighteenth-century European print culture. His story is worth recounting if only to emphasize the difference from the life experiences of Reid or Beattie. The Baron de Lahontan, like many Catholic radicals who ultimately sought refuge in Holland, came from an old but ruined aristocratic French family. One rumor had his mother running a gambling establishment in Paris in the 1680s, the era of the baron's youth. What is sure is that during his adolescence he left France to seek military glory by participating in campaigns against the Iroquois in Canada. There, over a decade of long, frigid winters, he got to know intimately a group of Algonquins with whom he regularly conversed and hunted. Simultaneously, he rose to the rank of *lieutenant du roi* for his services. But at age twenty-seven, after a dispute with the governor of Plaisance, Lahontan fled both Canada and his military career aboard a fishing boat bound for Europe. When he disembarked in 1693 in Portugal, he found himself without money, profession, or country since, as a deserter, he could hardly head home. Endlessly itinerant, Lahontan initially offered himself up as a spy to the English and the Dutch. Then, in the bureaucratic capital of The Hague just after the turn of the new century, Lahontan tried out the role of writer, publishing an extraordinary account of his American adventures, followed by a huge documentary collection on the physical, biological, cultural, and political life of North America, possibly to convince the English or Spanish to pay him for his knowledge.[46] But it was the third volume in this trilogy, entitled *Curious Dialogues between the Author and a Savage of Good Sense Who Has Traveled (Dialogues curieux entre l'auteur et un sauvage de bon sens qui a voyagé)*, that assured Lahontan a life permanently at the margins of the Catholic world and landed him on the Inquisition list. For in this dialogue, the protagonist standing for orthodox Catholic values (whom Lahontan cleverly named after himself) had an unusual challenger. That was Adario, an imagined Huron, described as the embodiment of natural, uncorrupted reason or, in the author's words, "good sense."[47] What ensued was a conversation in which the eloquent and cosmopolitan native American used his natural aptitude, all the stronger for its distance (as Charron would see it) from European material distractions, customs, and learning he had observed as a traveler, to uncover the true nature, which is to say the contradictions and absurdities of "civilized" European ways, especially when it came to the metaphysical and moral claims of the Jesuits. Registering surprise as much as indignation or horror at the illogic and non-sense of the cleric's and the assumed audience's values, Adario holds up European common sense to the pure light of his own, natural, anterior good sense.

Everything about Christian Europe, it turns out, looks upside-down from this vantage point, the generally unremarkable seeming crazy and the outlandish turning sensible. Hurons see obvious good sense in a world of total equality (in contrast to the obsession with social rank and hierarchy in France), in political liberty (in contrast to absolutist monarchical culture), in sexual liberty (in contrast to French marriage laws and the gap between precepts and behavior), and in freedom from things (in contrast to a culture marked by possessive pronouns). Above all, they identify good sense with natural religion, in which one of the few key articles of faith is that the creator of the universe provided the Hurons with "reason capable of distinguishing the good from the bad, just like the sky from the earth."[48] That it is Europeans, in this symmetrical inversion, who have lost track of good sense is demonstrated by the fact that the Hurons lead untroubled, peaceful lives and, unlike Europeans, need no fancy language to justify their positions. For as Adario points out, from the vantage point of natural, objective *bon sens*, even European languages are misleading; it is Jesuit teachings that truly seem like "fables." The frontispiece of Lahontan's collection shows an enormous man, with bow and arrow, standing with one foot astride a scepter and the other on top a European law code. He is at once the iconic eighteenth-century American Indian—strong, even-tempered, eloquent, indifferent to material pursuits—and the pure embodiment of human nature demolishing the work of civilization. Jules Michelet, the great Romantic historian, took one look and declared that he had found the opening blow of the principal intellectual battle of the eighteenth century.[49]

But this dialogue is not only an abstract morality tale pitting the caricatural voice of Scholastic orthodoxy against the logic of the natural man. It is also a story about authority in which Lahontan, the disillusioned colonial agent and outsider in the Dutch Republic, resides at the center. Adario would seem to be his likely mouthpiece, especially as the American savage employs a variant of a recognizably seventeenth-century rationalist, libertine, and even Pyrrhonist perspective against Christian dogma and tradition, including an unwillingness to defer to sacred texts that appear all too human and error prone upon close inspection. He also shares with his creator a penchant for travel and life outside "civilized" norms. But Lahontan gives himself the role of the perfect Christian, the proverbial straight man, in the dialogue. Perhaps this can be dismissed as nothing more than a means of protection, a tactic for absolving himself of responsibility for the attacks on religious and sexual values that he commits to paper. Yet this close identification between the author and his Jesuitical character, whose parodic theology sprinkles the text, could also be part of a very political game of reversal, a way to play the *doxa* against paradox and thereby keep the reader guessing. Both sides accuse the other of being seduced by appearances. Still Adario does not have to be fully right; he only has to defamiliarize what normally goes unquestioned or even unnoticed in order to undermine his readers' assurance in the natural order of things or the seats of authority. In the end, the prophet of good sense in the early eighteenth-century Dutch underground is not the person holding the most sensible doctrine but he who, by shaking readers' confidence in all the truths they take to be universal and absolute, enhances the space for agonistic politics.[50]

The radical possibilities inherent in this role were made even more apparent in the second edition of the *Dialogues* put together in 1705 in The Hague by a defrocked monk and libertine named Nicolas Gueudeville. Gueudeville described himself proudly as an ordinary man, "neither theologian, nor savant, nor *bel esprit,* I know . . . only black and white."[51] But we can learn something of Gueudeville's own extraordinary story from another form of self-serving autobiographical writing, his *Motives for Conversion* of 1689, which begs to be read alongside his other more explicitly polemical works. Its life-on-the-run narrative begins the night that the young man, born of a family with "more reputation than means," climbs down the walls of his monastery and flees the Benedictine order that he had joined as a teenager.[52] Once his eyes are opened to the falseness of Catholicism, and once he has had occasion to converse with a Protestant, Gueudeville determined, we learn, to set out and join the Huguenot exile community across the border. In Rotterdam he established himself at the edges of the local literary world, befriending Bayle, writing a bit, teaching Latin. Later, as Gueudeville moved away from Calvinism (it seems he was a bit too attracted to women, alcohol, and Bayle's more radical ideas), he took himself to The Hague, where he made a living editing a viciously anti-French and anti-Catholic political journal, working as a translator, and composing atlases, among other projects. It was in The Hague that Gueudeville was most likely hired to revise the work of Lahontan, who had already moved on as well. Not only did the former monk succeed in further radicalizing Lahontan's critique of European institutions, especially when the conversation turned to monasteries or oppressive kings and the right of revolt. (Shortly thereafter he would do the same to Erasmus's *In Praise of Folly,* in which the locus of *le bon sens* and agent of reversal took the more traditional form of the madman.) In the new edition of the *Dialogues,* the function of the author's *bon sens* also became more violent and defiant, a vehicle for a kind of emotional rage that would prove essential to populism in its later forms. As Gueudeville's Adario explains to his interlocutor, "good sense furnishes me with what's necessary to strike down your responses and beat them into ruins."[53] The "sensible" author could do more than expose the gap between the most taken-for-granted European norms and good sense. He could, with the same tools, also become a force of destruction.

But there was a second step in this ongoing project. That was to transform, at least in theory, the function of the reader as well. The goal of the underground French writers who used Holland as their base soon became teaching the reader how he (or she) might assume the role of the fictitious Indian himself. Where James Beattie offered his assurances to his disciples that they were already seeing the world in a way that corresponded to "reality" and urged them to continue to trust both their senses and the very words that they used to convey their perceptions of the world around them, the participants in the early eighteenth-century Franco-Dutch underground proposed that the enlightened needed to do the opposite. That is, they had to recover the infallible instinct for discerning truth from falsehood, good from bad, even beauty from ugliness, that civilization and the refinements of education had done their best to obscure. Then the reader—the ordinary, if newly enlightened, person rather than the scholar—could take matters into his or her own hands and become his or her own source of authority, official voices be damned. As in Aberdeen, it is not anachronistic to speak of an effort at democratizing the methods for arriving at truth or of social leveling through epistemology. Though not yet imagined in collective terms, this appeal to the reader's innate sense for thinking against the grain provided the seeds for one more component of what would, eventually, become a populist political idiom.

For how this transformation could be effected, we must jump slightly forward in time and meet another member of the large population of marginal former Frenchmen who helped make Dutch cities so intellectually vibrant in the first half of the eighteenth century. The astonishing Marquis d'Argens is now best remembered as the probable author of the great pornographic novel *Thérèse philosophe* of 1748.[54] But he was also a key figure in the early history of common sense. Once again, we encounter an aristocrat but perpetual outsider, a man seemingly always on the run well into middle age. Born into a *parlementaire* family in Aix-en-Provence, d'Argens spent his early adulthood in recognizable eighteenth-century forms of elite debauchery: shirking his legal studies, gambling, and chasing women with unsuitable provenances all across Europe. Only his intermittent military career held his interest for long. But that, too, ended abruptly after a fall from a horse while training with the Duke of Richelieu's regiment east of the Rhine. In the mid-1730s, d'Argens suddenly began to produce voluminous pages of worldly philosophical writing, the character of which made it necessary for him to flee Catholic Europe and to try to eke out a living, without family support, as one more writer for hire moving semiclandestinely among Holland's urban centers. In his memoirs, d'Argens placed the blame, such as it was, on his early travels. An encounter in Constantinople, first, with a thoughtful Spanish-Jewish doctor and former *converso* and, then, with an Armenian (or possibly Arminian) who had spent time in Amsterdam and discovered Spinoza, had turned the young noble tourist toward a "philosophic" cast of mind.[55] Soon he was on a boat bound for Livorno, in the middle of a storm, reading Bayle while everyone else prayed.[56] It is hard in this case to tell whether fact inspired fiction or fiction inspired fact. But many of d'Argens' most successful early works were to depend upon the motif of the exotic outsider—the Jew, the Egyptian, or the Chinese man, if not the Indian—to similar effect. In correspondence with their coreligionists and with Christian Europeans, these characters could be counted upon both to underline multiplicity of belief and, with their outsiders' good sense, puncture Europeans' "epidemic delusions."[57]

However, with his widely read *Philosophy of Good Sense, or Philosophical Reflections on the Uncertainty of Human Knowledge (Philosophie du bon sens, ou Réflexions philosophiques sur l'incertitude des connoissances humaines*), produced most likely in Maestricht and published

in The Hague in the same years as his volumes of fictional correspondence, the similarity between d'Argens and Lahontan or even the Montesquieu of *The Persian Letters* came to an end.[58] In simple, jaunty prose
admired by Voltaire, the reputed libertine attempted to turn *le bon sens*
from a rhetorical position employed by a fictional character who undermines unfounded truth claims into the foundation of a philosophical
method that the reader, or any ordinary person, might, with minimal
reeducation, use against any authority. Even the author himself was ripe
to be debunked.

The premise of the *Philosophy of Good Sense* is that thinking philosophically could, and should, be for everyone. That included women, the
generic stand-in for the uninformed and credulous across all classes.
D'Argens' expression is "the most ordinary minds."[59] All that was required was to demystify language, which, he claimed, had been stolen by
pedants and "demi-savants" eager to confuse the public, and then to
demonstrate the limits of reason for explaining all aspects of the world
around us. Thus far, we are not that far from the Aberdonians. But to this
end, d'Argens gave himself a seemingly arrogant, if fictional, task that
ran directly counter to that of Beattie, even as they both took on the residue of Scholasticism and its ivory-tower practitioners. D'Argens set out
to convince a lady (and hence a philosophical innocent, despite her previous reading of Montaigne, La Mothe le Vayer, and Bayle, which could
only have paved the way) that her chaplain was an ignoramus and that
his hero, Aristotle, was not much better. What is more, he proposed in
characteristically anti-intellectual fashion that this lady, with only her
"natural light" at her disposal, could know everything that there really is
to know, including more than most so-called savants and certainly more
than the heads of all the Parisian *collèges,* in a mere eight days. Then, in
a self-consciously breezy, unpedantic style aimed explicitly at both men
of the world *(cavaliers)* and polite women *(le beau sexe)* bored to death
by the dry and unintelligible tomes that normally passed for philosophy,
d'Argens showed how this might be done. For what he really hoped
to demonstrate for the hypothetical lady who stands for the reader is
"the little certainly that we actually have of those things that we often
believe are the most sure," whether their source is learned opinion, logic,

tradition, or common consent.[60] One by one, he undermines the truth claims of every field of human knowledge, from history to metaphysics to astrology to the art of happiness. With judicious use of contrary citations, faulty cross-references and notes, and other forms of wit, he even undermines himself. In effect, d'Argens sets out to save his heroine— and, by extension, any reader—from acceptance of any received knowledge and from credulity itself. The reader who has fully absorbed *The Philosophy of Good Sense* emerges an independent-minded and amused skeptic. Philosophy should lead us to laugh at everything, d'Argens implies, right down to ourselves.

Laughter and common sense already had a close and long-standing relationship at the time of the publication of *The Philosophy of Good Sense.* At the very start of the eighteenth century, the humanist theologian François de Salignac de La Mothe Fénelon had answered his own question—"What is common sense?"—by stating that it is the instinct that, when shocked, results in laughter. Ask a four-year-old child, Fénelon demands, if the table in his room can walk by itself and if it can play like him. The child will begin laughing. Or ask an "uncivilized laborer" if the trees in his field are his friends or if his cows give him advice on domestic affairs. He'll respond that you are mocking him. That is because, says Fénelon, such impertinent questions constitute an affront even to the most ignorant laborer and the simplest child. They violate the man's or the child's common sense, that sense that "prevents all examination, which renders the examination of certain questions actually ridiculous, which determines that, despite oneself, one laughs instead of examining, which reduces man to being unable to doubt, no matter what effort he makes to put himself in a state of doubt," that sense "which reveals at first glance and which immediately discovers the evidence or absurdity of a question." For it is this sense, Fénelon continues, that makes certain common first notions, including the existence of God, obvious to all.[61] Reid and Beattie would not have substantially disagreed. Remember the old saying, cited by Richelet: "As long as a man has good sense, he must confess that there is a God." But the Marquis d'Argens comes close to saying that good sense and humor work in exactly the opposite way. Only the basic senses are trustworthy. The boundaries between heterodoxy and orthodoxy, the acceptable and the unacceptable, fluctuate constantly. Truth has no relation to intersubjectivity, and community is transient anyway. It is laughter that should keep us, philosophically, on our toes, unsure of anything that seems to be self-evidently true but that cannot be seen, including perhaps even God.[62]

Was there anywhere to go from here? Recently the historian Jonathan Israel has argued that the real "radical Enlightenment," firmly rooted in Spinoza's Dutch Republic, ended shortly thereafter. The rest of what we designate as enlightened, including the intellectual movement centered in Paris after 1750, was but a pale imitation in a new setting. The "high" Enlightenment, he proposes, should be reconceptualized as simply "a summing up of the philosophical, scientific, and political radicalism of the previous three generations," an extension of the culture of the Dutch Republic beyond its initial center but without much innovation.[63]

Surely it is true that the world of the Baron d'Holbach, not to mention Voltaire, Diderot, and company, owes much more to eccentric aristocrats like Lahontan and d'Argens, hovering at the shadowy fringes of the Republic of Letters while seeking shelter and income in Protestant enclaves outside France, than has traditionally been acknowledged. Their causes, their techniques, their epistemologies, their rhetoric, indeed even their commitment to the deployment of a critical *bon sens* continued to reverberate in the better-known loci of enlightened Francophone culture that followed, from the Baron d'Holbach's Parisian mansion to the Potsdam of Frederick the Great, where d'Argens sought patronage and protection beginning in 1742. D'Argens and Frederick collaborated in 1767 on a new edition of Bayle's dictionary, described in their introduction as "the breviary of good sense" for the way it helped form judgment that began from doubt.[64] D'Holbach meanwhile set to work retranslating and publishing that most famous of Dutch underground manuscripts, "The Treaty of the Three Impostors," in which God is a human creation and all religion is a form of deceit perpetuated by unscrupulous priests and politicians, eager to exploit the common man's ignorance and fear. Clearly its vulgarized Spinozean worldview, infused with a fair amount of libertine skepticism, had a large influence on d'Holbach even as he made his own changes to the text, including substitution of the term *le bon sens* for reason.[65] Even the first French translation, in 1678, of Spinoza's *Tractatus Theologico-Politicus,* one of whose deliberately misleading titles was *Curious Reflections by a Disinterested Mind on the Most Important Matters for Public and Individual Salvation,* found an obvious echo (for those in the know) in the subheading of d'Holbach and company's *Portable Library of Good Sense* almost a hundred years later.[66]

Such dismissiveness regarding the second half of the eighteenth century is, however, misleading from the point of view of a political, rather than purely intellectual, history of common sense. The moment in which the *Portable Library of Good Sense* appeared was, in fact, the high-water mark for a radical conception of and use value for *le bon sens.* For one, the 1760s and 1770s saw a blitz of didactic publications, with an increasingly popular tone, launched with the aim of attracting new readers to a strain of ideas that went back to Bayle. Second, this understanding of good sense began in these same years to be directed toward a new, more constructive social purpose: founding an alternative moral order to replace that tied to the Catholic Church. Finally, Amsterdam emerged as the central node for this more political enterprise, even as the city began its slow financial and cultural decline.[67] (Voltaire himself, no fan of publishers, noted in an essay of 1770 that the Dutch had become "the agents of our thoughts as they were of our wines and salts."[68]) For it was in Amsterdam after the midcentury that a heterodox *bon sens* finally found its institutional base.

That institution was the book business of Marc-Michel Rey, a man with a serious financial interest in spreading the gospel of radical good sense in popular formats throughout Francophone Europe and beyond. By the 1760s, the former Genevan of Huguenot origins had become a well-established member of the bookselling community in Amsterdam, a burgher with a multistory house on a central canal. Partly this was a result of the extensive business that he did in fully legitimate books, most of them recent and in French, including Bibles, works of Protestant and Catholic theology, and even anti-Enlightenment diatribes. But it was also because Rey, simultaneously and quietly, commissioned and published a huge inventory of impious, anticlerical, even pornographic books, some still famous and others long forgotten, some original and others reprints or compendia, and then distributed them to other booksellers and individual readers situated from Russia to Rouen. His underground customer base even extended to the Dutch New World sugar colony of Surinam.[69] And to keep this complex business humming when speed and secrecy were both vital, Rey not only traveled regularly across the European continent; he also collaborated with or directly employed printers, copiers, editors, smugglers, shippers, bankers, and postal clerks, not to mention readers with risky tastes and writers with heterodox ideas, many of them based in other countries.[70] Together they formed an international network that was integral to the propagation of a radical form of good sense in the 1760s and 1770s.

On the one hand, Rey played patron and boss to yet another generation of French speakers in temporary exile or otherwise down on their luck in Amsterdam. Typical was Henri-Joseph Laurent (called DuLaurens), one more former French Jesuit with highly unorthodox religious views who had escaped to Holland as a refuge from the law. In the early 1760s, DuLaurens ended up in Amsterdam working for Rey as a jack-of-all-trades; his functions seem to have included indexing one of Rey's journals, writing theater reviews for another, copyediting manuscripts received, and even compiling heterodox essay collections in the style of the *Portable Library of Good Sense* and helping to arrange their shipment abroad.[71] And with Rey's backing, DuLaurens simultaneously inundated Europe with his own satirical and blasphemous publications—all written behind the mask of such pseudonyms as Modeste Tranquille Xan-Xung, a virtuous Chinese adventurer and clichéd embodiment of innate good sense—before spending the final twenty-six years of his own itinerant life imprisoned as a lunatic in Mayence and then Marienborn.[72] From *L'Arrétin* of 1763 (which had the subtitle "The Debauchery of the Mind as Regards Good Sense") to *Le Compère Mathieu* of 1766, DuLaurens specialized in stories, in the style of Candide, of young naïfs learning about the absurd ways of the world through one dreadful, disillusioning experience after another. The moral was always the same: priests and monks do terrible damage to the understanding, especially of the young, and it was *le bon sens* alone that should serve as "our Sorbonne."[73] With Rey's support, DuLaurens briefly situated himself as a leading European educator about the dangers stemming from books, universities, and faulty authorities of all kinds.

But not all of Rey's aid came at the local level, and he also made money by reaching outside of Holland. In the same years, Rey became the off-site publisher of key works by Voltaire, Rousseau, and other writers stymied by the French censorship apparatus. Most significantly for our purposes, it was Rey who set in motion d'Holbach's flurry of long-distance atheist publishing in the decade between 1766 and 1776. Or to put it differently, with d'Holbach's money, Rey helped facilitate the baron's vision, which was nothing less than a populist campaign, at the very same moment as those of Beattie and Oswald, to use the low-level capacity for common or good sense to destroy the (false) notion of God and all that followed from it.

What distinguished d'Holbach's and Rey's enterprise was their seemingly paradoxical attempt to reach a broad literate public with an attack on its most deep-seated beliefs. Where good sense had, in the pre-1750 Dutch underground, made itself heard mainly in esoteric manuscripts smuggled from reader to reader and in small printed editions of irony-laden prose, in d'Holbach's hands it became the driving force behind a blitz of didactic publication, much of it written in layman's terms and published in portable formats, to be distributed to a large—if necessarily primarily wealthy, given the cost of all underground books—international audience. Several factors conspired to make this possible in the 1760s and 1770s: expanded commercial networks for circumventing police and censors across national boundaries, a growing population of readers in France and elsewhere in Europe with an interest in heterodoxy, and the deep pockets of d'Holbach himself. That this effort in both vulgarization and secrecy succeeded to some degree is attested to by the excellent sales results for the legitimate and pirated editions of d'Holbach's *System of Nature*.[74]

Moreover, while the baron remained committed to hierarchy in all realms of life, including the world of ideas, he continually sent forth the message that the truths he had to impart were, at least in theory, accessible to every man or woman. All readers had to be willing to do was renounce their prejudices and listen to that minimal level of reasonableness inherent in all that d'Holbach called good sense. This was a considerably lower threshold than abstract reason or logic since, in his account, it had much more to do with effortlessly accepting obvious truths than with arriving at new ones, and it was most useful for eliminating questions that simply could not be answered. And d'Holbach did not doubt publicly that this was possible. One day in the future, d'Holbach insisted (in striking distance from the erudite libertines of the seventeenth century or even Bayle), with the advent of a government supportive of real education and eager to render the truth "common and popular," a world of enlightened "opinion" built upon the philosopher's good sense rather than custom and habit would become the norm.[75] As he envisioned it, "Sensible and peaceable persons become enlightened; enlightenment spreads little by little and succeeds in the long run in making an impression even on the eyes of the people [*le peuple*]."[76] The generalization and popularization of an ethos that began with an inherent capacity for *le bon sens* allowed for the idea that ordinary people, male and female, would also eventually be able to do without the aid of professional clerics. Then good sense and common sense, or *le bon sens* and *le sens commun,* now at odds, could become one once again.

But on the other hand, given the power of priests and the depths of popular ignorance, d'Holbach put little faith in this transformation happening any time soon. The baron actually had nothing but disdain for the current ideas of the majority of his contemporaries, especially those of common origins (*le vulgaire* or *le commun des hommes,* in his terms) whom he saw as superstitious, impulsive, irrational, and uninformed.[77] Moreover, the truths that Holbachian *bon sens* were intended to reveal were as estranged from late eighteenth-century commonplaces, even within enlightened circles, as could be imagined. *Le bon sens* became, in the late 1760s and early 1770s, in the hands of d'Holbach, a means by which to reveal the problematic nature of all religious beliefs and practices and to proselytize not simply doubt, beginning with the word "God," but also an explicit atheism, materialism, and related moral code with little obvious broad appeal.[78] Even the deism of d'Argens and, later,

Voltaire or the theism of Rousseau looked tame by comparison. No wonder that d'Holbach's writings were often lumped together with pornography and scandal sheets in the late Old Regime booksellers' category of "philosophical books."

It was to this complex and ultimately political project that d'Holbach stealthily devoted ten years of his life, employing a small circle of invisible collaborators, including his endlessly sycophantic secretary, Jacques-André Naigeon, and dispensing (rather than earning) an enormous amount of money in the process. Like our other French-speaking prophets of good or common sense, d'Holbach's efforts to address the public were aided by fortune of birth and education as well as an international orientation. Baptized Paul Henri Thiry, the philosopher entered the world in the Palatinate in 1723 and, upon being orphaned at a young age, became the adoptive son of an uncle named Holbach, who made enough money as a financier to be able to add an aristocratic "de" to his name and to send his young charge off to study law at the University of Leyden. It was a cosmopolitan, itinerant beginning to life for Thiry. But in most ways, the Baron d'Holbach's story reads as the inverse of that of our French émigrés to Holland. For after five years in the Dutch Republic frequenting the circles of Huguenot and English radicals, the wealthy, titled young d'Holbach abandoned his peripatetic ways and settled permanently in the center of Paris. Henceforth his comportment in daily life betrayed little (as demanded, given the period and place) of the adventurer about it. Neither did he play the debauched libertine. Instead, d'Holbach successfully made his way to the forefront of Parisian intellectual culture. In short order, he became a naturalized Frenchman. He married his first cousin (and, upon her death, his wife's sister, thanks to a papal dispensation). He even bought himself both a fancy office and fancy friends, literary and noble, local and international alike. D'Holbach passed his time as an independent working member of the Republic of Letters, a vocation that found him, among other tasks, weighing in on the musical quarrels of the moment and writing more than 400 articles for Diderot's and D'Alembert's *Encyclopédie,* the bulk of them on geology and chemistry. Above all, he fashioned himself into an extraordinary entertainer and promoter of enlightened sociability, operating what was known variously as his "hotel of philosophy," "synagogue," and "la Boulangerie" (in reference to the presence of the anticlerical Nicolas-Antoine Boulanger rather than to d'Holbach's baking skills) at his home in Paris as well as a country estate in nearby Grandval. The abundant food, the fine wine, the private library and art collection, the patronage possibilities, the cosmopolitanism of the guests (this was, after all, mainly a transplanted elite, with origins both international and provincial), even the family chaplain at his country estate: all this became the stuff of Enlightenment legend. So did the ongoing animated discussions that he fostered. D'Holbach's life was, it appeared, one of wealth, privilege, and relative ease, distinguished mainly by the free and lively conversation among well-connected men that famously flowed around his grand dinner table.[79]

It was only in his mid-forties, and only in the deepest secrecy, that d'Holbach traveled briefly to England to make the acquaintance of the emissaries of Rey and to begin his large-scale underground campaign to publicize atheism as a foundation for a new moral code. Not only the content but also the sheer volume of these publications came as a shock to contemporaries. Some of these publications were translations of key treatises by polemical, freethinking English writers, such as Thomas Hobbes and John Toland. Others were rewrites of earlier French-language texts, including some of the most famous heterodox manuscripts of the previous hundred years. Still others were brand-new works, composed alone or with the help of Naigeon and possibly Diderot. The original manuscripts made their way in hand-copied form from Paris to Amsterdam, via Sedan and Liège, and with the help of a small circle of allies, including a postal inspector named Bron and a Madame Loncin, whose job was to turn them over to Rey himself.[80] In all, d'Holbach was responsible for over thirty such anonymous or pseudonymous texts appearing on the market, almost all published by Rey and then diffused clandestinely well beyond Holland, in the ten years between 1766 and 1776—and all without their foreign author ever managing to call any attention to himself.

The old notion of "good sense" was, in one way, an aid in this task. The success of d'Holbach's publishing frenzy, much like the infamous manuscripts promoting atheism that preceded it, depended on avoiding originality in terms of either ideas or voice; this was to be an impersonal kind of wisdom, handed down without regard for authorship. Good sense, the cognitive authority with which d'Holbach most often associated himself, was, for this author, something like a useful disguise. It was a generic but universal epistemological position from which to speak to an undefined but potentially unlimited public, itself endowed with the potential to use its own good sense to similar effect.

But mainly good sense functioned more ambitiously: as a way to undermine the language of religion and all the certainty about the world that came with it. If, as members of the Académie française and the *philosophes* agreed, languages were codified as a result of usage or tacit consent and functioned to underline the prevailing common sense, then to undo the referentiality of religious language, starting with the word "God," was to destroy the key foundation of French Catholic public life.[81] D'Holbach imagined *le bon sens* as primarily a means to distinguish appearance from truth. In his hands, good sense became the minimal level of reason that would potentially allow all people to see through the nonsensical language at the heart of all religions—the chimeras (or things given reality only through imagination and words), the *galimatias,* the language games—and to build a new, atheistic, moral order out of the wreckage.

Now, it is essential to point out that the role of obscure or esoteric religious language in the obfuscation of truth was not d'Holbach's discovery. It had long been a key theme of anti-Scholastic rhetoric, and one might well challenge any claims about d'Holbach's distinctiveness by pointing to the long history of the idea that even biblical language was highly ambiguous. It is worth remembering that Lahontan, well before d'Holbach or even Rousseau, had depicted the primitive world of the Hurons without "yours" or "mine," thereby rendering even certain basic French pronouns perversions of nature. Similarly, d'Argens, in his *Philosophy of Good Sense,* had made fun of Scholastic argumentation by attacking demi-savants who use "a few unintelligible words against the attacks of reason and natural light," and he had offered a ringing critique of the dangers of words being taken for things.[82] In his contemporaneous

Cabalistic Letters, d'Argens had gone even further toward linguistic materialism and denounced prayer as misplaced faith in what was ultimately just a collection of sounds in the air.[83] The "difficulties" of defining even the most basic terms of the Christian religion, not to mention the social and moral "difficulties" generated by this imprecision, were central themes in the clandestine manuscript and print culture of the first half of the eighteenth century, a literature well known to d'Holbach.

But by the time d'Holbach turned his atheism into a public campaign, some fundamental changes in perceptions of language had taken place. The key source was Lockean sensationalism, especially as developed by the Abbé de Condillac in the mid-eighteenth century. What Locke had introduced was the concept that all ideas arrived in the mind by way of the senses; no ideas were innately there. In the case of Reid and company, who rejected this doctrine, an epistemological shift of this magnitude had necessitated a rethinking of the social function of language as well. For Condillac, it became apparent that language was not simply reflective, a way of conveying knowledge. Rather, language was vital to the formation and then the propagation of that knowledge. Or to put it another way, knowledge constituted itself and continually manifested itself in language; the two had an entirely symbiotic relationship. That meant that while words—the arbitrary signs that humans attach to their ideas and then use to link ideas together—could be a spur to truth, they could also produce and perpetuate falsehoods and prejudices, including giving a mistaken existence to things that we cannot, or can only partially, know given the limitations of our mental equipment. And while language could be used to spread knowledge and to foster social ties, it could also become a tool of deception, especially in the hands of the powerful, who might use the gap between words and things to their advantage. For Condillac, then, an effective philosophical method began with linguistic discipline; every word had to be made to correspond to a single, material thing. And every time language was employed in an equivocal, vague, or misleading way, whether as a result of habit or malice, it had to be denounced as what Locke and then Condillac called an "abuse of words."[84] That was the only way to conquer error and bring truth to light.

D'Holbach trumpeted an almost identical epistemology and rooted it in a picture of human psychology characterized by fear, ignorance, and a lively imagination. More importantly, he—like many of his generation— put this stance toward signs and things to polemical use in a crusade against specific "prejudices," with the hope that this tack would lead to actual social change. The project began with a form of literature entirely focused on language: a dictionary of the key words of religion. In part, d'Holbach's choice can be seen as a product of his intense interest in reaching a broad, literate public, since the fragmentary and condensed form of the dictionary was thought to aid in the process of vulgarization. However, d'Holbach's *Portable Theology or Abridged Dictionary of the Christian Religion* (*Théologie portative, ou Dictionnaire abrégé de la religion chrétienne*) of 1768—which was to be one of the central works reproduced in the composite *Portable Library of Good Sense*—operated principally as a vehicle of destabilization and desacralization by means of the significations, classifications, and organization of words. For d'Holbach set out to show that when it came to the language of Christianity, most words failed to hold up to the basic test of good sense.

Many of the key terms of religion turn out in this dictionary to mean nothing or to refer only to more words, all equally disconnected from true knowledge rooted in sense experience (which is why d'Holbach insisted that a sensationalist and nominalist theory of language necessarily led to atheism). Take the case of the soul (*l'âme*), explained as an "unknown substance which acts in an unknown fashion on our bodies that we hardly know," before d'Holbach segues to the joke that priests and monks seem to be too modest ever to show us theirs. More often, the terms of theology turn out to mean the opposite of what they are widely taken to mean, especially when the author speaks from the position of basic human reason or good sense rather than its antagonist, blind faith. Not the least of these is common sense itself. How does d'Holbach define *le sens commun* in his *Portable Theology?* "It is the most rare and most useless thing in the Christian religion; dictated by God himself, religion is not subject to the human and vulgar rules of good sense. A good Christian must enslave his understanding in order to subordinate it to his faith, and if his curate tells him that three makes only one [i.e., the

Trinity] or that God is bread [i.e., the principle of transubstantiation], he is obliged to believe it in spite of common sense."[85]

Indeed, over and over in d'Holbach's dictionary the language of religion—those invented words and obscure turns of phrase that clerics have long used to confuse and mislead the ignorant and credulous—and the language of good sense are set at odds. What is materialism, as understood by all those steeped in religion? "An absurd opinion, that is to say, contrary to Theology, which props up the unreligious who do not have enough intelligence to know what intelligence is." This leads one to ask what d'Holbach takes to be the religious conception of "absurdities." The answer is "They cannot exist in Religion, which is the work of the Word and of divine Reason, which, as one knows, has nothing in common with human reason. . . . The more a thing is absurd in the eyes of human reason the more it is suitable to divine reason or Religion." The goal of d'Holbach's definitions is not ultimately to try to overcome the gap between words and things but rather to expose and exacerbate it, to underline the rationality of what is typically dismissed and the absurdity of what is typically said and believed.

Both Voltaire and Helvétius, at almost the same moment, drew similar connections between a corrupt social order and the misleading language of priests and prelates. Both also played on the chasm between common and good sense and the different (and multiple) ways each appears depending on one's perspective. Voltaire had already famously included a definition of *le sens commun* in the second, 1765 edition of his own *Portable Philosophical Dictionary* and, after a deliberately debunking explanation of the various meanings of common sense in the modern world, also set out to show its distance from true reason.[86] Similarly, Helvétius, to illustrate the precept in his posthumous *Of Man* (1773) that religion "prohibits men from using their reason and makes them brute, unhappy and cruel at the same time," rehearsed the story of one act of Fielding's *Pasquin* to make the new point that though clerics depend for their survival upon a phony appeal to good sense, *true* good sense will always constitute religion's antagonist.[87] The play between good and common sense was on its way to becoming a critical, anti-establishment tool, at least on the page and among intellectual elites. One could even argue that d'Holbach, Voltaire, and Helvétius collectively established the model, circa 1770, for a new kind of intellectual provocateur (of which the twentieth- or twenty-first-century social scientist is only the latest incarnation). That is the person who takes his or her public task to be exposing the existing common sense, regardless of whether the subject is money or belief or anything else, as a collection of culturally variable illusions that stand in the way of real knowledge.

But with *Good Sense,* published just a few years later, d'Holbach's objective expanded. Here the title value itself is defined positively as "that portion of judgment sufficient to know most simple truths," as well as negatively as "the portion of truth necessary to reject the most striking absurdities and to be shocked by palpable contradictions."[88] And skepticism about words and meanings gives way to the invention of a purified idiom consonant with this positive conception of good sense. The (future) language of an atheist society, we discover, will be simple, concrete, impersonal, and accessible to all—in striking contrast both to the language of Christianity, with its embellishments and fables, and to an earlier language of elite heterodoxy, with its signature esotericism, hidden messages, and dissimulations. What this new language will provide is a more accurate view of reality; for without God to complicate matters, real clarity will finally become feasible. This simplified idiom will also make it possible to convey precisely the axioms of good sense that will form the basis of the new, atheistic ethical and political system that d'Holbach would go on to lay out in a quick succession of subsequent anonymous tomes, including *Natural Politics* and *The Social System* of 1773 and *Universal Morality* and *Ethnocracy, or Government Founded on Morality* (which was dedicated to Louis XVI) of 1776. For as d'Holbach argued repeatedly, once one's gaze is fixed toward the earth rather than the heavens and not obscured by prejudice or encumbered by the teachings of false prophets, "the true principles of politics are clear, [self-]evident . . . as sure as in any other area of human knowledge."[89] They needed now only to "be simplified to the point where they can be felt by the most ordinary of men."[90]

Unlike d'Argens, d'Holbach was ultimately not skeptical about the possibility of knowledge, except in the religious sphere. His epistemology, with its distinctive mixture of modesty about what humans can know and arrogance about the certainty of what they can, had become quite mainstream by the 1770s; like Beattie, d'Holbach saw himself building on the model of the natural sciences. D'Holbach's real radicalness, and his significance for a political history of common sense, comes from the fact that in his effort to do away with God, he reimagined the nature of politics, conceptualizing it not as an esoteric science but as a mundane realm of knowledge derived entirely from everyday life and concrete things. Then he tried, through publishing, to reach a large, trans-European, literate public and convince it that this vision of a simple, secular social order was a perfect match for its native common sense. That such consonance was possible would become an article of faith for all revolutionary movements to come.

But was anyone really listening in the early and mid-1770s? Here is where true irony enters the story. Despite all his money and effort, d'Holbach's proselytizing for the *bon sens* of atheism and a related moral code might have remained a marginal affair, a hypothetical conversation with only a small number of readers with access to (and interest in) underground books. D'Holbach himself put no faith in open confrontation or actual involvement with a wide public; democracy was another of his "chimeras," not least because "the imbecilic populace" was, at present, so very "lacking in common sense."[91] Even for Rousseau, the idea of a real rebellion, "a revolution . . . to bring men back to common sense," entered the picture only when the discussion revolved around linguistic jargons, not practical politics.[92] Except that d'Holbach's high-brow antagonists—of whom there were many—chose to respond in as public a fashion as possible, with competing treatises, competing dictionaries, even competing dialogues and novels, and with both sides claiming veritable good sense as their ally. Thus his opponents inadvertently accomplished just what d'Holbach and his few secret associates could not have done alone. They turned an imaginary battle into a real one and permanently destabilized, on the eve of the Age of Revolutions, any set notion of what good sense meant or who possessed it. D'Holbach's arguments may have begun life at the outer edges of public consciousness. But by the end of the 1770s, the relationship between good and common sense had become so confused that it was no longer possible to answer the question, as the author of one anti-Holbachian screed phrased it, "whose side is Good Sense on?"[93]

Even in the decades when the High Enlightenment turned into the ostensibly sedate culture of the European establishment, d'Holbach's *Good Sense* generated considerable alarm. As the French chronicler Louis Petit de Bachaumont said about this work, "it is a real catechism of atheism, but one within the understanding of everyone: women, children, and the most ignorant and stupid people; and for this reason it is to be feared that it will proselytize many and will be much more dangerous than learned treatises on the same subject."[94] The Baron Grimm was more succinct: "it is atheism put at the disposal of chambermaids and wigmakers."[95] Furthermore, it could be had at a cost of only "10 sous," added D'Alembert in a letter to Voltaire that Thomas Jefferson was subsequently to transcribe into his own, annotated copy of d'Holbach's tome.[96] Orthodox Catholics, Protestants, even deists had already been horrified by d'Holbach's more obscure and difficult *System of Nature*.[97] *Good Sense* was a work that, d'Holbach's peers fretted, threatened to spread the Baron's doctrine and methods to larger and potentially more credulous audiences, including that growing category of readers with significant influence over their households, women.

Nowhere was that anxiety more evident than within the Catholic Church. Its representatives responded, as they had to previous public declarations of impiety, by going on the defensive in two ways. One was through formal denunciations, accompanied by physical destruction of the offending texts. The other was through literary efforts at correction—even if participating in the conversation risked drawing new attention to d'Holbach's incendiary claims.

Censors, both clerical and governmental, tried their hand first at countering the "contagion" of the new philosophy that had turned *le bon sens* against traditional common sense. Official actions against the key works of the new *philosophie* punctuated the midcentury, especially in France, where the majority of this illicit literature circulated despite its usually foreign place of publication. In early 1759, the Parlement of Paris ordered all copies of Helvétius's *Of the Mind,* along with Diderot and D'Alembert's great *Encyclopédie,* d'Argens' now seriously passé *Philosophy of Good Sense,* and several other well-known works of impiety, to be publicly burned. Distribution and further printing were declared illegal as well. What needed to be blocked from public consumption, according to the censors, were the dangerous and mistaken ideas—whether atheistic, deistic, materialistic, or simply anti-Christian—contained within these screeds. But even more, the wrongheaded epistemology put forth to justify these ideas demanded public condemnation. As the censors' report explained, all of these works tended toward error because they depended on "systems that have for principles only human intelligence and sense impressions," rather than "first truths graven in our hearts by the hand of the Creator" and "certain principles" stemming from "divine light."[98]

Such rhetoric underwent little change following condemnations on similar charges of Voltaire's *Portable Philosophical Dictionary* in 1768, d'Holbach's *System of Nature* in 1770, and d'Holbach's *Good Sense* together with Helvétius's posthumous *Of Man* in 1774. In France, a plurality of censors, from the Parlement of Paris to the Assembly of the Clergy to the doctors of the Sorbonne, continued to root out and excoriate the same old impious claims and methods in almost identical terms before subjecting the offending volumes to laceration and burning. Such denunciations appear by the last years of the Old Regime to have become little more than a rote response in a system characterized by laxity (including lack of any real detective work to discern authorship), haphazardness, and even collusion. However, legal effectiveness aside, these cases gave the Catholic Church a coveted opportunity to try to reaffirm its power over the *doxa.*[99] That this was partly the motive for the challenge to *Good Sense* is made clear by the censors' report, in which the unknown author's appropriation of *le bon sens* "to attack the truths which hold together Society and console the human species, confound all notions of good and evil, rip apart the eternal boundaries that separate vice and virtue, and treat God as a chimera," which is to say to undermine all that constituted common sense from the Church's position, became the center of his crime. What is more, in the official response to tomes like *Good Sense,* a growing sense of panic is also discernible: that as a result of their newly vulgarized message, irreligion was spreading like a "terrible poison," infiltrating everywhere from the salons of well-heeled urban ladies (which may well have been true) to the cottages of vulnerable farmers (which is less likely).[100] According to the alarmist General Assembly of the Clergy of 1785, the lessons of the new *philosophie* could now be heard "even in the workshops of the artisan and under the humble roofs of peasants."[101] No space, it seemed, would henceforth be safe. Unchecked, a skeptical, anti-authoritarian *bon sens* seemed poised to render general a new, upside-down common sense, with the credulous its first victims.

Given this dire situation, the Catholic Church was also well aware that it was not sufficient simply to denounce existing works of impiety in report after report or to continue to burn copies of offending books (though *Good Sense* was put on the Index of the Church in 1774 and *Portable Theology* was burned alongside DuLaurens' *L'Arrétin* the following year in Cologne).[102] Truths that should go without saying—obvious assumptions about the existence of God and the immateriality of all thinking beings, for example—needed to be shored up. And just as importantly, the very idea of "good sense" needed to be seized and reappropriated for legitimate Christian purposes. Until very recently, after all, good sense had been considered a tool in the defense of faith and the status quo for Protestants and Catholics alike. In 1769, the "Reverend" Louis Dutens, in a French-language essay on how to refute the atheism, theism, and deism of contemporary false philosophers, had advised opposing their far-fetched ideas with simple, reassuring "good sense, which is the common inheritance of us all."[103] Even Stanislas Leszczynski, the Polish king and brother-in-law of Louis XV, who spent most of his days writing minor philosophical tracts while ruling in exile over the tiny state of Lorraine, had tried this tactic in his *Incredulity Combated by Simple Good Sense, a Philosophical Essay by a King* of 1760.[104] Across Europe, this fashionable phrase had long been marshaled, in conjunction with revelation and church teachings, in defense of Christianity. D'Argens and then d'Holbach had, however, changed the stakes by attaching the expression to impiety and then giving it an increasingly popular flavor. In response, writers with either a pecuniary or a moral stake in challenging the irreligious thought of the day felt compelled to change tactics. Many Catholic apologists continued to draw directly on the authority of church spokesmen or government censors in making their own case. But in an effort to reach a large lay readership, including women, they also increasingly couched their message in the form, style, and rhetoric of the best of the heterodox writers, among them d'Holbach and Voltaire.

As early as the 1750s, the Abbé Gabriel Gauchet had established a monthly journal dedicated to detailed refutations of popular works of impiety and aimed at a lay audience. In response to the Marquis d'Argens' *Philosophy of Good Sense,* for example, Gauchet had devoted a whole volume to showing how this book was in fact "good sense reversed" since it had separated this basic epistemological category from the Christian faith.[105] The real growth in this new genre of religious writing did not begin, however, until the late 1760s and early 1770s, when such skillful stylists as the Abbé Barruel, Madame de Genlis, and the Abbé Bergier began producing simply written and, at times, clever and entertaining responses to the new, vulgarized philosophy associated with the radical Francophone Enlightenment. Much of this literature, like the heterodox French language texts that it was designed to counter, was produced and published outside Paris, including in what one scholar calls the "Jesuit Amsterdam" of Avignon, among other eastern cities.[106] In these pages, a new common purpose also came to the fore. That was to restore the traditional union of the French language and common sense sundered by d'Holbach and others and to make the world referentially stable once again.

At the most general level, anti-*philosophes* sought to demonstrate that certain kinds of truths were fixed in language and that proof, or certainty, could indeed be found in the agreed-upon meaning of words, whether the subject was religion or the price of bread. As the ex-Jesuit Abbé Nonnotte, the author of a dictionary of religion that presented itself as a corrective to that of Voltaire, explained in a discussion of certainty, "when I say that two and two make four, I perceive that it is impossible that the thing be otherwise; because the idea that I attach to these words *two* and *two* represents for me precisely the same thing as the idea that I attach to the word *four.* I perceive in the same manner the truth of this proposition: *God cannot deceive us,* because *deception* indicates a vice and the idea of *God* excludes all vices and all imperfections."[107] Nonnette, like many other writers with similar sympathies, then tried to restore traditional, consensual meanings to particular terms that the *philosophes* seemed to have hijacked for their own purposes—a project that would be widely adopted in the early 1790s by counter-revolutionary dictionary writers. Among those contested terms were *common sense, good sense,* and *philosophy* itself.

After Voltaire's assault, and even more after that of d'Holbach, *le sens commun,* ostensibly the most obvious of notions given its relation to commonplace ideas, seemed to require redefinition. The simplest answer issued from the pen of the Jesuit writer and physicist Aimé-Henri Paulian: restore its Aristotelian meaning as an internal sense.[108] More often—as in the hands of another ex-Jesuit, the Abbé Barruel—both common and good sense were redefined as something very close to Cartesian natural light. When its "real" or spiritual meaning was distinguished from the arrogant "reasoning" of modern rationalists, as the unnamed author of *Anti-Good-Sense (L'Anti-Bon-Sens)* put it, good sense became the faculty that granted humans the ability to discover truths that are eternal and innate, including about God himself.[109] For anti-*philosophes* also imagined *le bon sens* and a more socially constructed *sens commun* being made one once again, albeit on different terms from d'Holbach. According to Barruel, the common sense faculty may have found itself under assault from its "mortal enemy," modern philosophy and its small coterie of adherents. Yet it remained the source of what he called (ironically) "the sad uniformity that reigns among us" about certain basic assumptions, not least of them about the truth of God. As one of the characters in his massive anti-philosophic novel *The Helviens, or Provincial Philosophical Letters (Les Helviennes, ou Lettres provinciales philosophiques)* of 1781–1788 points out, if you were to ask even the least religious provincials about the existence of God, they would retort incredulously, "Is there a sun? When light shines, is there a cause of its splendor . . . or even more simply, when there is a watch, is there a maker?"[110] In other words, the answer was obvious, indeed commonsensical, to everybody who was neither swept away by fashion nor mad. (In a reversal of d'Argens, this was the common sense lesson that it took a fictional provincial baroness with a passion for the new philosophy a full five volumes to learn.)

But the main word that became a battleground in this war over representation was *philosophe* itself. The charges were multifold. First, the *philosophe* erred by being an individualist. As Barruel noted, with a characteristic undercurrent of irony, there are no slaves in the new philosophy; everyone thinks exactly as he wants and speaks exactly as he sees it.[111] Nonnotte put it more forcefully. The new philosophy was characterized by "libertinage of the mind and heart," coupled with "an arrogant presumption [about one's own mental powers] which, without study and without examination, dares decide all."[112] The prideful *philosophe* thought nothing was more powerful than his own independent reasoning process.

As if this were not enough, the *philosophe* could also be tarred as an elitist who, though he might appeal to the public, had nothing but scorn for the common opinions of the common man. Dutens explained: "He who publishes his apparently new opinions, or disputes those which are generally received, flatters himself that he shall rank above the vulgar herd; and such an author, who is incapable of distinguishing himself by his knowledge or his genius, aims rather at exciting wonder in weak understandings by the singularity of his opinions than is satisfied with remaining in the class of men of moderate capacity who are strangers to a vanity which can make such glory a reward."[113] Barruel made the same position into an ironic question: has there ever before been "a school where one could flatter oneself for being less subject to vulgar opinion?"[114]

Indeed, in keeping with this tendency toward both self-regard and condescension toward the established, communal truths that constituted ordinary peoples' common sense, the *philosophe* was also frequently pegged as an obscurantist. Eager to obfuscate the difference between substances and appearances and dedicated to sophisms and paradoxes, the *philosophe* turned his back on the simplicity and directness of truth. What does one need today to have the name of *philosophe*, Louis-Mayeul

Chaudon asked rhetorically in his own anti-Voltairian dictionary, only to respond: "He needs simply to find bad what one has up until now found good, to jeer at ancient truths in order to substitute new or modernized paradoxes."[115] The *philosophe,* in other words, routinely chose unsettling language games over restoring the direct and long-established correspondence between words and things. His love of contradictions, like his refusal to follow either established authorities or the *consensus gentium,* pushed society in two directions: toward a generalized doubt about all that should be certain and toward the espousal of dangerous new absurdities under the banner of truth.

Never mind that none of this was really true, that the two supposed "sides" in this battle—the Holbachians and their opponents—were actually quite fluid, sharing many of the same literary techniques, same methods for reaching the public, same readers, even some of the same personnel. The Abbé Bergier, for example, remained an active participant in d'Holbach's social group at the same time as he kept busy publically attacking d'Holbach's materialism (not knowing its source) as a shock to common sense.[116] Never mind, too, the great internal divisions in both camps. The damage was done. Jointly, heterodox, Protestant, and Catholic writers managed to undermine what counted as common sense. By the mid-1770s, explicit agreement could be found only around one point: that what constituted good or common sense and where it was to be found were in a state of extraordinary dissolution. Given the many shocks to the status quo that continental Europeans experienced at this moment, from experiments in the deregulation of the economy to the launching of hot air balloons, no one was quite sure that anything like a single common sense could, in fact, be restored. As the author of one pamphlet written in response to the painting salon of 1777 noted, when it came to matters of public judgment even about taste, "there is no common sense" to be found.[117] Not that Queen Common Sense had been killed off once and for all. The existence of facetious announcements for "academies" of common sense and "courses" in common sense suggest that the idea, or, better yet, the ambition, was still very much alive in the last decades of the Old Regime.[118] It was just that no one was sure where this fabled queen lived or what she represented any more. And even if few in this conflict were yet to recommend *le peuple* taking matters into its own hands and crafting its own version of a common sense solution, the promotion of the rhetorical power of good sense, combined with the destabilization of its meaning, made it a spur to the very kind of conflict that it was supposed to negate.

The tight-knit, mid-eighteenth-century Protestant literati of Aberdeen proposed that philosophers should think in the same fashion as ordinary people, upholding a stable, collective *doxa* that left space for God. At almost the same moment, a small number of nonconformist writers with loose and primarily clandestine ties to the book business of Amsterdam, among other continental cities, suggested that ordinary persons should (on an individual basis) learn to think like the new philosophers, which is to say more like reasonable savages unschooled in Christianity than like traditional savants. As such, they helped legitimize nonexpert challenges to existing authority on the part of those dismayed by the status quo. And finally their orthodox Catholic opponents inadvertently aided them in making this case. All were to contribute to the formation of an epistemological basis for a rapidly developing populist worldview. Indeed, the incendiary modern political style that we now call populism was to depend upon the fusion of these different strands of Enlightenment culture more than any explicit development within the political theory of the moment. The only real surprise was that the explosion was to occur first in a fabled but little-known city on the other side of the Atlantic called Philadelphia.

CHAPTER 4

Building a Common Sense Republic

Philadelphia, 1776

We have it in our power to begin the world over again.
Thomas Paine, *Common Sense*

IN 1776, IN THE DISTANT colonial outpost of Philadelphia, "common sense" became a call to arms. The basic story has, over the last 235 years, become something of a historical cliché. In January of that year, nine months after the first skirmishes of the Revolutionary War, debate on the streets of the main colonial cities of North America was not yet focused on breaking free from the British. Fear, combined with residual loyalty and affection for the mother country, mostly ruled out this kind of thinking. But behind closed doors, and within radical circles such as those frequented by the bankrupt ex-corset-maker and émigré known familiarly as Tom Paine, the conversation about independence had already begun. After arriving penniless in the old Quaker city of Philadelphia as recently as late 1774, Paine had spent the better part of his first year in the New World writing essays for the *Pennsylvania Magazine* under such noms de plume as "Vox Populi" and "Justice, and Humanity"; hobnobbing with Benjamin Rush, Benjamin Franklin, and other colonial radicals; and growing increasingly enraged at British responses to colonial discontent. Finally, with the backing of some of his influential new Philadelphia friends, Paine began drafting a small pamphlet in which he set out to convert the large reading public in the colonies not only to the cause of independence but also to the even more extreme idea that a self-governed, unified America should be a republic, without king or nobility. When the first edition of this revolutionary call to arms appeared on colonial bookstalls that January, it came with a title suggestive of one of the immigrant author's chief forms of evidence. That, of course, was common sense.[1]

Paine's claim that his anonymous pamphlet had "the greatest sale that any performance ever had since the use of letters" may have been somewhat self-serving. But *Common Sense* was a publishing phenomenon even by modern standards, selling—Paine claimed—more than 100,000 copies in the first year alone.[2] "Common Sense for eighteen pence" became one of the great sales pitches of the late eighteenth century.[3] John Penn, a delegate to the Second Continental Congress, reported after a trip south in the spring of 1776 that he "heard nothing praised in the Course of his Journey, but Common Sense and Independence. That this was the Cry, throughout Virginia."[4] The Boston radical Sam Adams put it even more succinctly, albeit ambiguously: "Common sense prevails among the people."[5]

In effect, Paine's success was twofold. By most accounts, what Paine produced with his slim, cheaply printed pamphlet was an abrupt and massive shift in opinion up and down the Atlantic colonies. Soon after the appearance of *Common Sense,* according to standard histories, national independence came to seem not only viable but also essential—and did so to a public that ran the gamut from New England ministers to Philadelphia artisans and tradesmen. In a short span of time, the notion of the natural inequality of men, all of whom owed obedience to a king, was also largely replaced by a new vision of the world, no more inherently correct in its presuppositions, in which the people were at once the governed and the governors. This massive change of heart then altered the direction of the struggle between Britain and its North American colonies, forcing the recently formed Continental Congress meeting in Paine's adopted hometown to move toward the drafting of a Declaration of Independence the following summer. Thus Paine set the stage, or so the story generally goes, for a revolution that would produce an independent New World democracy to be called the United States of America.

There is, however, a second way to think about Paine's achievement, one that does not require accepting this exceptionally neat story in full. That is to focus on his linkage of this startling new political vision to a mundane, invisible, but increasingly valuable standard of truth. Paine's other great success stemmed from his decision to call upon "common sense" as both the rationale and the name for the then-revolutionary political sensibility that he hoped to instill. The transplanted English stay maker also invented the myth that there was common sense in a form of government that began from common sense, a myth that was to have a very long life in modern democratic politics. Paine did not actually use the expression much in his pathbreaking pamphlet. He only employed it three times apart from the title, which was supplied, according to Benjamin Rush, by the Philadelphia doctor himself, who had vetoed Paine's own, more straightforward suggestion of "Plain Truth."[6] Moreover, some contemporaries insisted that Paine had adopted the term in a way that was entirely ambiguous. As the author of one hostile response, *The True Merits of a Late Treatise,* pointed out, it was not even clear whether the bard of common sense had meant to imply with this phrase "that his Opinion is the Common Sense of all America, or that all those who do not think with him are destitute of Common Sense."[7] From one perspective, Paine seemed to be evoking in his own defense a set of commonplace, collectively held assumptions, the quotidian wisdom of a preexisting community of ordinary people. From another, he seemed to be referring to a basic human faculty that allowed individuals to make elemental judgments about basic matters—judgments that sometimes aligned themselves with conventional wisdom but just as often did not.

Arguably, though, it was precisely this manipulation of the modest, yet semantically slippery notion of common sense—his peculiar mixing of the common sense of the Scots and the *bon sens* of radical continental philosophers in the new circumstances of the New World—that lay at the heart of Paine's textual sleight of hand. With a fashionable and multivalent claim to common sense or self-evidence being on his side, Paine was able, in the remote Enlightenment city of Philadelphia, to transform himself from a marginal, foreign writer for hire into a legitimate spokesman for an amorphous "American" public. Then he was able to persuade a large number of his new compatriots that they actually desired something contrary to what they thought they did. That was not only a change in their own national identities but also the idea that their own collective common sense ought to rule the day.

The impact of this approach to politics would be felt most immediately and concretely in the new constitution for the state of Pennsylvania that a small coterie of Paine's allies in Philadelphia drafted later that same year. This legal text set in motion a major experiment in the justification and implementation of the republican notion of the sovereignty of the people independent of any king. And though it did not survive as a literal framework for government, the consequences of this initiative have endured to the present day. The fixing of a paradoxical conception of common sense to a democratic vision of politics as authoritative cause *and* effect must be counted as one of Paine's and his cohort's chief and most lasting legacies. Certainly this was not the ghost that Fielding had had in mind, though sovereignty would remain the fundamental issue. What require explanation are the origins and consequences of the unexpected marriage that began in Philadelphia in 1776 between self-evidence, on the one hand, and self-rule, on the other—a pairing that, by now, has become largely invisible to us because it is so thoroughly internalized and embedded in what might be called "democratic common sense."

When Paine's little pamphlet made its debut, it was hardly alone, of course, in offering up one obscure individual's political views for public consumption. The stark title might have been unique in American publishing history prior to 1776. But it joined a very crowded (by eighteenth-century standards) urban public sphere in which information, protected by English-style liberty of the press, flowed in every direction. Philadelphians had, in the 1770s, access to five fairly regular newspapers, books and broadsides produced from Paris and Amsterdam to Philadelphia's own Front Street, and port gossip from around the world. City residents also had at their disposal a leading college, lending libraries, philosophical clubs committed to testing the new science, taverns and coffeehouses famous for their chatter, and a battery of different kinds of churches, a reflection of the colony's early commitment to religious toleration and the flourishing of evangelism. The Continental Congress meeting in Independence Hall only increased the flow of news and opinion in the city's streets after 1774. Regular trade with the West Indies, Britain, and continental Europe; the presence of enslaved Africans; and a heavy quotient of recent immigrants among the city's 33,000 or so residents rendered this information international as well.[8]

In such a setting, no one "common sense" on any subject could ever easily have prevailed, especially as tensions with a distant British crown grew. French elites idealized Philadelphia in the eighteenth century as the land of Quaker simplicity and economic equality. But this orderly brick provincial crossroads was, by 1776, a city of great ethnic, racial, and religious diversity, a place rife with class tensions and political divisions, both recent and long-standing, that made themselves felt in newspapers, local assemblies, boycotts, and occasional riots. In the eyes of colonial contemporaries, Philadelphia was the most cutting-edge and pluralistic urban space in British North America, a place of social and cultural invention.

How, then, could Paine's message have struck anyone in Philadelphia as inexorably, indisputably true or commonsensical? Why did he, after more than a year in the thick of public life in that city, even imagine that it could? Paine was not, after all, a man of deep learning, formal or otherwise, though he certainly picked up a lot in the way of current ideas in the newspapers and public houses of London and then his new hometown.[9] He always claimed, in keeping with his later self-identification as the embodiment of common sense, to have read little before taking up a pen himself.[10] Moreover, Paine's investment in common sense seems, in retrospect, to be in many ways a commonsensical point, a commitment that transcends the need for research and analysis of the sort in which scholars are typically invested precisely because so much of its content has, over time, become *our* common sense.

But even putting aside Paine's own contribution, it should by now be evident that Paine's personal trajectory intersected with one of the great ages of thinking about common sense and its meaning and function. By the start of the 1770s, the concept as well as the expression had become

staple ingredients of polemical writing of all sorts. The formulaic evocation of "a reverence for our great Creator, principles of humanity, and
the dictates of common sense" at the opening of *A Declaration by the
Representatives of the United Colonies of North-America, now met in General Congress at Philadelphia, Setting forth the Cause and Necessity of
their taking up Arms*, published in Philadelphia just six months before
Paine's famous pamphlet, is typical in this regard.[11] From the perspective of rhetoric, Philadelphia was no different than London, Edinburgh,
or the cities of continental Europe.

One possibility, then, is that Paine in the mid-1770s was just following
the style of the moment and borrowing the concept of common sense
from the most expected of places: contemporary Aberdonian thought.
This argument has particular appeal for those eager to see Scottish
(rather than Lockean or republican) influence on revolutionary America
at every turn. And, in fact, all kinds of evidence can be marshaled to support the idea of the long strain of anti-skeptical British thought that culminated in the widely diffused common sense claims of Reid and Beattie's beloved Wise Club as the primary source for Paine's political
utilization of the concept in 1776.[12]

At the most literal, biographical level, it is worth noting that Paine,
during the months he was engaged in writing his brief diatribe in favor
of the common sense of independence and republican governance, remained an employee of Robert Aitken, a bookseller and the publisher of
the *Pennsylvania Magazine*. Aitken was himself a recent arrival from
Aberdeen, where the chief tenets of Common Sense philosophy had
taken form. Benjamin Rush, the Philadelphia physician and Presbyterian
republican who nurtured Paine's project and subsequently took credit
for the title change from "Plain Truth" to "Common Sense," also spent
formative years in Scotland, undertaking medical training in Edinburgh
as well as in Paris and Philadelphia and steeping himself in Scottish
thought. It was Rush who helped negotiate the arrival at the College of
New Jersey of John Witherspoon, who would do so much to bring the
philosophy of Reid and his disciples to the new nation.[13] What is more,
Rush's vested interest in the subject of common sense, and specifically
in the claims of Reid and Beattie, prompted the Philadelphian, years

later, to include the subject in his medical teachings and to compose his own reflective essay entitled simply "Thoughts on Common Sense."[14] A glance at the catalogue of the city's main libraries of the eighteenth century or the books lined up behind Rush in his 1783 portrait by Charles Willson Peale make the popularity of Scottish epistemology in late colonial Philadelphia abundantly clear.

But more generally, and without insisting on any specific chain of individual conduits or intellectual influences, one can identify several hallmarks of this extensive British common sense philosophical and literary tradition simply by reading Paine's own words. The first reference to common sense in *Common Sense* opens chapter 3, "Thoughts on the Present State of the American Affairs," where the topic of the fate of the American colonies is first broached. "In the following pages," Paine states, "I offer nothing more than simple facts, plain arguments, and common sense."[15]

Common sense is here clearly intended to signify, following mid-eighteenth-century British usage, a basic, instinctive, immediate, and irrefutable form of perception and judgment natural to all humans. It also means the basic axioms or maxims derived from this universally shared human capacity. But more to the point, Paine's tripartite pairing suggests that common sense constituted, for Paine as for his Aberdeen contemporaries, a critical source of incontrovertible and self-evident knowledge, the best kind of evidence of all. Beattie had, of course, strongly suggested that in times of crisis, these primary truths could be brought to light as a bulwark against the social and moral failures of the modern world, such as those brought on by rampant commercialism, licentiousness, and irreligion. With this introductory reference to common sense, Paine indicates that his basic perceptions and principles will operate in a similar fashion: as foundations on which to build shared and unassailable communal understandings. Only in this instance, they will do their work at a time of perceived political crisis.

Paine's "common sense," in conjunction with "simple facts" and "plain arguments," is also intended to signal his commitment to a straightforward, unambiguous, even naked style of expression that is faithful to the elemental quality of these perceptions and the principles derived from them. Here is a variant of Reid's and Beattie's attachment to the ordinary, everyday language in which common sense manifested itself, as well as to the "plain style" associated with the Royal Academy and with certain kinds of Protestant preaching in the previous century. Except that in this case, too, Paine was determined to apply one of common sense's chief qualities in support of a political platform rather than an abstract moral philosophy.

It was this effort to present his positions, no matter how unconventional and hyperbolic in reality, as simple in form, obvious in content, and consequently universal and indisputable in effect, that constituted the most distinctive aspect of Paine's pamphlet.[16] In his defense Paine made no use of logical expositions or carefully reasoned arguments or even suggested that his opinions were open to debate. He equally avoided relying on specialized knowledge or learned references to history or political theory to justify his claims. Rather, in language that was by turns unadorned, satirical, prophetic, metaphoric, and violently indignant but never dry, Paine crafted a partisan manifesto that presented itself as an exposition of what was, or should have been, entirely self-evident to all, based simply on their experiences living in the world.

From the beginning, Paine continually reminds his readers that the opinions on offer in *Common Sense* are nothing more than "plain truth" presented in "plain terms." Often the analogy is to scripture, which, in his telling, is also "direct and positive . . . [and] admit[s] of no equivocal construction." At other times, the example is the "simple voice of nature" that indicates instinctively what is right. Again and again, Paine denounces complexity or ambiguity in reasoning or expression as evidence of falsity or manipulation. In contrast, bluntness and simplicity are, as in most Protestant traditions, equated with indisputable truth.[17]

Then, when it comes to argumentation, Paine turns his energies toward making his pamphlet a case study in the application of common sense judgment and principles to current events. In the latter half of the pamphlet, this strategy entails nothing more than insisting upon the moral and financial benefits to be derived from his doctrine of national independence; common sense is primarily a form of practicality and prudence. But in the opening sections, Paine tries, by adage, injunction, prescriptive maxim, or concrete analogy with the natural, physical world, to turn political calculation into a matter of applying the precepts of common sense to social processes and power relationships. His goal is to introduce the "first principles" that make the need for separation from Britain and, especially, republican governance across the American expanse both obvious and sure.

Many of the most famous lines in the pamphlet illuminate the political truths that can be derived from universally recognized elementary principles. Sometimes they are stated in the affirmative. "Youth is the seed-time of good habits," Paine notes bluntly, "as well in nations as in individuals." Or, in regard to the English Constitution, it is a "principle in nature, which no art can overturn, viz. that the more simple any thing is, the less liable it is to be disordered" and "the greater weight will always carry up the less." Yet equally his dicta illustrate what, following nature, cannot be true for politics without violating or upending a fundamental common sense principle. For example, on maintaining ties with Britain: "There is something absurd, in supposing a continent to be perpetually governed by an island." Here the principle that small things should not rule bigger ones proves universal and irrefutable whether in nature or in social life; after all, continents are necessarily bigger than islands, and larger things naturally govern smaller ones. Similarly, against hereditary monarchy, he remarks: "In point of right and good order, it is something very ridiculous, that a youth of twenty-one (which hath often happened) shall say to several millions of people, older and wiser than himself, I forbid this or that act of yours to be law." To argue the opposite or to assert anything contrary to such claims would, according to Paine, simply be "repugnant to . . . the universal order of things."[18]

Paine sounds here much like his Scottish contemporary, Beattie, who noted that it was impossible to say that "a man sees with the soles of his feet" or "a part is greater than a whole," precisely because to do so would be to contradict common sense.[19] Throughout *Common Sense*, all propositions contrary to those that Paine calls self-evident are labeled if not ridiculous or absurd, then unnatural, useless, childish, farcical, or a kind of folly. With these expressions of moral and epistemological indignation, Paine tries to obviate the need for further argument ("the period

of debate is closed," he notes at one point)[20] or even further demonstration, even though he is obviously also inviting counter-responses through
the very act of publication. From the opening distinction between society and government to Paine's numerous folksy adages, politics is here
reduced to seeing things for what they are and naming them accordingly.
Paine may be offering one unsubstantiated opinion or "fiction" after another,[21] but he frames them all, both rhetorically and conceptually, as
obvious extensions of similarly indisputable and self-evident principles
about size, quantity, power, or prudence.

This approach is not, however, all that seemingly links Paine to the
mid-eighteenth-century epistemology of Aberdeen. Reid's defense of what
"every man understands by the principles of his nature" sets the stage, in
Paine's usage, for what appears to be a politics of class resentment or, at
least, a defense of the silent majority as against a powerful minority.[22]
Tributes to the instinctive perceptions, unschooled logic, and simple
style of what Reid called "plain sensible men" could be used against all
those of elevated or privileged status whose actions and language no
longer seemed governed by a recognizable common sense.[23] This is exactly what Paine did. With his plebeian syntax and vocabulary alternately redolent of popular sermons and the popular press, his constant
references to the elemental foundations of his ideas, and his strident
disdain for both hierarchy and rhetoric (despite his own mastery of it),
Paine introduces a very modern fusion of egalitarian epistemology and
social biases into the debate about the future of the American colonies.
He repeatedly tries to distance himself from philosophers, aristocrats,
clerics, and thinkers of the past by claiming that their obfuscating,
pompous language displaces common sense (a subject he had already
broached in an earlier article entitled "Reflections on Titles," which he
had written under the pseudonym Vox Populi).[24] Then, with debatable
sincerity, Paine paints himself, the Quaker English émigré, not as an
outsider but as one of the crowd. In his telling, he is a man capable of
seeing and articulating ordinary Americans' collective assumptions and
point of view from within. This stance is a function less of geography
than of a shared and mutually reinforcing social and cognitive position.
His intended audience is people like himself, which is simply to say all

ordinary, clear-sighted colonists who, by virtue of quotidian experience rather than wealth or formal learning, can recognize truths that are universally accessible and already largely self-evident. In numerous ways, including his preference for the collective pronoun "we" (for example, "Wherefore, what is it that we want? Why is it that we hesitate?"),[25] Paine suggests that it is his mission to speak simultaneously from and to this burgeoning popular common sense community, linking it to independence and republicanism, the two causes of the day.

Though common sense did not yet belong to any one faction in the debate about Britain's relations with her colonies in January 1776, it had already acquired these intellectually anti-elitist connotations. Consider the two political pamphlets on the American problem that made substantial use of the idea prior to Paine. The unnamed author of the pro-colonist *A Defense of the Resolutions and Address of the American Congress* (1775) explicitly draws his argument from "common sense and experience" rather than a more highbrow source. He then deems merchants, a "class of men distinguished for liberality both of sentiment and manners," far better qualified to comment on public business than "the college clown and bigot." This latter category includes "the lettered pensioner [a.k.a. Samuel Johnson, the author of *Taxation No Tyranny*], with the refined sentiment and language of his brother beef-eaters."[26] Once again it is the man of the world—and not the fancy pedant or aristocrat—who embodies the position and language of common sense, and this worldly common sense turns out to be uniquely suited to the realm of political judgment and decision making. Similarly, the plainspoken British merchant-conversationalist in Jonas Hanway's pro-British *Common Sense: In Nine Conferences, between a British Merchant and a Candid Merchant of America* (1775) insists that one can learn far more about the truth and coherence of things from the "useful knowledge" and "common sense" born of the "honest simplicity" of the hosier or the blacksmith than one possibly could from the "learned disputant" with "fine-spun reasonings," "crooked pride," and motives for misrepresentation. Moreover, the commoner's common sense, declares the merchant mouthpiece for the author, is not overmatched by taking on "the glory and interests of a mighty nation."[27]

It is thus but a short stretch to see Paine building on this set of associations, alongside his own experiences of British and American urban life, to establish a communitarian and democratic foundation for an as-yet-to-be-realized political culture. *Common Sense*, as Robert A. Ferguson aptly puts it, "celebrates an orchestrated solidarity of the right-minded in a new type of participatory republic" (which might explain why there is no mention of anything as divisive as voting or even potential differences of opinion).[28] Paine arguably uses an anti-skeptical common sense tradition of rhetoric and philosophy to help foster an imagined community of "common" (ordinary) people ready to establish a new kind of political order firmly grounded in their "common" (shared) perceptions, judgments, and assumptions.

Yet there is something very partial about this genealogy. What is so striking about this political pamphlet is ultimately how Paine manages to use such appeals to popular sentiment and popular language to argue *against* the dominant assumptions of his moment and place. At the end of the day, Reid and his fellow moderate Presbyterian academics and ministers evoked common sense as a leveling but essentially conservative device, a defense against a fashionable skepticism and perceived moral decline, much as Shaftesbury and Addison had done at the start of the eighteenth century and liberal Anglican divines had done as far back as the mid-seventeenth century. By and large, common sense was employed to safeguard the legitimacy of views about right and wrong and true and false that were, among British elites, already widely accepted. In contrast, we see just the opposite in Paine: common sense used in the service of a radical, even iconoclastic agenda, with the author positioning himself as the forward-looking, anti-establishment agitator. In Paine's able hands, common sense became a weapon to be deployed against the sense of things that was, in the late-eighteenth-century Atlantic world, actually common, whether in numerical or class terms.

The very first lines of *Common Sense* make this desire clear. The essay opens with a declaration of the fact that almost nothing that the author has to say actually accords with reigning or customary opinion: "Perhaps the sentiments contained in the following pages, are not *yet* sufficiently fashionable to procure them general favor; a long habit of thinking a thing *wrong*, gives it a superficial appearance of being *right*, and raises at first a formidable outcry in defense of custom." Quickly it becomes evident that the purpose of common sense thinking is, for Paine, precisely to cut through this fog of habit, convention, and "inattention" that normally passes for common sense language and belief in order to reveal the naked reality beneath for the benefit of the future. The sentence that follows that first reference to "simple facts, plain arguments, and common sense" indicates that the reader is expected to employ his basic, innate sense of truth and goodness to shatter his own complacent, status quo assumptions. He is to "divest himself of prejudice and prepossession, and suffer his reason and his feelings to determine for themselves" so as to "generously enlarge his views beyond the present day." The two subsequent references to common sense continue this theme. The case for independence must be examined "on the principles of nature and common sense" rather than according to habit, tradition, or the obfuscating rhetoric of those currently invested with authority. In the end, "common sense," meaning the faculty rather than the set of basic assumptions typically resulting from the collective use of this faculty, "will tell us, that the power which hath endeavored to subdue us, is of all others, the most improper to defend us."[29]

The main body of the text, far from being an apology for the status quo or even a plan for reform, then constitutes a scathing and often satirical attack on precisely those beliefs that Paine's assumed readers generally took for granted because of misplaced faith in the rightness of history and of language. He makes this case in the name of humans' underutilized capacity for instinctively detecting error and duplicity either in actions or in the words used to describe them. With common sense as his ally, Paine upends many of the most basic assumptions, habits of thought, and even expressions governing local, colonial political life, including the intuitive understanding his readers had of themselves as British subjects. Key concepts, beginning with monarchy, are revealed as products of nothing more than tradition and fear. Vital words in the current conversation, such as "mother country," turn out to be misnomers or empty terms, "jesuitically adopted" by the powerful as a means to bolster their authority and devoid of any meaning beyond their sound, especially when applied to the place known as England. Biblical stories are frequently turned on their heads as Paine makes them mean the opposite of what they generally do. Even the idea of continuity is obliterated with a specious, folksy analogy: "We may as well assert that because a child has thrived upon milk, that it is never to have meat, or that the first twenty years of our lives is to become a precedent for the next twenty." Under the rubric of common sense, Paine makes natural what had been almost unthinkable before—and unnatural, even laughable, what had seemed obvious.[30]

Here is also where Paine's common sense breaks company with the Scots in the most fundamental of ways. Like the Common Sense philosophers of Aberdeen, Paine clearly paints common sense as a universal faculty and true common sense principles as outside the vicissitudes of history. For Paine, though, what goes by the name of common sense at any given moment is rarely transhistorical or universal in terms of its contents; the dictates of true common sense are only widely adopted or even revealed over time as mass prejudice, misinformation, and inequity recede. As he explains, what may "appear strange and difficult" at one moment—for example, the death of kingship—becomes "familiar and agreeable at another." Paine's common sense is ultimately rooted neither in mass behavior nor in common usage nor in universal consent. For all his false modesty in promising "nothing more" than simple facts and for all his devotion to the pronoun "we," Paine positions himself as an individual at odds with the values of the dominant political culture, and as a prophetic individual at that. Paine sees clearly what others cannot yet see. And he takes his job to be jolting his readers' sense not only of space (in terms of relations with Britain) but also of time and progress. Rather than an end unto itself, shock is a device, a means of catapulting his readers and new countrymen out of the fog of prejudice and habit. For the outraged author seems to believe that once average Americans have been "expose[d]" to what Paine himself has already seen (including all the ways they have contributed to their own delusions and resulting oppression), they will be ready to go out and change the course of history in keeping with a new, not yet self-evident common sense. Or, as Paine puts it, "begin the world over again." In *Common Sense,* common sense becomes an arm of a future-oriented revolution.[31]

These are, then, the secret ingredients of Paine's dualism. In Paine's polemic, we see common sense function not only as a foundation for certain knowledge but also as a way to undermine what passes for unassailable fact in the present. We see common sense as the corollary of commonplace language and simultaneously as a means to cut through the filter of words, especially those that serve to obfuscate or disguise reality. We see common sense as the voice of the people as a whole and as the voice of the clear-sighted, prophetic individual who intuits what the people should be able to grasp but cannot by themselves. And we see common sense mean not only what is common in the here and now but also what is antithetical to the common until some later moment in time.

Here, too, one can look for precedents to a long British tradition of radical Whig politics, of satirical literature, of Protestant dissent. But Benjamin Rush, in his 1791 essay on common sense, turns our attention in a wholly contrary direction: back toward the words of the late seventeenth-century French Protestant skeptic Pierre Bayle. In defense of his own debunking of common sense as generally no more than collective error, Rush writes: "Mankind are governed, says Mr. Bayle, by their prejudice, and not by their principles." Otherwise, Rush notes with the American War of Independence firmly behind him, it is impossible to explain the variety of views that now pass for self-evident around the world, that, for example, "it is contrary to common sense to speak or write in favour of republicanism, in several European countries; and it is equally contrary to it to speak or write in favour of monarchy, in the United States of America." Or similarly, "The common sense of the planters in Jamaica, is in favour of the commerce and slavery of the Africans. In Pennsylvania, reason, humanity and common sense, have universally declared against them." Only within some utopian state in which knowledge has been perfected and universalized will truth and common sense routinely coincide. For now, he insists, they are largely antithetical. Contrary to Reid's claims, muses the Philadelphia doctor, those who will change history for the better, like Galileo, have no choice but to set themselves in opposition to the reigning notions of their time and place and to attempt, against the odds, to institute a different common sense in the future.[32]

We cannot know if Paine or even Rush ever read the work of Bayle, though Bayle was certainly well known to contemporary readers in Philadelphia as well as in London and Edinburgh.[33] But Rush's appropriation of Bayle brings to light the dualism that ran more generally through eighteenth-century discussions of common sense up to their collision point in 1776. That is, Rush's single reference to Bayle suggests an alternative or second path by which common sense worked its way into the nexus of epistemological and political change that underlay the transition to democracy in the northern Atlantic world. Here we must look again toward the almost antithetical (and considerably less cohesive) continental Enlightenment trajectory that took the French cognate *le bon sens* as a key concept. As we have seen, this style of philosophizing also saw its apogee in the 1770s, most especially in Bayle's Holland, which the equally peripatetic Paine himself praised in *Common Sense* for its avoidance of both monarchy and war. But in the last quarter of the century, as the radical Enlightenment extended across much of northern Europe, from the Netherlands to France to England and, finally, to its overseas dominions, *le bon sens* came to stand for the capacity, common to all regardless of educational, economic, gender, and status differences, to pierce through both the prejudicial "common" sense of the day and the misleading language that corresponded to it in every realm. This, clearly, is just what Paine tried to do—even as he insisted that he was only speaking for common sense.

Moreover, it might also be said that Paine owed something substantial to local tradition. After all, Paine found himself writing in a public sphere already defined by the plainspoken, pragmatic, and anti-aristocratic wisdom and morality of Benjamin Franklin's great creation, Poor Richard, not to mention Franklin himself.[34] By 1776, Franklin had achieved iconic status, especially among Philadelphia's working classes. He had also been instrumental in fostering the myth of the synergy between himself and his and Paine's adopted city, the epicenter not only of New World practicality but also of Quaker plainness and anti-authoritarianism (a fantasy that would endure despite the actual lack of Quaker support for independence). In this setting, a tribute to common sense could hardly have seemed out of keeping.

Paine's great revolutionary gesture was thus an act of synthesis. The success of Paine as a polemicist stemmed in large part from his bringing together the individualist with the collective and the conservative with the subversive strains of common sense—or sometimes good sense—thought and expression current on both sides of the northern Atlantic.[35] Here was British common sense, with its pseudo-egalitarian consensualism, and a radical continental *bon sens,* with its elite attack on the status of all presumed universal truths, melded into a locally inflected tour de force: an argument for a scarcely tested form of government in which a radical interpretation of the sovereignty of the people was to be the essential principle. What Paine crafted was the beginnings of an epistemological as well as social justification for a populist democracy. North America—and, more specifically, Philadelphia—would simply be its first testing ground.

Tom Paine's own reputation faltered soon thereafter as he became embroiled in a series of scandals. Yet the duality of the common sense on full display in his cheap and hastily composed pamphlet of January 1776 endured. The little tract known as *Common Sense* had an almost immediate and demonstrable influence on the political history of common sense. Within weeks it provided a story and a language with which to assimilate the breaking away from Britain and the establishment of a functional republicanism within the North American colonies. Then, as the work of crafting a new government for the new "state" of Pennsylvania began that same spring, it suggested a populist foundation for instituting a remarkably democratic but also self-contained polity. We should be careful not to exaggerate the premeditation or even impact of Paine himself. However, before the year 1776 was over, common sense had become an essential prop to one new (and destined to be very influential) form of popular rule in which the people, or citizens, were sovereign by virtue of their inherent capacity for practical and sound judgment, but these judgments were also defined and circumscribed by the terms of common sense.

The transformation began immediately. Paine's rhetorical conceit of instinctive commonality and indisputability was strikingly successful in the days that followed in shaping American political ideals as well as American ways of talking about them. Whether Paine's little pamphlet actually changed minds overnight, it was certainly mythologized as such in rapid order, by Paine himself (who quickly ceased to be anonymous and gave himself the patronymic "Common Sense") and by sympathetic commentators both famous and obscure. Contemporary accounts suggest sudden mass conversion. Edmund Randolph of Virginia, for example, claimed "the public sentiment, which a few weeks before had shuddered at the tremendous obstacles with which independence was environed, overleaped every barrier" on the appearance of *Common Sense*.[36] George Washington, too, described the pamphlet as "working a powerful change there in the Minds of many Men."[37] Here literally was evidence of a "revolution in men's minds," a dramatic transformation in people's way of thinking that would surely lead to parallel revolutions in the social and institutional spheres, according to eighteenth-century theorists of historical progress.

But Paine did not always get credit for his personal foresight. On the contrary, many early commentators suggested that the immigrant polemicist, rather than acting as a prophet or a creator of "miracles" (the traditional opposite of common sense), had succeeded by conjuring up the resentments and longings that American colonists had simply not realized that they already felt.[38] Their residual prejudices just had to be vanquished for their true feelings to be revealed. Typical was the reaction of a Connecticut man: "In declaring your own, you have declared the sentiments of Millions: Your production may justly be compared to a land-flood that sweeps all before it. We were blind, but on reading these enlightening words the scales have fallen from our eyes."[39] A nationwide, antideferential, antihistorical, and ultimately democratic common sense was understood to be not only an effect but also a root cause of the forty-six pages of *Common Sense*.

The first historians of the revolutionary era, including Rush's onetime student at the College of Philadelphia, David Ramsay, replicated this heuristic device, eager to show that the War of Independence, far from being a departure, was the result of continuity and consensus, the inevitable consequence of the values already shared by all Americans. "The new system was not so much forcibly imposed [in 1776] or designedly adopted, as introduced through necessity, and the imperceptible agency of a common danger, operating uniformly on the mind of the public," Ramsay explained. In Ramsay's hands, Paine's pamphlet was transformed into an instrument of this process: "In union with the feelings and sentiments of the people, it [*Common Sense*] produced surprising effects." The great majority came to the side of independence with "surprising unanimity," and "the voice of the people," rather than a few ambitious politicians, forced the uprising's leaders to undertake a veritable revolution.[40]

Even the Declaration of Independence, with its celebrated "self-evident truths" and insistence upon popular rule, would be retrospectively assimilated to this story. According to Thomas Jefferson, the Declaration, far from being his own creation, was better perceived as "an expression of the American mind." In a famous letter to Henry Lee written many years later, Jefferson noted that the Declaration of 1776 was intended to be simply "the common sense of the subject."[41] Furthermore, though the common sense of a broad, anonymous public was understood to be at the roots of this experiment in self-rule, democracy was also celebrated, in theory and in practice, as an incubator of common sense. In the early republic, it became a prized American value, something to be touted (despite its ostensible self-evidence) in sermons, almanacs, and collections of proverbs, sayings, and practical wisdom.[42] It also became a successful commercial slogan.[43] Arguably, reliance on common sense remains part of the ideal image of modern Western democracies, which typically present themselves as rooted in the wisdom of ordinary people.

Of course, this is hardly the way 1776 unfolded. There is, after all, always a danger in taking claims to represent common sense too literally. For one, claims to speak for or to common sense always depend—as early champions of *le bon sens* knew—on a certain level of deception. Whatever goes by this name is rarely popular in any true sense, never universal or fully consensual, and generally just as abstract as the rhetorical

abstractions it is designed to replace. Evocations of common sense always work to favor one segment of society at the expense of another.
Most of all, they are always polemical, which is to say political. Far from
being impervious to challenge or even argument, common sense is typically reactive, something brought back to the table from which it has
been displaced, something that will then demand a counter-response.
Even the Presbyterian thinkers of mid-eighteenth-century Aberdeen
used the idea of common sense to partisan advantage, hoping to sway
middling public opinion in one particular direction, especially when it
came to religious and moral questions, and away from another. The
radical continental Enlightenment forged common sense into a public
weapon for the enlightened few. That it sounded objective and indisputable yet widely accessible was the source of its success as an organ of
subjective, partisan, and always potentially demagogic political action.
With the aid of common sense, any well-placed individual or collectivity,
with any particular point of view, could pretend to represent the whole
social body's sentiments and promise an end to all dispute as a result.

And predictably, a very public struggle over the locus of common
sense ensued. The innovative and iconoclastic Paine did not actually
speak for any particular preexisting set of common sense tenets when
he composed his pamphlet. In practice, no popular consensus about independence or about republican government actually took immediate
hold either in Britain or in the American colonies after the pamphlet's
appearance in early 1776. Even if Paine's *Common Sense,* along with the
extensive commentary about it, persuaded many fence sitters, it also
produced something diametrically opposed to what the title seemed to
promise. No sooner had the first edition appeared in colonial bookshops
and other public places than a transatlantic mini-industry of published
commentary, much of it hostile, emerged in response. The pamphlet's
language, not to mention its argument, was denounced in articles, pamphlets, and letters from Dublin to New York by loyalists and hostile patriots alike. John Adams predicted that *Common Sense,* with its "crude,
ignorant Notion of a Government by one Assembly, will do more Mis-
chief in dividing the Friends of Liberty, than all the Tory Writings together."[44] Furthermore, insofar as each side claimed to speak for the

true, single, authentic vox populi—and rejected the similar claim of the opposition—the colonial struggle over ownership of common sense did nothing to limit a new, heightened style of ideological combat that, in turn, intensified an already partisan and increasingly polarized political contest. Witness the subsequent appearance of such pro-British, and consequently anti-Paine, diatribes as Thomas Bull's *Resolutions of Common Sense about Common Rights* and the anonymous *Memorial of Common-Sense, upon the Present Crisis between Great-Britain and America,* in which common sense was reclaimed from London on behalf of an entirely different set of propositions.[45] Here the argument was that Paine constituted the violator, abusing words, playing on public credulity, and leading the world down the garden path. Indeed, common sense was soon used to discredit Paine, who in effect encouraged this kind of treatment by wrapping himself for the rest of his career in the mantle of this popular epistemic value.

This was especially true in Paine's new hometown. The Anglican clergyman and New York loyalist Charles Inglis, writing as "An American," set the terms for this kind of oppositional polemic in *The True Interest of America Impartially Stated,* which appeared on Philadelphia newsstands just weeks after Paine's first edition in the winter of 1776. Inglis accused "The Englishman" (Paine) of violating common sense at every turn; of trafficking in "absurdities and falsehoods"; and of writing in the tradition of "fanatic[s]," "enthusiasts," and "visionary assertors of paradoxes, who were conscious that the common feelings of mankind must revolt against their scheme." Here were all the clichés typically used in early eighteenth-century British Protestant political discourse as antonyms for the prized common sense of the postrevolutionary settlement era. Then Inglis concluded with an attack on the very language of Paine's title: "to make his pamphlet go down better, he prefixes the title of *Common Sense* to it by a figure in rhetoric, which is called a *Catachresis,* that is, in plain English, an abuse of words. . . . I find no *Common Sense* in this pamphlet but much *uncommon* phrenzy. It is an outrageous insult on the common sense of Americans; an insidious attempt to poison their minds, and seduce them from their loyalty and truest interest."[46]

Others, most of them Philadelphians, took this same tack in 1776: Paine's common sense was best understood as its opposite, "a total perversion of the understanding," in the words of an opponent calling himself Rationalis.[47] Or it was patent "Non-Sense," in the words of Cato (later revealed as the Philadelphian and Scottish native William Smith).[48] "Under the specious name of Common Sense," Cato raged, "[the pamphlet's author] is constantly dealing out paradoxes, and setting himself up, not only in contradistinction to the sober sentiments of the wisest of mankind, but often in contradiction to himself."[49] What all these pseudonymous commentators ultimately hoped to do was to wrench the term back from Paine and prove their own legitimate connection to this ideal. They labored to show that they instead spoke for the true sentiment of Americans—or at least "nine-tenths of the people of Pennsylvania," in the words of Cato.[50] And they took care to point out that they did so in ways that should be self-evident, though Paine had encouraged new absurdities and prejudices to take root. Inglis, for example, in an effort to prove that his own position was steeped not only in scripture, the English constitution, and the principles of 1688 but also "common sense, reason and truth," could not resist employing the same kind of plainspoken, folksy, analogic reasoning that had worked so well for Paine. In defense of unity and prudence, this antagonist noted: "The remedy [separating from the mother country] is infinitely worse than the disease. It would be like cutting off a leg, because the toe happened to ache."[51]

In this debate, much as in Paine's pamphlet itself, claims to common sense became central to a style of political reasoning and expression that would play a key role in the invention of democratic politics in North America, once again reinforcing both its redemptive and its pragmatic faces. It is tempting simply to recall London almost half a century earlier and to see a replay of the fight for mastery of common sense that characterized the extraparliamentary political struggles of the 1730s. There, as we have seen, conflicting parties claimed the sense of the people for conflicting ideologies, even though no one imagined England embarking on a plan of government as foolish as a democracy. But before the year 1776 was out, Cato and his allies would find themselves on the losing side. The fight revolve around independence for the former colonies.

It would also concern the establishment of a new institutional frame of government, one that would become a touchstone for revolutionaries across the northern and, eventually, southern Atlantic, too. Paine's version of the rule of common sense—what a writer in the *Pennsylvania Packet* of May 1776 explained as a government in which power resides in "every individual inhabitant of this colony who *has a will and understanding of his own* capable to manage his affairs"[52]—soon became America's great contribution to Europe's political development. Ultimately, it would provide a template for popular democracy, not to mention popular challenges to democracy, that would be global in reach.

The transformation began before the ink used to write the Declaration of Independence was even dry. For at the same time and in the very place that Paine—arguably the first international revolutionary—was suggesting the "common sense" of a radical reorientation of the transatlantic imperial order, local, urban politics within the province of Pennsylvania was also reaching a crisis point. The early months of 1776 constitute the moment when the tussle with England ceased to be simply a contest over home rule. An internal revolution, a struggle against provincial authority, broke out in Britain's North American colonies simultaneously.[53] Moreover, the city of Philadelphia, that cosmopolitan if remote commercial center where Paine's pamphlet first entered the world, was the location where this second revolution was to be most profoundly felt. There a new form of politics, harnessed to a new understanding of common sense, rapidly took form in practice as well as theory. In the framing of a constitution for what was, in the course of that great year, to become the state of Pennsylvania, the nascent populism of Paine and his champions helped fuel a first experiment in the translation of a radical reading of popular sovereignty into institutional terms. That is, a small group of Philadelphians tried to create a legal armature for a form of rule that would eventually come to be called, without any intended insult, democracy.

There were several deep-seated causes for the unusually radical political notions that took root in 1776 in Pennsylvania, and especially in its chief city, Philadelphia. Certainly a tradition of religious freedom originating with the Quakers, not to mention a tradition of freedom from royal prerogative, had long allowed new ideas to circulate in the colony without real impediment. Equally significantly, over the preceding two decades profound changes in the economic sphere, including a long depression in the years following the Seven Years' War, had altered Philadelphia's old class structure. The working classes or laboring poor had been especially hard hit, their share of the city's wealth declining from midcentury. But even many craftsmen and "mechanics" had had trouble maintaining their standard of living in the 1760s and early 1770s. Philadelphia in the era of the Continental Congress was an increasingly polarized city culturally and economically. Moreover, the rise in all kinds of associational activity and committee formation among the "middling" classes and, then, the politicization of poorer artisans and laborers around the new militia system set up to send volunteers to the Continental Army: these developments also played a role in altering the nature of politics in wartime Philadelphia, not least in giving a voice to shared resentments on all sides. Tradesmen, craftsmen, laborers, and farmers looked increasingly not only to break free of imperial control but also to participate in a political process in which they had long had little say.[54]

The most immediate impetus for the decision to craft a new plan of government for Pennsylvania was, however, the refusal of the colony's provincial assembly to throw its support behind the move toward independence. Unlike colonial elites in other British North American cities, the wealthy property owners and established political leaders of Philadelphia—the same men who had been the primary backers of the city's great Enlightenment institutions, including its libraries, schools, fire companies, and learned societies—continued in 1776 to reject the vision of a fully independent, republican America proposed by Paine. This reluctance to embrace the patriot cause allowed the rise (much to the dismay of most of those who casually identified themselves as "thinking people")[55] of new political spokesmen, clustered in new, extralegal, organizations, with new kinds of rhetoric and new political agendas. The principles of these upstarts would ultimately fail to provide the dominant institutional framework for the new United States. But this distinctive mode of politics, with its populist thrust, would find its way into the first constitution of Pennsylvania and would provide inspiration for other revolutionary democratic movements and challenges to the ruling class in America and abroad for years to come.

May 1776 proved to be the turning point. On the first day of that month, a slew of anti-independence candidates yet again won assembly seats in special Philadelphia by-elections. With the advance of British troops looming in the background and no help seemingly forthcoming from the local ruling elite, a small number of radical republicans, many with close ties to artisanal or military interests, set their sights on curtailing the power of the assembly and of Pennsylvania's proprietary government more generally. Some of these men (and they appear to have been entirely men), such as Rush and the math teacher James Cannon, a native Scot who had emigrated in 1765 and had risen to the position of secretary of Philadelphia's Committee of Privates representing the interests of the militia, were themselves college-educated professionals. Others, including the painter Charles Willson Peale, the watchmaker-turned-astronomer David Rittenhouse, the activist physician Thomas Young, and the shopkeeper and cockfighting expert Timothy Matlack, were, like Paine, largely self-taught. Similarly, some—like Young and Matlack—were freethinkers, while others were committed Quakers or, more often, evangelical Protestants, particularly of the Presbyterian variety. What they shared was an intellectual commitment, typical of the late Enlightenment culture in which most of them were steeped, to the idea of government rooted in a few basic, invariable, and simple-to-grasp principles. They also formed the ambition of appealing to a broad and considerably less well-educated public both as a practical form of support and as an abstract source of legitimacy.

These men were, though, too pragmatic to make the case for an overhaul of Pennsylvania politics simply by depending on the prevalence of the new republican "common sense" that Paine had supposedly created overnight. Surely they realized this would be insufficient in the current climate, especially since "the people" hardly existed as either a distinct social group or a political force. So instead they looked for help to the Continental Congress, then meeting in the city's center. Two weeks later, John Adams answered their hopes—with the ambition of furthering the cause of independence more generally, not the realization of the radical political ideas of Paine and his cohort. In part to force the hand of the Pennsylvania Assembly, the Continental Congress adopted, at Adams's urging, a resolution recommending that in all provinces "where no government sufficient to the exigencies of their affairs have been hitherto established," representatives should craft a new one of their own devising. The catch, in the words of the preamble, was that the legitimacy of all such governments was to rest on "the authority of the people of the colonies" alone.[56]

John Adam's rhetoric provided the opening for which radical Whigs and committeemen outside the assembly like Matlack, Marshall, Rittenhouse, and Cannon were looking. Immediately they began to issue calls for the creation of a special convention, in lieu of the existing legislative body, to be given the specific charge of producing a written constitution for a new government for Pennsylvania. The Assembly's disqualification for this job rested, according to an anonymous incendiary pamphlet of that May entitled *The Alarm*, on two facts: that the Assembly's power did not reside in "the AUTHORITY of the PEOPLE," as demanded by Congress, and that, as a single body, it had to date shown an absence of both "judgment" and "wisdom," the most essential traits of any legislature, especially around questions of independence. What was needed in its place was a new representative body that was responsive first and foremost to the people and its collective wisdom—or, in the words of *The Alarm*'s author, a "REVOLUTION" in government comparable to what had occurred on English soil less than a hundred years before.[57]

Amazingly (given what we know of how differently the American Revolution was ultimately to play out) this radical logic prevailed in Philadelphia in 1776. By mid-June, the Pennsylvania Assembly, despite some last-minute backpedaling, had been rendered defunct. The powers of its most prominent members, with the exception of the now-legendary Benjamin Franklin, declined alongside it. By mid-July, a constitutional convention made up of elected members from across the state, all of them friendly to the cause of independence that had just days earlier been made official by the Continental Congress, was ready to begin the work of creating a republican framework for the free and independent state of Pennsylvania.[58]

But Adams and other leading patriots, with their repeated references to the increasingly banal principle of popular sovereignty and the authority of "the people," had opened up what they, in retrospect, must have seen as a veritable can of worms.[59] Indeed, they created a controversy that would eventually split Pennsylvania's Whigs, or supporters of independence, apart—and in the process give new political salience to the old notion of common sense. Already, on May 20, the day after the appearance of *The Alarm*, radical spokesmen associated with Philadelphia's Committee of Observation and Inspection had managed to orchestrate a mass outdoor meeting to "take the sense of the People" on just how the notion of popular sovereignty articulated in Adams's congressional resolve should be interpreted.[60] Other town meetings, demonstrations, committee negotiations, and the drafting of a flurry of pamphlets, broadsides, newspaper columns, and petitions soon followed. Radicals worked hard with these tools to mobilize "the people," in whose name they were eagerly crafting a new political vision, into an actual force. The provincial congress that met in June to determine the rules for holding a constitutional convention only magnified the issues at stake. For what ensued in the second half of 1776 can best be described as a public fight over not only what a republican constitution should promise but, first, whose ideas the new constitution should represent and how.

Up and down the eastern North American seaboard, the drafting of state constitutions opened up profound divisions of opinion about the nature, source, and distribution of authority in a government that was, in principle, to be based on popular consent.[61] But it was in Pennsylvania alone, at first, that these questions prompted an argument for direct popular rule that would ultimately tear the body politic apart. The explicit procedural question that consumed the delegates to the June provincial congress concerned suffrage requirements: who, among the residents of Pennsylvania, should be able to choose those who would write the state's new constitution? However, this question soon turned more general for the members of the constitutional convention: what subset of the sovereign public should ultimately govern

Pennsylvania, whether indirectly as voters or directly as officeholders? Or, to put it differently, in what sense were "the people" to rule? The answers crafted in 1776 under the leadership of Philadelphia's radical political agitators marked a decisive break with traditional thinking about questions of representation—and the emergence of a surprising new view of where the judgment needed for effective and responsible political decision making was to be found.

In a classic book on Paine, the historian Eric Foner detects the influence of the author of *Common Sense* on the stances adopted by Philadelphia's radicals. Pointing to the desire for "social leveling" on display in the bids for an expanded franchise on the part of the most ultraist members of the provincial congress and then the constitutional convention, Foner argues that the constitution of 1776, which they took the lead in framing, would ultimately put into practice the egalitarian social theory and, indeed, class hostility inherent in Paine's political outlook.[62] That may well be the case. Yet that is not the only concern that these men seemingly inherited from Paine. The debate about suffrage throws us once again into the realm of epistemology, that is, into a set of claims about the capacities for judgment (or lack thereof) of ordinary people. From Paine to Matlack, Young, and Cannon, we also see the crafting of a new argument for popular political participation and inclusion that cannot be reduced entirely to the rhetoric of class antagonism rooted in economic and social competition. It is this link that brings us back to another abstraction that would have greater play in Philadelphia than in any other colonial city at the time of the war of independence: common sense.

The traditional answer, for colonial Whigs as for everyone else, was that the privilege of participating in political decision making, whether as a voter or as an officeholder, was contingent on personal wealth.[63] In English thought on the subject, only those in possession of income-producing land could truly be called independent. And only those who were independent could be counted on to make good judgments in matters of community interest. Those without personal property or those who were dependent in terms of their livelihoods—a category that included not only women but also children, slaves, tenants, servants, journeymen, and apprentices—could not be expected to have the independence of mind necessary, according to American as well as British Whigs, to make rational political decisions of their own, especially when it came to civic matters. They were simply too subject to the influence (or coercion) of others. As John Adams famously pointed out in a letter of May 1776, "Men in general, in every society, who are wholly destitute of Property, are also too little acquainted with public Affairs to form a Right Judgment, and too dependent upon other Men to have a Will of their own. . . . Such is the Frailty of the human Heart, that very few Men, who have no Property, have any Judgment of their own. They talk and vote as they are directed by Some Man of property, who has attached their Minds to his Interest."[64] In fact, in the eyes of many of the incipient nation's staunchest advocates of popular sovereignty, including Adams, men with limited property were better off being represented by those with superior means. What ordinary people owed their social betters was actually political deference based on the latter's presumed superiority in education, wisdom, *and* judgment, which were, in turn, all understood to flow from their distinctive experience as men of wealth.

But in the spring and summer of 1776, a radical minority of spokesmen—most notably, Matlack, Cannon, and Rittenhouse—seized the lead in overturning this logic. The ground for their arguments had been prepared in large part by the advocacy work of popular associations, such as those of the state's militiamen, which had been actively trying to expand the franchise to include all tax-paying associators, or civilian reservists, regardless of their property holdings, since well before the provincial congress ever met.[65] Their political allegiances and commitment to the community's interest, it was argued, earned them this right. The new thinking was not, however, worked out fully until the provincial congress and constitutional convention forced the issue. In the buildup to electing delegates to the constitutional convention, and then more fully in the process of constitution writing that lasted from midsummer to the end of September 1776, an entirely new vision of the relationship between ordinary people and government emerged. This vision marked an explicit rupture with prevailing assumptions not only about voting rights but also about the nature of politics itself. At its center was the idea that the best decisions resulted from the full, equal, and direct participation of all adult men in the business of law making; for only then would law reflect men's basic and fundamental agreements about the nature of right and wrong, true and false.

The full articulation of this argument required looking backward: to the remote past of Anglo-Saxon England. In this largely imaginary time and space, English people—much like the "noble savages" evoked by Scottish and continental political theorists at much the same moment— had been uniformly free and equal. The men had also been actively and cooperatively engaged in crafting their own government and laws. As explained by the anonymous author of a pamphlet titled *The Genuine Principles of the Ancient Saxon, or English Constitution* that appeared in Philadelphia in the middle of the suffrage controversy of the summer of 1776, the ancestors of today's colonists had met regularly to exchange their thoughts and sentiments with one another. They had also all routinely voted without any aid from their superiors (since, in this world, even an inability to write had posed no obstacle to casting a vote). What had made these people such stakeholders in their government was not the extent of their property; it was their intense involvement in the business of ruling, which, in turn, was rooted in their basic epistemological capacities as humans in conversation with one another. According to the author of *The Genuine Principles,* itself a pastiche of an almost contemporaneous radical English tract, the collective wisdom produced by the Anglo-Saxon system of participatory governing had the power to amaze even today:

> In their small republics, they often met in council upon their common concerns; and being all equally interested in every question that could be moved in their meetings, they must of course be drawn in to consider, and offer their sentiments on many occasions. It is from the prevalence of this custom among the savages, that they have been enabled to astonish our great lawyers, judges and governors, commissioned to treat with them, by displays of their sublime policy.[66]

It was but a short step from this image to the argument (made first by associators and then by the leaders of the provincial congress) that *all* male citizens who displayed loyalty to and engagement in a republican state should gain the right to make decisions about their own futures by means of the vote.[67] The humble, on the basis of their convictions, not money, were the political equals of their economic superiors.

Indeed, some radical Whig spokesmen went even further that summer in dismantling a political theory built on the close link between intellectual deference and socioeconomic distinction. James Cannon, already known for his advocacy of militia interests, issued an anonymous broadside in June 1776 on behalf of the associators' Committee of Privates that entirely inverted this coupling. The purpose of his one-page circular was to suggest which delegates would best serve the people's interest in the constitutional convention. And rather than argue in terms of deference or even equity, Cannon explicitly built on Paine's hostility to the pairing of inherited privilege with expertise, as well as his conviction about the value of a politics rooted in "first principles of things."[68] What Cannon proposed was nothing less than the superiority of ordinary people over specialists and elites in the realm of political judgment.

It is, in this brief but fiery broadside, the rich and mighty and connected who are not to be trusted. In Cannon's telling, they have lost the ability to think and feel like ordinary people and thus to empathize with the collective interest; their natural intellectual impulses have been corrupted precisely as a result of their privilege. Men of great learning, warns the math professor, are even more suspect as they are liable to engage in the wrong kind of reasoning: "Gentlemen of the learned Professions are generally filled with the Quirks and Quibbles of the Schools; and though we have several worthy men of great learning among us, yet, as they are very apt to indulge their Disposition to refinement to a Culpable Degree, we would think it prudent not to have too great a Proportion of such in the Convention."[69] In much the same way, "Pretenders to rank and gentility," whose vulgarity is seated in their "minds" rather than "manners," also came in for suspicion in a contemporaneous address, possibly also by Cannon.[70] And men of special interests, covetous men: they too set off alarms. What was needed, according to Cannon, was just the opposite:

lawmakers who thought, felt, and lived just like their constituents, men whose judgments about the world stemmed primarily from the experiential knowledge of everyday life. For insofar as governance itself was a practical science, the necessary conditions for writing a constitution, according to the author of this broadside, were astonishingly simple: "Honesty, common Sense, and a plain understanding, when unbiased, by sinister Motives, are fully equal to the Task."[71] What Cannon did in a few short strokes was turn a concept long associated with a plainspoken, pragmatic, anti-aristocratic, and anti-expert way of seeing the world—that is, common sense—into an ideal foundation for a new, and distinctly American, political order.

Is this approach best understood as radically egalitarian or demagogic? Neither precisely, despite the claims of more than two centuries of avid champions and detractors of the 1776 Pennsylvania Constitution. Or, better yet, both simultaneously.[72] For here, in the radical Whig rhetoric of revolutionary Pennsylvania, we can locate the apotheosis of a brand-new and decidedly modern form of political legitimation known as populism. Cannon and his associates—through their rhetoric and actions alike—initiated a style and form of politics that depended upon wrapping itself in the moral and epistemological notion of the collective common sense of common men more than any economic argument. That way, what might otherwise be a sign of inferiority—lack of refinement and inexperience in the workings or even language of politics—became instead a symbol of the people's dignity and undiminished connection to the good and the true. Indeed, it became part of the United States' founding creed. The idea of the people's basic agreement about simple-to-grasp truths—just as much as the idea of individual rights so essential to disciples of Locke or the common good to which classical republicans were so attached—was to provide an armature, in the 1770s, for a new kind of political order that would come to be known as democracy.

All the hallmarks of what we now call populism were already in evidence in Philadelphia in 1776, despite the claim of many historians that populism is a late nineteenth-century mode of persuasion and legitimation.[73] The radical writing of that spring is distinguished by repeated

direct appeals to an abstract audience called "the people" and its unerring understanding of circumstances, including what can only be called
self-evident truths. Witness, for example, the author of *The Alarm* declaring in stirring defense of what is actually his own argument: "Fellow
countrymen, it must occur with the fullest force of conviction to every
honest, thinking man, that the persons delegated with proper powers to
form a plan of government, ought to possess the entire confidence of the
people."[74] In this instance, since the common sense of the collective
people is called upon to grasp the fact that government requires the support of all, common sense is employed as both a mode of persuasion and
a proposed solution.

Such appeals to "the people" were then typically followed by a defense of the authority of this abstraction—or, more precisely, those elements of the collective people who are still endowed with the spirit of
the community and an infallible instinct for what is right and just and
true. (It is, of course, this logic that makes it possible to advocate popularly sovereignty but also preclude uppity elites, experts, plutocrats,
entrenched politicians, people of unusual backgrounds, and all those
who lack the people's spontaneous and "real" knowledge rooted in the
experience of daily life and communication with others or who have
forgotten their role as part of "the people.") As in Cannon's broadside,
resentment, outrage, and deep suspicion of the motives and values
of others outside the majority are simply the flip side of the exaltation
of the unity of an abstract people and its equally abstract common
sense. There remains little space for real dissent or difference. The
"common people"—meaning, generally, ordinary, white, Christian
men employed in ordinary jobs, rather than any particular class—exist
only in symbolic opposition to the untrustworthy and "uncommon"
ones.[75]

The radical arguments of 1776 also typically involved a call for rupture, that is, a break with the immediate past in which the exploitative
rulership of those who hold themselves apart from the people and are
estranged from common sense in all its meanings, whether as princes
or as legislators, comes to an end. From the perspective of Cannon and
Young, tyranny and enslavement, not to mention the failure of wis-

dom, were currently under threat from domestic institutions as well as external powers. The very need for a new "state" constitution stemmed from the existing assembly's failure to respond to the true people's true concerns.

Finally, in typical populist fashion, the restoration of a primitive golden age, long lost to the expanding commercial society of the late eighteenth century, was held up as the ultimate goal by its modern, urban advocates. In 1776, this fantasy, with its pre–Norman Conquest trappings and its faith in political rather than economic remedies, had two further components typical of later populist arguments. Nostalgic advocates imagined the return to a world of pure, unmediated self-government, in which there would be no distinction or distance between the governed and governing, much like audience and author in these texts. And this sovereign people would find its way by recognizing and living in accordance with a small set of "fundamental" and "original and first principles," the kind that should be self-evident to all.[76] Of course, these principles had been threatened often enough in history that they needed now to be documented, in written form, for the people's future protection. But once they became operative, politics in an antagonistic mode would finally end, and the realm of the good, the natural, and the consensual—as defined by the overwhelming majority—would finally prevail.[77]

And after several months of back and forth arguments, revisions, and compromises, the constitutional convention finally, in September 1776, unveiled a new written state constitution, complete with "first principles," that can be said to mark the first effort to institute a populist government in practice. This designation is not primarily a result of the class position of its authors (who fancied themselves intellectuals for the most part, though they certainly harbored a good share of social resentments). Neither is it a product of the broad support behind its ideas; in the end, despite submitting a draft version to the public and publishing it in the newspaper for comment, the people of Pennsylvania were not given a chance even to ratify the document.[78] As the historian Edmund Morgan pithily notes, the success of the concept of popular sovereignty in eighteenth-century America was less the result of popular demand than "a question of some of the few enlisting the many against the rest of the few."[79] The populist aura of the Pennsylvania Constitution of 1776 inheres in the distinctive kind of political system that Cannon, Matlack, and Young, among others, tried to forge on behalf of the heterogeneous citizens of Pennsylvania, a system in which the single voice of a mythic people and its imagined common sense will rule the roost.[80]

The framers of the Pennsylvania Constitution who met at the State House in Philadelphia during the hot summer of 1776 rejected the idea of a strong executive with veto power. It was not "consonant to reason," argued one of the constitution's great defenders, George Bryan, "to set up the judgment of one man above all the people."[81] Instead, almost all authority was vested, unusually, in a unicameral legislature intended to represent the single, shared, indivisible interest of "the people."[82] "There is no room [in Pennsylvania]," explained a commentator identified only as One of the People, "for an Upper House with lordly powers to direct and control the Commons, whom they will *hardly* allow to have common sense."[83] Moreover, elections to this single body were to be annual. Constant rotation of membership in the legislature, or what we could call strict term limits, was intended to curb the chance of the emergence of a ruling class, committed to abusing its power, or any permanent cleavage between the governed and the governing. For the same reason, publicity (as opposed to secrecy) was to be the order of the day. Open doors for all legislative debates, weekly publication of roll-call votes, the printing of all bills for public notice and discussion prior to their passage, the maintenance of a free press: these policies were specifically designed to guarantee the kind of easy communication and transparency of functioning necessary, it was thought, to protect the interests of the people outside the meeting hall. The only kind of censorship was to be that of the public itself; an elected watchdog body to be called the "Council of Censors" was to make sure that the "first principles" of the constitution were constantly upheld and also, as the constitution's preamble put it, that government remained for "the people, nation or community," not any subset within.[84]

Then there was the question of suffrage and competency to vote. Under the new constitution, the franchise in the state of Pennsylvania was to be both expanded and contracted. That is, eligibility to vote was to be determined in new ways. Following on the heels of the provincial conference, which had enfranchised all taxpaying associators, the Pennsylvania Constitution gave the chance to participate in elections to all adult men, including free blacks, who had lived in the state for one year and paid some taxes, whether or not they were property owners or independent in terms of their livelihoods. The same held true for officeholders. In theory, day laborers, shoe makers, tailors, seamen, and all other male residents of the state engaged in ordinary work, even sons of freeholders who had not yet paid taxes, were henceforth entitled to participate in the political nation. This decision might not have substantially transformed the actual votership. It did, however, amount to a dismantling of the older argument for the close relationship among financial independence, capacity for judgment, and political power. And it marked a greater effort to derive the "sense of the people" as a whole as the foundation for laws and policies.

But at the same time, the framers of the constitution also produced new forms of exclusion from the sovereign political body in the form of oaths of allegiance. The new constitution, to the immediate horror of some delegates, required every member of the assembly to subscribe to an oath professing his belief in one God, "the Creator and Governor of the Universe, the rewarder of the good and the punisher of the wicked," and the divine inspiration behind the Bible. Officeholders, and soon voters, too, were also obliged to swear loyalty to their state and their support for its new constitution. Finally, if that were not enough, in June 1777 a Test Act required all white, male inhabitants to renounce loyalty to the British king, swear fealty to Pennsylvania, and even promise to inform on traitors—or else lose a battery of civil rights and risk arrest as a spy.[85]

In other words, the realm of common sense in which political decision making was to take place was itself to be circumscribed and restricted to those who accepted the ruling "principles" of both religion as laid out in the Old and New Testaments and republican governance. In an effort to control the odds, the Pennsylvania Constitution simultaneously expanded the definition of the body politic by pulling in new voters, some of whom still needed to be convinced to give up their old loyalties, *and* limited divisions within that body by rejecting old voters who refused to change their minds and go along with the new common sense. The result was the formal exclusion of Quakers, Loyalists, neutrals, and deists, among other kinds of dissenters, from the political body of the state. Moreover, most of the old limitations on voting remained in place, including legal restrictions on the political participation of unfree laborers, children, and women, groups who arguably became that much less visible in the context of the universalizing language of the populist republicanism of 1776. At the time of the American Revolution, intolerance of dissent and the segregation of different social groups from each other went hand in hand with professions of the unity of the people, from the taverns to the meeting halls of Pennsylvania's leading city. Paine's *Common Sense* had created a populist language for justifying the rule of the people. The framers of the Pennsylvania Constitution succeeded in giving institutional form to this communitarian populism, crafting a plan for government in which common sense was to be both a justification for a broad, involved, pluralistic electorate and a means of curtailing individual liberty of expression and delimiting the boundaries of debate.[86]

Not surprisingly, this founding document, much like Paine's *Common Sense,* produced an immediate backlash, creating—in its effort at producing unity—new divisions that cut across class lines, religious distinctions, even occupational groups.[87] Many moderates and conservatives simply refused to participate, either as voters or officials, in the kind of government that the new constitution created. In effect, opponents made it unworkable from the start. The press and public spaces of Philadelphia, meanwhile, filled with denunciations of the more unusual aspects of this framing document. Challengers stressed the lack of continuity with prevailing assumptions and habits, the "strange innovations" and "singular principles" that seemed to characterize Pennsylvania's experiment in constitution writing.[88] "Absurdities" became the foil to all the claims of common sense, much as it had been for Paine's critics just months before.

But much of the animus was directed toward the men who had been responsible for (and consequently empowered by) the framing process itself. What the constitution reflected, according to many opponents, was the lowly intellectual as well as social status of its authors. They were, in this view, disastrously without either past experience in government or formal education in political ideas. This ignorance, not to mention a deep desire for "popularity," then led them to believe that expertise and knowledge were not simply irrelevant but actually detrimental in the construction of a new government.[89] "Damn simplicity," in principles as in men, was to rule the day instead.[90] As Thomas Smith, a participant in and then opponent of the framing process, wrote to a friend in August 1776, "Our principle seems to be this: that any man, even the most illiterate, is as capable of any office as a person who has had the benefit of an education; that education prevents the understanding, eradicates common honesty, and has been productive of all the evils that have happened in the world. . . . You learned fellows who have warped your understandings by poring over musty old books, will perhaps laugh at us; but, know ye, that we despise you."[91]

This bias against formal education, it was said, manifested itself in various aspects of the plan. But most egregiously, in the minds of many of the critics who responded that autumn, the framers' anti-intellectualism had been institutionalized in their insistence on a single legislative chamber to be made up of ordinary men, voted into office by men just like themselves, and regularly replaced by more of the same. A writer to the *Pennsylvania Journal* that September drew out the implications. Farmers, mechanics, merchants—men who knew nothing of law, history, or politics but were "busied with the common concerns of rural or mercantile life"—may well be honest and possess that capacity for determining right from wrong called common sense, he conceded. But such men would, in the legislature, be incapable of "weighing so critically the probable causes or consequences of any proposed measure," or what Cato had earlier that year called "cooler reflection."[92] For this task, they needed, as Whig theory had long suggested, a second body, an upper house representing "all the *wisdom* of the most learned and experienced members of the state" (which was to say also the most wealthy and socially prominent) to serve as a check on the people.[93] It was a bicameral solution, rather than a change in suffrage requirements, according to critics, that would "secure the state from the fatal influence of hasty, incorrect, passionate and prejudiced determinations" and protect against the "weakness and depravity of human nature."[94] Without, the result was likely grievous error and even majoritarian tyranny.

For Foner, again, this is the language of class antagonism in which property and its fate are key.[95] Yet what draws our attention here is the way this fight over the meaning of popular sovereignty was filtered through and, indeed, constructed as a struggle over access to ideas and over the relative value of the exceptional individual's specialized knowledge—the product of education, reason, and leisure—and ordinary men's collective common sense. In the end, the implementation of the Pennsylvania Constitution produced a cultural war among committed and more moderate revolutionaries over the relationship between rank and judgment in the specific domain of politics.

The writings of Benjamin Rush are particularly instructive in this regard. For Rush seems to have changed his mind very soon after the ratification of the new state constitution—and not only about this document but also about the idea of a populist appeal to common sense as the starting point for effective republican governance. At the end of 1775, it was, after all, the excitable Philadelphia physician who had urged Paine to wrap his arguments in the mantle of common sense and to change the title of his about-to-be-published screed. Clearly Rush had seen the notion of common sense as a perfect complement to Paine's call for democracy; it had suggested a link to the collective people and the existence of indisputable, self-evident principles, two essential props to the emergence of the new political logic.[96] Rush had also been a close associate of Cannon, Young, and other radical Whigs throughout the remarkable year that stretched from the articulation of the need for new state governments through the establishment of a new constitution for Pennsylvania. He had been selected by Philadelphia's Committee of Inspection and Observation as a delegate to the provincial conference of June, and he had then been appointed to Congress by the members of Pennsylvania's constitutional convention.

But in Rush's correspondence for 1777 and beyond, and more publically in his anonymous articles for the *Pennsylvania Journal,* we can trace his increasing dismay at the direction in which local politics had evolved over the previous year.[97] Quite possibly swayed by the influence of his more recent friendship with John Adams,[98] Rush decried what he took to be the potentially demagogic aspects of his state's new constitution. Calling Cannon, in particular, a "fanatical schoolteacher" (which may indicate Cannon's modest class position but may also suggest the irony of what Rush took to be an anti-intellectual stance on the part of an educator), Rush denounced the new constitution that both he and Cannon had helped bring about. Its principles were "absurd" rather than commonsensical, Rush wrote to his friends. Moreover, the social context for the government's functioning was the "mob" and the "porter shop" rather than an abstract people or public.[99] It was not that he suddenly became a defender of aristocracy. But for Rush, there remained an important difference, as he explained it to his Philadelphia readers, between power derived from the people in the abstract and power actually seated in the people. Much like Adams, he was convinced that to protect liberty and property, a legislature had to be divided into two houses or chambers, one, for balance, to be reserved for men of formidable mental capacity, education, *and* wealth. The key was to find a way to argue for these positions without seeming to turn his back on popular sovereignty.

This ambition forced Rush to address the question of wisdom and social status head on. As he noted, "The idea of making the people at large judges of the qualifications necessary for magistrates . . . proceeds upon the supposition that mankind are all alike wise, and just, and have equal leisure." But in Rush's estimation, nothing could be further from the truth. "Natural distinctions of rank," which followed from inequality of property and, consequently, knowledge, experience, virtue, and even intellect, were the reality of life even in a republic. Better, Rush insisted, that a government reflect the world that actually exists and give the guiding role in policy making over to elites, men of special "obligations to wisdom and integrity." For even if the bulk of men were fine at judging basic principles, they were—as the framers of the constitution of 1776 seemed to have forgotten—incapable of judging political forms, which (*pace* Cannon) are always "difficult and complicated."[100]

And by the time Rush revisited the idea of common sense, quoting Bayle in his own defense, he had become highly skeptical about this concept as the foundation for any workable politics, not to mention science or morality. Rush himself noted at the start of the 1790s, perhaps in a veiled commentary on his former friend Paine, that when wise men "do homage" to common sense it is often "where advantages are derived from it in promoting their interest or fame."[101] For Rush, an evangelical Christian as well as enlightened scientist, common sense was just another name for custom, and a potentially demagogic one at that. On the contrary, the task of leaders in all domains was to restructure and, occasionally, to shatter the ordinary perceptions of ordinary people since they only rarely had anything to do with truth.

Even James Wilson, the "Founding Father" best known for his attachment to the ideal of common sense as the bedrock of republican governance, refused to accept the interpretation of it offered by the Pennsylvania Constitution's champions. The Scottish-born Philadelphia lawyer and fellow "republican" (as opponents of the constitution's unicameralism were soon known) held on much more explicitly than did Rush to the notion of government by regular consent. Wilson also remained committed for the rest of the century to the idea that common sense—"that degree of judgment, which is to be expected in men of common education and common understanding"—was sufficient for determining the first principles, or self-evident truths, vital to reasoning in all domains, including law; reason, with its potential to mislead, was only necessary as problems grew extremely complex.[102] These notions cropped up repeatedly in his political writings, his teachings, even his judicial opinions once he joined the new nation's first Supreme Court. In the 1770s and 1780s, they even gave him ammunition to suggest that his opposition to the new constitution of Pennsylvania stemmed from the fact that this frame for government simply was not democratic enough: it was insufficiently responsive to the people and, from the loyalty oaths to the Council of Censors, failed to give them the opportunity "of declaring their sentiments, free and unbiased" at every turn.[103] But into the

1790s, Wilson's unfailing touchstone for questions of language, evidence, and human nature was still, as for many conservative republicans and committed Protestants into the nineteenth century, the anti-skeptical arguments of Thomas Reid. Wilson saw them as pillars not only of democratic governance but also of social order. In other words, Wilson's dream of a politics of collective reasoning beginning from common sense principles remained rooted in the loosely consensual, well-heeled, and orderly sociability of the Scottish philosophical clubs of his youth, not the noisy tumult of the Philadelphia beer hall or the mass meeting place.[104] Ultimately, in the opinion of this increasingly socially prominent Philadelphian, only divergent voices, in polite dialogue across two houses of a legislature and at some formal remove from the people, could prevent "rash, hasty, passionate or artful proceedings" (as Adams had warned) and make sure "public business will be more maturely considered."[105]

Histories of the American Revolution, especially those written from the left, tend to tell the story of the next phase of the nation's founding as one of the ultimate triumph of Rush's and Wilson's more exclusionary form of democracy—and of the failure of radicals to keep alive the utopian vision of popular sovereignty as more-or-less direct rule expressed so forcefully in Philadelphia meeting halls in 1776.[106] Indeed, in many accounts, the first Pennsylvania Constitution plays a central role in producing its opposite: stronger curbs on legislative power in subsequent state constitutions and finally, in 1787, the checks and balances and limits to popular political participation characteristic of the new United States Constitution. The Pennsylvania Constitution of 1776, which was finally abandoned in 1790, gained much of its domestic renown as a theoretical counterpoint in early national political and legal wrangling. It also left the authority of its prominent opponents, including Rush and Wilson, greatly enhanced.

However, there is more to this story—and that is what brings us back to common sense. In fact, Pennsylvania's first constitution, with its anti-elitist epistemological and moral thrust, marks the inauguration of a style of politics and set of ideals that would have a long afterlife, reap-pearing in various guises at intervals throughout the history of American politics. Just as the story of the unanimous support for the American Revolution and then the Declaration of Independence was kept alive by the idea of common sense that Paine's *Common Sense* helped to popularize, so an alternative political mode most easily described as democratic-populist has been repeatedly brought back into existence through appeals to and celebrations of the public's common sense, much as radical Whigs first tried to do in the framing of the 1776 Pennsylvania Constitution.[107] In the 1780s and 1790s, Anti-Federalists resuscitated many of the same themes in the same style as they fought both against the complexity of the new federal constitution (which they saw as an explicit betrayal of the principles contained in the first state constitutions) and against its advocates' perceived desire to reserve positions of power for those of superior virtue, wisdom, accomplishment, and wealth. The writings of the leading Anti-Federalists are filled with familiar counterimages: of government as "evident to simple reason, as the letters of our alphabet"; of a homogenous population trained to think primarily in practical terms; and of the closest possible relationship between the rulers and the ruled, the judgments of political leaders and the people's common sense.[108] Oppositional or protest movements in the nineteenth century would return repeatedly to this storehouse as well, using it to challenge all efforts to tip the scales in favor of technocracy, constitutionalism, and representative government rather than direct, popular rule.

Of course, this mode of politicking, in which native smarts matter more than expertise or formal education and simplicity is prized over complexity, now exists independently of its sources. It has, by now, been used by every major political party and candidate for office as well as by those who are pushing for change from outside. It has been coupled with demands for economic justice, and it has been offered as an alternative to efforts at social or economic leveling or the politics of class. And it has fueled efforts at national union and local, grassroots initiatives alike. But this mutability exists only because faith in an indisputable, plainspoken, popular common sense, along with an accompanying egalitarian impulse, remains unmistakably linked to the idea of democracy as it initially took root in North America. It belongs to a democratic idiom that can continually be used to advance the cause of "the people" against the existing order even as that order develops in new ways. More than 200 years later, it remains an intrinsic, if largely unspoken, part of America's political imaginary, continually fostering both greater inclusivity and new forms of conformity and exclusion in its wake.

What is more, the flow of ideas would soon go two ways across the Atlantic. Paine brought divergent European conceptions of common sense into play in the American context and, after mixing in some local elements, crafted them into something new. Similarly and almost simultaneously, an American politics of common sense in practice offered its example to would-be revolutionaries on the other side of the ocean. Critics warned already in 1776 that "the eyes of Europe and America" were on the electors of Philadelphia, the most famous city of the New World.[109] The Pennsylvania Constitution fulfilled this prophesy, for better or for worse, by becoming a marvel in Europe. It was published, republished, and commented upon by a series of French *philosophes.* Despite his lack of active involvement in the proceedings surrounding its framing or passage, Benjamin Franklin, the great symbol of the ordinary American made good on his own, became both its chief overseas promoter and its figurehead. By the 1780s, the French writer and future revolutionary Jacques Pierre Brissot de Warville had become convinced that this foundational text could have applications in Europe as well.[110] (By contrast, the Constitution of the United States had none of this impact when it, too, finally arrived on the other side of the ocean at the end of that decade; it struck contemporaries as considerably less democratic.) And well into the nineteenth century, Paine's own invention, the revolution staged in the name of the common sense of popular rule, was adopted, modified, and used as much to fan the flames as to cool them in Europe and then in Latin America. The contents of *Common Sense,* too, became known from French, German, British, Spanish, even Polish editions, offering an example to eager readers that could be adapted with relative ease to new contexts.[111] What the Pennsylvania Constitution demonstrated, on the heels of Paine's *Common Sense,* is that popular sovereignty would henceforth require a faith not only in the existence of the rational individual and his rights but also in the common sense of the people considered as a whole. Furthermore, the chief public questions confronting the modern world were ideally suited to resolution by means of this shared capacity for making practical judgments and distinctions because they were really not so different from the kinds of questions one confronted every day in private life. The resulting populism is still part of our dominant creed.

XLII.

The outward and Inward Senſes.

Seuſus externi & interni.

The Outward and Inward Senses, in Johann Amos Comenius, *The World Seen through Pictures,* trans. Charles Hoole (London: Charles Murne, 1685), 86, plate 42. Numbers 1 through 5 refer in the customary order to the outward senses, as they were known in post-Aristotelian psychology. Numbers 6 through 8 show the location in the human brain of the three inward senses, including the common sense (number 7), "which apprehendeth things taken from the outward senses." *By permission of the Folger Shakespeare Library.*

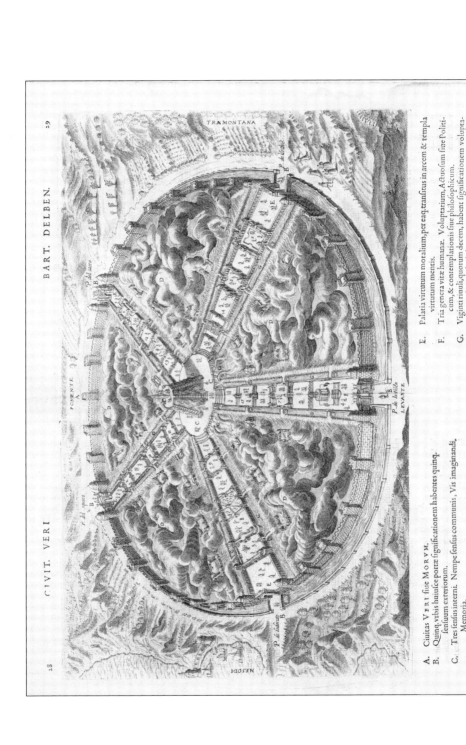

TRAMONTANA

PONENTE

LEVANTE

NESODI

A.   Ciuitas Vᴇʀɪ ſiue Mᴏʀᴠᴍ.
B.   Quinq.vrbis huiuſce portæ ſignificationem habentes quinq.
     ſenſuum exteriorum.
C.   Tres ſenſus interni. Nempe ſenſus communis, Vis imaginandi,
     Memoria.
D.   Valles in quib. atria vitiorum.

E.   Palatia virtutum moralium, per eaq. tranſitus in arcem & templa
     virtutum mentis.
F.   Tria genera vitæ humanæ. Voluptarium, Actuoſum ſiue Politi-
     cum, & contemplationis ſiue philoſophicum.
G.   Viginti riuuli, quorum decem, habent ſignificationem volupta-
     tum: decem alij dolorum.

D iij

Sensus Communis, emblem designed circa 1711 by Anthony Ashley Cooper, the third Earl of Shaftesbury; executed by Henry Trench; and engraved by Simon Gribelin, in Shaftesbury, *Characteristicks of Men, Manners, Opinions, Times,* 2nd ed. ([London], 1714), 1:312. The triptych is intended as an attack on Hobbes's skepticism, which is juxtaposed with Shaftesbury's own philosophy and its signature commitment to toleration as well as to ridicule as a path to truth. The central oval refers to a passage in the essay *Sensus Communis* in which Shaftesbury imagines a "native of Ethiopia" witnessing carnival in Paris or Venice and then ponders the question of who would "laugh with better reason" at whom. On the sides of the triptych, mankind is depicted in two contrasting lights: on the left as Shaftesbury saw it and on the right as envisioned by Hobbes. *Special Collections, University of Virginia Library.*

Left: *The Soul as City,* in Bartolommeo Del Bene, *Civitas Veri sive Morum* (Paris: Drouart, 1609), 28–29. Here the soul, or mind, is represented allegorically as a city surrounded by five sensory portals or gates. Each gate is linked by an axial roadway to the center of the city, where sit five elevated temples (dedicated to science, art, prudence, reason, and wisdom). Access to the temples is provided by three ladders representing the three internal senses responsible, respectively, for receiving, ordering, and retaining sense impressions. In the valleys between roads are houses of vice surrounded by fogs of error. *By permission of the Folger Shakespeare Library.*

Third Dialogue Vignette, in George Berkeley, *Dialogues entre Hylas et Philonous,* trans. Jean-Paul de Gua de Malves (Amsterdam, 1750 [1713]), 175. This illustration of a dialogue before a vertical fountain represents the movement of thought from skepticism to common sense (in this case, the common sense of Berkeley's philosophy of immaterialism). The original passage that accompanies the engraved illustration reads: "You see, Hylas, the water of yonder fountain, how it is forced upward, in a round column, to a certain height; at which it breaks and falls back into the basin from whence it rose: its ascent as well as descent, proceeding from the same uniform law or principle of *gravitation.* Just so, the same principles which at first view lead to *scepticism,* pursued to a certain point, bring men back to common sense." *Courtesy of Houghton Library, Harvard College Library.*

The Judgment of the Queen O' Common Sense. Address'd to Henry Fielding Esquire. A Satire on Pantomimes, and the professors of Divinity, Law and Physic (1736). This anonymous engraving shows a kneeling Fielding offering his drama *Pasquin* to the Queen of Common Sense, who is showering gold coins on the successful playwright. According to the verse below, "Wit, Humour, Satyr, in their own defence, Are all Ariv'd to wait on common Sense." *Copyright Trustees of the British Museum.*

The Festival of the Golden Rump, designed by the Author of Common Sense and published according to an Act of Parliament in 1737. This anonymous engraving is based upon a description of a scene of the same name published in the London political journal *Common Sense* in March of 1737. In this famously nasty satire, Queen Caroline injects a magic calming potion into the "rump" of her husband, George II, while Walpole, holding a magician's wand, supervises. *Copyright Trustees of the British Museum.*

Portrait of James Beattie, engraving by James Watson after Sir Joshua Reynolds's 1773 painting, *The Triumph of Truth*, published in 1775 by John Boydell of London. Beattie noted in his *London Diary* of 1773: "Sir Joshua [Reynolds] proposes to paint an Allegorical picture representing me and one or two more lashing Infidelity & c. down to the bottomless pit" (80). But Reynolds's finished work shows Beattie alone holding his *Essay* (here labeled simply "TRUTH") under his arm. Behind him hovers a female personification of truth, who pushes to the ground the faces of three men representing sophistry, skepticism, and folly. The men were widely interpreted to be Voltaire, Gibbon, and Hume, but Reynolds confirmed the identity only of the first. *Copyright Trustees of the British Museum.*

Frontispiece to [Louis-Armand de Lom d'Arce, Baron de Lahontan], *Dialogues curieux entre l'auteur et un sauvage de bon sens qui a voyagé,* in *Suplément* [sic] *aux voyages du baron de Lahontan* (The Hague: chez les frères l'Honoré, 1703). In this celebrated image, a nearly naked Huron, the embodiment of good sense, stands with one foot on a scepter and the other on a law code, the twin symbols of European civilization. *Special Collections, University of Virginia Library.*

COMMON SENSE;

ADDRESSED TO THE

INHABITANTS

O F

A M E R I C A,

On the following interesting

S U B J E C T S.

I. Of the Origin and Design of Government in general, with concise Remarks on the English Constitution.

II. Of Monarchy and Hereditary Succession.

III. Thoughts on the present State of American Affairs.

IV. Of the present Ability of America, with some miscellaneous Reflections.

Man knows no Master save creating HEAVEN,
Or those whom choice and common good ordain.

THOMSON.

PHILADELPHIA;

Printed, and Sold, by R. BELL, in Third-Street.

MDCCLXXVI.

Title page of *Common Sense: Addressed to the Inhabitants of America* (Philadelphia: printed and sold by R. Bell, in Third Street, 1776), the first edition of Thomas Paine's best-selling pamphlet. *The Library Company of Philadelphia.*

Zion Besieg'd and Attack'd, an anonymous etching by a "friend of the people," offered for sale by William Poyntell of Philadelphia in 1787 along with a broadside explanation, the whole intended to illustrate the ongoing struggle over the 1776 Pennsylvania Constitution. In this elaborate allegory, the controversial document, or Zion, is represented by a fortification built on a rock. It is being defended by a battalion of mechanics with a flag reading "Franklin and Liberty" but also attacked on all sides by "besiegers," including (on the far left) "a BAND of A-r-tocrats, led by Doctor Benjamin playing on a RUSH reed" and (on the right) a band of bankers who see the constitution as "too democratic." Paine (described as "SENSE-able Janus, formerly an Officer in the Constitutional service, but lately raised to a Post of Profit in BANK-ers life guards") is stationed sprawled on the ground at the foot of a pedestal erected for another battalion. He is also represented by a "bird of wisdom . . . expressive of his elevation and influence" who is shown exclaiming, "What uncommon sensations have I suffered for the loss of my reputation," concrete evidence of the shifting perception of Paine in this era even among supporters of the original state constitution. *The Library Company of Philadelphia.*

L'Optique naturelle et artificielle, ou le microscope de la rage, le telescope de l'orgueil et les yeux de la raison et du sens commun (Natural and Artificial Optics, or the microscope of rage, the telescope of pride and the eyes of reason and common sense), an anonymous French water-colored engraving (September 1791). This pro-revolutionary image plays on different ways of looking, or optics, to demonstrate variety in points of view regarding the new constitution, which is being presented by the nation to the king. With their artificial instruments, the figures representing the clergy and nobility are literally blinded with rage and pride; they can see the constitution only in a skewed manner ("Oh! That monster will devour everything," says the priest; "Oh! Oh! It is not yet as close as one thinks," says the nobleman). Without the aid of any instruments, just his native common sense and reason, the figure representing the people alone sees what is evident and true ("Oh! It is beautiful, it will be the happiness of the People"). *Bibliothèque nationale de France.*

ah! il est temps que chaqu'un fasse son metier,
et les Vaches seront bien gardées

Ah! Il est temps que chaqu'un fasse son métier, et les Vaches seront bien gardées (Ah! It is time for everyone to attend to his own affairs, and then everything will go alright), anonymous French aquatint (April 1792). According to the *Journal de la cour et de la ville* of May 9, 1792, this counter-revolutionary caricature represents an honest cobbler whose head has been turned by revolutionary ideas and who has been neglecting his duties until events cause "the scales created by Jacobin patriotism to fall from his eyes." Then, "having come back to his good sense, he crossly rids himself of his military dress, tears away his wig and pigtail, and returns peacefully to his small workshop, to the great happiness of those who had heard him making motions, and above all that of his wife and children" (cited in Claude Langlois, *La Caricature contre-révolutionnaire* [Paris, 1988], 199). *Bibliothèque nationale de France.*

Tom Paine's Nightly Pest, engraving and aquatint by James Gillray, published in London by Hannah Humphrey in late 1792, in anticipation of Paine's trial for seditious libel in response to the English publication of *Rights of Man, Part II*. Paine, wearing a cap that says "Libertas," lies sleeping on a dilapidated wooden bedstead, covered only by his coat, in a depressing and impoverished room. A nightmarish vision of his forthcoming judgment and punishment, complete with dungeon and shackles, appears above him. We can read the title of the pamphlet stuck in his coat pocket: "Common Sense or Reason destructive to Free Government" (or, in later versions, "Common Sense or Convincing Reasons for Britons turning Sans-Culottes"). This is one of many British anti-Paine caricatures that appeared in 1792 and 1793, a good number of them playing on his former association with common sense. *Copyright Trustees of the British Museum.*

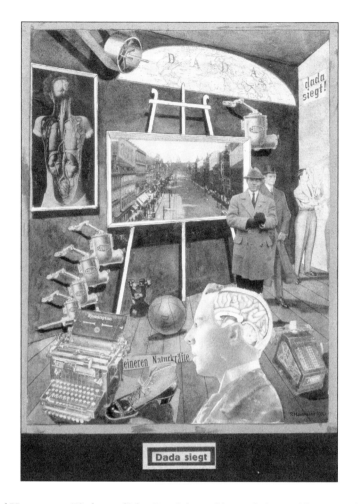

Raoul Hausmann, *Ein bürgerliches Präcisionsgehirn ruft eine Weltbewegung hevor* (A Bourgeois Precision Brain Incites a World Movement, later known as *Dada siegt* or *Dada Triumphs*), montage and watercolor, 1920. At once programmatic and satirical, this image makes explicit the idea of Dada as an ambitious global political campaign aimed at domination. With its prominent display of an anatomical model of the mind, it also identifies the human perceptual apparatus as the source and subject of this campaign. But what *Dada Triumphs* makes clear in formal terms and in its iconography alike is that the apotheosis of the mechanized "precision brain" will not result in order, clarity, and common sense. Hausmann uses a variety of avant-garde aesthetic techniques—pictures within pictures, odd juxtapositions of scale, and the linking of the unrelated debris of modern life (a football, typewriters, mass-produced door locks)—to suggest that a temporally appropriate confusion of perspectives and knowledge is what the politics of Dada is actually about. *Private collection, courtesy Neue Galerie New York. Artists Rights Society (ARS), New York/ADAGP, Paris.*

CHAPTER 5

Making War on Revolutionary Reason

Paris, 1790–1792

> Mother Duchesne . . . your good sense is worth more than all the
> intellect of our so-called *philosophes.*
>
> Abbé Buée, *Le Drapeau rouge de la Mère Duchesne*

L EST WE FORGET, however: common sense always belongs to the language of reaction, which is to say opposition. That means it can, in altered circumstances, be used equally well to push back against democratizing currents as to support them. Nowhere was this irony more evident than in the first years of the French Revolution, as the nation, and especially France's largest city, hurtled toward the undoing of its centuries-old power structure. Surprisingly, the fate of the concept of common sense in Paris in the early 1790s was to be remade as a foundation for a political movement that hoped to reverse the order imagined by Paine, Cannon, and their French counterparts. Its primary job would be bolstering a self-conscious defense of the pre-revolutionary status quo, the very world that revolutionaries were eager to leave behind.

In France as in Pennsylvania just a few years earlier, the democratization of public life, aided and abetted by an ideology of popular sovereignty combined with new legal protections for individual expression, propelled the abstraction known as common sense into an increasingly authoritative position in the last decades of the eighteenth century. But as soon as the initial blush was off the events of 1789 in France, the appeal to the simple, unshakable wisdom of the rural everyman, and eventually everywoman, became a prop in a battle against the new regime, with its perceived urban and philosophical roots. Paradoxically, this campaign for traditional ways also made its initial home in that nation's capital city, the largest city in continental Europe and the Revolution's power base. In the early years of the French Revolution, Paris produced the first stirrings of a populist critique of democracy, in the name of the people's common sense, that has existed on the underside of democratic politics in the West ever since.[1] This counter-revolutionary impulse has become integral to our understanding of the dynamic of the French Revolution, especially as Jacobinism's foil. It deserves now to be seen as one of that revolution's, and indeed the Enlightenment's, principal (and still relatively overlooked) legacies.

Let us first look back to the vital years between the American and the French Revolutions, as the example of Philadelphia made itself felt on the other side of the Atlantic Ocean. But then we need turn our full attention to the transformation of common sense into the centerpiece of what would become a second international populist idiom, this time on the political right. For this antidemocratic mode of popular appeal, too, would prove crucial to the future shape of politics in North America and Europe alike.

The continental reworking of common sense did not start as either a conservative gesture or an effort to thwart the march of instrumental reason. It did not even start in Paris. After 1776, it took almost no time for a universalizing politics of common sense to recross the Atlantic and to take root in multiple, modified forms in Western Europe's most important towns and cities. There, in conjunction with the growth of a new non-noble elite (fueled in large part by transatlantic commerce), an increase in literacy rates, and a more general rethinking of human nature and psychology, the concept of common sense greatly aided the entrance of common or ordinary people into the political strife that began, in the final decades of the eighteenth century, to characterize urban centers from London to Amsterdam to Brussels to, finally, Paris. In all of these settings, just as in Philadelphia, the invocation of common sense served initially to justify the expansion of the political power of these same ordinary people on a local level and a rethinking of the nature of politics itself.

Traditionally, it is the abstract notion of the individual as an autonomous, rational being that has been taken to be the fundamental social-epistemological aid to this cause, especially around questions of "rights." But the myth of a unified people, endowed with an irrefutable and consensual folk wisdom born of its collective quotidian experience, also played a significant role in fueling a defiant print culture, rioting, and eventually battles in the streets of European cities in the years between the American Declaration of the Independence and the end of the eighteenth century. The slow growth of that strange hybrid of representational politics, constitutionalism, and popular sovereignty that we have come to call democracy would require the people's collective common sense as well as individual reason as its prop.[2]

The independent Calvinist city of Geneva offers an important prerevolutionary example. When an extraordinary pamphlet war broke out over constitutional questions in the late 1770s and early 1780s, anonymous commentators seized immediately on common sense, claiming to speak in its name as well as that of truth, impartiality, the public voice, and a variety of other unassailable sources of impersonal and ahistorical authority.[3] These new spokesmen did so in an effort to justify the employment of "I" in an inhospitable context—one in which participation in the formal business of governing was still largely restricted to a small ruling class and where the expression of unorthodox political ideas frequently ended in jail sentences for authors and booksellers, as well as in bonfires for the texts themselves. Public speakers were well advised, at the very least, to disguise themselves as anonymous representatives of collective values. What is more, the recourse to shared epistemological categories, such as common sense, provided the city's burghers with the foundation for a case for a more expansive public politics. That would be a politics where a true "republican spirit" would prevail and the voice of the people (limited in practice to mean the adult male bourgeoisie or those distinguished by age, sex, education, fortune, and enlightenment alone) could make itself formally heard within an oligarchical city-state.[4]

Pre-revolutionary advocates of common sense did not entirely disavow history, however. Despite their deep aversion to anything that suggested "a pure revolution towards democracy," these Genevan writers chose to make their case armed not only with, in many cases, the contract theory of local hero Jean Jacques Rousseau and his idea of a general will but also with a sense of shared purpose with their Philadelphia brethren.[5] It is hard to know for sure whether Paine was the model for the *Appeal to Common Sense (Appel au sens commun)* issued anonymously in 1777 by Etienne-Salomon Reybaz, a Protestant minister who had an interest in physics and poetry and was a strong supporter of the *représentant* or burgher cause. Like Paine, he made good rhetorical use of the great Protestant virtues of prudence, moderation, clarity, and consensus, not to mention the "supreme law" of *le bon sens,* to denounce the reigning logic of his city's political status quo and its sophist defenders.[6] As Reybaz put it in a subsequent tract, "it is to principles, and not to persons, that we accord our confidence."[7] But the *représentant* cause was directly linked by a good number of Reybaz's colleagues with developments in the new United States and, especially, the revolutionary city of Philadelphia.[8] To associate one's position with Philadelphia was to conjure Quaker simplicity, American constitutionalism and liberty, and popular common sense all at once. What Philadelphia offered—whether one wrote in Geneva or elsewhere on the Continent—was a new vision of politics in practice, a politics that had thrown off the yoke of older authorities in favor of an arrangement whereby the sense of the people, at least as an abstraction, held sway.

Indeed, when revolution broke out in Paris in the summer of 1789, this pattern was to endure, though Paine had not yet left Britain for France or thrown himself into a second dramatic overseas political struggle. To speak of common sense in 1789 or 1790 was to advocate keeping alive the (moderate) democratizing movement begun by the Americans two decades earlier. Only rarely were references to *le sens commun* in French discourse intended to evoke the example of the English, with their socially divisive and aristocratic bicameralism. Generally, the reference point was either Paine, or that other great representative of the practical virtues of Philadelphia, Benjamin Franklin, or one of their plainspoken alter egos. In the first years of the French Revolution, several pamphlets and periodicals, all ostensibly authored by "Le Bonhomme Richard" (a.k.a. Franklin's Poor Richard), offered up a simple man of the people, armed only with liberty, honor, and common sense, to address a like-minded audience about the events of the day.[9] That this character was so closely attached to the unicameralist Pennsylvania Constitution only underscored the connection between his American values and what one French editor of a collection of American constitutions called "the purest democracy which ever existed."[10] *Common Sense (Le Sens commun)* a satirical one-issue journal of early 1790, made the link even more explicit. Channeling Paine instead, the eponymous main character promised to do for the French what he had already done for the Americans, that is, restore "simple truths" and clear notions of good and evil destroyed by journalists and various other "people of intellect"; foster "unity of opinions, desires, and means"; and finally give the public a name—his name, Common Sense—to rally around.[11] In France, the association of the idea of common sense with the great political experiment begun by Paine's incendiary pamphlet and given legal heft in the writing of state constitutions lasted through the first phase of the Revolution.[12]

Yet the connotations of invoking "this common reason which links all of humanity"[13] and promising a new consensus in its wake were very different in Paris in 1789–1790 than in Pennsylvania in 1776 or even Geneva in 1777–1778. Not only was this a question of a predominantly Catholic as opposed to Protestant society. In Paris, the appropriation of common sense as a political ally belonged to a sudden effusion of political expression—itself made possible by the abrupt curtailment of a centuries-old formal censorship apparatus in the summer of 1788—that was to dwarf these other locations in terms of its volume, diversity of content, and suddenness. Moreover, in Paris and other major French cities, the mantle of common sense helped a new kind of spokesperson or *porte-parole* both to actualize this abstract right to speak without fear of official reprisal and to get others to listen.[14]

As Quentin Skinner has succinctly noted, "what it is possible to do in politics is generally limited by what it is possible to legitimate."[15] Common sense worked rhetorically, at a time when the most prominent voices remained those of people already in possession of considerable stature, to legitimate the efforts of those even farther from the corridors of power than the Genevan bourgeois or the Philadelphian militia member as they tried to mobilize their compatriots. That included those whose origins and limited literacy had long kept them outside the traditional Republic of Letters as well as any legislative bodies. At a minimum, *le sens commun* (or *le bon sens,* as the reference point also became less explicitly American after 1790) offered a modest vantage point from which *les gens du peuple,* unable to address their fellow citizens from the more exalted position of high social standing, special knowledge, or even reason, with its suggestion of formal education and leisure, could justify their efforts to manipulate another emerging authority known as public opinion.

But more than that, the claim to be able to speak from common sense was to prove vital to the development of the "inverted inegalitarianism," or reversal of expectations whereby ordinary people are deemed not equal to but actually superior to their rulers and social betters, that was destined to become a staple of modern populist politics.[16] For in the early years of the French Revolution, the possession of common sense became a special asset, a way to insist upon the particular value of what one had to say *and* its suitability to the particular problems at hand. Here, its evocation suggested, was the wisdom not of the complicit insider but of the true Bon Homme Richard, the descendant of the mythical noble savage, whose simple, infallible pronouncements had been obscured until now both by the formal mechanisms of censorship and by the informal processes by which a hierarchical, corporate, and stratified society operated. This was the voice of *les choses* rather than *les mots*; of sensory experience rather than philosophy, theology, or formal book learning; of commonality rather than self-interest or individuality. Speaking as "an organ of the public voice and of good sense,"[17] to the good sense of other ordinary people, became, much like speaking as a patriot, a way to suggest that what one was peddling were the shared values of the community, on the one hand, and the uncorrupted language of truth, on the other.

A self-proclaimed "old man of good sense," born to humble parents in Marseilles, offers us one example of how this epistemological self-transformation could work.[18] Like others of his sort who were eager to address a broad public in 1790–1791, this revolutionary made a point of introducing himself to his readers with a disclaimer about his own inadequacies, beginning with the fact that everything he knew was a result of quotidian experience rather than erudition. But in his telling, his distance from culture or capital, coupled with the extensiveness of his experiential knowledge, quickly became the source of his greatest strength: unadulterated perceptual capacities, especially at the level of vision. With his so-called eye of good sense, the octogenarian from the south of France promised that he possessed the now-rare ability to pierce the appearance, physical or rhetorical, of circumstances or individuals and to perceive things for what they really were. Popular images of this era often made this same point through depictions of vision itself. For it was this capacity for clear-sightedness, associated particularly with the laboring classes, that allowed the author to paint himself as the ideal eyewitness, the disinterested nobody who could objectively see the (political) truth that constantly eludes the socially embedded somebody. He is the man whom the people can literally look through to glimpse the reality behind.[19]

The style of expression used to convey this experiential knowledge hewed closely to this model of transparency as well. Unlike professional journalists (a perennial populist target from this point forward), "Me, I will not deceive you," the "old man of good sense" told his audience.[20] For an individual armed with good sense "calls a cat a cat," according to another writer of the same moment.[21] He may not be gifted with words. He may not even speak properly, and his thoughts might well be dictated to a third party better equipped to use a pen, as in the case of our man from Marseilles. But as the author of a 1789 pamphlet called *Solid Good Sense Addressed to the National Assembly (Le Gros bon sens, adressé à l'Assemblée Nationale)* explained, neither eloquence nor study is necessary to make this quality heard.[22] The ordinary man's lack of pretense makes for a special ability to translate his perceptions into simple, unembellished prose that does not betray the elemental quality of those perceptions or shade off into lies and distortions. This was a precursor to the stridently anti-rhetorical (and anti-aristocratic) position that was to characterize much subsequent revolutionary writing; style and ornament are banished in the name of the people and of truth.[23] But then the point in almost every instance was to articulate what everybody should already know from instinct and experience if they were not so blinded by prejudice (meaning what had passed for common sense just months earlier in many cases). Our anonymous popular spokesmen—not unlike Paine or Jefferson—took their job to be the laying out of simple, theoretically self-evident principles that needed neither to be logically proved nor legitimated by external authorities, whether religious, political, intellectual, or social, in order to be perceived as true. That was because they accorded so well with the basic cognitive capacities and experiences of the social body to whom they were addressed. As a different self-declared "old man of good sense" asked his readers rhetorically in another pamphlet of circa 1790, "And good sense and reason, as simple and pure among you as your manners, have they not told you one thousand times that the abuses [of the clergy] were revolting and that they were soiling and dishonoring the Religion to which you are most sincerely attached . . . ?"[24] His audience, he implied, needed only to be reminded of the dictates of good sense by one of their own for these simple, unvarying principles to cease to be obscure. To speak from *le bon sens* in 1790–1791 was to speak a collective language on behalf of collectively held and thus indisputable principles regarding both self and community.

And this time women were among the great beneficiaries. The notion of common sense, along with sentiment, offered an especial advantage to women across class and geographic differences as they, too, tried to make themselves into citizens (if only rarely voters or officeholders). Women, of course, had a particular need to justify their incursions into the new world of political debate and the direct address of any segment of *le peuple*. Their credibility as spokespeople was constrained regardless of their class of origins. It was harder for them than even for provincial octogenarians to claim to speak from the elevated perch of reason when their literacy was frequently limited, even for those from the fanciest of families, and their capacity for sustained reflection or generalization was frequently met with doubt.[25] Furthermore, they risked compromising their feminine modesty through the very act of publicizing their ideas and their selves. But in the context of the Revolution and its suspicion of language, to be associated with the homely and the mundane and the instinctive could also be turned into an advantage. A humble-sounding *bon sens* became a trump card for female *porte-paroles* in the early Revolution, an epistemological category that allowed them to construct a new identity in which it became an actual asset to think and to write *as women*.

The trick was not to deny one's outsider status or constraints but, rather, as for the old man from Marseilles, to draw attention to them precisely because they connoted distance from common sense's opposites: insincerity, metaphysics, and verbiage. Consider the illiterate washerwomen who declared in the *cahier de doléance* written on their behalf before the meeting of the Estates-General that "our rejoicings exalt our king better than all the beautiful sentences that have been addressed to him."[26] Or reflect upon the Dutch feminist Etta Palm d'Aelders, who opened one of her speeches in Paris in 1790 with the ringing words "If the construction of my sentences does not follow the rules of the French Academy, it is because I have consulted my Heart rather than their dictionary."[27] By emphasizing their lack of rhetorical refinement, women could simultaneously underline their authenticity. And this quality, in turn, suggested an exceptional capacity to be vehicles of truth and virtue to others like themselves. The author of *The Patriotic Woman or Solid Good Sense (Le Femme patriote, ou le gros bon sens)*, imagining a challenge to her status as writer, answered her own question with an assertive "Why not?" and went on to demonstrate that she, a "simple woman" armed with no big words, no beautiful turns of phrase or education, only basic good sense, was uniquely situated to "make people see things as they are" and grasp the advantages of the Revolution in ethical terms.[28] The common sense political theory that followed turned out to be what, she claimed, should be obvious even to the most humble in her audience: kings rule only because they take power by force; hereditary privileges are unjust; and everyone needs bread. This is precisely how Antonio Gramsci, writing in prison in Italy in the 1920s, imagined an effective revolutionary making his (or her) case. Rather than disdaining an often contradictory and *retardataire* common sense, which he called "the philosophy of non-philosophers," revolutionaries needed to do as the woman of "basic good sense": identify with the sentiments of ordinary people and build directly upon those precepts of folk wisdom that are nascent and feel true but are currently obscured or immobilized by other basic conceptions embedded in the collective mind. In this manner, a new practical consciousness or common sense should come into being for a people as a whole.[29]

Even Olympe de Gouges, the most famous of female voices in the era of constitutional monarchy, worked from this playbook, elevating her own stature as director of opinion by seemingly disparaging her formal qualifications to do so. In the legions of posters and pamphlets that she composed (via dictation to a secretary) and distributed at her own expense across Paris in the early 1790s, she, too, made herself—as a woman—the issue. She did so in good part because her issues generally concerned the very possibility of women as active citizens; she is, in her writings, her own proof. But she also was able to use this stance to disparage, by means of contrast, that of her (often more exalted) opponents.

To take one example, in a pamphlet called *French Good Sense (Le bon sens françois)* that she published in the spring of 1792, six months after her notorious *Declaration of the Rights of Woman*, de Gouges repeatedly insisted that she was merely in the business of repeating what she had discovered with the aid of a long-lost "tutelary angel" called good sense. But though she remained fervently attached to hierarchy and rank in her political thinking, she was also happy to point out all the trouble she had had in locating this guidepost in the expected places: among doctors of the Sorbonne, monks, *parlementaires,* so-called nobles, savants, journalists, and other specialized elites.[30] Over and over Olympe de Gouges capitalized on her supposed artlessness and painted herself, with her conversational style, as something mundane but rarer, especially in "the midst of the violent upheaval [*le bouleversement*] of all things and in the time of the reign of party." That is, "the voice of a just and sensible woman."[31] In her repeated first-person interventions, she regularly suggested that her lack of refinement, her proximity to nature and to *le bon sens,* in short, all her distinctly feminine qualities made her an especially efficacious mediator between the king and his subjects (whom she called alternately "the people," "the French," and "citizens"), especially when it came to the causes of women and the expansion of the suffrage to all without distinction of sex.[32]

Of course, it is highly likely that many who claimed to be writing in the first years of the 1790s as semiliterate women, not to mention as poor male farmers or humble octogenarians, were actually neither what they claimed they were nor as incapable of wielding a pen as they made themselves out to be. Some were certainly just trying on these roles with the hope that it made them more likely to be able to thrust revolutionary values down the throats of people who actually were what these authors were pretending to be, especially in a context in which much propaganda was self-consciously (and paradoxically) aimed against ideology. It was an open secret, for example, that the almanac associated with Père Gérard—one of the very few deputies who actually made his living in agriculture—was written by the Jacobin leader Jean-Marie Collot d'Herbois, who had devised the strategy of writing in the voice of this "venerable" peasant and "man of exquisite good sense" with the hope that it would help win provincial public opinion over to the embattled constitution of 1791.[33] In this clever text, an immediate best seller aimed at rural men and women alike, the moralizing deputy answers the naïve but always reasonable questions of a group of villagers gathered in his garden and gradually converts them to his cause through a language that they recognize as their own: *le bon sens populaire*.

Such didactic propaganda, structured around adages and analogies and aimed specifically at "inhabitants of the countryside," had itself a precedent in the revolutionary weekly *The Village Newssheet (La Feuille villageoise)* founded in 1790 by a group of enlightened elites. Even though the peasantry as a whole was still associated with backwardness and superstition, and even though this journal never displayed any interest in increasing the political participation of its own rural readers, its editors had been playing a major role in advancing the physiocratic notion that "good sense is the spirit of the people. . . . [It] is the sole bulwark against contagious imagination, against corrupting charlatanism, against disruptive revolts."[34] What the editors hoped was to turn *le bon sens villageoise,* a flattering idealization of the simplicity, inherent morality, and practical wisdom of the agricultural people of France's hinterland, into a platform upon which enlightened revolutionary values could be permanently established. Applauding the persuasive (and fake) naïveté with which the *Almanac of Père Gérard* was composed, the editors of *The*

Village Newssheet compared it with Franklin's *Poor Richard's Almanac* and explicitly wished that Franklin's literary invention, the musings of the common man speaking for common sense, would now have the same effect in France that they had in America not long before.[35]

It matters little, then, from our perspective, that the representative of the people, speaking to and from *le gros bon sens* or *le bon sens populaire* or *le bon sens villageoise* failed to exist as a sociological reality behind every text that assumed this authorial voice. It is not authenticity that is our chief concern. (Still today spokesmen for "the people" are frequently not really "of the people" in any meaningful way.) Rather, it is the way that the perceived common sense of peasants or women or any social group deemed closer to nature than the old ruling elite helped to foster a new populist ideal, a stereotype to be favorably contrasted with the aristocrat, the wordsmith, the sophist, and all others whose erudition or self-interest had caused them to lose sight of the simplicities that ostensibly unite most other humans. And it is the way new hierarchies and new kinds of inclusions and exclusions were created in the wake of this invention.

At the most basic level, the rhetorical figure of the simple "man of good sense" offered a means by which ordinary persons and exalted persons alike could reach out to other ordinary persons, a critical first step in revolutionary proselytization. Note the direct appeal to fellow people of good sense, male and female, that figures in all of these pamphlets: "free men, reasonable and sensible men—it is time to wake up" or "you, whose good sense and reason [are] as simple and as pure as your manners."[36] Then, once established, this association between author and audience became a vehicle through which to push populist principles and ultimately policies onto this same audience. These included a collective national veto and freedom of the press, both of which could be described as mechanisms for righting past injustices (namely, the silencing and subordination of ordinary people) and for translating common sense, or common reason, or even the public spirit, into formal law. For in the end, the agent of common sense almost always promises that the result of listening to him or her will be consensus, the bringing together of a fractured people around a small set of common ideas and values that no one can reasonably oppose because they are, for all sensible and honest persons, unassailable and self-evident. The spokesperson for common sense was ultimately promoter both of the revolution and of its successful conclusion.

Yet this pose still left room for enemies, those who refused to appreciate this particular interpretation of good sense and insisted on another version because of their commitment to party or self-interest or their malleability at the hands of duplicitous priests, nobles, and charlatans. As we have seen repeatedly, common sense, like all populist motifs, allows ample room for imagining conspirators socially both above and below the (ostensibly united) virtuous people of the large middle. But it remained axiomatic to revolutionary spokesmen that unanimity was essential to political order; and the triumph of good or common sense offered the possibility that it would ultimately be possible to overcome division of opinion, acrimonious debate, and maybe even politics itself in its adversarial or agonistic form—an idea that would become another platitude of populist thinking. Sounding much like James Cannon fourteen years earlier and an ocean away, a member of the Society of 1789 explained that ideal on the first anniversary of the storming of the Bastille: "Society essentially needs laws that bind equally all of its members and that, dictated by good sense and open to even the most simple of men, bring them together around the goal of the social state: the greatest happiness for the individual and the generality."[37] With the possibility of the reign of good sense on the horizon, a new potential relationship among epistemology, social structure, and political order opened up in France.

In the end, however, common sense did not have the same trajectory in Paris that it had had in Philadelphia. Neither common sense nor good sense ever became a key term, like Reason, Liberty, Truth, or Nation, in the ideology of the French Revolution. Common sense failed to capture either the rationalist utopianism or the verbal inflation that increasingly characterized the revolutionary vanguard of the 1790s. Especially for the Revolution's Jacobin leadership, common sense ultimately sounded too mild and homely to be widely useful as a rhetorical ideal. Robespierre certainly agreed that it was better to root politics in "the first principles of good sense" than in "vain metaphysical abstractions"; that was a constant theme of revolutionary culture from the first days of the National Assembly.[38] But he also insisted that France had not yet arrived at the point where such principles were self-evident to all. And though Robespierre repeated on occasion the familiar refrain that the people have more *bon sens* than their social superiors, he also emphasized that good sense was inadequate to see through the artificial, deceptive politics of the current moment, especially since so much of the population was still hampered by ignorance and superstition.[39]

Here we are not so far as it sometimes seems from the politics of the leading deputy, the Abbé Sieyès, who had argued persuasively back in the summer of 1789 that though the principles of the new order were potentially intelligible to all, citizens had necessarily to be divided between the passive and the active, depending on their contribution to the public establishment (that is, wealth) and their related capacity to judge what is in the nation's best collective interest.[40] Even the great early champions of republicanism and suffrage rights, such as the Marquis de Condorcet, had trouble shedding their old anxieties about whether *le bon sens* or irrational ignorance really prevailed in village life. Condorcet was not unusual in his eagerness to find ways, within the context of popular sovereignty, to keep a certain amount of decision-making power in the hands of the enlightened few, like himself, at least until superstition and fanaticism began to recede.[41] The proper relationship between "the people" in the political sense and the diverse individuals who flooded France's streets and marketplaces remained one of the great problems of the entire decade. Can we be surprised that reason, with its superior cultural and social trappings and greater distance from lived experience, stepped into the place that common sense could potentially have held as the great epistemological foundation for the rest of the Revolution's advances?

Yet the chief explanation for the failure of common sense to lead the people of France collectively to the Revolution was surely that none of its early innovations, from the division of France into geometric departments to the writing of a national constitution, appeared to contemporaries to have anything much to do with the realm of self-evident truth. In North America, too, the inventions of the war years, including the new state constitutions, were experienced as disruptions of established norms. However, these transformations did not reach as profoundly into daily life as they did in revolutionary France, and for all their talk of rupture, the past remained a conscious reference point for most of the leading American revolutionaries. In contrast, from the very beginning of the summer of 1789, the changes wrought by the new National Assembly and other French revolutionary institutions were posited as bold new innovations. They were also, despite propagandists' claims to the contrary, experienced as profoundly unsettling to old habits of mind even among those who welcomed many of their benefits. Amidst all the emotions that those summer months produced, according to contemporary accounts, the one that stands out as a constant is disorientation—about what exists, about what is good, about what is possible. Commonplace assumptions about order, hierarchy, manners and comportment, the division of space and time, the boundaries between public and private, even the nature of the self were profoundly shaken or upended in the countryside as well as in urban centers.[42] Moreover, within the space of just months, both the status of the king, the key symbol of political power, and that of the *seigneur,* the primary symbol of noble power, were overturned from below. Even the meanings of the words used to evoke ordinary, everyday relationships began to change. Surely, common sense could not be easily located in this setting.

Once again the problem became that much more acute in the context of the introduction of a new form of ideational control, one that had, just as in Philadelphia in 1776, initially been justified as a step toward the production of unity: the administration of state-sponsored loyalty oaths. Only this time the target was not newly elected legislators or even voters but the French clergy, who were soon forced into the impossible position of choosing between fealty to the revolutionary state and fealty to the Catholic Church. The Civil Constitution of the Clergy was originally voted into law by the National Assembly in the summer of 1790 with the idea not of doing away with the Catholic Church but rather of making it and its clerics a faithful part of the new regime; henceforth they were to be popularly elected. But the Civil Constitution quickly opened up new questions of allegiance, thus upsetting what had been one more source of certain authority in the lives of the faithful as well as their spiritual leaders. For when the decision to turn priests into functionaries was met with resistance on the part of much of the French clergy, the idea emerged from within an impatient (and largely undevout) National Assembly that another provision of the Civil Constitution should be the requirement of an immediate loyalty oath on the part of every priest in France. By January 1791, following reluctant royal sanction, this oath of allegiance to the new, national constitution became the law of the land. It has often been described since as one of the Revolution's great misjudgments.

The effect was not only to split the clergy into opposing factions, constitutional and refractory, depending on individual priests' willingness to defy the pope (who formally condemned the measure that spring) and to swear their loyalty to the entire constitution. It was also to sever much of the rural population of France from the Revolution's considerably more anticlerical, urban, and enlightened leadership and, in effect, to divide the nation as a whole into two new factions: supporters of the church and supporters of the state. The Civil Constitution inadvertently functioned as a referendum on the new "revolutionary" church and, indeed, on the Revolution as a whole, region by region, parish by parish.[43]

In much of the French countryside, where many villages suddenly lost their beloved nonjuring priest, the Civil Constitution soon produced a backlash. Significantly, this backlash gave a popular, provincial, and ultimately disproportionately female dimension to the struggle against the tide of Revolution. Starting in 1791, rural women, in particular, found themselves at the forefront of protest, sometimes in conjunction with male members of their own families, sometimes in opposition.[44] Many rural women were angry at those local priests who had seemingly betrayed their congregants by accepting the Constitutional Church. Many also blamed the Revolution's leaders, who seemed to have imposed these assaults on private consciousness and the rituals of daily and village life on an unwilling population and from a distant, largely secular, urban space. And in various corners of France, ordinary women found themselves taking direct, collective, and often illegal action, at the local level, to express their displeasure. Tactics included refusing to baptize infants or bury family members within the Constitutional Church but also protecting nonjuring priests from arrest and shunning or harassing the constitutional clergy who showed up to fill newly vacant slots. In early January 1792, for example, the Constitutional priest of Isle-sur-Serein just escaped being deposited in the village fountain by an angry crowd led by women supporting the local nonjuring or refractory priest.[45] It was enough to cause juring priests to complain about rural women's new social roles, despite the fact that women had always taken the lead in certain forms of popular resistance.[46] It was also enough to introduce a reversal by the start of 1791: a campaign against the tide of the Revolution (perceived to be staged in the service of Parisian lawyers enamored with abstract reason, science, and philosophy) in the name of the common sense of France's *real* people.

The intellectual impetus behind this campaign was not itself a product of the countryside. The anti-revolutionary ideology of the early 1790s—an effort to produce a populism of the right aimed at ordinary men and women disenchanted by the Civil Constitution and loyal to church and king—also made its home in the political and literary center that was Paris, much as other revolutionary currents did. Furthermore, this reactionary movement, largely the product of elite propagandists who saw the potential for building a popular base for counter-revolution in rural resentment, borrowed many themes from urban revolutionary discourse, including the notion of *le gros bon sens,* the superior sense of the world endemic to ordinary people as a whole. But the Parisian architects of the language of counter-revolution ultimately attached this notion to a different vision of the people—rural rather than city-based—and to a different representative of that culture—the pious and virtuous woman rather than her supposedly easily swayed husband. And with even less popular foundation but a similar intention of popular appeal, these activist writers directed this image to entirely different ends: against the loyalty oaths that came with revolutionary politics but also against democracy in any form.

A coterie of well-born moderates, committed to constitutional monarchy and angered by the overheated rhetoric emanating from Parisian Jacobin clubs in the wake of the Civil Constitution of the Clergy, tried its hand first at remaking *le bon sens* as a term of collective reaction during the winter of 1790–1791. In a manner reminiscent of the Whigs in the aftermath of the Glorious Revolution, these *monarchien* deputies and their supporters sought to redefine this term as synonymous with the sentiments of the vast (and largely silent) majority of French people.[47] The idea was to fashion good sense into a bulwark against a small minority: aristocrats, certainly, but also Jacobins, club participants, street prophets, and all others who sowed disorder or favored fancy, impassioned, or abstract words over simple truths and were using the deregulation of speech to lead the "respectable majority" of farmers, property owners, and heads of households astray.[48] If these hyperbolic voices could no longer be directly eliminated through the old repressive mechanisms of the state, perhaps ordinary men could be persuaded not to listen, that is, to turn their collective back on what popular politics had become. This was the paradoxical message of a large number of anonymous and "pseudo-populist" (in the words of one historian) short-lived journals, pamphlets, and posters with names like *The Sensible and Patriotic Town Crier, Good Sense: Free Thoughts on Current Events,* and *My Patience Is at Its End: A Word of Good Sense* that moderates began distributing for free across Paris in the first half of 1791.[49] Like Addison and Steele eighty years earlier, the acerbic author of an anti-Jacobin pamphlet of 1791 was only partly joking when he detailed the bylaws of an imaginary underground club, a "Society of Friends of Good Sense," in which political discourse would be limited to the basic truths of the "lower region," where human life occurs, and language was to be stripped of all hyperbole and tours de force.[50] Here was a platform for an end to active revolution, an extralegal way to bring all sensible parties around to a common, consensual ground from which a very circumscribed discussion could emerge. The idea was to reverse the tide of the Revolution, if not its civil libertarian gains, through a kind of informal censorship, rooted in good sense, that would allow for the resurrection of a single national voice representative of (moderate, elite) community norms.

At best, this kind of rhetorical coercion might be just as effective as "real" censors insofar as it would ultimately result in something like self-censoring, an internalization of those values that conformed to dominant social norms. But here, as in England at the other end of the century, we can also glimpse a desire to stake out a middle ground between the regulation of speech and total license to say anything, between state or church control of ideas, on the one hand, and unmitigated freedom of thought and expression, on the other. Good or common sense was intended to work outside the mechanisms of regulatory law to provide limits on what could sensibly be articulated and what could not, of what fell within the realm of the sensible and what was purely, surely to be sidelined as *le non-sens*. If applied to politics, *le bon sens* promised to result in the collective agreement of all people (with the exception of those who were imbecilic, mad, perverse, or thoroughly deceived) to support the basic premises of what had begun to take form, before being derailed by popular agitation and unreliable *porte-paroles,* as a new orthodoxy.

But good sense had no lasting success as a synonym for moderation, despite the best efforts of *monarchien* propagandists. After the Civil Constitution of the Clergy and then the king's flight to Varennes, little space remained in the revolutionary schema for a consensual middle ground to emerge, and "good sense" alone could not do this work, especially as revolutionary rhetoric became more heated on both sides. Plus, solutions borrowed from the playbook of British constitutional monarchy, Parliament, or even English literary culture held decreasing value as the center failed to hold or find any kind of popular basis. Perhaps, though, this is simply the way of appeals to common sense. Just as in England after the Glorious Revolution, such appeals work better as the foundation of scorched-earth crusades directed against their opposites than they do as forms of informal, centrist regulation.

The great victors in the struggle for the mantle of common sense in the first years of the Revolution were, in fact, the Revolution's staunchest opponents, those who rejected even the legal dismantling of the Old Regime that began in mid-1789. After all, the anti-Enlightenment polemicists of the late Old Regime had already been making use of appeals to this value for several decades, beginning with the tracts of the 1760s and 1770s in which they aggressively took on the new philosophy of the day. Both the satirical style and the network of writers and patrons dedicated to combating the dangerous expression of anticlericalism, deism, atheism, materialism, libertinism, and other kinds of free thinking could be, and were, redirected toward the live enemy that was the Revolution, the seeming realization of their long-standing fears. Moreover, operating with the same Manichean logic as the Jacobins, only set in reverse, royalist, Catholic agents of counter-revolution found it easier than did fans of constitutional monarchy to appropriate *le bon sens populaire* for their needs, especially in the wake of rural resentment of the Civil Constitution of the Clergy. By the spring of 1791, common sense had become firmly attached to the nostalgic idea of restoring a lost world centered on church, king, and the spirit of the village and a key element in the defense of traditional values and ways of life. It had also become the epistemic centerpiece of an angry populist propaganda campaign, engineered in Paris by entrepreneurial Catholic publishers, refractory priests, disgruntled nobles, and hack writers and aimed at turning the popular eastern *faubourgs* of Paris and villages all across France against the new ruling class.

The Counter-Revolution (if we can speak of such a thing without suggesting a single coherent movement) was slow to gain a popular base or even popular aims. It came to life as a philosophical and literary current first.[51] From the middle of 1789, a smattering of opponents of the National Assembly, of its upstart deputies, and of their Declaration of Rights of Man and Citizen had made a concerted and generally uncoordinated effort to derail the whole enterprise. Apart from hatching a few ill-fated plots, anti-revolutionaries did so primarily by taking advantage of the very liberty of the press that many of them despised and, just like their ideological foes, trumpeting by pamphlet or periodical their profound displeasure at the course of events and the people at the helm.[52] The October Days of 1789, when the king and his family were forced back to Paris at the behest of an armed crowd, much of it female, proved particularly catalytic in this regard for the old Parisian anti-Enlightenment establishment, just as it was for Edmund Burke, viewing events from across the Channel. Only days after King Louis XVI had been effectively imprisoned in the Tuileries, the prototypical early counter-revolutionary journal, the *Acts of the Apostles (Actes des Apôtres)*, came into being, the product of a close-knit coterie of several dozen royalist writers who began meeting regularly for convivial but dyspeptic banquets in the cafes and restaurants of the Palais-Royal, as well as at the bookstore of Gattey, "royal and apostolic bookseller," in the same square.[53]

The result—much of it left scribbled on the tablecloth for the printers to cart away—was reactionary in terms of both methodology and ideology, though battle lines had not yet hardened at the inception. It was also the first piece in what was to become a counter-revolutionary intellectual crusade for the restoration of good sense as it had long been understood. From one vantage point, the *Acts of the Apostles* was one more upstart revolutionary newspaper, closely following the events of the day, albeit from a hostile perspective. The fact that Pennsylvania was holding a new convention to reconsider its misguided attachment to a one-house assembly was, for example, duly reported in the winter of 1790, when some of the *Acts'* writers still believed a compromise between crown and revolution possible.[54] But most of the journal, as its very name suggested, was given over to satire and irreverent parodies—of the Assembly, of clubs, of decrees, of constitutions, of festivals, even of letters to the editor—much of it laden with sexual double entendres.[55] Laughter was to be the right's ticket, it was determined early on, to the restoration of a much-aggrieved common sense.

The journal's well-born writers, led by Jean-Gabriel Peltier and that great defender of the common sense structure of the French language, Antoine Rivarol, generated their aristocratic and often bawdy brand of humor in several ways. They juxtaposed the sacred with the scatological. They also turned the jargon of the Revolution against itself, indirectly confounding its logic in the name of the greater good sense of authors and readers alike. This was an old technique that had been widely employed by Voltaire and then d'Holbach (himself the author of a satirical *Acts of the Apostles*), as well as by their most clever detractors. Indeed, its pedigree stretched from Lucian to Shaftesbury to the conversations held in the great Parisian salons over the previous century. Should we be surprised that a list of fake books offered for sale included "Of the Superiority of Metaphysics over Common Sense" by the "author of the Declaration of the Rights of Man"?[56] Or that a list of fake laws included such pseudo-rational efforts to legislate away common sense as these: "Beginning next July 14, days will be equal to nights on the whole surface

of earth" and "As soon as the day finishes, the moon will start to glow
and it will be full until the sun comes up"?[57] The intended effect of all
this derisive laughter was deflation—of a phony philosophy characterized by pretentious and quasi-metaphysical mumbo jumbo and of the
demagogic and self-aggrandizing ambitions of the men behind this philosophy (a category that expanded to include orators, legislators, and
journalists as well as *philosophes*). Every novel and "democratizing"
term, value, institution, or political practice of the moment was potentially opened up to ridicule, mockery, and exposure as non-sense. The
educated reader became complicit in what was essentially a mild act of
debasement with the understanding that he (or she, since a good percent-
age of the readers of highbrow, anti-revolutionary satire were women)[58]
would contribute to the restoration of normal, familiar ways of thinking
in the aftermath. Though Carnival had been outlawed on Parisian
streets by the end of 1790, the impulse toward temporarily scrambling
the status quo in the name of the future return to order survived on the
counter-revolutionary page.

In the long run, though, this aristocratic mode of subversive political
writing, in which even Catholic liturgy was not safe from parody, proved
no more popular with the court of public opinion than did the heavy
style of the venerable conservative literary journal, the *Année littéraire*,
which failed to survive in the new commercial marketplace of 1789–1790.
Its primary audience—provincial nobility, army officers, the upper ranks
of the clergy, and parts of the upper bourgeoisie, including landowners
and state agents—was simply too small, especially as emigration sapped
its numbers all across France.[59] These journals also all depended upon
subscribers to thrive, making them available only to those with funds for
a full year in place at the start. What is more, in the wake of the Civil
Constitution of the Clergy, the internal needs of Paris-based counter-
revolutionaries began to change. Already, after the Great Fear of the summer of 1789, many rural people of humble backgrounds had begun to
view the Revolution as an urban assault on what they perceived as traditional, local ways and to distance themselves from the politics of the
National Assembly. But it was the provisions of the Civil Constitution
that exacerbated and, indeed, formalized this breach—and provided

Parisian opponents of the Revolution with an opportunity. By the fall of 1790 and increasingly into 1791, there seemed, from the perspective of Paris, an ever greater chance of forging some kind of ideological solidarity between the denizens of France's countryside and urban anti-revolutionary crusaders. What was needed was a new kind of propaganda directed at the less-educated masses and intended to convert them to the cause of the refractory church and its nonjuring clergy, arm them with arguments for combating the revolutionary notions of their confreres, or even just prop them up in their efforts to thwart change at a grassroots level. The solution arrived at by a small number of polemicists, many of them clerics themselves, was to turn the old notion of good or common sense to new ends, ones only loosely related to the techniques of the *Acts of the Apostles* or to *monarchien* newspapers. In the hands of hired Parisian scribes, the resentments remained the same. But common sense became a key element of a populist style of conservatism that celebrated authoritarian governance alongside the traditional ways, values, and language of ordinary people. This idiom would long outlast the Counter-Revolution itself.

Most of the creators of this genre remain as anonymous today as they were in late 1790 and 1791. One great exception is the Buée brothers. Neither Adrien-Quentin nor his older brother, Pierre-Louis, ever signed a polemical word they wrote, and their names surely never rang a bell even in their heyday outside of their small orbit of Catholic, royalist, Parisian writers. But the Buée brothers should be seen as belonging to a long transatlantic tradition of quasi-anonymous eighteenth-century prophets of common sense stretching back to include Fielding, Beattie, and d'Holbach, as well as Tom Paine, James Cannon, and Olympe de Gouges. All three Paris-born Buées were trained to be priests, though only two seem to have developed sidelines in which they took up a pen. Pierre-Louis devoted himself more fully to his calling, becoming register of the chapter of Notre-Dame in Paris, then canon at several other Parisian churches.[60] Adrien-Quentin, a devotee of Newton as well as a devout and orthodox Catholic, seems with hindsight always to have been more interested in politics, music, and science than in theology. When he emigrated to Bath, England, in 1792 following a brief career as a church organist in Tours and a stint as secretary of the chapter of Notre-Dame in Paris, he remade himself as a minor composer of keyboard works and writer on mathematics.[61] It took him twenty-two years to return to Paris and take up another clerical position.

What linked the Buée brothers to politics in the early 1790s was the Imprimerie de Crapart, located not in the Palais-Royal but across the river in the Place Saint-Michel, number 129.[62] Jean-Baptiste Nicolas Crapart, the son of a publisher and bookseller, had made a name for himself almost as soon as he received his printing license in December 1789. Motivated by politics and economic survival alike, he soon became one of Paris's foremost producers and distributors of royalist, Catholic, and counter-revolutionary journals, pamphlets, and other tracts, an entrepreneur in the realm of anti-Constitutional Church materials, which he sent by post all across France. For disenchanted nobles and well-placed clergy, Crapart was the source of the exalted anti-Enlightenment organ, the *Année littéraire*, and, when that folded, a new right-wing political journal called *Friend of the King, of the French, of Order and especially of the Truth (Ami du Roi, du français, de l'ordre et surtout de la vérité)*, created by the same editors. Crapart also became known for printing and distributing the many pamphlets, journals, and collections of anti-Constitutional Church writings produced by the noble-born former Jesuit, the Abbé Barruel. Adapting the message that he had developed earlier in his best-selling *The Helviens*, Barruel now applied himself, with Crapart's backing, to denouncing the workings of the Assembly and the Civil Constitution of the Clergy as the results of a plot by immoral, atheistic *philosophes*.[63] Priests from around France and even the pope followed suit, entrusting the dissemination of their own denunciations of the Civil Constitution and its loyalty oath to Crapart. Adrien-Quentin Buée first entered these elevated ranks in late 1790, when he was hired as one of Crapart's authors. But Crapart, who was also an activist in revolutionary terms, directing his proceeds partially to anti–Constitutional Church causes,[64] was clearly not content to reach only the same small pool of clerical and aristocratic, urban readers targeted by journals like the *Acts of the Apostles*. Starting in the second half of 1790, when the issue of the oath required of priests had begun to

dominate political conversation across the country, Crapart must have
seen the potential for both profits and political payoff in producing and
distributing a more popular form of propaganda aimed squarely at inhabitants of Paris's poorer neighborhoods and the countryside, pamphlets and images in which the embodiment of *le sens commun* was no
longer the Parisian or even the priest or the *procureur de la commune*
speaking for urban ways but, instead, the peasant himself. It was in this
domain that Adrien-Quentin Buée would find his niche.

Dialogues, as every publisher in Paris knew, were a particularly useful genre for reaching a wide audience. This much had been discovered
from the earliest days of the Revolution by its opponents as well as the
monarchien center and the radical left. (Even the *Almanac of Père Gérard* of Collot d'Herbois could just as well be described as a dialogue
between a deputy and his constituents.) In practical terms, short pamphlets labeled *dialogues* or *conversations* or *entretiens* could be sold
cheaply by the piece rather than by subscription. In addition, their titles
and often their entire contents demanded to be cried out by *colporteurs*
in the street looking to make a sale and then read aloud, in cities and villages across France, either in political clubs or after Mass. Like popular
plays, these dialogues typically opened with an indication of the encounter's setting (a kitchen, a garden, a cabaret, a market, a club) and a
list of the cast of characters. What distinguished the explicitly political
dialogues of the early revolutionary era is that their stock characters
tended to present themselves as representatives of different worldviews,
different social stations or professions, different places of origin, and different forms of speech and even reasoning. The dialogue form offered an
opportunity to set in play a series of binary oppositions drawn from
these differences: the ideas of priests in contrast to those of the Revolution's agents, the language of the learned as opposed to the popular, ungrammatical language of Parisian marketplaces or villages, the mores of
the city or *les grands* versus those of the countryside. But in contrast to
those penned by early skeptics, the conclusion of these newer dialogues
was always marked by consensus and resolution. Their plots may have
turned on confusion or a misunderstanding, typically of the innovations
of the Revolution and its novel language. Eventually, though, through

questions, answers, observations, and debate, the sensible character or characters succeeded in converting the others to the position that the author deemed consonant with good sense.[65]

The question—to which Adrien-Quentin Buée was eventually to have an innovative answer—was who should lead the way. In the earliest royalist and anti-revolutionary pamphlets, whether published by Crapart or one of his many competitors in the Place Saint-Michel, the job of embodying counter-revolutionary *bon sens* (in contrast to the nonsensical ideas and language espoused by the representative of the Revolution) was often, very literally, given to a noble, a *seigneur*, a cleric, or traditional authority figure. In one case, M. Bon Sens is actually the name of the priest who leads his interlocutor to conclude that "in losing our legitimate clergy [*pasteurs*], we are losing at the same time the Gospel, the laws of our consciences, and the best friends that we have in the world."[66] For the partner in dialogue in these first examples is typically an ignorant tenant farmer or other, less exalted type, who is told what to believe and finally offers his thanks for the clarification. In *The Only Good Sense: M. Franckin, Barrister; Piccard, Master Carpenter; and Jean Berdaulou, Winegrower* (1790 or 1791), for example, the barrister converts an illiterate and not very bright master carpenter (explaining "you have been made dizzy by pompous verbiage that you admire because you have not understood it") to the position that the oath is the work of a cabal that has pulled the wool over the eyes of common people. The dialogue ends with the carpenter's desire to return to his place and "always display good sense," just like the barrister.[67] Such conclusions were entirely in keeping with the elitist tone and hierarchical message of most early anti-revolutionary, royalist polemics. In journals like the *Acts of the Apostles* and the *Gazette de Paris*, "the people" made their entrance as the *canaille* (the rabble) or violent brigands, at best deluded or easily manipulated until shown the light by their superiors and, at worst, no better than beasts.[68] Certainly, with their lack of developed judgment or political experience, they were seen as incapable of perceiving independently what was in their own best interest or participating directly in public life. This message accorded well with a view of church and state in which the preservation of hierarchy was essential both to morality and to social order.

But as early as 1790, some anti-revolutionary writers of dialogues, often clerics themselves like Buée, began inverting this rhetorical schema while still denouncing the sovereignty of the people, or even the popular election of clerics, as a chimerical idea. In part, they followed the lead of the Abbé Barruel, who had employed an ignorant provincial baroness in *The Helviens* to raise naïve but common sense objections to the fashionable new philosophy of her clever Parisian interlocutor, only to rediscover the value of the teachings of her local *bon curé*. Equally, though, popular anti-revolutionary polemicists drew on a formula patented by the writers of burlesque pamphlets of the late Old Regime in which *le jugement des ignorants,* including women, children, peasants, and the disabled, often speaking in a low, ungrammatical language, revealed serious truths, especially in matters of taste.[69] And surely one can trace a debt to the contemporaneous revolutionary tradition of writing from *le gros bon sens* in which it is the outsider to power, armed only with rudimentary logic, folk wisdom, and the experience and perceptions of daily life, who knows best. The Parisian writers of cheap anti-revolutionary, Catholic, and royalist dialogues found new traction by engaging in a similar kind of role reversal and making the plain or even ill-spoken, unlearned, lowborn resident of the countryside show up his social superiors by incarnating the (counter-revolutionary) *bon sens* of the true people of France. The trick was to invent a more flattering and less contemptuous or paternalistic image of the masses, even as the ultimate message was the importance of restoring hierarchy, expertise, and older forms of deference and authority in social and political life.

What happens in more clever versions is that characters identified as "men of the countryside," unsullied by Parisian norms or still able to see through them as outsiders, end up judging the world around them more accurately than, in many cases, that agent of urban revolution and representative of the new French legal system, the *procureur,* or procurator. In one such dialogue, Bon-Sens becomes the name not of a priest but of a national guardsman, whom the author describes as "full of good sense" and "incapable of lying" to the people of his village about what he has glimpsed in the big city.[70] In another, a villager named Pierre la Raison (Peter Reason) reasons using simple analogies much better than the big-city *procureur,* who "[falsely] imagines himself possessing all the common sense of the village."[71] Pamphlets like *The Good Sense of the Village, a Visit and Colloquial Conversation between an Officer of the National Guard and a Female Villager* (1790) then further advanced the genre by adding a new twist: the female villager, a humble version of Barruel's baroness, becomes the stand-in for the vox populi. Her primary function is to "open the big eyes" of her male relative, a national guardsman temporarily seduced by urban ways, and, with her naïve questions about the meaning of unknown words like "liberty" and "equality," convert him back to the position of true good sense or *le bon sens du village.*[72] The message, which Buée was shortly to turn to his advantage, was twofold. Simple rural people needed to watch out for all the misleading and mystifying talk coming from Paris, as it would ultimately do nothing to assuage their most basic need: satisfying hunger. And those farthest from the urban direction of this Revolution and most limited in their powers of expression—unsung, unnamed rural women with concrete preoccupations—often saw best what was in "the people's" interest.

La Mère Duchesne (Mother Duchesne) was Adrien-Quentin Buée's literary contribution to this popular genre. Père Duchesne, a foulmouthed, violent, and deeply patriotic working-class Parisian character with roots in fairground theater, had already in the course of 1790 become an icon of the radical journalistic left, spewing his entertaining and abusive revolutionary sentiments in several competing versions.[73] What Buée did was give him a wife—a peddler of old hats who would, with a scabrous dialect borrowed from the market women of Les Halles and the threat of a few smacks with a broom, "open his eyes" and bring her husband back around to his (counter-revolutionary) senses.[74]

Mère Duchesne seems to have made her first appearance as a female icon of resistance in a four-page dialogue, quite possibly invented by Adrien-Quentin Buée, in which she, too, called upon an utterly rude, ungrammatical, and richly imagistic, proverb-filled style of speech to score political points.[75] Four more such dialogues followed in early 1791, loosely forming a periodical of sorts, and they were in turn followed by a few occasional dialogues in 1792–1793, all published by Crapart and probably authored by Buée. Each can be seen as a freestanding verbal duel—and quite possibly a means to incite real violence among sympathetic readers. One side features a changing cast of imaginary pro-revolutionary characters armed with a novel political jargon that they have ignorantly swallowed without full comprehension. On the other stands a series of anti-revolutionary and virulently anti-Constitutional Church figures, representatives of long-standing good sense.[76]

What ensues is not, however, only a struggle over ideology. It is also a matter of gender. Frequently, realistic women characters, in defense of nonjuring priests, are lined up against their own menfolk. Mère Duchesne, who leads the former pack, often gets assistance in these dialogues from a male intermediary, a cultivated man of the people (in several cases, M. Recto, or Mr. Right Hand Page, the bookseller), who reinterprets what she has said in more formal language. But this figure also never fails to praise the mother's innate good sense ("you reason better, all alone, than the entire ecclesiastic committee put together," "In truth, Mother, you speak like a preacher," or "Really, Mother, there are some scholars who do not reason better than you")[77] or her ability to express herself clearly and forcefully ("Really, that is very well said")[78]—especially when juxtaposed with the utterances of (male) learned idiots who believe everything they have read. Mère Duchesne's message was ultimately not far from that of the Abbé Barruel: the Revolution, with its "idiotic inventions" *(bougre d'inventions)*, is a plot against the good people of France led by new political elites, including philosophers, lawyers, and journalists, but also freemasons, Protestants, Jews, and venal, debauched clerics, all of whom come in for abuse.[79] Other authors managed to add blacks in France's colonies to this list as well.[80] In these dialogues we find an early taste of what will become the populist trope of hostility to all outsiders to traditional social hierarchies or mores, in this case used against the false notion of "the people" as a unified whole. As Mère Duchesne points out, it is the restoration of the old social and religious order, with its highly differentiated categories, not the fiction of "the nation" (or "c'te nation," as she puts it), that will put bread on the table.[81] Yet what is worth stressing is that Mère Duchesne operates as more than simply an empty vessel for these messages. She is intended to be a model of identification, especially for women of the lower classes, a populist heroine who stands for the common sense of ordinary people confronted with the upheaval, in the form of the Revolution, of all that they know and cherish.[82] Here is Fielding's allegorical Queen Common Sense come back to life in an extremely earthy and only semiliterate form.

Typical is this scene from *The Red Flag of Mother Duchesne (Le Drapeau rouge de la Mère Duchesne)* of early 1792, the high point of popular counter-revolutionary expression.[83] One of Buée's stock characters, a M. Lefranc, announces that the problem with everything stems from the fact that "this miserable constitution has no common sense," and "since the world became the world, there is no example among any people of a similar *galimatias*" (which, as we have seen, is a classic word of opposition to common sense that makes repeated appearances in these reactionary dialogues as well as in the writing of the pre-revolutionary *philosophes*).[84] Predictably, these utterances immediately lead another character, inflamed by the Revolution, to announce the opposite point of view, inadvertently pointing out yet another contradiction between language and fact in the process: "But that's, however, very strange, that, because we are, everyone says at the moment, in the century of lights [or what we call the Enlightenment]." It is then left to Mère Duchesne, in her rough patois with its phonetic misspellings and mistaken verb agreements, to cut through official speech and to set the record straight, explaining how she arrives at her superior understanding though she is only a woman of the people:

> Oh, if that's true, it is the devil who is holding the candle . . . that's clear because even with all their lights, we only ever see calamities everywhere, and I say it is not the good God who has made them. I is only a poor woman, I haves no intellect, I haves no understanding, [and] I haves never read no big books; but my reason tells me that all of this is a big muddle of bums and such that the devil and those rascals there have contrived.

In case any reader or listener missed the point, M. Lefranc responds, "You are absolutely right, Mother Duchesne," adding that her good sense is worth more than all the intellectual posturing of our "so-called *philosophes.*" From the point of view of M. Lefranc, the Revolution will one day offer a great lesson about what it means to have been governed by fake philosophers who are without faith, religion, manners, or common sense. But it is Mère Duchesne who is leading the battle.[85]

That this formula worked is evidenced by the imitators. Not only did the *monarchiens* and the Catholic right set to work producing their own versions of Père Duchesne in 1791 and, to a limited degree, early 1792, some of them to be distributed for free along with bread so as to reach as wide an audience as possible.[86] Mère Duchesne also became a hero of the right, appearing even in the *Acts of the Apostles,* while also being appropriated by the radical left and refurbished with a gun and a new revolutionary vocabulary starting in February 1791.[87] Other popular counterrevolutionary female characters, such as Mère Saumon, doyenne of the market, followed in this path, essentially inverting the formula of Olympe de Gouges. Even that semireal figure of the people, old Père Gérard, found himself in early 1792 outfitted with a royalist, Catholic wife, a Mère Gérard. Not only was she eager to show that the language of the Revolution signaled, from the perspective of the common sense of the countryside, a world that had been turned upside down, beginning with a Jacobin mayor called "Brûletout," or Burn-everything. She was also given the role of urging other women of the countryside, by means of simple analogies, proverbs, and definitions, to follow her example in setting their menfolk right and reestablishing "domestic happiness" through a return to the old order.[88] The populism of the right could be as socially expansive in its base as that of the left, extending in the era of the French Revolution to encompass women and rural peoples when politically sympathetic. It could also be as absolute in constructing categories of the excluded.

But the Buée brothers did not stop with Mère Duchesne in their campaign for common sense as a tool of populist reaction in confrontation with the institutions, laws, and language of the Revolution, from the Civil Constitution to the Jacobin clubs. Instead, they kept returning to this message while retrofitting it to a variety of ready, preexisting polemical genres, appropriating and inverting the often satirical or ironic forms staked out by d'Holbach, Voltaire, and others (not to mention their contemporary opponents) a quarter of a century earlier and giving them a wide reach. By the end of the eighteenth century, even activists on the right, eager to reverse social and cultural change, wanted to be able to generate and claim popular support for their cause. They found in common sense a particularly efficacious legitimating mechanism.

Like his predecessors and, indeed, many of his counter-revolutionary contemporaries, Adrien-Quentin Buée saw especially formidable opportunities in the radically simplified form of the dictionary. In early 1792, while all the while denouncing freedom of the press as the most dangerous of liberties, he also went on the attack with a satirical dictionary dedicated to "friends of religion, the king, and common sense." Buée's first goal was to show that, at the hands of the Revolution, language itself had been turned upside down, violating the laws of sensible usage and leaving only contradictions and absurdities in its wake. This he accomplished (like the authors of other virulently royalist and even *monarchien* dictionaries) with a series of logically illogical, deadpan definitions in the spirit of Voltaire or d'Holbach. *Refractaires,* for example, were in the present order "the name that one gives to priests who have refused the oath only in order to obey all laws." *Philosophes* were "prompters in the tragic-atrocious-absurd-comedy-parade called the Revolution." *Clubs* were "associations that have hatched the new constitution, which does not want any [associations]."[89]

Buée's second goal was then to show the nefarious effects on contemporary life of the acceptance of these nonsensical or inverted terms. Throughout his dictionary, he charged "the very syllables" that made up words from *aristocrat* to *ça ira* with nothing less than "producing the Revolution" and "changing the habits, prejudices, usages, passions, [and] manners of twenty-five million individuals and reversing the empire under which they have prospered for fourteen centuries."[90] That is, he linked the disruption of semantic sense with the disruption of actual common sense in daily existence. Fault, Buée insisted, lay not with the "the people" but with revolutionary leaders, who treated social life as if it were an abstract puzzle. As he explained in his dictionary's entry for "equality," "the National Assembly, in order to lead us to perfect equality, has imitated the monkey of Lamotte who, to make two morsels of cheese equal, always ate the excess of one to match the other, and never found perfect equality."[91] Here we are not so far from the critique of Edmund Burke or any number of French disciples who repeatedly stressed that regeneration in the name of reason and other abstract terms had produced nothing but the transgression of every kind of norm, including that of good sense.[92]

A similar plea of distress at the demise of both formal and customary or linguistic laws formed the basis of the appeal that Adrien-Quentin Buée's brother, Pierre-Louis, made that same winter directly to the laypeople of Paris. In a topsy-turvy world where the people were given the charge of choosing who was to govern them, and atheists and nonbelievers were to regenerate religion, among other absurdities, what, he asked his audience, was he to do? How could he, a priest, reconcile the fact that "conversion" required swearing to maintain the Civil Constitution of the Clergy—and thus endorsing this new world—with the fact of his deep commitment to "the rule of common sense [*une règle de sens commun*] that you must take care to follow [even] for the most minor temporal objects?"[93] The answer, of course, was that he could not.

The ultimate goal of both brothers' many polemical writings was to urge ordinary men and women to find a new source of authority and restraint in the most steadfast and quotidian of places: not simply tradition, or history, or even faith, but "good sense," which, in the words of Pierre-Louis Buée, remains "above you" and "must govern your heads" even when the people are mistakenly deemed sovereign.[94] For what both brothers ultimately saw in good or common sense was a synonym for the law in the absence of a formal legal system in which one could hold any faith. In Adrien-Quentin's counter-revolutionary dictionary, the article "law" can best be described as a tribute to the value of what is visible, consistent, long believed, and widely accepted without objection: in other words, common sense itself. This was the standard that his brother and he urged for decision making on every front. Indeed, it was the very same criterion for coming to sound conclusions upon which Adrien-Quentin was to insist just a few years later in one of his scientific treatises: a kind of probability about one fact following another that approaches certitude,

comparable to the assumption that the sun will rise tomorrow.[95] The
message of all of the Buée brothers' writings is that when formal regulations no longer exist to do what they should—when there are no legal
constraints on self-expression or even language itself—the self-regulating
rule of common sense becomes the only hope, the only way to restore
the undisputed norms and sense of normalcy that it is the job of common
sense to bolster. At the start of the 1790s, with the Revolution spinning in
unanticipated directions and expanding its reach into daily life and belief, common sense became a last-ditch stopgap, a plea for a socially imposed and popular mechanism of reaction in the absence of more traditional forms of regulation, whether royal or clerical or even customary.

This story is, however, ultimately rife with ironies. The Counter-
Revolution's strong defense of the self-evidence of hierarchy and established authority necessarily contained, from the beginning, an unavoid-
able concession that these values had become anything but. Not only
should such ideas require explicit defending. They should surely not
need to be presented to a broad public for its consideration and approval, particularly since the intended message was the unsuitability of
ordinary people to the judging process required by political life. Moreover, the case for the indisputability of these principles should not need
to be made in the fashion of English Protestants, anticlerical *philosophes,*
American revolutionaries, and, worst of all, terrorists: with the people's
common sense as its prop and chief authority. In this sense, the Counter-
Revolution may be said to have helped foster its own demise.

For in a further irony, the right-wing press, especially in its populist
incarnation, fell victim shortly thereafter to the very kind of formal legal
censorship of unpopular ideas of which it had long been in favor. The
state-sanctioned dismantling of royalist presses began in August 1792,
when the massacre at the Champ de Mars gave the Commune of Paris an
opportunity to shut down radical left-wing presses as well as royalist
ones. That month, Crapart's offices were sacked and his presses smashed,
and Crapart soon found himself in prison (though he was to survive the
Terror and return to counter-revolutionary publishing soon thereafter).[96]
The Buée brothers, Barruel, and many other right-wing journalists fled
abroad, just as Voltaire and radical writers had before them when faced

with the Old Regime's censorship apparatus. Counter-revolutionary publishing became an increasingly clandestine affair during the next few years, heading underground or overseas, especially to London.

One might thus be tempted to conclude that the lifespan of right-wing common sense populism in Paris was even shorter than that of left-wing common sense populism in Philadelphia fifteen years earlier. Populism is, after all, always a protest position and thus likely to diminish with time as it succeeds or is superseded. But, in fact, both versions produced lasting legacies, and not only in the cities of their origin. The Philadelphia-style crusade for the judgment of the working man, applied to a set of principles that should be self-evident to all, remained a staple of later movements for popular sovereignty and suffrage rights in Europe in 1830, 1848, and beyond. So, too, did right-wing populism find itself adaptable to new circumstances, first as an effect and then as a challenge to democratizing initiatives in the Atlantic world. The French Revolution, understood as the ultimate example of reason applied to politics without concern for common sense, would structure this international cleavage for decades to come.

In England, for example, where Burke had articulated a withering critique of excessive rationalism divorced from tradition, denouncing its "enthusiastic" propagators and its accompanying jargon in turn, the common sense of the English people became—once again in the 1790s—a contrasting refrain. That nation's proclivity for sensibleness was first turned against Tom Paine in the wake of the publication of his *Rights of Man, Part II* in early 1792. In tract after tract, the collective English people were called upon to stand up to those who, like Paine, "rejecting the plain and simple language of Common Sense" that was their birthright, "have bewildered themselves and their readers in the dark mazes of abstract theorems, and in the wily labyrinths of metaphysical disquisitions," hell-bent on French-style "universal destruction."[97] In a series of devastating caricatures and cartoons, England's leading graphic artists— Isaac Cruickshank, James Gillroy, and Thomas Rowlandson, among others—echoed this point, repeatedly displaying the tormented author of the *Rights of Man* wrestling with or perverting his beloved common sense rather than espousing it.

Then, with backing that stretched all the way to the upper reaches of the British government, this line of attack was generalized as a means to dissuade all in the English-speaking world who would defend the French Revolution—or fail to see Britain's existing political and legal system as, conversely, the very embodiment of common sense. In November 1792, a pro-government London newspaper ran an advertisement, placed by a former chief justice of Newfoundland named John Reeves, announcing the formation of the unwieldy-sounding Association for the Preservation of Liberty and Property against Republicans and Levellers. Over the next year, with support from high places, this anti-Jacobin movement morphed from a gathering of like-minded souls in a single London tavern into the largest political organization in England, with branches in the west, then the Midlands, north, and east and a surprisingly large popular following. Its (primarily middle-class) leadership urged its more socially heterogeneous adherents to undertake a certain amount of direct action of the sort that had become common to revolutionary and counter-revolutionary associations alike: rioting, acts of intimidation, the burning of undesirables like Paine in effigy. But mainly Reeves and his collabora-tors were attached to the power of print as a means of secular proselytiz-ing. Starting in the winter of 1792–1793, the Association for the Preser-vation of Liberty and Property against Republicans and Levellers became the leading sponsor, printer, and distributor of a wave of cheap tracts, addressed to the mechanics, day laborers, and journeymen of Great Britain, in which common sense stood for loyalism, national pride, and conservatism—in strict opposition to French "nonsense."[98]

And it was a real-life woman, Hannah More, who anonymously penned perhaps the most influential of these popular pamphlets touting common sense, *Village Politics,* just as Louis XVI's trial was progressing across the Channel. The recipe for this tract, which the Bishop of London called "better calculated for the understanding of the lower classes of the people than anything that has [y]et been published," was very close to something that might have been concocted by Buée.[99] Take two stock rural characters—one a pro-French villager who barely understands the Painite language he has picked up from reading "a book," the other a sensible English workingman who can expose the ludicrousness of everything the other espouses, from the pursuit of abstract equality to the value of philosophy to the ideal of perfection itself.[100] Then get them to converse about politics in the simplest of terms until they are both persuaded of the position of the sensible one (e.g., "Tom: What is it to be an enlightened people? Jack: To put out the light of the gospel, confound right and wrong, and grope about in pitch darkness."). No women figure in this dialogue. But More's idea, which she was to continue to advance for the rest of the century, was that, through everyday language and logic, and with a little help from influential female friends like the patroness Mrs. Montagu, a broad public could be persuaded of the perfect match between the status quo—including the existence of social distinctions—and its own native common sense.[101]

Reeves echoed many of the same points in his own writings, including his subsequent *Thoughts on English Government,* which he addressed to "the Quiet Good Sense of the People of England" in 1795. Common sense, not reason, was the great quality of the English people, possessed by all ranks. The obvious explanation for their happiness was that all of their institutions, including a mixed government and social inequality, had been shaped in the image of common sense. Now, in its typically unobtrusive fashion, common sense must become their guardian against French ways and ideas, which were absurd in principle and destructive in result.[102] For Reeves, as for More, the goal was to develop a new style of politics, aimed directly at "the people." Ordinary English men and women were to be simultaneously flattered into believing in "the [experiential] wisdom of the unlettered man" (as Burke put it, despite his antipathy to what he otherwise termed the "swinish multitude") *and* rendered politically impotent, convinced of the rightness of being represented by their social and economic betters in the difficult business of managing the state.[103] The end result was to win more adherents in the 1790s than either the more grandiose rhetoric of the elitist Burke or the demotic radical propaganda of Paine.[104]

Meanwhile, in the new United States, where the French Revolution also heated the temperature of political discourse and split the public into hostile camps, Federalists publically attacked their opponents as *philosophes,* shorthand for persons who were deeply invested in

French-style abstract theories to the detriment of what actually worked. Jefferson was a particular target for this kind of invective. According to Massachusetts Congressman Fischer Ames, Jefferson—like Condorcet, Marat, and Paine before him—had been carried away by system building and a zeal for generalization. The philosopher of Monticello had failed to proceed "like common men of practical sense, on the low, but sure foundation of matter of fact," and he had mistakenly treated the "plodding business of politics" as a matter of fine art. It all came down, once again, to a problem of optics: Jefferson, the visionary, observed the world at too great a distance from the eyes of the common man and consequently had lost touch with common sense. As Ames explained, "[Jefferson] sees the stars near, but loses sight of the earth; he sails his balloon into clouds and thick vapors, above his business and his duties, and if he sometimes catches a glimpse of the wide world, it seems flattened to a plain, and shrunk in all its proportions. . . . He strains his optics to look beyond its circumference, and contemplates invisibility, till he thinks nothing else is real."[105] Jefferson's chief crime, in other words, was failing to recognize that politics was best approached as a matter of simple, everyday perception and judgment.

The broad outlines of this form of attack against the overtly pro-French Jefferson had already been developed by the youthful John Quincy Adams. As early as 1791, under the pen name Publicola or Friend of the People, John Quincy Adams had published a series of letters in Boston's *Columbian Centinel* in which he not only denounced "visionary politicians" but also implied that the current secretary of state (Jefferson) was a wild, French-style revolutionary for appearing to have endorsed Paine's scandalously democratic and irreligious *Rights of Man, Part II*.[106] These essays were widely reprinted in the United States and Europe alike.

But then what goes around comes around. For out of this kind of anti-French Federalist oratory, a new tradition was born. The first true master of an American populist idiom, Andrew Jackson, was able, decades later in the presidential election of 1828, to present himself as a man of the people—and deride his opponent, John Quincy Adams, as an intellectual who had permanently lost sight of the practical reason of daily life, in contrast. In the telling of Jackson's supporters, the diplomat, professor, and ex-Federalist from the famous Boston family became an overly learned and unmanly cosmopolite, better suited to presiding over Harvard than the nation. The western Jackson, in contrast, fashioned himself as a latter-day Adario (Lahontan's idealized Huron chief), armed with nothing but experience and instinct and immune to the tortured reasoning of gentlemen, experts, and specialists on account of their money and book learning alike. Moreover, Jackson and his partisans successfully argued that his "American" common sense approach to knowledge was ultimately the perfect match for the questions confronting the young nation. As the Republican General Committee of the Young Men of the City and Country of New York put it in its campaign propaganda of 1828, "Jackson is recommended . . . by his *capacity.* He possesses in an extraordinary degree, that native strength of mind, that practical common sense, that power and discrimination of judgment which, for all useful purposes [that is, politics], are more valuable than all the acquired learning of a sage."[107]

In one sense, then, when Jackson emerged victorious over John Quincy Adams later that year, it represented what the historian Sean Wilentz calls "the culmination of more than thirty years of American democratic development."[108] The rise of Jackson to the presidency seemed to suggest the egalitarian ethos of Paine and the framers of the Pennsylvania Constitution finally coming to fruition. But the presidential election of 1828 also marked, it might be said, something else: the consolidation and triumph of a newer, reactionary-populist, style of politics born in the French Revolution's shadow and aimed at an ever-widening electorate to go along with it.

In the early nineteenth century, this right-wing, common sense mode was to gain new steam in Europe, too, often in the hands of the same people who invented it, like the Abbé Barruel, when they returned from exile to take up their pens once again. If the dominant myth of the American Revolution (like the Glorious Revolution before it) was that it constituted a revolution of common sense, the dominant myth of the French Revolution for Anglo-Americans, and for many early nineteenth-century Europeans as well, was that it had been directed against common sense—and that the restoration of the reign of this important source of knowledge and traditional social glue was the critical job for posterity. As one reactionary Dutch "friend of common sense" explained in 1809, the source of the problem went all the way back to the sophisms and paradoxes of Spinoza and Bayle, and the fight was not over yet.[109] That was to be the message of much subsequent populist politics.

Indeed, we might say that Napoleon Bonaparte, whose accumulation of power after the turn of the new century was to depend upon a series of symbolic plebiscites, represents a third or composite populist strain to emerge from the Age of Revolutions. Napoleon never turned his back on the revolutionary tradition of soliciting the people's support or speaking in their name; when necessary, he, too, could sound like a latter-day Paine. In Italy in the 1790s, he even adopted the still-controversial word "democracy" to describe his initiatives.[110] But at the same time, in keeping with the long-standing wishes of many counter-revolutionaries, he rejected the direct involvement of ordinary people or even their representatives in the business of political judgment. And he did so even as he courted their support. Napoleon's great innovation, as Alexis de Tocqueville was to underline later, was to make these two impulses compatible, that is, to keep alive the idea of unlimited popular sovereignty not despite but in the service of the curtailment of individual liberty and his own personal seizure of power.[111] He successfully mobilized "the people" in support of policies that disempowered them. And like all early populist regimes, Napoleon's was, regardless of its often autocratic tendencies, vital to the long-term growth of democracy in that it maintained the question of the proper relationship between common sense and expertise, or between "the people" and the state, at the forefront of public consciousness. Such problems would animate the rest of the nineteenth century.

CHAPTER 6

Königsberg to New York

The Fate of Common Sense in the Modern World

[C]ommon sense [is] the political sense par excellence.
Hannah Arendt, "Understanding and Politics"

J UST AS THE EVENTS OF 1789 were unfolding in France, a well-
known professor of logic and metaphysics at the University of Königsberg (today Kaliningrad) busied himself putting the finishing touches on
his third magnum opus. That professor was Immanuel Kant. The book
that appeared from a Berlin publishing house at Easter 1790 was his *Critique of Judgment (Kritik der Urteilskraft)*. What linked this difficult
philosophical tome with the distant rumblings of revolution was, in part,
Kant's effort to return the very old idea of *sensus communis* to the domain from which it had so egregiously escaped in recent years. Kant,
greatly excited about events in Paris some thousand miles away from
his coastal Baltic homeland, found in this Latin concept a means to
explain the social dimension of the act of judging. But the celebrated
philosopher also made abundantly clear that the workings of this public sense applied exclusively to the matters of aesthetic taste and properly played no role in moral or political determinations. In this regard,
Kant might be said to have ushered in the end of an era. Was this, in
fact, the case? Let us, in this final chapter, follow the story of common
sense episodically, from the 1790s to the present, in an attempt to
answer.

For Kant, common sense, in its by-then-ordinary meaning as either the elemental, shared assumptions or basic intellectual capacity of ordinary people, held no appeal as a philosophical principle. Despite his parallel situation as a professor in a provincial Protestant university town, and despite the fact that the Common Sense philosophy of Reid, Beattie, and Oswald had become well known in German lands over the previous few decades, Kant dismissed his Scottish colleagues' dependence on the authority of common sense in their responses to Hume.[1] In his *Prolegomena to Any Future Metaphysics,* written after his reading of Beattie in translation in the early 1780s, Kant had denounced the turn to ordinary common sense *(gemeinen Menschenverstand)* as a desperate appeal to the judgment of the masses in which "the popular charlatan glories."[2] Far from a tribunal of truth, common sense constituted to his mind little more than a rhetorical expedient that served to cut off critical investigation of knowledge claims; it might have its uses in judgments that applied immediately to experience, but it had no positive role to play in metaphysics. Similarly, in his *Critique of Judgment,* Kant complained that "common human understanding, which, as mere sound (not yet cultivated) understanding, is looked upon as the least that we can expect from anyone claiming to the name of man" now had "the doubtful honour of having the name of common sense bestowed upon it." To make matters worse, he continued in the same scathing vein, the meaning we give to "the word common (not merely in our own language, where it actually has a double meaning, but also in many others) . . . makes it amount to what is vulgar . . . a quality which by no means confers credit or distinction upon its possessor."[3] Philosophy was, for Kant, the son of an east Prussian master craftsman, not to be grounded in a popular principle. Nor was it to be a popular enterprise unto itself.[4]

Yet at the end of the 1780s, when this increasingly famous Prussian scholar took up the challenge of composing a companion volume to his celebrated critiques of pure and practical reason, he found an important use for the older notion that he continued to call by its Latin name, *sensus communis,* in an effort to distinguish it from what he took to be the colloquial meanings of its closest German synonyms. Returning to Shaftesbury, whose reflections on this subject at the other end of the century had already generated great interest among an earlier generation of German thinkers, including Thomas Abbt and Moses Mendelssohn, Kant insisted that the *sensus communis* is a "common" sense only insofar as it is communal.[5] Kant explained it, variously and perplexingly, as "the effect arising from the free play of our powers of cognition" and as "a critical faculty which in its reflective act takes account *(a priori)* of the mode of representation of everyone else, in order, as it were, to weigh its judgment with the collective reason of mankind."[6] In Kant's telling, all judgments of taste both depended upon and were actually synonymous with this kind of common sense.

On the one hand, Kant, ever focused on the individual, insisted on taste as a distinctly private matter. In Kant's view, judgments of beauty have their unique ground; they cannot be subsumed by either understanding or reason. In deciding on questions of beauty and sublimity, or what might otherwise be called aesthetic questions, the individual becomes aware of his or her freedom in relation to the physical world and also his or her freedom from any rule. That is precisely because judgments of taste are always highly personal, the product of singular sensory and emotional experiences and circumstances. They make manifest our subjectivity, our differences from others.

At the same time, though, these judgments can have no meaning or validity without other people. Indeed, in Kant's telling, in judging aesthetic matters we become unusually aware of our links to others. For we necessarily compare our own judgments with the (conjectural) "collective reason" of humanity as a whole. Though judgments of taste are perforce subjective, they always presuppose and refer to an ideal of universal assent, the possibility, if not the fact, of consensus among all. *Sensus communis* is ultimately the name that Kant gives to this faculty of judgment that leads us, without reflection, to make this comparison or to think from a universal standpoint. It is thus also the source of a social feeling, a sense of sharing something with others, that Kant described as the "necessary condition of the universal communicability of our knowledge."[7] And therein lies its importance: the *sensus communis,* or taste, illustrates the possibility of agreement founded on affective identification with the other, or intersubjectivity. It is a distinct way of knowing that has no rational ground. As such, it hints at the possibility of an undogmatic public sphere, a space of free discussion that is not mediated by any rule but in which the possibility of agreement always exists at least on the horizon. Kant's *sensus communis* can be read as a creative effort to imagine what might hold together a self-regulated community compatible with the opening salvos of the French Revolution.

And yet Kant was also very clear: the focus of the *sensus communis* is the judgment and appreciation of the beautiful. It can be activated only through participation in discussions of aesthetic questions and has no bearing on determinations of either truth or moral feelings. Despite the dominance of political and even legal metaphors in his account of taste, Kant does not offer in the *Critique of Judgment* a political philosophy to follow from this principle. The revolution in human rights that the Prussian state servant eagerly talked about "with great frankness and fearlessness" even at Königsberg's "noble tables" (as one contemporary noted in amazement) never explicitly entered this philosophical discussion.[8] On the contrary, Kant made explicit in the *Critique of Judgment* that he meant to restrict the purview of the *sensus communis,* or common sense, to the aesthetic alone.

What is also evident from the vantage point of history, however, is that he did not succeed in maintaining these limits either in practice or in theory. (And this is what will ultimately bring us back to Hannah Arendt, the greatest twentieth-century theorist of the politics of common sense.) Essentially, it was too late: Kant was engaged in a battle that had already been lost even though he was ultimately to challenge the philosophical orthodoxies of his own moment in numerous ways. The French Revolution politicized every dimension of European thought, including that of Kant himself, who soon turned to openly political subjects and endorsed the Revolution's intellectual program, with its emphasis on freedom of speech, even as he continued to reject the right of revolution on the part of the people.[9] Moreover, in the writings of his immediate disciples, the kind of judgment the sixty-six-year-old Kant associated with the aesthetic was pulled steadily toward the political, with various interpretations of common sense in tow.

To take one important example of how quickly common sense and politics rediscovered one another: just several years after the appearance of the *Critique of Judgment*, the celebrated dramatist Friedrich Schiller, then a professor at the University of Jena, published a series of letters on aesthetic education. In them, he built directly on Kant's conception of the *sensus communis* as both foundation and product of the appreciation of art. But Schiller refashioned this concept so as to make it the basis of a solution to what he took to be the key political problem posed by the French Revolution, namely, how to achieve popular sovereignty and social equality without a descent into violent struggle.[10] Schiller's *On the Aesthetic Education of Man in a Series of Letters (Brief über die aesthetische Erziehung des Menschen)* of 1795 is sometimes read as part of a particularly German retreat into the aesthetic, an abdication of political responsibility in favor of the cultivation of the few. Schiller was, after all, in no way a democrat; he found himself as alarmed by the actions and attitudes of the common man as most Enlightenment thinkers were, especially in light of the unfolding of the French Revolution beyond its earliest stages. Yet in what began in the summer of 1793 as a series of letters to a Danish prince who was also Schiller's patron, the German playwright and poet tried to imagine a new role for art in the modern world: as a means of transforming individuals so that they were ultimately prepared to craft a republic in which true equality would reign. In Schiller's hands, the contemplation of the beautiful object became not an entirely distinct mental activity from the contemplation of the moral or the political but rather a path to liberation, a way to draw people together and to renew the social order. Indeed, by the end of the published version of these letters, art has been established as the end as well as the means. The final "letter" concludes with a utopian vision of the "aesthetic state," a society governed by taste that, by bringing harmony between the rational and the sensible to each individual, brings harmony and equality to society as a whole and produces the triumph of common sense. As Schiller explained in grand fashion,

> No privilege, no autocracy of any kind, is tolerated where taste
> rules. . . . From the Mysteries of Science [i.e., Scholasticism], taste

leads knowledge out into the broad daylight of Common Sense [*Ge-meinsinn*], and transforms a monopoly of the Schools into the common possession of Human Society as a whole. In the kingdom of taste even the mightiest genius must divest itself of its majesty, and stoop in all humility to the mind of a little child. . . . In the Aesthetic State everything—even the tool which serves—is a free citizen, having equal rights with the noblest.[11]

That day has not yet arrived, nor is it even on the near horizon, Schiller was quick to point out. For now, it concerns but a tiny, rarified portion of the population. But here, in these pages, common sense, in opposition to the esoteric knowledge of "the Schools," paves the way to a more egalitarian and more just future.

And far from the domain of philosophy or poetry, Schiller's hunch that common sense would one day form the backbone of a new social order turned out to be right, though certainly not in the way he prophesied. In fact, common sense—both in the colloquial senses of the basic, shared assumptions or intellectual capacity of ordinary people *and* in the technical, philosophical sense of the presumed original bond of any community—was destined to venture in the opposite direction from where Kant had tried to push it. That is, it was to move increasingly into the political domain until, finally, it turned into such a frequent and unremarkable reference point for political life that commentators ceased to talk much about it. First an element of post-Aristotelian epistemology, then a mode of persuasion aimed at flattering the multitude about its own cognitive abilities and capacity to reimagine the world, common sense became, in the postrevolutionary era, an article of political faith. In the nineteenth century, it would simultaneously help redraw the social foundation of Western political life and play a key role in redefining the nature of politics itself. Fielding actually had it right back in 1736 when he insisted that though Queen Common Sense might be killed off in spectacular ways at particular moments in time, she was destined, as an ideal, to haunt the modern world. The concept of common sense, as first imagined in various eighteenth-century European and colonial cities, has continued to shape the nature of democratic politics, at some moments as stimulus, at others as foil. The practice of democratic politics has, meanwhile, permanently altered our own common sense.

The template for what would later be termed populism, with its (sometimes explicit, sometimes indirect) hallmark appeal to the collective common sense of the "true" people, was already in place at the opening of the nineteenth century. Soon it would be adopted by a wide variety of different political constituencies armed with mutually exclusive agendas and vocabularies.[12] What makes it possible to talk about the endurance of a particular "common sense" style of politics, across two centuries of scientific and philosophical ruptures and the obvious divisions of religion, ideology, nation, language, and social group, is the continued existence of a few basic suppositions for which the groundwork had been laid in the revolutionary as well as counter-revolutionary ferment of the previous century.

One of these suppositions is that "the people" or "citizens" in the aggregate possess something called common sense, born of their common experiences and shared faculties as humans, that is not to be confused with individual reason, though the two might coincide at moments. (It is the indistinctness and even hypothetical nature of this kind of common sense that makes it not as far from Kant's *sensus communis* as is often supposed.) Another is that the realm of politics or governance, when properly defined, squares perfectly with the people's common sense judgments and the basic axioms derived thereof. Or to put it differently, arriving at good and universally applicable solutions to real political problems is often simply a matter of listening to the collective common sense and ignoring outlying opinions. As one conservative English commentator, wondering in the late nineteenth century whether it were possible to constitute an actual Party of Common Sense, noted bluntly: "on the whole, the stupid people have been right; and even the clever people are now beginning to find out that in politics very little cleverness suffices; for politics is nothing more than knowledge of human nature applied to the safety and welfare of the state."[13]

These optimistic assumptions about both human nature and the nature of politics then typically culminated in a kind of cheerful faith in the future, even when, rhetorically, common sense was invoked in anger about the absence of the recognition of these truisms in the present world. The final supposition is that when these (still unheeded) facts about the mental acumen of the "real" people are finally recognized, strife in politics will end. Then the reign of universal contentment and social harmony, apart from party or creed or class interest, will begin. None of these claims should, by this point in our account, seem unfamiliar.

And yet, the social context in which this approach to politics could be deployed was to change dramatically in the northern Atlantic world in the course of the nineteenth century. The result was that the nascent mythology of a future politics rooted in common sense was to prove increasingly useful from the 1830s in the United States and the 1840s in Europe onward. Two broad developments, neither of them occurring in a straight, unabated line and both of them simultaneously dependent on and generative of the exaltation of a politics of common sense, played a central role in this story.

The first is the expansion of the definition of citizenship and, with it, the expansion of the franchise or opportunity to vote. Across the area that was coming to be known as "the West," the great issue of the nineteenth century has sometimes been said to be democracy and its dangers or, more specifically, the fitness of white men of the laboring classes, not to mention women, people of color, the impoverished, and other types of legally dependent peoples, for the job of political judging.[14] Much handwringing accompanied early efforts to decipher exactly what knowledge, experience, and cognitive capacity an individual would need to exhibit in order to have an aptitude or even minimal qualifications for voting. Fear concentrated on the question of what might happen should large numbers of the ignorant, illiterate, confused, misled, or even apathetic—in other words, the majority of the population—decide to weigh in on the critical issues of the day or, more often, the choice of representatives charged with confronting the critical issues of the day. Even those ostensibly sympathetic to the democratic idea could not shed the anxiety that anarchy, physical assault, and the destruction of private property were the only likely result. As Alexis de Tocqueville remarked in an 1841 manuscript fragment, "I have an intellectual preference for democratic institutions but . . . I hate demagogy, the disordered action of the masses, their violent and uneducated participation in [public] affairs," a sentiment shared by many anti-populists to this day.[15] Gradually, though—in some places as a result of popular agitation, in others as a result of imperial decree—the idea of universal manhood suffrage won the day. It happened in America in the 1830s (if one overlooks exclusions based on race, which lasted in practice until the Voting Rights Act of 1965); in France in 1852 (following several abortive earlier attempts); in England over a series of bills in 1832, 1867, 1884, and into the twentieth century; in Germany in 1867; in Spain in 1890; in Italy in 1912; and in the Netherlands not until 1918. In other words, nation by nation in the course of the century that followed the French Revolution, "the people" ceased to be simply objects of political rhetoric and became subjects of political action, collectively and individually.[16] What had been a revolutionary condition—the political mobilization of the masses—became an element of daily life. Moreover, the subset of the people known as "citizens" itself eventually grew to encompass whole categories of individuals who had previously been excluded. Over time that included the poor or propertyless, the nonwhite, and finally (in most cases, not until well into the twentieth century) women—even as all sorts of new and entrenched hierarchies remained essential to the world outside the voting booth.

The second, not unrelated, development of importance for the political history of common sense is institutional. The nineteenth century saw the rise across the Americas and Europe of a host of new institutions whose primary function was to win the allegiance of these same individuals whom enfranchisement had transformed from observers to potential political participants. The list includes political parties, social clubs and workers' organizations, and public schools. It also includes an increasingly unfettered commercial press. The communication, transportation, and consumer revolutions of the nineteenth century, not to mention the accompanying invention of leisure time, cannot be separated from the expansion of the realm of politics both in terms of people and in terms of space. Consider the entrance into everyday, urban life of mass rallies and demonstrations, of leafleting, of election campaigns complete with parades, handshaking, and baby kissing. Many elites, including those who positioned themselves in liberal as well as conservative camps, surely resented having to work so hard to mobilize voters in whom they had little faith. Yet on all sides it was conceded well before the end of the century that new strategies were necessary for reaching this expanding public of readers and voters, teaching them how to exercise their new political rights, and then persuading them of one point of view or another—while still promising the eventual harmony of the body public as a whole.

The appeal to common sense, as originally formulated in the eighteenth-century Atlantic world, offered one potentially highly effective means to political leaders or pundits, whatever their class background, who found themselves courting an amorphous popular constituency in the new consumerist world of electoral politics.[17] This was especially true at moments of crisis in the ongoing revolution of human rights begun in the previous century. For questions of human rights immediately opened up questions of epistemology on two levels. The first had to do with mental capacity: can the individuals who make up the subset of "the people" being considered for admission to the political nation (peasants, the working poor, blacks, women, or any other subordinate identity group) judge properly themselves? That is, do they have the ability to make the common sense determinations essential to meaningful participation in the political process and the production of good outcomes? The second had to do with the nature of knowledge: insofar as we are talking about a basic question about human nature and right and wrong, is not the answer to the preceding question itself self-evident, at least for all reasonable people?

The year 1848, the next great moment of transnational and potentially democratic European revolution after the 1790s, provides a case in point. At stake everywhere from Paris to Naples to Berlin was the abstract question of how much political power should be accorded to ordinary people, generally meaning urban working men and men of the peasantry. Conservatives and liberals alike insisted on the need for limits to enfranchisement, not least for reasons of stability; government, it was still argued in the spirit of John Adams, was best left to those of superior means, social status, professional experience, or time for learning (which were all typically one and the same). But radicals, now including socialists as well as republicans, demanded universal manhood suffrage, a position that required explicit justification given the lingering bad reputation (outside North America) of democracy as but another name for anarchy or mob rule. And where this left-wing ambition actually became the law of the land—France, initially in the midst of the tumult of 1848—these new voters had to be appealed to, cajoled, and ultimately convinced of what was in their best interest. Good sense or common sense worked on both fronts, anchoring a burgeoning language of mass persuasion.

As in 1776 and 1789, good or common sense was trotted out in mid–nineteenth-century France both as an authoritative source of specific political stances and as the promised result of those same political stances, should the intended audience vote the correct way. Authors claiming this mantle continued to paint themselves as disinterested, humble, nameless members of the crowd. "I am nothing," without education or riches, announced the voice behind *The Good Sense of the People (Le Bon Sens du Peuple)* (1849), before pointing out that despite his suffering, he was in possession of the "ray of light of His [God's] wisdom" necessary for talking about "national issues."[18] From this common vantage point, whether God-given or natural, these same authors could then legitimate begging the attention of similar folks—those, in the words of the author of *Socialism in Confrontation with Popular Good Sense (Le Socialisme devant le bon sens populaire)* (1849), "without the time to read big books" but who could, without stopping working, "discern the true from the false."[19] The promise was the production of a politics rooted in simple language and their mutually agreed-upon ideals. Before insisting that the solution to their troubles lay in good behavior, hard work, and perseverance, not socialism, the author of a tract called *Socialism and Common Sense (Socialisme et sens commun)* (1849) declared with only a touch of condescension: "I have found, in consulting only the simple lights of common sense, what the simplest laborer or the least educated worker would also have found, just like me, if he had the leisure to devote himself to the same examinations."[20] In the new world of political advertising and competition, the cult of the common man—the tribune of the people—was on the ascendancy in direct proportion to the growing distrust of the professional politician.[21] For whether good sense meant expanding suffrage in anticipation of "universal conciliation"[22] or rejecting the nonsense of the new in favor of a preexisting solidarity across classes, common sense's perceived antagonists remained the same: fancy folks, insiders, charlatans, journalists, but also parties, coteries, divisions of opinion, excessive production of print, the seductive powers of money, big words, complexity, exaggeration, and ingenious, unrealistic theories. Reflecting on what had become of politics as of late, the author of *A Whit of Good Sense* (*Un grain de bon sens*) of 1849 exclaimed quite typically: "what a shower of manifestos, what abundance of circulars, what obscure, tangled, insignificant phraseology, when our health depends on clarity, uprightness, and sincerity!"[23] And in the end, the promise remained the same as well, even as elections made explicit the competitive basis of politics and the threat of class war became increasingly real.

The popular Parisian journalist Emile de Girardin put it this way early in 1848, after denouncing a past politics built on duplicity and individual genius: "Nothing is more radical *and* more conservative than Good Sense. Good Sense is radical because what it wants is the reform of all abuses, the abandonment of all errors. Good Sense is conservative because what it wants is the conservation of all that pertains essentially to the duration of societies, the well-being of peoples, the progress of civilization."[24] In other words, good sense stood for the meeting point of left and right, progressive and traditional, rich and poor, the very point at which such terms would become meaningless. In response to railroads, steam engines, an improved post office, electric telegraphs, and the press and its advertisements, Girardin claimed, politics was on its way to becoming simpler, easier—and more and more suited to the people's good sense and good faith alike. What was new was really only the scope of common sense's potential reign. Even if it remained fashionable in France to despair over the banishment of an allegorical "King Good Sense" from the realm of politics, it was becoming increasingly axiomatic, even among anti-democrats, that only his return would save the nation and end politics in its current agonistic form.[25] To not only the immediate benefit of the tide of democracy but also to the ultimate advantage of all forms of populist politics, the nameless multitude was well on its way to becoming the imagined source of all legitimate and effective political solutions. By the middle of the nineteenth century, common sense was what dictated the establishment of democracy, and common sense was what democracy would—theoretically—produce.

But soon new questions emerged in the realm of practical politics: Who exactly was the universal man behind the collective common sense?[26] Just how expansive was this political community to be? The difficulties attendant upon answering proved particularly acute in the new United States. For there the clash between the republican and human rights principles of the founding creed, on the one hand, and the continued existence of chattel slavery, on the other, soon necessitated new thinking about what qualified one, or not, for the prerogatives of citizenship or even manhood. In particular, such questions demanded novel intellectual resources for those determined to justify the maintenance of the peculiar institution. Here is where common sense once again mattered on two levels.

The struggle over the legitimacy of slavery and, more specifically, over the exclusion of men of color from the rights and prerogatives associated with citizenship, focused almost immediately on questions of human nature or psychology. In the intensified search for justifications for slavery, it was always possible to turn to traditional authorities: history or scripture, for example. A key strategy on the part of slavery's defenders was, however, to consider the emotional and cognitive capacity of the black man or woman, much as Jefferson had done back in the 1780s in his *Notes on the State of Virginia*.[27] Well into the nineteenth century, this approach typically involved reasserting traditional notions of dependency, which is to say the linkage of intellectual and moral incapacity to economic subordination. The same logic applied to women, children, and household servants; denying them the full attributes of personhood functioned as an effective way to keep them out of the body politic and away from the vote. But increasingly in the antebellum period, in popular and scientific discourse alike, claims of dependency were naturalized and rendered commonsensical as an attribute of something called "race" that people of color possessed whether they were enslaved or not.[28] This meant that white as well as black abolitionists tended to spend much of their energy in the first half of the century asserting the opposite against prevailing (white) sentiment: the universality of human intellectual and moral capacity and the possibility—with a change in material and educational circumstances—of former slaves joining the family of men endowed with civil and political rights.[29]

However, a second wave of nineteenth-century Anglo-American abolitionists, under the sway of a combination of evangelical Protestantism and the Common Sense philosophy of the Scots, challenged this whole line of reasoning, at least rhetorically. Rather than simply make logical arguments about the capacity of people of color to employ common sense, they declared that the problem of slavery could be solved by actually following the precepts of common sense: theirs and that of all other citizens, if they would only take the blinders away from their eyes. For the moral wrong of slavery belonged to the category of truths that should feel so self-evident or instinctively correct to all sensible people that it precluded the need for demonstration at all.

James Beattie himself had made this case repeatedly throughout his career. In his late *Elements of Moral Science* (1793), he had insisted, "It is impossible for the considerate and unprejudiced man to think of slavery without horror. . . . In arguing against slavery, it may perhaps be thought that I dispute without an opponent."[30] From the 1830s onward, abolitionists throughout the Anglophone world borrowed this approach of the Scots, backed up by both biblical aphorisms and the alleged "self-evidence" of the principles of the Declaration of Independence, to similar ends. From the black American abolitionist (and former slave) J. W. C. Pennington, who told a cheering English crowd in 1843 that the "monopoly of suffrage [by the white man] was an insult to common sense," to the editor of the *Fitchburg Daily* of Massachusetts, who made the paper's motto in the early 1850s that "No person of common sense will deny that slavery is the greatest curse on earth, next to Romanism," the future of the slaveholding system was transformed by the midcentury into another one of those weighty political questions that really required nothing more to solve than the application of the people's common sense.[31] The *Anti-Slavery Manual* (1848) of the Southern abolitionist preacher John Fee was typical in this regard; after festooning his title page with a citation from Isaiah 5:20 that seemingly disparaged those who attempt to confuse the categories of common sense ("Woe to them that call evil good, and good evil; That put darkness for light, and light for darkness"), Fee introduced his text with a quotation from "Prof. Miller [*sic*] of Glasgow." The quote, which would seem to mitigate against the long discussion that was to follow, read, "The human mind revolts at a serious discussion of the subject of Slavery. Every individual, whatever be his country or complexion, is entitled to freedom."[32] More influentially, from the very first issue of the fiery abolitionist journal the *Liberator* (1831–1865), the fabled abolitionist William Lloyd Garrison took the same line and made the Declaration of Independence his touchstone, openly admiring its authors' conviction that there were some wrongs that they deemed "so palpable as to scorn to argue the matter," even as they (and he) championed free inquiry and debate. For as Garrison put it in a later essay, "However perplexing in casuistry some questions may be, there are such things as 'self-evident truths'; there are some human duties too plain to be mistaken. THE SLAVE IS A MAN!"[33]

Such declarations, of course, posed the immediate question of why so many felt and behaved differently, of why the subject of slavery had, to date, produced nothing but strife. Fee, Garrison, and others responded by blaming recognizable enemies of common sense: not human nature or mass behavior but rather circumstances external to "the people," including corrupting institutions (schools and courtrooms among them), the self-interest of social and political elites, and especially the euphemistic, mystifying language of slavery's apologists.[34] Then these abolitionists returned to the old claim that a nation's political discourse, as well as its laws, must stem from the simple, self-evident, and consensual moral-intellectual domain that they called common sense. Only then would harmony and justice prevail. The problem was that slavery's justifiers had little trouble proposing the same, appealing to the common sense of the American public to grasp the obvious point that "until the leopard can change his spots and the Etheopian [*sic*] his skin, white men and negroes must act in different spheres, unless one is subordinate to the other."[35]

The American women's movement, whose roots both organization-
ally and rhetorically were firmly planted in the abolitionist movement,
found itself in similar straits around the end of the century. In 1894, the
well-known women's rights activist Thomas Wentworth Higginson tried
taking up every objection to granting women the vote—including the
traditional notion that "women don't have enough sense to vote"—and
debunking each in turn. He then titled his compilation *Common Sense
about Women*, suggesting that none of this was (or should be) very controversial in the first place.[36] That same year, the prominent New York physician Mary Putnam Jacobi insisted that the cause of women ran parallel
to that of the insurgents of the American Revolution; it pitted those few
women who naïvely believed that "as soon as we saw that woman's suffrage was right, everyone would soon see the same thing" against "the
entire organized system of traditions, beliefs, prejudices, convictions,
habits, laws, and customs which has hitherto existed from the beginning
of history down to the year of grace, 1848 [the moment of the first wom-
en's rights convention as well as various European revolutions]." To help
bridge this divide, she penned the important suffragist tract *"Common
Sense" Applied to Woman Suffrage; a Statement of the Reasons Which
Justify the Demand to Extend the Suffrage to Women*, consciously echo-
ing and quoting Paine throughout.[37] As the editor of the second edition
put it in 1915, this essay reaffirms "all that is universally and permanently
true with respect to the claims of women for enfranchisement."[38] But
such claims aside, opponents of suffrage also fixed on this traditional
ground of persuasion in feminine prescriptive literature, seeing no contradiction in appealing to female as well as male readers to use their common sense to see the dangers of expanding the franchise to impulsive,
highly emotional people like themselves.[39] (As we have seen, reactionary
forms of populism often simultaneously expand roles for women in the
public sphere in practice and reinforce traditional gender distinctions
and divisions in theory.) As in the debate about slavery, the struggle over
female suffrage suggests that common sense could work equally well to
prop up efforts at increased democratization or to undercut them, to
render obvious the similarity of all humans (not least in possessing common sense) and to reaffirm ostensibly self-evident distinctions rooted in
race, gender, religion, or nationality.

Indeed, it was the rising tide of nationalism that seemed, by the turn of the new century, to mark the culmination of a politics of an ever-protean, populist common sense. Partly this impulse to attach the cause of "the nation" to the rule of common sense originated among those who still felt unheard and unseen by ruling forces. Resentment in the American Heartland at the concentration of wealth and power in the cities of the Eastern Seaboard, for example, fueled an unprecedented third-party protest movement in the early 1890s with the striking name of the People's or Populist Party. The promise held out by the party's leaders was that national unity, or government built on "the love of the whole people for each other and for the nation" across the divisions of class and region, if not race and religion, was no longer out of reach. Neither was the end of all forms of oppression. The solution lay, as in all subsequent populist movements with a patriotic dimension, in (re)establishing the isomorphism between the common sense of the nation and the work of the state. What was needed, according to the preamble to the party platform read in the midwestern city of Omaha before a crowd of thousands on the highly symbolic date of July 4, 1892, was twofold. Politics had to be "restored" to "the hands of the 'plain people,' with which class it originated"—a coded way of signaling hardworking Protestants of all classes but also leaving out foreigners and people of color, on the one hand, and East Coast "millionaires," on the other. Then the power of the federal government had to be extended "as rapidly and as far as the *good sense of an intelligent people and the teachings of experience* shall justify."[40] The advertised result would be a new kind of postpolitical politics, a politics of national reconciliation.

But by the turn of the century, the notion of the common sense of the people—known increasingly as the nation—was also being appropriated by political leaders already in power, not just those fighting for access or greater responsiveness. And ultimately the value of the common sense of the nation became part of the creed of the modern state itself, which eagerly tried to promote loyalty and social cohesion among the newly politicized masses regardless of whether that state had more authoritarian or more democratic tendencies. Common sense can, as we have seen, be called upon and used as a conceptual tool in the creation of communities out of strangers; as such, it proved a boon to government servants eager to break down old right-left divides and to foster national integration as a universalizing political project. But it can also serve a narrowing, restrictive function, highlighting the common sense of particular peoples in opposition to the perceived nonsense of others.[41] Recall the long tradition of British, American, and even German claims of exceptionality based on a purported national tendency toward a special purchase on common sense (usually meaning a tendency toward valuing practicality and lived experience over "theory," but also signaling a taste for their own norms over those of competing nations).[42] For evocations of common sense always imply an Other, a shared antagonist outside the boundaries of this sense—whether the proponent is Fielding, Paine, Hannah More, or, most recently, Sarah Palin. One of the leitmotifs of populist thought, after all, is the division of the world into two opposing camps, even as one claims to be the whole.[43] In the late nineteenth century, the excluded were simply defined in ever more xenophobic terms, making the foreigner (whether as immigrant or as colonial subject or as racial minority) into the new associate of the banker, the philosopher, and the opposing party politician in common sense's enemy camp, even by those on the inside.

And as we approach World War I, we can see heads of state and government spokesmen across Western Europe as well as the United States using, encouraging, affirming, and even celebrating common sentiments, habits, and prejudices, along with explicit customs and traditions, to define, at once, the particular and the universal elements of specific national peoples. Vico had, long before the age of nationalism, imaged the *sensus communis* as holding together nations, or groups of people, prior to the imposition of politics. This sense of union is just what seemed to come to fruition simultaneously, on the eve of war, in formal and informal political spheres alike, as ordinary citizens became fascinated with the virtual image of themselves as part of a single people, the bearers of a shared set of national values and common categories for making sense of the world around them. It is enough to recall the famous descriptions of the "August Days" of 1914, when German citizens, upon hearing the news of the declaration of war against Serbia and Russia and then France and Britain, filled the streets of Germany's main cities in what one historian calls "an upsurge of popular nationalism . . . in which differences of class, confession, and region seemed erased and the people, the *Volk*, appeared to be all of one piece."[44] By the start of the twentieth century, the nationalist state and its outreach institutions, from mass parties to public schools, had made it their business to craft a new, integrated sense of national belonging through rhetoric, symbols, and rituals alike.[45] And as these norms were internalized in the years leading up the outbreak of the war, the existence of distinct nations with distinct cultures, like the existence of distinct races and sexes, became a fact beyond dispute, widely accepted across all other lines of division, and a key feature of a burgeoning democratic common sense.

World War I is, however, a turning point in our story. Among the many profound shocks it delivered to European and American consciousness, not least was the shock to the idea that politics and common sense had something important to do with one another. When Voltaire's hero Candide wanders the globe in the mid-eighteenth century, he is gradually disabused of all of his acquired platitudes about everything in the world happening for a legitimate, comprehensible reason. What he discovers is a world governed by greed, meanness, base drives, dogma, and prejudices disguised as truth. So it was for many people, reeling even before the war was over from the seeming senselessness of it all. Modernity, with its crowd-pleasing politicians, mass parties, advanced technology, addiction to entertainment and advertising, love of consumption, and sophisticated financial industry, had seemingly left little but mass destruction and carnage in its wake. Such disillusionment generated a crisis that was at once moral and epistemological, a collective version of the experience of Candide: the shattering discovery of the vast hypocrisy and untruth hiding behind bourgeois rationality and regulatory systems.

How, then, could common sense—the great foundation of modern "enlightened" politics and morality—be resurrected in the war's aftermath? One of the most important collective answers, partly German but really international in inspiration, was that it could not. The artistic and literary movement known as Dada was born of disillusionment and anger at the state of the modern world. But rather than propose a withdrawal from mass politics into the private and subjective or even the aesthetic *sensus communis* of Kant and Schiller, the artists and writers associated with the Dada movement from the war years into the 1920s energetically pursued an alternative course. Facing the modern world head on, they advocated an intense confusion of the boundaries between art and politics and a concerted effort to undermine the very norms, values, and language of the dominant culture, right down to its attachment to the term "common sense" to describe any of these qualities.

Dada came into being as the brainchild of a multilingual group of antiwar refugees and expatriate artists and intellectuals who found themselves spending the war years in the politically neutral city of Zurich, a place of escape and political refuge much like Amsterdam two centuries earlier. Their point of contact was not, though, a printing shop. Instead it was a bar located in a seedy entertainment district renamed for the occasion in honor of the greatest of the eighteenth century's parodists and deflator of pieties, Voltaire. The writer Hugo Ball later referred to the cabaret as "our kind of Candide against the times."[46] There, in the so-called Cabaret Voltaire, Ball, along with the poets Tristan Tzara, Emmy Hennings, and Richard Huelsenbeck and the artists Hans Arp and Marcel Janco, created a space for a small alternative community of performers and audience to take form. The thrust of their collective efforts was, however, hardly communal in spirit. Dada represented an unmitigated assault on all collective values or norms, including the very possibility of meaningful communication or community building in the present world. Through inexplicable performances and bodily gestures, bizarre costumes, and the recitation of poems without obvious meaning because they were in three languages simultaneously or made up only of nonsensical sounds or constructed by chance, the pioneers of Dada joyfully challenged existing codes of representation and communication ("the foundations of the civilization responsible for the war" down to "speech, syntax, logic," in the words of Max Ernst, writing much later of Dada in Cologne[47]). What linked these spectacles was the idea that the subversion of "sense" and the undermining of comprehension were the starting point for undoing all structures of authority, including that of the dominant common sense, much as they had been for d'Holbach and Vol-

taire a century and a half before. This is not to say that the originators of
Zurich Dada put their stock in the Enlightenment *tout court*. With their
nonmimetic language and imagery, the original Dadaists sought nothing
less than to liberate their small, shell-shocked public from the oppressive, inherited, bourgeois *Begriffswelt,* or conceptual world, of the early
twentieth century and all that came with it. That included its hypo-
critical moral platitudes, its outdated social conventions, its misleading
words, images, and gestures, and its everyday, habitual assumptions
about the nature of things that ran counter to real experience.[48]

Like Kant, Dada's originators put no stock in populist pandering.
They saw themselves as outsiders, immersed in the modern world, on the
side of the mythic "people" but also critically distant from them, playing
the role once accorded to the madman, the idiot, the savage, or the clown
and more recently accorded to the avant-garde. Unlike Kant, they expressed deep skepticism about any collective judgments, moral, political,
or aesthetic, in a social order for which they had nothing but disdain.
Even the appeal of the term Dada stemmed from its suggestion of nonref-
erentiality and absurdity, the end of collectively agreed-upon meaning
and consensual truth. Dada "signifies nothing" according to Romanian
immigrant and Dada impresario Tristan Tzara. It is a signifier without a
signification, an emblem of noninstrumental speech. As Tzara further
clarified (or not) in his "Dada Manifesto," a declaration of purpose otherwise built out of contradictions and semantically mystifying statements
that he first read in July 1918 at the Cabaret Voltaire: "I do not explain
myself because I hate common sense [*gesunden Menschenverstand*]."[49]

Tzara's text, once published in *Dada 3,* one of many nascent Dada
propaganda vehicles, functioned as the advance notice of a new cultural
movement. And in the aftermath of the war, Dada would spread beyond
expatriate centers like Zurich and, later, New York, to the heart of urban
Europe, its preoccupations and techniques expanding along with its geographical boundaries. In Berlin, once the chief city of Kant's Prussia and
now the capital of Weimar Germany, the parodic and anti-authoritarian
strain of Dada would also leave the enclosed space of the cabaret to begin the work of dismantling the boundaries between art and life, including the mass media and parliamentary politics, where common sense

had for some time made its home. Tzara and Austrian anarchist Walter
Serner had already taken advantage back in Zurich of the gullibility of the
press, steadily feeding it with false, sensational news. Now Berlin Dada,
relying on techniques borrowed from the world of political parties, advertising, and newspapers but without the standard appeal to or representation of "the people," explicitly made art into politics and politics
into art, directly provoking ever larger urban crowds with challenges to
the sense perception and judging capacities of the modern human brain.

In early 1918, against the backdrop of the revolutionary insurrections
and street fighting that accompanied the birth of the Weimar Republic,
Raoul Hausmann and Huelsenbeck announced in the Berlin press the
formation of a "Club Dada" that was open to everyone, across nations
and all other divides. All that was required was a common commitment to a certain "state of mind." We might well recall here the "common sense clubs" imagined at similar moments of strife in the pages of
London's *Spectator* at the beginning of the eighteenth century or Paris's
revolutionary press at that century's end. On this occasion, though, the
shared purpose was not to be the overcoming of division and conflict but
rather the "tearing to pieces of all the platitudes of ethics, culture, in-
wardness which are merely cloaks for weak muscles," as Huelsenbeck
put it in his "Collective Dada Manifesto" of that same year.[50] Club Dada
took as one of its major goals the disruption of the familiar, clichéd rhetoric, symbols, institutions, and ritual gestures of modern mass politics
and capitalist public life, primarily by means of parody or subversion. And
in this, neither painting nor poetry nor performance proved effective
enough by itself. Political common sense needed to be tackled head on.

One strategy associated with Club Dada involved the production of
fake candidates for office, fake bureaucracies and parties, fake rallies,
and fake political propaganda (much of it fed, once again, to an unsus-
pecting mainstream press). Johannes Baader, a key participant in Club
Dada, remade himself as a phony politician with the fabulous name "Ober-
dada" and deemed himself nothing less than President of the World and
Commander of the Empire of the Soul (when he was not insisting that he
was Christ or demanding the Nobel Prize for Dadaists). Public announcements of pseudo-institutions mocking their real-life, bourgeois

counterparts followed: the Dada Sex Center and the Dada Institute for the Dissolution of Countries, among them. Another method was to re-produce the banal, nationalist rituals of public life while simultaneously undermining them by mixing them with incongruous elements. Why else did Baader, when he presented himself as a candidate for the Reich-stag, donate a large picture of Schiller to the National Assembly with an inscription prophesying the destruction of the Weimar Republic? Why else would Walter Mehring have given his "New German Anthem" the subtitle "Coitus in the House of Three Lasses"? Not even revolutionary republicanism was given a pass. Perhaps most spectacularly, on April 1, 1919, Hausmann and Baader declared the wealthy Berlin suburb of Niko-lassee a "dada republic" to demonstrate how a republic might be founded "with nothing but a typewriter," an act that caused the mayor to call out 200 soldiers to protect the town hall.[51]

All of this could be seen as simply a series of stunts by an antinational-ist, more or less communist avant-garde invested in invented personas, mock rituals, and satirical humor of different sorts, a kind of early per-formance art designed primarily to *épater le bourgeois*. But by introduc-ing a politics of nonsense, that is, a politics that not only aggressively dramatized the absurdity and hypocrisy of contemporary political life but also actively tried to overthrow existing structures of thought and action through unreasonable behavior and language, Dadaists offered the first concerted, collective challenge to a politics of common sense that had been developing for the previous 200 years. Indeed, Dada can be seen as a profound assault on the nature of politics altogether in the age of democracy. No actual political movement, right or left, came any-where near such a radical revolt against any of the dominant creeds, with their populist trappings and potentially phony faith in "the people," prog-ress, and collective sense, that early into the twentieth century. (And it is worth bearing in mind that populist imagery and tropes were to attach themselves to authoritarian and democratic regimes with equal ease in the first half of the twentieth century—with often catastrophic results.[52]) Arguably, Dada set the terms for all subsequent avant-garde resistance movements that were at once political and aesthetic in orientation, move-ments that would, well beyond World War II and into the second half of the twentieth century, reject mass support and appeals to mass reason and turn in their stead to the counter-strategies of absurdism, irrationality, or the surreal.

And yet, in the aftermath of the horrors of World War II and then the beginning of the atomic age, something quite unanticipated happened. North American and Western European interests manufactured a revival of common sense, that increasingly clichéd product of the "true" people. They did so in a self-conscious effort to provide support for representative democracy in the wake of its confrontation with the evils of fascism, on the one hand, and Stalinism, on the other. This revival happened on the level of rhetoric and political praxis. It also occurred on a theoretical one.

In the second half of the twentieth century, common sense became, more than ever, a way to sell products and policies. As Michael Kazin points out in his history of populism in America, "defining what the people want and then selling it to them has long been the forte of both merchandisers and politicians."[53] After the war, this lesson was absorbed by Europeans as well.[54] Common sense became a lasting critical tool in a populist rhetorical arsenal available from main streets to capital cities in all mass consumer societies. (At the start of the twenty-first century, "Le Gros Bon Sens," once a slogan of French revolutionary politics, has become a character, described in the promotional material as "a typical consumer," with "no pretensions" and "an obvious natural logic," whose job is to sell you a Nissan in French Canada. My local Virginia phone company drives trucks emblazoned with arrows and the meaningless phrase "This way to common sense.") There is nothing really new here. We are fully immersed in the realm of banalities. As first discovered in London in the aftermath of another great political turning point—the Glorious Revolution—the appeal to common sense in the context of the deregulation of speech constitutes a seemingly unthreatening, nonpartisan, and modern way to push one very particular point of view or commodity at the expense of another. Common sense has, by now, long existed as a fake normative criterion for making choices, whether the subject is soaps or candidates for office.

What is more intriguing is that, during these same decades, a new political theory of common sense, dependent on a self-conscious return to the conceptual innovations and experiments of the eighteenth century, came into being as a prop for a revived democratic politics. Its postwar advocates worried about both the threat of communism and a potential resurgence of fascism. But they rejected as insufficient a kind of liberalism that sees citizens as autonomous, rational actors and democracy as but a means to private, individualistic ends. They also turned their backs on Kant's famous separation of aesthetic judgment from ethical or political judgment. Instead, they saw in that quintessentially Enlightenment category, common sense, or *sensus communis,* a way to revive democracy with a community-oriented, participatory, and ultimately humanist face. Their first order of business became exposing the political prehistory of this aestheticized concept, a prehistory that, to use literary critic Joel Weinsheimer's familiar metaphor, continued to "haunt" the field "like a ghost that is not to be exorcised."[55]

Weinsheimer was referring at the time to the great hermeneutic project of Hans-Georg Gadamer. In 1960, when *Truth and Method (Wahrheit und Methode)* appeared, Gadamer was a professor of philosophy in Heidelberg, yet another German university town. He had also been an observer at close range of precisely sixty years of German regime changes, including the rise and fall of the Third Reich. Ostensibly, though, his subject bore little direct connection to politics at all. *Truth and Method* offered intense scrutiny of the experience of understanding, particularly in the case of those truths that cannot be verified by "the methodical means of science."[56] The onetime student of Martin Heidegger began this task by returning to the realm of aesthetics, as originally constituted by Kant in his *Critique of Judgment.*

However, far from endorsing Kant's efforts to cordon off the judgment of art from other forms of discerning knowledge or truth—a move that Gadamer saw as having had lethal results for the so-called human sciences ever since—he made it his project to reclaim the older meanings of the humanistic concepts out of which Kant had constructed his third *Critique.* First in the order of presentation came *Bildung,* or cultivation, then, in quick succession, common sense, judgment, and taste. What interested Gadamer was not only that these mental operations had an important cognitive claim that, he argued, we hardly recognize anymore because of the triumph of the intellectual methods of science. Critical to Gadamer's endeavor was the restoration of their (long-lost) ethical and political salience.

In the case of what Gadamer, too, called *sensus communis* out of dismay at the lack of moral resonance of the equivalent German terms (as opposed to "common sense" or "le bon sens"), this meant reviving an alternative intellectual tradition. This tradition had begun with the Romans but had taken its usable form in the writings of the last great humanist thinkers, Vico and Shaftesbury, who had already adapted this legacy to suit the new intellectual and social circumstances of modernity.[57] The trajectory of science, ever since Descartes, had, to Gadamer's dismay, denigrated community sentiment or "prejudice" as that which stood in the way of the individual pursuit of objective truth. Kant, according to Gadamer, had perpetuated this mistaken approach to knowledge by allowing the *sensus communis* to play a role in the communication of subjective aesthetic judgments but then denying it any function in the determination of the kinds of truths that mattered to social life. Yet Vico, in a challenge to the reason of modern science, had rightly noted that moral and political existence depended upon a common sense, by which he meant not just a faculty common to all men but a "sense" of right and wrong, of proper and improper, and ultimately of the common good that evolves in concert with history. As Gadamer interpreted Vico, this *sensus communis,* unlike universal reason, theory, or logic, was a product of life in an actual, concrete community. It was also "the sense that founds community." Indeed, it had fundamentally shaped the "moral and historical existence of humanity, as it takes shape in our deeds and works."[58] And Gadamer points out that Vico, though obscure in his day, was not alone in according this resonance to common sense. The postwar German philosopher took as one of his first tasks constructing a genealogy of modern thinkers who, like Vico, saw what the modern obsession with science had obscured for so long: the centrality of the *sensus communis,* not to mention judgment and taste, to the business of society and the state.

Most of the names in Gadamer's account will sound familiar as we arrive at the end of the book that you have before you. Vico's counterpart is Shaftesbury, for whom common sense is "not so much a capacity given to all men, part of the natural law, as a social virtue, a virtue of the heart more than of the head."[59] In Hutcheson and Hume, this "virtue of the heart" turns into moral sense. But as Gadamer points out, Shaftesbury's appropriation of *sensus communis* also had an impact on Reid and the common sense thinkers of Aberdeen, who preserved the connection between common sense as an epistemological category and social concerns: "In their eyes, the philosophy of sound understanding, of good sense, is not only a cure for the 'moon-sickness' of metaphysics, but also contains the basis of a moral philosophy that really does justice to the life of society."[60] In France, too, "the classical land of *le bon sens*," this moral element remained intact into the twentieth century; Henri Bergson is simply a late exemplar of a long tradition of taking seriously the social function of common sense.[61] Only German thinkers (with the important exception of Friedrich Christoph Oetinger and the Pietists in the middle of the eighteenth century) continually refused "the political and social element contained in *sensus communis*" and "emptied [it] of all political content." For in a further effort to link the *sensus communis* to the real world, Gadamer proposed that it is impossible to contemplate common sense in humanist terms when and where receptive social and political conditions are "utterly lacking," as they were for most of German history.[62]

Gadamer did not, however, develop a full-fledged explanation of how such conceptual recovery might be effectively translated into political theory, not to mention practice. From the point of view of postwar politics, his chief contribution was to urge epistemological modesty upon human actors, rooted in acceptance of the fact that, *pace* Descartes, we possess no way to make judgments about the world around us from outside of history, language, or "prejudice" (his provocative terms for our historically bounded assumptions). In *Truth and Method*, readers are left only with the vague sense that common sense, as a product of history and community traditions, should be considered enabling rather than restraining and a positive balance to the claims of science—a position that has caused some commentators to label Gadamer a traditionalist, if not a reactionary. It was left to another former student of Heidegger—in this case, one who was female, Jewish, and living in forced exile from the late 1930s onward in Paris and then New York—to build a political theory rooted in common sense. That student was Hannah Arendt.

Like Gadamer, Arendt eventually went back to Kant and, specifically, the section of the third *Critique* concerned with aesthetic judgment or *sensus communis,* to help clarify her own thinking. But rather than rebuke Kant for depoliticizing the old notion of common sense, Arendt claimed to find in his aesthetic theory a model for political judgment, a subject that would occupy her for much of her career. Moreover, Arendt adopted this sense not as a hermeneutic principle with political implications. She hoped instead that it would provide a foundation and goal for a politics that began with the active participation of "the people" in community making.[63] For Arendt, the cultivation of what she too called common sense set the stage, at least potentially, for true democracy.

The question that dominated the early years of Arendt's postwar career was the crucial one of that moment: what particular modern conditions had made the totalitarianism of both Hitler and Stalin possible? Or, to reverse the question, why had democracy in its twentieth-century incarnation failed? Arendt approached this dilemma in idiosyncratic fashion. She probed the nature of modernity with constant glances backward through history, especially to the eighteenth century. From the beginning, she also took an active interest in the link between politics and habits of mind, the way certain mental operations or orientations fostered specific political formations, and vice versa. (It might be said that Arendt's spirit hovers over all subsequent efforts to write politically engaged histories of epistemology, the present book being no exception.)

At a time when they were rarely discussed in tandem, the American and French Revolutions loomed large in this endeavor. In the 1950s and early 1960s, living in New York and teaching at the New School, Arendt found a vivid illustration of the active political life that she sought in what she took to be a central feature of eighteenth-century American political culture. Conjuring a fantasy past with echoes of the Anglo-Saxon mythology that urban radicals had exploited at the start of the American Revolution, Arendt paid tribute to the "council" or "ward" system of New England town governments in which citizens had come together to share their common concerns and, as she quoted Jefferson saying, "the voice of the people" was "fairly, fully, and peaceably expressed, discussed, and decided by the common reason" of all citizens.[64] Yet Arendt also stressed that this ideal was not to last, in America or elsewhere. In *On Revolution* (1963), Arendt made clear that after some initial experimentation with grassroots clubs and municipal councils, the French revolutionaries had rather quickly failed in their efforts to develop a participatory and truly republican political culture. "The people," starving, entered the scene as a mob or mass aggregation, concerned with economic survival alone. And as in all subsequent revolutionary movements, direct governing was soon replaced by revolutionary "parties," politicians, and a large administrative apparatus that functioned quite apart from citizens, who were left with the vote alone. Mass society, which was Arendt's pejorative term for a world without meaningful politics or public life, was already on its way to being realized. Capitalism, and the market culture created by the Industrial Revolution of the nineteenth century, furthered the people's estrangement from the public sphere. Modern science, insofar as it removed the world of nature as a stable reference point for all, played an important role in breaking down mental and social bonds as well. For Arendt, totalitarianism marked simply an extreme version of what had become the modern condition: the emergence of a vacuum that was at once political and epistemological. Shut off both from reality and from each other by means of government-ordered terror and ideology, unable to exercise their capacity to judge, the "masses" (as opposed to "the people") finally ceased to share even a portion of what a healthy political life required: anything worthy of the name common sense.

Arendt made this point again and again. In *On the Origins of Totalitarianism* (1951), it is precisely the gradual withering of common sense along with any sense of community or connection to others that results in the rise of ideological thinking.[65] In an essay originally published in the *Partisan Review* in 1953 called "Understanding and Politics," the emergence of totalitarianism is tied to the replacement of common sense with a coercive attachment to abstract logic in which basic axioms seem to fit all situations without regard to real-world circumstances:

> If it was the peculiarity of the ideologies themselves to treat a scientific hypothesis like "survival of the fittest" in biology or "survival of the most progressive class" in history, as an "idea" which could be applied to the whole course of events, then it is the peculiarity of their totalitarian transformation to pervert the "idea" into a premise in the logical sense, that is, into some self-evident statement from which everything else can be deduced in stringent logical consistency.[66]

The result was a context in which actors could no longer tell right from wrong, fact from fiction, and even the historian, looking retrospectively, is left flummoxed. In *The Human Condition* (1958), Arendt again describes the pain of the modern situation, declaring: "What makes mass society so difficult to bear is not the number of people involved, or at least not primarily, but the fact that the world between them has lost its power to gather them together, to relate them and to separate them." And she attributes this phenomenon to the disappearance of common sense understood as anything more than a basic rational capacity, or the ability to determine that two plus two make four, apart from consideration of the judgments of others.[67]

This diagnosis then sets up the outlines of a solution, although Arendt never claimed that true politics could be restored under contemporary conditions. Arendt's proposed response to the politics of "barbarism" hinges not on the imposition of more rules, whether self-generated or from outside. What individuals require is the return to a kind of public life that forces them to constantly weigh and consider things from the perspective of other people or, in the terms of *The Human Condition*, a public life that really does "gather them together, to relate and to separate them."[68] In other words, any meaningful countermeasure had to begin with the revival and cultivation of common sense.[69] If genuine politics could be envisioned as something like a New England town meeting, in which "the people" spoke, acted, and decided in public and in conditions of plurality, revealing themselves as they went, that was because the result—common sense—was the antithesis of the uniform ideology associated with totalitarianism. In Arendt, political action and common sense stand and fall together.[70]

But what *is* this common sense in Arendt's telling? Here is where things get tricky. Arendt defined this key concept—which she once called the "Ariadne thread" guiding all thinkers through the "labyrinth" of their results—in multiple ways over the years.[71] Indeed, she seems to echo at different points almost every major strand that we have identified in the history of thinking about common sense. At times, she sounds like a latter-day Aristotelian, reviving the original notion of common sense as the meeting ground of the five external senses, the "inner sense" responsible for fitting together distinct sensations so as to orient us in reality and help us cope with the world. In her discussion of thinking in *The Life of the Mind* (originally given as lectures in 1973), Arendt relates her conception of common sense directly to that of Aquinas, calling it a "sixth sense needed to keep my five senses together and guarantee that it is the same object that I see, touch, taste, smell, and hear."[72] In this account, it is also what makes private sensations public and allows us to share them, via language, with others. She makes much the same point in *The Human Condition,* where the common sense is "the one sense that fits into reality as a whole our five strictly individual senses and the strictly particular data they perceive" and thus reveals to us the world we hold in common, not to mention our own commonality.[73] Elsewhere, though, she sounds more like Edmund Burke or even Gadamer, suggesting that common sense is common wisdom, born of experience and custom, neither irrefutable nor permanent but evolving right along with the popular language that expresses it. In the essay "Understanding and Politics," common sense becomes "that portion of inherited wisdom which all men have in common in any great civilization" or something closer to unquestioned, everyday assumptions.[74] Still other times, Arendt links her ideas, much like Gadamer, back to a long "classical" tradition of French *bon sens* that extends from Montesquieu to Paul Valéry, who is given credit for first detecting the bankruptcy of what passes as common sense in the modern world.[75] And ultimately, Arendt takes up the Kantian notion of *sensus communis,* calling it the "community sense" to which judgment appeals in every case and which, in turn, gives judgments their special validity or impartiality.[76] It is both what links us to other people and what makes true originality go unheard. Here Arendt brings us neatly back to the metaphor of common sense as "judge and censor" with which the present book began, even though we have now moved far from seventeenth-century political or psychological theory.

From one perspective, this is an impossibly messy set of definitions upon which to build any coherent theory. Yet there is one trait that every one of Arendt's attempts at defining common sense share and that explains why this notion has such an extended shelf life in Arendt's work. That is her conviction that common sense has a "high rank in the hierarchy of political qualities," indeed, that it is "the political sense par excellence."[77] Notice that there is only one conception of common sense that she rejects: the idea that common sense can be reduced to an "inner faculty without any world relationship," or nothing more than a basic capacity for logical reasoning apart from other people, as has been the tragic "characteristic of the whole modern age."[78] Unlike thinking, which for Arendt is primarily an isolating experience, common sense keeps people related to the real world. It also keeps them related to one another. And it sets the parameters in which their public life can unfold. Common sense, for Arendt, is ultimately a noncoercive but vital form of social glue suitable to a pluralist and talkative world. Its significance for her lies in the fact that, in its very formation, it safeguards "the people"—without collapsing all differences among them and making them a mass—against the kind of mental separateness that allows totalitarian politics and a totalitarian mental life to flourish. True common sense, Arendt insists, can be produced only in the context of a robust public sphere, governed by freedom of speech and exchange. But then the reproduction and reinforcement of common sense under these conditions is also what makes possible the workings of a politics free from dogmatism, ideology, excessive conformity, or coercion. In other words, common sense is simultaneously a means and an end, the ground on which true democracy forms and the product that true democracy creates.

This may well explain why, in the final stages of her lifelong quest to understand the relationship between human mental activities and political life, Arendt turned formally back to Kant (with whom she shared both a place of origin and a fascination with the Age of Revolutions), insisting that far from retreating from politics in his *Critique of Judgment*, Kant provided the best blueprint we have for how to conceptualize the practice of politics itself. As early as 1957, Arendt mentioned in a letter to Karl Jaspers that she had found Kant's missing political philosophy "hidden" in his treatment of aesthetic judgment.[79] What Arendt left unfinished upon her death in 1975 is her own account of what she called Kant's "nonwritten political philosophy": an essay on judging in the Kantian spirit that was to have formed the third volume, after "Thinking" and "Willing," of *The Life of the Mind*.[80] Its outlines can be made out from the lectures on Kant that Arendt delivered at the New School in New York in the winter of 1970 and that may well have been a first draft. The lesson that Arendt took from Kant is that *all* judging is political. Why? The answer is threefold: because one judges as a member of a community (since "one can only 'woo' or 'court' the agreement of everyone else"); the judgment is itself rooted in a sense of community or common sense; and the judgment is open to communication—which means it ultimately helps to reconstitute common sense as long as the judgment exhibits the existence of what Kant called an "enlarged mentality" in the first place.[81] For Arendt, it was not a big step to say that Kant's account of common sense could, despite his claims to the contrary, be transferred to the political sphere and used, in conditions of unfettered speaking and listening, to give intersubjective validity to the judgments of ordinary people when it came to the pressing questions of their social and moral, as well as aesthetic, life.

Out of these unlikely elements, Arendt thus tried to save democratic practice from a solely liberal justification or a framework dependent on rules. Arendt cannot be labeled a strict communitarian or republican; her interest in plurality makes this impossible. Neither does it make sense to deem her a populist, as if this were a job description one did or did not fill (and one need only recall Beattie to remember the problems that any populist philosopher, even one who eschewed both terms, was likely to face).[82] Populism remains much more a style of political persuasion than a set doctrine. However, one can find versions of several key populist motifs in Arendt's thought as it developed in the wake of both World War II and her life as a foreign scholar in New York: the appeal of an earlier, Edenic moment of direct democracy; the dismay over the alienated quality of modern political life, with its rationalist, technocratic ethos; the commitment to the idea of the people (though not the mob, crowd, mass, or any one class) as the great actors of history; the disdain for parties and labels; and, not least, the attachment to the people's collective common sense, born of free speech and quotidian experience in the world, as the source and guarantee of a healthy political life. Critiques of these positions range from the charge of hopeless idealism to the charge of a dangerous aestheticization of politics that actually leads back to fascism. But the attraction is also obvious. Late in a career that spanned much of the twentieth century in Europe and the United States, Arendt provided her readers with a vision of a kind of participatory democracy in which the common sense of ordinary folk could accomplish wonders.

Of course, all this might have little to do with the realm of real politics as lived today, except that an odd thing has happened as of late. The ghost of common sense has hardly disappeared, Fielding can rest assured. In fact, quite the opposite has transpired. Those questions that we define as political arguably grow more complex and technical all the time. Even sophisticated economists and scientists have trouble figuring out why the financial sector or the biosphere has gone so wrong and what should be done about it. In the age of the Internet, the public realm has also gotten more and more crowded with discordant voices responding to fragmented information. Opinion polls only further manifest our cleavages. The idea of a common culture as either the basis or result of public discourse is starting to sound quaint. Yet as democracy has turned into the only acceptable global norm, common sense has become more valued than ever, both conceptually and rhetorically, in public life.

What is odder still is that, in the West, the appeal to common sense as the foundation for effective political solutions has also, since Arendt's time, become increasingly the province of the right, from Jean-Marie Le Pen's xenophobic celebrations, starting in the 1980s, of the "good sense" of authentic Frenchmen, to Ontario Premier Mike Harris's so-called Common Sense Revolution of the late 1990s and early 2000s against taxes and big government, to the "common sense conservatism" touted circa 2010 by American pundits Sarah Palin, Mike Huckabee, Glenn Beck, and their Tea Party supporters. In recent years, even the great "American" apostle of common sense, the radical Englishman Tom Paine, has been appropriated as a sage of the right. For the first 200 years that followed the publication of his *Common Sense,* Paine had served as the patron saint of radicals and revolutionaries everywhere, from the French and German republicans who called for the return of his spirit in 1848 to the New York intellectuals who launched a socialist magazine at the height of the Depression under the banner, once again, of revolutionary common sense. But beginning with Ronald Reagan, Paine and his "common sense" approach to politics began a second American afterlife.

In a startling change of course for a self-proclaimed conservative, Reagan, during the years of his presidency, frequently mined the pages of the original 1776 *Common Sense* for pithy, patriotic quotes about the necessity of limited government or the spirit of revolution. Then he often added his own simple, Paine-like homiletic messages, seeming truisms on which his own policies could be justified and built. Consider these explanations for his political choices: "Common sense told us that when you put a big tax on something, the people will produce less of it" and "Common sense also told us that to preserve the peace, we'd have to become strong again after years of weakness and confusion."[83] From his days as governor of California in the 1970s, when he claimed to have relied on "the belief that government was no deep, dark mystery, that it could be operated efficiently by using the same common sense practiced in our everyday life, in our homes, in business and private affairs," to his Farewell Address to the Nation in 1989, when he described the so-called Reagan Revolution as "the great rediscovery, a rediscovery of our values and our common sense," the Great Communicator kept returning to the idea that the simple, shared, quotidian logic of ordinary people provided him with an unerring political compass.[84] Indeed, he constantly told audiences, in fine populist form, that he was less a politician than one of the people, a political insider and outsider at the same time.

Someone must have been listening. For at the end of the first decade of the twenty-first century, common sense remains a leitmotif of a politically conservative strand of populism. And Paine is more popular than ever, spawning a cottage industry of videos and books updating his form and message for the present moment. The connection lies not so much in Paine's actual ideas (he was, after all, both an economic radical and a nonbeliever, as his eighteenth- and nineteenth-century critics never tired of pointing out). It is a matter of rhetoric and style and of thinking about politics in the first place. Today Paine symbolizes power to the fed-up people as opposed to the powers that be. Moreover, Paine stands for simple, everyday solutions—the answers that bankers, intellectuals, foreigners, politicians, journalists, scientists, urbanites, experts, scholastics, and other traditional foes of populists cannot see because their vision is so clouded and their language so obscure—to the pressing political questions of our times. Inevitably the left will have to find a way to adapt, or reappropriate, this same language for its own ends.

Therein also lies the dilemma. Democracy requires for its success both the promotion of common values and the very notion that there is something out there called "common sense" that has an important role to play in political life. In tension with liberal constitutionalism and expertise, it is the other, more collective, side of the democratic coin. At the same time, common sense, as both an informal regulatory system and a political authority, also always threatens to undermine the democratic ideal: blocking out truly new ideas, cutting off debate, convincing us that simple, kitchen-table solutions formulated by everyday people are necessarily better than complex or specialized or scientific ones. As Arendt conceded in her reflections on Kant, "The less idiosyncratic one's taste is, the better it can be communicated."[85] Common sense ultimately works to help us talk to each other but also to limit what we can hear and from whom. No thinker has tried to call our attention to this phenomenon with more sustained energy than the sociologist Pierre Bourdieu, who made his career demonstrating the way our lives, thoughts, and public discourse are invisibly restrained by the commonplace,

shared assumptions that pass for our common sense (or, as he more frequently called it, *habitus* or *doxa*).[86] Common sense, as concept and as
expression, has become part of our standard political arsenal in ways
that would have been unimaginable at the start of the eighteenth century, where our story began. It appears it is here to stay at least as long as
the resurgent idea of self-rule does. However, antagonists from Tristan
Tzara to Pierre Bourdieu have, in the very different fashions of the artist
and the social scientist, reminded us of another truth. It is vital that some
individuals in the modern world consciously position themselves outside
of the reigning common sense and keep a close eye on the complex and
powerful work that it does.

Notes

1. On the definition and significance of common sense, see Karl R. Popper, "Two Faces of Common Sense," *Objective Knowledge: An Evolutionary Approach* (Oxford, 1973), 32–105; John Kekes, "A New Defense of Common Sense," *American Philosophical Quarterly* 16, no. 2 (April 1979): 115–122; Mark Kingwell, "The Plain Truth about Common Sense: Skepticism, Metaphysics, and Irony," *Journal of Speculative Philosophy* 9, no. 3 (1995): 169–188; Marion Ledwig, *Common Sense: Its History, Method, and Applicability* (New York, 2007); and especially Nicholas Rescher, *Common Sense: A New Look at an Old Philosophical Tradition* (Milwaukee, 2005). All engage at some level with the classic essay by G. E. Moore, "A Defense of Common Sense," in *Contemporary British Philosophy,* 2nd ser., ed. J. H. Muirhead (London, 1925), 193–223.

2. See Bruce B. Wavell, *Language and Reason* (Berlin, 1986), on how common sense is "implicit in the structure and uses of ordinary language" (xxi). On the ways certain primordial suppositions become embedded in the basic practices of everyday life, see Peter L. Berger and Thomas Luckmann, *The Social Construction of Reality: A Treatise in the Sociology of Knowledge* (New York, 1966).

3. On the tendency of the contemporary social sciences to be directed against common sense, see Pierre Guenancia and Jean-Pierre Sylvestre, eds., *Le Sens Commun: théories et pratiques: actes du colloque de Dijon* (Dijon, 2004); and Frits von Holthoon and David R. Olsen, eds., *Common Sense: The Foundations for Social Science* (Lanham, MD, 1987). On the (parallel) censorious attitude of literary critics toward the taken for granted in "everyday life," see Rita Felski, "The Invention of Everyday Life," *New Formations* 39 (1999–2000): 15–31, and more generally, Antoine

Compagnon, *Literature, Theory, and Common Sense,* trans. Carol Cosman (Princeton, NJ, 2004 [1998]), esp. 193.

4. Clifford Geertz, "Common Sense as a Cultural System," *Antioch Review* 33, no. 1 (1975): 5–26, reprinted in *Local Knowledge: Further Essays in Interpretive Anthropology* (New York, 1983), 73–93. Historians have generally used other terms to refer to a culture's fundamental and often unarticulated principles and values, including historical psychology, *mentalité,* collective representations, structures of belief, and the social imaginary. But for a prominent example of a historian adopting this Geertzian framework, see Robert Darnton, *The Great Cat Massacre and Other Episodes in French Cultural History* (New York, 1985), 23. The historicity of our seemingly timeless, natural common sense was also, in the 1970s and 1980s, a frequent theme of cultural theorists from Roland Barthes to Stuart Hall.

5. John Rawls insists in *A Theory of Justice* (Cambridge, MA, 1971), 25–28, and *Political Liberalism* (New York, 1996), esp. 14, that a stable conception of justice must begin from the recognition of certain implicit assumptions or "common sense convictions" held by the vast majority of citizens of modern democracies. Nicholas Tampio calls this Rawlsian category "democratic common sense" in "Rawls and the Kantian Ethos," *Polity* 39, no. 1 (January 2007): 72–102, quote 88.

6. On Arendt, see Chapter 6.

7. Thomas Paine coined this term in *Rights of Man: Being an Answer to Mr. Burke's Attack on the French Revolution* (London, 1791), 162, to suggest that the American and French Revolutions should be seen as parallel struggles against monarchy. R. R. Palmer famously developed this idea in the 1950s, arguing that the thrust of a whole range of transatlantic revolts and revolutions of the late eighteenth century was against privilege and toward democracy; see *The Age of Democratic Revolution: A Political History of Europe and America, 1760–1800* (Princeton, NJ, 1959–1964). Recent critiques of Palmer's periodization, geography, and especially his claims about democratization include Wim Klooster, *Revolutions in the Atlantic World: A Comparative History* (New York, 2009); and David Armitage and Sanjay Subrahmanyam, eds., *The Age of Revolutions in Global Context, c. 1760–1840* (Basingstoke, UK, 2010). My own preference is for an age of revolutions that begins considerably earlier than Palmer's (or Paine's) and that has a more ambiguous relationship to democracy even within the limited horizons of the northern Atlantic world.

8. Immanuel Kant, *Prolegomena to Any Future Metaphysics,* trans. Lewis White Beck (Indianapolis, 1950 [1783]), 7.

9. On the prestige of ocular experience and quotidian life and, ultimately, their significance for a democratic political imaginary, see, respectively, Yaron Ezrahi, *The Descent of Icarus: Science and the Transformation of Contemporary Democracy* (Cambridge, MA, 1990), 61–68; and Thomas Dunn, *A Politics of the Ordinary* (New York, 1999).

10. The term "epistemic authority" is borrowed from Don Herzog, *Poisoning the Minds of the Lower Orders* (Princeton, NJ, 1998), 532.

11. On the relationship between democracy and populism, see Francisco Panizza, ed., *Populism and the Mirror of Democracy* (London, 2005); Yves Mény and Yves Surel, *Par le peuple, pour le peuple: le populisme et les démocraties* (Paris, 2000), and their

edited volume *Democracies and the Populist Challenge* (New York, 2002); and Jack Hayward, "The Populist Challenge to Elitist Democracy in Europe," in *Elitism, Populism, and European Politics,* ed. Hayward (Oxford, 2003).

12. Among the key works attempting a definition of populism, see Ghita Ionescu and Ernest Gellner, eds., *Populism: Its Meanings and Natural Characteristics* (London, 1969); Paul Taggart, *Populism* (Buckingham, UK, 2000); and especially Pierre-André Taguieff, *L'Illusion populiste: de l'archaique au médiatique* (Paris, 2002); and the following works by Margaret Canovan: *Populism* (New York, 1981); "Populism for Political Theorists?" *Journal of Political Ideologies* 9, no. 3 (October 2004): 241–252; and *The People* (Cambridge, 2005).

13. Ernesto Laclau, *On Populist Reason* (London, 2005), makes the vital point that populism, while constantly appealing to a unified "people," actually has no true referent, and "the people" is better understood as an aspiration than as a social reality. That "the people" is a fictional construct, a creation of politics rather than the inverse, is also central to Edmund S. Morgan, *Inventing the People: The Rise of Popular Sovereignty in England and America* (New York, 1988); and Patrick Joyce, *Democratic Subjects: The Self and the Social in Nineteenth-Century England* (Cambridge, 1994), who note, too, that part of the appeal stems from the term's ambiguity: does it refer to all humans? a national body or citizenry? or a plebian class? and in the singular or the plural?

14. Michael Kazin, *The Populist Persuasion: An American History* (New York, 1995).

15. On *Begriffsgeschichte,* see especially Melvin Richter, *The History of Political and Social Concepts: A Critical Introduction* (Oxford, 1995); Mark Bevir, "Begriffsgeschichte," *History and Theory* 39 (2000); and Reinhart Koselleck, *The Practice of Conceptual History: Timing History, Spacing Concepts* (Stanford, CA, 2002).

16. On the social history of knowledge, the starting point is Peter Burke, *A Social History of Knowledge: From Gutenberg to Diderot* (Cambridge, 2000), as well as his article "A 'Social History of Knowledge' Revisited," *Modern Intellectual History* 4, no. 3 (2007): 521–535. There is a close parallel here with the philosophical field known as "social epistemology"; see, for example, Alvin I. Goldman, *Knowledge in a Social World* (New York, 1999). The term *les usages commun* is borrowed from Antoine de Baecque and Françoise Mélonio, *Lumières et liberté: les dix-huitième et dix-neuvième siècles,* vol. 3 of *Histoire culturelle de la France,* ed. Jean-Pierre Rioux and Jean-François Sirinelli (Paris, 1998), and might best be understood as a reformulation of the history of mentalities to reflect the demise of the idea of distinct "popular" and "elite" cultures.

17. The term "historical epistemology" was coined by historian of science Lorraine Daston; see "The Moral Economy of Science," *Osiris* 10 (1995): 3–24. It has been adopted by scholars ranging from Mary Poovey to Arnold Davidson. Ian Hacking traces a closely related agenda with attention to the social sciences in *Historical Ontology* (Cambridge, MA, 2002).

18. On this question, see my "Politics, Epistemology, and Revolution," *Intellectual News,* no. 11/12 (Summer 2003): 64–69, as well as *A Revolution in Language: The Politics of Signs in Late Eighteenth-Century France* (Stanford, CA, 2001).

19. On the cultural significance of the Protestant concern with "ordinary life" in partic-ular, see Charles Taylor, *Sources of the Self: The Making of Modern Identity* (Cam-bridge, MA, 1989), 211–233.

20. On the changing meaning and epistemological value of common experience in the course of the Scientific Revolution, see Peter Dear, *Discipline and Experience: The Mathematical Way in the Scientific Revolution* (Chicago, 1995).

21. On *doxa* as a term for commonly held yet unexamined presuppositions about the world (as opposed to what we can speak and disagree about), see Ruth Amossy, "Introduction to the Study of Doxa," *Poetics Today* 23, no. 3 (Fall 2002): 369–394. For Maurice Blanchot, writing about common sense is inherently paradoxical, or a challenge to the *doxa,* insofar as one is making the everyday sensational and the im-plicit explicit; see his "Everyday Speech," *Yale French Studies,* no. 73 (special issue on Everyday Life) (1987): 12–20.

22. My approach to Atlantic history (which is still too often restricted to the English-speaking world) is best described, using the terminology of David Armitage, as "cis-Atlantic" in that it "studies particular places as unique locations within an At-lantic world and seeks to define that uniqueness as the result of the interaction be-tween local particularity and a wider web of connections (and comparisons)"; see his "Three Concepts of Atlantic History," in *The British Atlantic World, 1500–1800,* ed. David Armitage and Michael J. Braddick (London, 2002), 11–27.

23. For a summary of the large literature on the emergence of public opinion as a politi-cal variable in eighteenth-century Europe, see James Van Horn Melton, *The Rise of the Public in Enlightenment Europe* (Cambridge, 2001). Attitudes toward "the people" will be discussed place by place in subsequent chapters.

24. On social norms, see Cass Sunstein, "Social Norms and Social Roles," 96 *Colum-bia Law Review* 903 (1996); Eric Posner, *Law and Social Norms* (Cambridge, MA, 2000); and Eric Posner, ed., *Social Norms, Nonlegal Sanctions and the Law* (Chel-tenham, UK, 2007).

25. On Bourdieu's approach to common sense as a menacing form of restraint and ruse of bourgeois ideology, see Robert Holton, "Bourdieu and Common Sense," in *Pierre Bourdieu: Fieldwork in Culture,* ed. Nicholas Brown and Imre Szeman (Lanham, MD, 2000), 87–99. See too Bourdieu's own *Pascalian Meditations,* trans. Richard Nice (Oxford, 2000 [1977]), esp. 97–98, and *The Logic of Practice,* trans. Richard Nice (Stanford, CA, 1990 [1980]). On the notion of informal censorship, including in the work of Bourdieu, see my "Writing the History of Censorship in the Age of Enlighten-ment," in *Postmodernism and the Enlightenment: New Perspectives in Eighteenth-Century French Intellectual History,* ed. Daniel Gordon (London, 2001), 117–145.

26. See Françoise Gaillard, "The Terror of Consensus," in *Terror and Consensus: Vi-cissitudes of French Thought,* ed. Jean-Joseph Goux and Philip R. Wood (Stanford, CA, 1998), for a critique of consensus as a conservative regulatory idea that leads to a devitalization of the political. For a related argument from an opposing political perspective, see Glenn Loury, "Self-Censorship in Public Discourse: A Theory of 'Political Correctness' and Related Phenomena," *Rationality and Society* 6, no. 4 (October 1994): 428–461.

27. On the relationship between social crises and common sense, see Pierre Bourdieu, *Outline of a Theory of Practice,* trans. Richard Nice (Cambridge, 1977).

28. This term is borrowed from Bruce Mazlish, "Philosophical History," *Intellectual News* 8 (Summer 2000): 117–122. As defined here, "philosophical history" involves framing historical subjects in terms of philosophical questions and wrestling with philosophical issues through the empirical methods of the historian.

1. THE GHOST OF COMMON SENSE

1. On the latent dimension of history, see Jacques Rancière, *The Names of History: On the Poetics of Knowledge,* trans. Hassan Melehy (Minneapolis, 1994).

2. Aristotle, *De Anima* 3.1–5. On the Aristotelian conception of common sense, see Deborah K. Modrak, *Aristotle: The Power of Perception* (Chicago, 1987), 55–80; J. Brunschwig, "En quel sens le sens commun est-il commun?" in *Corps et âme. Sur le De anima d'Aristote,* ed. Gilbert Romeyer Dherbey (Paris, 1996); Danielle Lories, *Le Sens commun et le jugement du Phronimos. Aristote et les stoiciens* (Louvain-la-Neuve, 1998); Pavel Gregoric, *Aristotle on the Common Sense* (Oxford, 2007); and Daniel Heller-Roazen, *The Inner Touch: Archeology of a Sensation* (New York, 2007), 31–45.

3. On medieval and Renaissance understandings of common sense, see David Summers, *The Judgment of Sense: Renaissance Naturalism and the Rise of Aesthetics* (Cambridge, 1987), esp. 71–109, as well as Henry Austryn Wolfson, "The Internal Senses in Latin, Arabic and Hebrew Philosophical Texts," *Harvard Theological Review* 28, no. 2 (April 1935): 69–133.

4. On the location of the *sensus communis,* see Edwin Clarke and Kenneth Dewhurst, *An Illustrated History of Brain Function: Imaging the Brain from Antiquity to the Present,* 2nd ed. (San Francisco, 1996).

5. André Du Laurens, *Oeuvres de Me André du Laurens* (Paris, 1646), 527 (originally published in Latin as *Opera Anatomica* in 1595); and Helkiah Crooke, *Mikrokosmographia: A Description of the Body of Man,* 2nd ed. (London, 1615), 502, 608, 611, 696, in various combinations, certainly borrowed from Du Laurens. In Robert Burton's *The Anatomy of Melancholy* (Oxford, 1621), the common sense is also described as "judge or moderator of the rest" to whom objects are conveyed "to be censured" (pt. I, sec. I, memb. II, subs. 6).

6. On the significance of the body to political theory, see Leonard Barkan, *Nature's Work of Art: The Human Body as Image of the World* (New Haven, CT, 1975), esp. chap. 3.

7. On uses of the model of the court or city in anatomy, see R. K. French, *Dissection and Vivisection in the European Renaissance* (Aldershot, UK, 1999); and Peter Mitchell, *The Purple Island and Anatomy in Early 17th-Century Literature, Philosophy and Theology* (Madison, NJ, 2007).

8. See Bartolommeo Del Bene, *Civitas Veri sive Morum* (Paris, 1609), esp. 28–29.

9. Crooke, *Mikrokosmographia,* 453, 432.

10. Heller-Roazen, *Inner Touch,* 163–168. See, too, Jean-Robert Armogathe, "Les Sens: inventaires médiévaux et théorie cartésienne," in *Descartes et le Moyen Age,* ed. Joël Biard and Roshdi Rashed (Paris, 1997), 175–184.

11. Nicholas Amhurst, *Terrae-Filius: or, The Secret History of the University of Oxford* (London, 1721), no. XX, 100.

12. On the Stoics' understanding of *sensus communis,* see Lories, *Le Sens commun.* On the Ciceronian understanding of the term, see S. E. W. Bugter, "Sensus Communis in the Works of M. Tullius Cicero," in *Common Sense: The Foundations for Social Science,* 83–97, which is itself an extended response to C. S. Lewis, "Sense," in *Studies in Words,* 2nd ed. (Cambridge, 1996 [1960]), 146–150.

13. Edward Phillips, *A New World of Words: or, Universal English Dictionary,* 6th ed., revised by J. K. Philobibl (London, 1706), defines common sense as "those general Notions that arise in the Minds of Men, by which they know, or apprehend things after the same manner," a direct translation of the definition of *le bon sens* offered by Antoine Furetière in his *Dictionnaire universel* of 1690 and a standard for the rest of the eighteenth century. On the evolution of English definitions of common sense, see Helga Körver, "Common Sense. Die Entwicklung eines englischen Schlüsselwortes und seine Bedeutung für die englische Geistesgeschichte vornehmlich zur Zeit des Klassizismus und der Romantik" (PhD diss., Bonn, 1967).

14. On the social dimension of Augustan understandings of common sense, see William Bowman Piper, "Common Sense as a Basis of Literary Style," *Texas Studies in Literature and Language* 18, no. 4 (Winter 1977): 624–641.

15. Shaftesbury, "Sensus Communis: An Essay on the Freedom and Wit of Humour" [London, 1709], reprinted in vol. 1 of his *Characteristicks of Men, Manners, Opinions, Times* [London, 1711; 2nd ed. 1714], ed. Lawrence Klein (Cambridge, 1999), 48, 60, and 61, respectively.

16. On Shaftesbury's *sensus communis,* see Richard Voitle, *The Third Earl of Shaftesbury, 1671–1713* (Baton Rouge, 1984), 330–331; Lawrence E. Klein, *Shaftesbury and the Culture of Politeness: Moral Discourse and Cultural Politics in Early Eighteenth-Century England* (Cambridge, 1994), 96–97, 196; Isabel Rivers, *Reason, Grace and Sentiment: A Study of the Language of Religion and Ethics in England, 1660–1780,* vol. 2, *Shaftesbury to Hume* (Cambridge, 2000), 124–131; and John D. Schaeffer, *Sensus Communis: Vico, Rhetoric, and the Limits of Relativism* (Durham, NC, 1990), 41–46. It is variously defined in the scholarly literature as love of humanity, of society, of the community, and of the public or common good.

17. Roy Porter, *London: A Social History* (Cambridge, MA, 1995), 131.

18. The classic text is J. H. Plumb, *The Growth of Political Stability in England, 1675–1725* (London, 1967).

19. "The Earl of Manchester's Speech to His Majesty . . . at His Arrival at Whitehall [1660]," cited in P. K. Elkin, *The Augustan Defense of Satire* (Oxford, 1973), 7.

20. On the reasoning behind the Licensing Act of 1695, the starting point is Frederick Seaton Siebert, *Freedom of the Press in England, 1476–1776: The Rise and Decline of Government Controls* (Urbana, IL, 1952).

21. On Tory and Whig distinctions in civic spaces, see Geoffrey Holmes, *The Making of a Great Power: Late Stuart and Early Georgian Britain, 1660–1722* (London, 1993). On the problem of party spirit or pluralism at the level of discourse, see J. A. W. Gunn, *Factions No More: Attitudes to Party in Government and Opposition in Eighteenth-Century England, Extracts from Contemporary Sources* (London, 1972); Pasi Ihalainen, *The Discourse on Political Pluralism in Early Eighteenth-Century England* (Helsinki, 1999); and Mark Knights, *Representation and Misrepresentation in Later Stuart Britain: Partisanship and Political Culture* (Oxford, 2005).

22. Klein, *Shaftesbury and the Culture of Politeness,* 12.

23. On politeness, see J. G. A. Pocock, "The Problem of Political Thought in the Eighteenth Century: Patriotism and Politeness," *Theoretische Geschiedenis* 9 (1982): 14–17; Paul Langford, *A Polite and Commercial People: England, 1727–1783* (Oxford, 1989); and John Brewer, *The Pleasures of the Imagination: English Culture in the Eighteenth Century* (New York, 1997), esp. 99–114.

24. *The Spectator,* ed. Joseph Addison and Richard Steele, no. 126 (July 25, 1711); see the edition prepared by Donald F. Bond (Oxford, 1965), 2:1–4.

25. *The Spectator,* no. 125 (July 24, 1711), 1:509–510.

26. Shaftesbury, *Characteristicks,* 53.

27. On denominational strife, see J. D. C. Clark, *The Language of Liberty, 1660–1832: Political Discourse and Social Dynamics in the Anglo-American World* (Cambridge, 1994).

28. Benjamin Whichcote, *Moral and Religious Aphorisms* (1703), cited in *Enthusiasm and Enlightenment in Europe, 1650–1850,* ed. Lawrence E. Klein and Anthony L. LaVopa (San Marino, CA, 1998), 159. On the problem of enthusiasm, see, too, Michael Heyd, *"Be Sober and Reasonable": The Critique of Enthusiasm in the Seventeenth and Early Eighteenth Centuries* (Leiden and New York, 1995).

29. On the epistemological position of seventeenth-century Anglican Latitudinarians, see Henry Van Leeuwen, *The Problem of Certainty in English Thought, 1630–1690* (The Hague, 1963); Robert T. Carroll, *The Common-Sense Philosophy of Religion of Bishop Edward Stillingfleet, 1635–1699* (The Hague, 1975); Barbara Shapiro, *Probability and Certainty in Seventeenth-Century England: A Study of the Relationships between Natural Science, Religion, History, Law and Literature* (Princeton, NJ, 1983); and Frederick C. Beiser, *The Sovereignty of Reason: The Defense of Rationality in the Early English Enlightenment* (Princeton, NJ, 1996).

30. See Wilbur Samuel Howell, *Eighteenth-Century British Logic and Rhetoric* (Princeton, NJ, 1971), 441–502; Brian Vickers, "The Royal Society and English Prose Style: A Reassessment," in *Rhetoric and the Pursuit of Truth: Language Change in the Seventeenth and Eighteenth Centuries* (Los Angeles, 1985), 1–76; and Richard Foster Jones, "The Attack on Pulpit Eloquence in the Restoration: An Episode in the Development of the Neo-Classical Standard for Prose" [1931], in *The Seventeenth-Century: Studies in the History of English Thought and Literature from Bacon to Pope* (Stanford, CA, 1951), 111–142.

31. The term "mitigated skepticism" is taken from Richard Popkin, *The History of Skepticism: From Savonarola to Bayle,* new ed. (Oxford, 2000), 29–50.

32. Carroll, *The Common-Sense Philosophy of Religion,* 11. On the emergence of this notion of moral certainty, see Steven Shapin, *A Social History of Truth: Civility and Science in Seventeenth-Century England* (Chicago, 1994), 208–211.

33. Cited in Norman Sykes, *Church and State in England in the XVIIIth Century* (Hamden, CT, 1962 [1934]), 258. In late seventeenth-century English religious writing, "reasonableness" meant in accordance with common sense; see, for example, Richard Bentley's first Boyle lecture, reprinted in his *The Folly and Unreasonableness of Atheism* (London, 1693), 16, in which he argues that it would be reasonable to quit religion only if its principles were "repugnant to Common Sense."

34. John Tillotson, "Sermon I: Of the Duties of Natural Religion, with the Ways and Means of Knowing Them," in *Eighteenth-Century English Literature,* ed. Geoffrey Tillotson, Paul Fussell, and Marshall Waingrow (New York, 1969), 209.

35. James Downey, *The Eighteenth-Century Pulpit: A Study of the Sermons of Butler, Berkeley, Secker, Sterne, Whitefield and Wesley* (Oxford, 1969), 15.

36. Armhurst, *Terrae-Filius,* 180–181, sounding very close to Berkeley, Shaftesbury, and especially Locke, for whom "native rustic Reason . . . is likelier to open a way to [knowledge], and add to the common stock of Mankind rather than any scholastick Proceeding by the strict Rules of Mode and Figure"; see *An Essay Concerning Humane Understanding* (London, 1690), bk. IV, chap. xvii, sec. 6. On anti-Scholastic sentiment in Augustan culture, see, too, Barbara J. Shapiro, *A Culture of Fact: England, 1550–1720* (Ithaca, NY, 2000), 160–165 and 261, n. 113; and the notes of Charles Kerby-Miller to his edition of John Arbuthnot, Alexander Pope, et al., *Memoirs of the Extraordinary Life, Works and Discoveries of Martinus Scriblerus* (New York, 1966), 243–246.

37. Joel C. Weinsheimer, *Eighteenth-Century Hermeneutics: Philosophy of Interpretation in England from Locke to Burke* (New Haven, CT, 1993), preface, x.

38. George Berkeley, "Philosophical Commentaries," Notebook, A 751 [1707–1708], in *The Works of George Berkeley, Bishop of Cloyne,* ed. A. A. Luce and T. E. Jessop (London, 1948), 91. In his *Three Dialogues between Hylas and Philonous in Opposition to Sceptics and Atheists* (Cleveland, 1963 [1713]), Berkeley's character Philonous similarly refers to enlightenment as requiring a "revolt from metaphysical notions to the plain dictates of nature and common sense" (50).

39. J. L. of Lynn Regis, *The Principles of a Rationalist, Digested into stated Articles, containing the Laws of Reason, and the Elements of Religion, Morals, and Politicks: Together with the Whole Art of Reducing all disputable Cases to Self-Evident Propositions . . . Being A Practical Method of Teaching the Use of Common Sense, as the First Principle of all Knowledge, and an effectual Way to prevent the Arbitrary Imposition of Ignorance and Error in Religion and Politicks, and the Introduction and Support of Tyranny and Slavery* (London, 1721), 30.

40. *The Spectator,* no. 259 (December 27, 1711), 2:508; and no. 156 (August 29, 1711), 2:112.

41. *The Spectator,* no. 62 (May 11, 1711), 1:269.

42. *The Spectator,* no. 124 (July 23, 1711), 1:508.

43. *The Spectator,* no. 70 (May 21, 1711), 1:297.

44. On the identification of common people with not only ignorance but also cognitive incapacity, see Shapin, *A Social History of Truth,* 77.

45. On early eighteenth-century English understandings of "the people" as an abstraction, see Morgan, *Inventing the People* and Knights, *Representation and Misrepresentation in Later Stuart Britain.*

46. Cited in William Bowman Piper, *Common Courtesy in Eighteenth-Century English Literature* (Newark, DE, 1997), 187, n. 17.

47. Erin Mackie, *Market à la Mode: Fashion, Commodity, and Gender in* The Tatler *and* The Spectator (Baltimore, 1997), 21.

48. Rosenfeld, "Writing the History of Censorship in the Age of Enlightenment," in *Postmodernism and Enlightenment.*

49. *The Free-Thinker: or, Essays of Wit and Humour,* no. 58 (October 10, 1718) in the 3rd ed. (1740), 2:10. The three-volume reprint had the title *The Free-Thinker: or, Essays on ignorance, superstition, bigotry, enthusiasm, craft, etc: Intermixed with several pieces of wit and humour: Design'd to restore the deluded part of mankind to the use of reason and common sense* (London, 1733).

50. *The Spectator,* no. 253 (December 20, 1711), 2:484.

51. The roots of this kind of criticism can be traced back to Thomas Rymer's *Tragedies of the Last Age: Consider'd and Examin'd* (London, 1677), in which the author insisted that art must correspond to "the common sense of all ages," as well as the rules of the ancients, in order to please.

52. Mr. Savage, *The Art of Prudence: or, a Companion for a Man of Sense. Written Originally in Spanish by That Celebrated Author, Balthazar Gracian,* 2nd ed. (London, 1705), esp. "Maxim LX: Good Sense," 64–65. "Good sense" is sometimes described as a specifically manly attribute in this period. But similar ideas were promulgated in contemporaneous advice books for women, such as Lady Mary Lee Chudleigh, *Essays upon Several Subjects in Prose and Verse* (London, [1710]); the author announced in her introductory address that "My whole design is . . . to persuade my Sex . . . to prefer Wisdom before Beauty, good Sense before Wealth, and the Sovereignty of their Passions before the Empire of the World."

53. See, among others, William Combe, *Plain thoughts of a plain man, addressed to the common sense of the people of Great-Britain* (London, 1727); John Wilkes, *The North Briton makes his appeal to the good sense, and to the candour of the English nation* ([London], [1763]); Anon., *An Appeal to the Good Sense of the Inhabitants of Great Britain* (London, 1770); Anon., *Plain Facts, Submitted to the Common Sense of the People of England* (London, 1785); Anon., *British Common Sense* (London, 1791); and John Stewart, *Good Sense: Addressed to the British nation, as their pre-eminent and peculiar characteristic, in the present awful crisis* (London, 1794). For a foreign reference to "that truly English attribute, good common sense," see Oloff Napea, *Letters from London: Observations of a Russian* (1816), 28, cited in Paul

Langford, *Englishness Identified: Manners and Character, 1650–1850* (Oxford, 2000), 75.

54. On the common-law mind and custom, see J. G. A. Pocock, *The Ancient Constitution and the Feudal Law: A Study of English Historical Thought in the Seventeenth Century*, 2nd ed. (Cambridge, 1987); Glenn Burgess, *The Politics of the Ancient Constitution: An Introduction to English Political Thought, 1603–1642* (Houndsmills, Basingstoke, UK, 1992); and J. W. Tubbs, *The Common Law Mind: Medieval and Early Modern Conceptions* (Baltimore, 2000). See, too, Gerald J. Postema, *Bentham and the Common Law Tradition* (Oxford, 1986), esp. 66–77, on the enduring importance of a social conception of knowledge in common law theory.

55. Thomas Shadwell, "Dedication to Charles, Earl of Dorset and Middlesex," *Bury-Fair* [1689], in *The Complete Works of Thomas Shadwell*, ed. Montague Summers (London, 1927), 4:294; this theme is also central to the play's prologue.

56. Markku Peltonen issues a similar warning about assuming that politeness remained (if it ever was) an exclusively Whig preoccupation; see his "Politeness and Whiggism, 1688–1732," *Historical Journal* 48, no. 2 (2005): 391–414.

57. "Of Common Sense," *Applebee's Journal* (March 11, 1732), reprinted in *Gentleman's Magazine* 2 (March 1732): 647. Again one hears echoes of the *Spectator*, where praise is lavished on "Notions that fall in with the common Reason of Mankind, that are comfortable to the Sense of all Ages, and all Nations, not to mention their tendency for promoting the happiness of Societies, or of particular Persons" (no. 185 [October 2, 1711], 2:230).

58. [Herbert Lawrence], *The Life and Adventures of Common Sense: An Historical Allegory* (London, 1769), 2:113. The idea of writing an allegorical history of common sense and his family may well also have been derived from the *Spectator*, no. 35 (April 10, 1711), 2:145–158, in which Addison offers a genealogy for both Good Sense personified, a descendant of Truth, and for Nonsense personified, a descendant of Falsehood.

59. G. M. Trevelyan, *The English Revolution, 1688–1689* (London, 1938), 7. For a recent reassessment of this argument, see John Morrill, "The Sensible Revolution," in *The Anglo-Dutch Moment: Essays on the Glorious Revolution and Its World Impact*, ed. Jonathan Israel (Cambridge, 1991), 73–104.

60. See Melvin Richter, "Le Concept de despotisme et l'abus des mots," *Dix-huitième siècle*, no. 34 (2002): 373–388.

61. The classic text here is W. B. Gallie, "Essentially Contested Concepts," *Proceedings of the Aristotelian Society* 56, no. 167 (n.s. 1955–1956).

62. Benjamin Hoadly, *A Preservative against the Principles and Practices of the Nonjurors Both in Church and State. Or, an Appeal to the Consciences and Common Sense of the Christian Laity* (London, 1716), 99, 2.

63. Most of these titles are listed in "An Account of all the Considerable Pamphlets that have been published on either side in the present controversy," in *The Works of Benjamin Hoadly* (London, 1773), 2:381–401. See too Rosenfeld, "Before Democracy: The Production and Uses of Common Sense," *Journal of Modern History* 80, no. 1 (March 2008): 1–54.

64. Joseph Smith, *Some Considerations Humbly Offer'd to the Lord Bp. of Bangor* (London, 1717), 1; and Thomas Pyle, *A Second Vindication of the Lord Bishop of Bangor* (London, 1718), 55, respectively.

65. For contrasting views on the membership of the Opposition, see Archibald S. Foord, *His Majesty's Opposition, 1714–1830* (Oxford, 1964); Linda Colley, *In Defiance of Oligarchy: The Tory Party, 1714–60* (Cambridge, 1982); and J. C. D. Clark, *English Society, 1660–1832: Religion, Ideology, and Politics during the Ancien Regime,* 2nd ed. (Cambridge, 2000).

66. John Gay, "Fable IX: The Jackal, Leopard, and Other Beasts. To a Modern Politician" [1728], in *The Poetical Works of John Gay,* ed. G. C. Faber (London, 1926).

67. Claude Adrien Helvétius, in *De l'Homme, de ses facultés intellectuelles et de son éducation* (London [The Hague], 1773 [posthum.]), vol. 2, sec. 7, note B, retells the story of an English play whose title he gives in French as "La Reine de Bon Sens" but is clearly one act of Fielding's *Pasquin.*

68. Henry Fielding, *Pasquin. A Dramatick Satire on the Times: Being the Rehearsal of Two Plays, viz., A Comedy call'd The Election; and a Tragedy, call'd the Life and Death of Common Sense* (London, 1736), prologue to Act I; see the edition of O. M. Brack, William Kupersmith, and Curt A. Zimansky (Iowa City, 1973), 5. On the connotations of this play, see, too, the varied readings of Jean Ducrocq, *Le Théâtre de Fielding: 1728–1737 et ses prolongements dans l'oeuvre romantique* (Dijon, 1975), 332–378; Bertrand A. Goldgar, *Walpole and the Wits: The Relation of Politics to Literature, 1722–1742* (Lincoln, NE, 1976), 150–153; Robert D. Hume, *Henry Fielding and the London Theatre, 1728–1737* (Oxford, 1988), 209–213; and Martin C. Battestin with Ruth R. Battestin, *Henry Fielding: A Life* (London, 1989), 192–199. Battestin links Fielding's political sympathies to the Boy Patriots and his religious sympathies to Hoadly's moralizing Christianity at the time of the writing of this play; others see less firm commitments.

69. Fielding, *Pasquin,* act V, 49.

70. Ronald Paulson, *The Life of Henry Fielding: A Critical Biography* (Oxford, 2000), 46, 63.

71. Advertisement for an April 1736 benefit performance of *Pasquin,* cited in Thomas R. Cleary, *Henry Fielding: Political Writer* (Waterloo, ON, 1984), 88.

72. *Common Sense: or, The Englishman's Journal,* nos. 1–354 (February 5, 1737–November 16, 1743). On the history of this journal and its competitors, see George Hilton Jones, "The Jacobites, Charles Molloy, and Common Sense," *Review of English Studies,* n.s. 4 (April 1953): 144–147; Goldgar, *Walpole and the Wits,* 156–159; and Vincent J. Liesenfeld, *The Licensing Act of 1737* (Madison, WI, 1984), 92–93.

73. Lord Bolingbroke, *A Dissertation upon Parties* (London, 1735), first printed serially in the *Craftsman* in 1733–1734. On Bolingbroke and Opposition theory and discourse in the era of Walpole, see especially Quentin Skinner, "The Principles and Practice of Opposition: The Case of Bolingbroke v. Walpole," in *Historical Perspectives: Studies in English Thought and Society, in Honour of J. H. Plumb* (London, 1974), 93–128; H. T. Dickinson, *Liberty and Property: Political Ideology in Eighteenth-Century Britain* (New York, 1977); J. A. W. Gunn, *Beyond Liberty and*

Property: The Process of Self-Recognition in Eighteenth-Century Political Thought (Kingston, 1983); and Alexander Pettit, *Illusory Consensus: Bolingbroke and the Polemical Response to Walpole, 1730–1737* (Newark, DE, 1997).

74. On the Whig dissident political ideology of Lyttelton and his circle, see Christine Gerrard, *The Patriot Opposition to Walpole: Politics, Poetry, and National Myth, 1725–1742* (Oxford, 1994), esp. 34.

75. George Lyttelton, *Letters from a Persian in England, to His Friend at Ispahan*, 2nd ed. (London, 1735), 40.

76. *Common Sense*, no. 8 (March 26, 1737): 2.

77. Precedent for the idea of common sense as a tribunal can be found in such Civil War texts as *The Plain Case of the Common-Weal Neer the Desperate Gulf of the Common-Woe. Stated and Exhibited, to the People and High Court of Parliament . . . Also, the Oath to the Parliament Extricated, and the Case Resolved to Common Sense* (London, 1648 [1649]). On the function of this trope in relation to the better studied notion of public opinion, see Gunn, "Public Spirit to Public Opinion," in *Beyond Liberty and Property*, 260–315.

78. "Common Sense," *Common Sense*, no. 1 (February 5, 1737): 1. The epigraph for this opening essay was "Rarus enim fermè sensus communis" or "Nothing so rare as common sense" of Juvenal.

79. Ibid.

80. "A Letter from Common Honesty to Common Sense," *Common Sense*, no. 87 (September 30, 1738), reprinted in *Gentleman's Magazine* 8 (October 1738): 527, and later with the same title as a separate pamphlet (Boston, c. 1756).

81. "Common Sense," *Common Sense*, no. 1 (February 5, 1737).

82. See *Common Sense*, issues no. 1 (February 5, 1737) and no. 14 (May 7, 1737), respectively; the latter definition is provided by a character named "Age and Experience."

83. On the widely circulated print, see Paul Langford, *Walpole and the Robinocracy* (Cambridge, 1986), 130–131. For the original description of the ceremony, see *Common Sense*, no. 7 (March 19, 1737) and no. 8 (March 26, 1737).

84. *The Champion: or British Mercury*, nos. 1–63 (November 15, 1739–April 8, 1740), continued as *The Champion: or Evening Advertiser* from April 1740 to 1743, but without Fielding's participation.

85. Shaftesbury, *Characteristicks*, 59.

86. On this stance, and the heated debates it provoked at the time, see especially Elkin, *The Augustan Defense of Satire;* and James A. Herrick, *The Radical Rhetoric of the English Deists: The Discourse of Skepticism, 1680–1750* (Columbia, SC, 1997), esp. 60–65. Reprinted in *Common Sense*, no. 16 (May 21, 1737) is a letter, originally addressed to the *Daily Gazetteer,* in which the author supports the idea (attributed here to Pierre Bayle) that "Ridicule is a kind of Fiery Trial, by which Truth is most certainly discovered from Imposture."

87. *Common Sense*, no. 1 (February 5, 1737).

88. C. John Sommerville, *The News Revolution in England: Cultural Dynamics of Daily Information* (New York, 1996), 155.

89. "To Mr. Common Sense," *Common Sense*, no. 16 (March 22, 1740), reprinted in *Gentleman's Magazine* 10 (March 1740): 132. As Benjamin Norton Defoe's *A New English Dictionary* of 1737 makes clear, "common" continued to hold the double meaning of "that which belongs to all alike" and "ordinary."

90. On the trope of the "sense of the people" or the "sense of the nation" as used by both Court and Country, see J. A. W. Gunn, "Court Whiggery-Justifying Innovation," in *Politics, Politeness, and Patriotism*, ed. Gordon J. Schochet (Washington, DC, 1993), 125–156; and Kathleen Wilson, *The Sense of the People: Politics, Culture and Imperialism in England, 1715–1785* (Cambridge, 1995). On the older idea of a vox populi, see George Boas, *Vox Populi: Essays in the History of an Idea* (Baltimore, 1969).

91. The term "protesting" populism is borrowed from Pierre-André Taguieff, *L'Illusion populiste*, who uses it to distinguish the kind of populism discussed above, with its characteristic critique of the illegitimacy of elites, calls for greater democratization, and exaltation of the instinctive wisdom of the people, from a later, more xenophobic "identity" populism.

92. *Common Sense*, no. 142 (October 20, 1739); this statement is briefly discussed in H. T. Dickinson, "Popular Politics in the Age of Walpole," in *Britain in the Age of Walpole*, ed. Jeremy Black (London, 1984), 57.

93. *Common Sense*, no. 141 (October 13, 1739), cited in M. M. Goldsmith, "Faction Detected: Ideological Consequences of Robert Walpole's Decline and Fall," *History* 64 (1979): 7.

94. The editors of *Common Sense*, in between laying out "certain plain Rules of Common Sense, which [they] strictly charge and require all Persons to observe" regarding proper comportment dependent on gender, age, rank, and station in life (no. 4 [February 26, 1737]), frequently throw out comments to the effect that whatever good sense is left in the nation is now to be found mainly among women (no. 58 [March 11, 1737]) or more often among cobblers than statesmen (no. 33 [May 6, 1738]). Precedent for such comments goes back to Rymer and Sprat, among others, in the seventeenth century.

95. *Common Sense* (February 24, 1739), reprinted in Anon., *The National Dispute; or, The History of the Convention Treaty: Containing the Substance of All the Proceedings, Debates, Pamphlets, Journals, Daily, and other Papers, published both for and against the late Convention . . . Shewing the true Sense of the Nation, concerning the same* (London, 1739), 238.

96. On newspapers' efforts to monitor the state on behalf of the nation as both cause and consequence of the widening political awareness among ordinary people, see Wilson, *The Sense of the People,* esp. 12, 31, 41–42.

97. *Gentleman's Magazine* 9 (March 1739): 112.

98. On the insistence on impartiality and national interest as hallmarks of partisan discourse in this era, see Knights, *Representation and Misrepresentation in Later Stuart Britain*. Ditto John Brewer's brief comments in *The Sinews of Power: War, Money, and the English State, 1688–1783* (London, 1989), on the appeal of the idea of

"universal" or "public" knowledge among those most dedicated to private and selective agendas.

99. [Lord Hervey], *A Letter to the Author of Common-Sense; or The Englishman's Journal, of Saturday, April 16* (London, 1737), 8, 27–28.

100. Jacques Rancière, *Disagreement: Politics and Philosophy,* trans. Julie Rose (Minneapolis, 1999 [1995]), preface, x.

101. Anon., *The Country Correspondent. Being, a letter from a Country Gentleman to a Friend in Town. In Which is contained, a Short Reply to Mr. Common Sense, occasioned by his Paper of Saturday April 7, 1739,* no. 1 (London, 1739), 4.

102. [Hervey], *A Letter,* 10.

103. [Lady Mary Wortley Montagu], *The Nonsense of Common Sense* (December 16, 1737–March 14, 1738); see, in the edition of Robert Halsband (Evanston, IL, 1947), no. 2 (January 17, 1738), 7–8, and no. 1 (December 16, 1737), 1.

104. *London Journal,* no. 784 (July 6, 1734). See Gunn, *Beyond Liberty,* 309–311; and Ihalainen, *Discourse of Political Pluralism,* 80–85, on the ongoing Whig discourse about the Opposition's abuse of language. But see, too, the similar charges leveled in the other direction by the *Craftsman,* no. 405 (April 6, 1734), and *Common Sense,* no. 24 (July 26, 1737) and no. 86 (September 23, 1738), where Locke's warnings about words as arbitrary signs are evoked as the prelude to an offer to provide "true" definitions "under the Patronage of Common Sense."

105. On the difference between misunderstanding and true disagreement, see again Rancière, *Disagreement,* x–xii.

106. [Montagu], *The Nonsense of Common Sense,* no. 7 (February 14, 1738), 30. Such comments echo William Pitt's earlier complaints in the *London Journal* (see "Thoughts on the Independency and Wealth of the Parliament, and the Sense of the Nation," no. 784 [July 6, 1734], and "The Sense of the People Further Considered," no. 787 [July 27, 1734]) that the sense which accords with the Whig-Patriot position is better described as "Mob-Sense" and that "The [real] Sense of the Nation hath already been shown to be with the Court, if by sense is understood the Opinions of those who have any Knowledge of Public Affairs."

107. Thomas Newcomb, *A Miscellaneous Collection of Original Poems, Consisting of Epistles, Translations, etc. Written Chiefly on Political and Moral Subjects* (London, 1740), 34.

108. Marforio [pseud.], *A Historical View of the Principles, Characters, Persons, etc. of the Political Writers of Great Britain* (London, 1740); reprinted in an edition by Robert Haig (Los Angeles, 1958), 10, 23.

109. Letter to the *Daily Gazetteer,* no. 148 (March 25, 1740), reprinted in *Gentleman's Magazine* 10 (March 1740): 133–134.

110. Anon., *The Country Correspondent,* 11.

111. Letter to the *Daily Gazetteer,* no. 148 (March 25, 1740), reprinted in *Gentleman's Magazine* 10 (March 1740): 133–134.

112. [Montagu], *The Nonsense of Common Sense,* no. 5 (January 17, 1738): 21. On the actual relationship of political writers to the market, see J. A. Downie, "Walpole, 'the Poet's Foe,'" in *Britain in the Age of Walpole,* 171–188.

113. Anon., *The Country Correspondent*, 8.

114. "Printer to the Reader," in *Common Sense; or, The Englishman's Journal. Being a Collection of Letters, Political, Humourous, and Moral, publish'd weekly under that title, for the first year* (London, 1738–1739), vi.

115. Edmund Burke famously declared this skirmish with Spain the first and only war of the century that began as a result of popular pressure. This claim has subsequently been disputed, but there is no doubt that popular political agitation grew around this issue in the late 1730s; see Dickinson, "Popular Politics in the Age of Walpole"; Nicholas Rogers, *Whigs and Cities: Popular Politics in the Age of Walpole and Pitt* (Oxford, 1989), esp. 56–61; and Wilson, *The Sense of the People*, 140–165.

116. Anon., *Common Sense: Its Nature and Use. With the Manner of bringing all disputable Cases in Common Life, to a Trial and Final Detemination* [sic] *by it. Applied to the Spanish Affair* (London, 1738), 8; the second part of this pamphlet had previously been printed in the *Daily Gazetteer* of November 21, 1737.

117. Ibid., 8.

118. See [C. Ferguson], *A Letter Address'd to Every honest Man in Britain . . . With proper Remarks on a Pamphlet lately published for the Service of the Plunderers of the Subjects of Great Britain* (London, 1738), 3–4, in which an Opposition writer also accused the author of *Common Sense: Its Nature and Use* of sinning on the title page against his much vaunted common sense by calling "Spanish depredations" simply "the Spanish Affair."

119. This distinction is borrowed from Margaret Canovan, "Trust the People! Populism and the Two Faces of Democracy," *Political Studies* 47, no. 1 (1999): 2–16.

2. EVERYMAN'S PERCEPTION OF THE WORLD

1. On Shaftesbury's years in Rotterdam, see Voitle, *The Third Earl of Shaftesbury, 1671–1713*, 86–91 and 220–21, as well as Shaftesbury's correspondence with Bayle in Rex Barrell, ed., *Anthony Ashley Cooper, Earl of Shaftesbury (1671–1713), and le "refuge français"* (Lewiston, NY, 1989), 13–39.

2. On the possible relationship between Vico and Shaftesbury, see Schaeffer, *Sensus Communis*: Vico, *Rhetoric, and the Limits of Relativism*, esp. 41–54; and Voitle, *The Third Earl of Shaftesbury*, 393–395. On the context for *The New Science*, see Harold Samuel Stone, *Vico's Cultural History: The Production and Transmission of Ideas in Naples, 1685–1750* (Leiden, 1997); and John Robertson, *The Case for Enlightenment: Scotland and Naples, 1680–1760* (Cambridge, 2005), esp. 201–255.

3. Giambattista Vico, *The New Science,* 3rd ed. [1744], trans. G. Bergin and Max H. Frisch (Ithaca, NY, 1944), bk. I, axioms XI–XIII, 63–64.

4. Felix Paknadel, "Shaftesbury's Illustrations of Characteristics," *Journal of the Warburg and Courtauld Institute* 37 (1974): 290–312.

5. On the roots of moral sense theory in Shaftesbury's insistence on a distinctive mental faculty responsible for infallible judgments in matters of aesthetics and morality, as well as the debts to moral sense theory on the part of later theorists of common

sense, see David Fate Norton, "From Moral Sense to Common Sense: An Essay on the Development of Scottish Common Sense Philosophy, 1700–1765" (PhD diss., University of California, San Diego, 1966); Laurent Jaffro, ed., *Le Sens moral. Une histoire de la philosophie morale de Locke à Kant* (Paris, 2000); and Peter Kivy, *The Seventh Sense: Francis Hutcheson and Eighteenth-Century British Aesthetics,* 2nd ed. (Oxford, 2003).

6. On communitarian anxiety about toleration as a recurrent issue, see Roger Crisp, "Communitarianism and Toleration," in *Toleration: Philosophy and Practice,* ed. John Horton and Peter Nicholson (Aldershot, UK, 1992), 108–125; and Cary J. Nederman and John Christian Laursen, eds., *Difference and Dissent: Theories of Toleration in Medieval and Early Modern Europe* (Lanham, MD, 1996).

7. Thomas Reid, *An Inquiry into the Human Mind, on the Principles of Common Sense* (Edinburgh, London, and Dublin, 1764); see the reprint of the 4th ed., edited by Derek R. Brookes (University Park, PA, 1997), 68, for this quote and all subsequent ones. Reid also calls common sense the "sovereign mistress of our opinions" (93) and endows her with her own "dominion" (20).

8. John Coates, *The Claims of C. S. Moore, Wittgenstein, Keynes, and the Social Sciences* (Cambridge, 1996), 17.

9. Roger Emerson gives the population figure for Aberdeen of 10,000 in 1700, 22,000 at midcentury, and 27,000 at the century's end, in "The Contexts of the Scottish Enlightenment," in *The Cambridge Companion to the Scottish Enlightenment,* ed. Alexander Broadie (Cambridge, 2003), 21. Richard B. Sher, in *The Enlightenment and the Book: Scottish Authors and Their Publishers in Eighteenth-Century Britain, Ireland, and America* (Chicago, 2006), gives the even lower figure of 15,000 at midcentury (118).

10. On moderate Presbyterianism in general, see Richard B. Sher, *Church and University in the Scottish Enlightenment: The Moderate Literati of Edinburgh* (Edinburgh, 1985). On Aberdeen's particular combination of religious moderation and social conservatism, see Stephen A. Conrad, *Citizenship and Common Sense: The Problem of Authority in the Social Background and Social Philosophy of the Wise Club of Aberdeen* (New York, 1987).

11. On Aberdeen's universities, see Jennifer J. Clark and Joan H. Pittock, eds., *Aberdeen and the Enlightenment: Proceedings of a Conference Held at the University of Aberdeen* (Aberdeen, 1987); Roger Emerson, *Professors, Patronage, and Politics: The Aberdeen Universities in the Eighteenth Century* (Aberdeen, 1992); and Paul B. Wood, *The Aberdeen Enlightenment: The Arts Curriculum in the Eighteenth Century* (Aberdeen, 1993), and "Science and the Pursuit of Virtue in the Aberdeen Enlightenment," in *Studies in the Philosophy of the Scottish Enlightenment,* ed. M. A. Stewart (Oxford, 1990), 127–149.

12. On the importance of clubs and learned societies in eighteenth-century Scotland, see David Allan, *Scotland in the Eighteenth Century: Union and Enlightenment* (New York, 2002), 128–131 (quote from the *Spectator,* no. 10 [March 12, 1711], 1:44, on 130). On the social dimension of Scottish philosophy more generally, see John Dwyer and Richard B. Sher, eds., *Sociability and Society in Eighteenth-Century*

Scotland (Edinburgh, 1993); and John Dwyer, *Virtuous Discourse: Sensibility and Community in Late Eighteenth-Century Scotland* (Edinburgh, 1987).

13. For this formulation, see the introduction to Burke, *A Social History of Knowledge.* On the "Wise Club," see Conrad, *Citizenship and Common Sense;* H. Lewis Ulman, ed. and intro., *Minutes of the Aberdeen Philosophical Society, 1753–1773* (Aberdeen, 1990); and Peter J. Diamond, *Common Sense and Improvement: Thomas Reid as Social Theorist* (Frankfort, 1998), esp. 28–36. Many discourses and abstracts of papers have been preserved in the David Skene Papers, MS 37 and MS 540, and the Thomas Gordon Papers, MS 3107, in the Aberdeen University Library (AUL).

14. Richard Sher points out in *The Enlightenment and the Book*, 100–101, that few Scottish Enlightenment authors came from the titled elite; a substantial number were children of Presbyterian ministers, and most were tied to institutions as professional men during their own careers—a marked contrast from England, where writers ranged socially from aristocrats to Grub Street hacks and were considerably less likely to be university professors.

15. MS 539/1 (AUL), "Questions proposed in the Philosophical Society of Aberdeen," is reproduced in Ulman, ed., *Minutes*, 189–198. This list includes "In What Cases and for What Causes Is Lime a Proper Manure?" (July 24 and August 14, 1759) and "What Is the Origine [*sic*] of the Blacks?" (March 13, 1764).

16. "Rules of the Philosophical Society of Aberdeen" (written partly by Thomas Reid in 1758), in Ibid., 78.

17. On the problem of authority in Aberdeen, see Conrad, *Citizenship and Common Sense.*

18. This passage from Skene's discourse (AUL, MS 37, fol. 173r) is reproduced in ibid., 203.

19. Reid, *An Inquiry into the Human Mind*, 12.

20. See, for example, Anon., *The Scheme of Justification by Faith Agreeable to Common Sense* (Edinburgh, 1753).

21. Anon., *An Appeal to the Common Sense of Scotsmen, especially those of the landed interest, and more especially freeholders, if their own conduct be not the source of their misery? And, if their own vigorous efforts be not the only mean of their relief?* (Edinburgh, 1747); Anon., *Patronage Demolished, and the Rights of Christian People Restored; or, Eight Reasons, drawn from Scripture, common sense, and experience, why the ensuing General Assembly should apply to Parliament for the repeal of the Act restoring patronages in Scotland* (Edinburgh, 1769); Citizen, *Common Sense. A Letter to the Fourteen Incorporations of Edinburgh* [Edinburgh, 1777]; and Anon., *An Essay on Parliamentary Representation, and the Magistrates of Our Boroughs Royal; shewing, that the abuses at present complained of, respecting both, are late deviations from our constitution, as well as from common sense; and, the necessity of a speedy reform* (Edinburgh, 1784). Similarly, see [Henry Brooke], *Liberty and Common Sense to the People of Ireland, Greeting* (Dublin, 1759).

22. Humanus, *A Strange and Wonderful Account of an Inhuman Murder Committed in the Canongate [Theatre] of Edinburgh, on Monday, March 15th, by James Scoogy on the person of common sense* [Edinburgh, c. 1765].

23. On Reid's teaching responsibilities and career trajectory, see P. B. Wood, *Thomas Reid and the Scottish Enlightenment: An Exhibition to Celebrate the 200th Anniversary of the Publication of Thomas Reid's Essays on the Intellectual Powers of Man, 1785, Thomas Fisher Rare Book Library, University of Toronto, 25 February–24 April 1985,* esp. 8–9; as well as Alexander Broadie, "Reid in Context," in *The Cambridge Companion to Thomas Reid,* ed. Terence Cuneo and René van Woudenberg (Cambridge, 2004), 31–52.

24. Thomas Gordon's notes on Reid's 1758 discourse, "The Difficulty of a Just Philosophy of the Human Mind" (AUL, MS 3107/1/1, 18), are reproduced in part in Ulman, ed., *Minutes,* 52. Shortly thereafter, in a letter to Lord Kames of February 14, 1763, Reid referred to the "first Ages of the World when Common Sense reigned uncontrolled by the Subtleties of Philosophy" (see *The Correspondence of Thomas Reid,* ed. Paul Wood [College Park, PA, 2002], 27). Diamond, *Common Sense and Improvement,* discusses the evolution of Reid's uses of common sense, 103, 112–114, though metaphor is not his focus.

25. John Stewart repeatedly took up the topic "The Nature and Various Kinds of Evidence, and the Proper Subjects of Each" from February 1759 to 1766; see Ulman, ed., *Minutes,* table A-4; and Conrad, *Common Sense and Authority,* 273–275.

26. Reid's *Inquiry* was translated as *Recherches sur l'entendement humain, d'après les principes du sens commun* (Amsterdam, 1768) and then as *Untersuchung über den menschlichen Geist* (Leipzig, 1782), at almost the same moment as Voltaire's strikingly opposed essay on common sense from his *Dictionnaire philosophique* was being translated and printed in full in the British *Monthly Review* (see xxxi [July–December 1764]: 503–515), along with an essay, probably by William Kenrick, defending its printing but also declaring that much of this dictionary deserved to be sent up in flames.

27. On George Campbell's *A Dissertation on Miracles* (Edinburgh, 1762), an effort to defend orthodox religion based in part on the "common sense of mankind," see especially Jeffrey M. Suderman, *Orthodoxy and Enlightenment: George Campbell in the Eighteenth Century* (Kingston and Montreal, 2001).

28. The idea of a "school" of common sense philosophers was originally advanced by late eighteenth-century commentators, including the critic Joseph Priestley and the Reid disciple Dugald Stewart. It has subsequently been defended in such classic works as James McCosh, *The Scottish Philosophers, Biographical, Expository, Critical, from Hutcheson to Hamilton* (London, 1875); S. A. Grave, *The Scottish Philosophy of Common Sense* (Oxford, 1960); and George Davie, "The Social Significance of the Scottish Philosophy of Common Sense" [1972], reprinted in *The Scottish Enlightenment and Other Essays* (Edinburgh, 1991), 51–85; as well as Norton, "From Moral Sense to Common Sense"; and Conrad, *Citizenship and Common Sense.*

29. Commentators seized particularly on Hume's *A Treatise of Human Nature* (1739–1740) and *An Enquiry Concerning Human Understanding* (1748), esp. sect. I and appendix I. Within the voluminous literature on Hume, see especially David Fate Norton, *David Hume: Common-Sense Moralist, Sceptical Metaphysician* (Prince-

ton, NJ, 1982), who insists on the close connection between Hume and the Aberdonians as common sense moralists, accepting of the validity of instinctive feelings in morality, even as he defines Hume as a skeptic in epistemological terms, unwilling to accept the validity of such feelings in matters of metaphysics or theology.

30. Within the huge secondary literature on Reid's *Inquiry* and his conception of common sense, see especially Louise Marcil-Lacoste, *Claude Buffier and Thomas Reid: Two Common-Sense Philosophers* (Kingston and Montreal, 1982); Daniel Schulthess, *Philosophie et sens commun chez Thomas Reid, 1710–1796* (Bern, 1983); Melvin Dalgarno and Eric Matthews, eds., *The Philosophy of Thomas Reid* (Dordrecht, 1989); Keith Lehrer, *Thomas Reid* (London, 1989); Weinsheimer, *Eighteenth-Century Hermeneutics,* chap. 5 ("Reid on Common Sense"); Diamond, *Common Sense and Improvement;* and Nicholas Wolterstorff, *Thomas Reid and the Story of Epistemology* (Cambridge, 2001) and "Reid on Common Sense," in *The Cambridge Companion to Thomas Reid,* 77–100.

31. Thomas Reid, *Essays on the Intellectual Powers of Man* [1785], in *The Works of Thomas Reid,* 7th ed., ed. William Hamilton (Edinburgh, 1872), 1:421. Reid presented part of this text to the Glasgow College Literary Society in 1769–1770; the rest was developed subsequently in the course of his teaching career in Edinburgh.

32. On the importance of common language for revealing common sense, see Henning Jensen, "Common Sense and Common Language in Thomas Reid's Ethical Theory," *The Monist* 61, no. 2 (April 1978): 299–310.

33. Wolterstorff, "Reid on Common Sense," 90.

34. Reid, *An Inquiry into the Human Mind,* 33.

35. Reid, *Essays on the Intellectual Powers of Man,* 1:234.

36. Reid, *An Inquiry into the Human Mind,* 21.

37. On Reid's universality, see Alexander Broadie, "George Campbell, Thomas Reid, and Universals of Language," in *The Scottish Enlightenment: Essays in Reinterpretation,* ed. Paul Wood (Rochester, 2000), 351–371, esp. 354.

38. On Beattie as a philosopher of common sense, see Everard King, *James Beattie* (Boston, 1977); N. T. Phillipson, "James Beattie and the Defense of Common Sense," in *Festschrift für Rainer Gruenter,* ed. Bernhard Fabien (Heidelberg, 1978), 145–154; and Pierre Morère, "James Beattie," in *The Dictionary of Eighteenth-Century British Philosophers,* ed. John W. Yolton, John Valdimir Price, and John Stephens (Bristol, 1999), 1:61–67, based on his voluminous *L'Oeuvre de James Beattie: tradition et perspectives nouvelles* (Lille, 1980).

39. James Beattie, *An Essay on the Nature and Immutability of Truth, in Opposition to Sophistry and Scepticism* (Edinburgh, 1770); see the 6th ed. for this quote (xxiv) and all subsequent ones.

40. Ibid., 6.

41. Ibid., 11–12.

42. That this was a key principle of Beattie's epistemology from the beginning can be determined by his letter of January 30, 1766, to William Forbes, in which he states, "My doctrine is this: that as we know nothing of the eternal relations of things, that

to us *is* and must be *truth,* which we feel we must believe"; see Forbes, *An Account of the Life and Writings of James Beattie, including Many of His Original Letters* (Edinburgh, 1806), 1:78.

43. Beattie, *An Essay on the Nature and Immutability of Truth,* xxx.

44. Ibid., 111–112 and 35, respectively.

45. Beattie to Thomas Blacklock, January 9, 1769, in Forbes, *An Account of the Life and Writings of James Beattie,* 1:129.

46. See National Library of Scotland (NLS), Fettercairn Papers, acc. 4796, box 100, F5 ("Professor Dugald Stewart on Beattie's Essay on Truth," n.d.).

47. See Phillipson, "James Beattie and the Defense of Common Sense," 145, in which Phillipson makes a strong case for Beattie's provincial hostility to Edinburgh. Beattie is conventionally seen—in comparison to Reid—as more of a moralist and polemicist than epistemologist. But Peter Diamond, in *Common Sense and Improvement,* describes Reid, too, as a social theorist, and Knud Haakonssen, in his edition of Reid's writings entitled *Practical Ethics* (Princeton, NJ, 1990), makes a good case for Reid as a practical moralist, especially later in his career.

48. Beattie to Thomas Blacklock, September 22, 1766, in Forbes, *An Account of the Life and Writing of James Beattie,* 1:88. Beattie makes the same point in his "Postscript" (November 1770) to *An Essay on the Nature and Immutability of Truth.*

49. See, for example, John Gregory to James Beattie, December 26, 1768, in which Gregory calls skepticism "the Bane of Virtue, Public Spirit, Sentiment . . . every solid foundation of Human Happiness" (NLS, Fettercairn Papers, acc. 4796, box 91).

50. Beattie to Thomas Blacklock, September 22, 1766, in Forbes, *An Account of the Life and Writing of James Beattie,* 1:88.

51. Beattie, *An Essay on the Nature and Immutability of Truth,* 296.

52. Ibid., 274.

53. Ibid., xvi.

54. "Dedication," in Reid, *An Inquiry into the Principles of the Human Mind,* 4.

55. On James Oswald's *An Appeal to Common Sense in Behalf of Religion* (Edinburgh, part I, 1766; part II, 1772), see Gavin Ardley, *The Common Sense Philosophy of James Oswald* (Aberdeen, 1980), who points out that though Oswald was moderator of the General Assembly of the Church of Scotland starting in 1765, he was also deeply linked to the mercantile men of Glasgow and thus, more than Beattie, able to offer a critique of the modern, commercial world from inside.

56. Beattie, *An Essay on the Nature and Immutability of Truth,* 225–226.

57. Ibid., postscript, 317. The defense of freedom of inquiry and speech constitutes one of the major subjects throughout part III and the postscript to *An Essay on the Nature and Immutability of Truth.* Similar sentiments appear in the writings of Beattie's fellow Wise Club members; see, for example, in AUL, Thomas Gordon Papers, MS 3107/2/3, Gordon's answer to question 36, which opens with the statement: "It is the happiness of the present age to have got itself entirely disengaged from Philosophical thralldom; and to encourage and countenance freedom of inquiry."

58. AUL, David Skene Papers, MS 37, f. 190v–191v and r: abstract response to question 91.

59. Wolterstorff, "Reid on Common Sense," 77.

60. Reid, *An Inquiry into the Human Mind*, 39, 68.

61. Ibid., 18.

62. Reid, *Essays on the Intellectual Powers of Man*, 1:415, 438.

63. Beattie to Forbes, April 19, 1769, in Forbes, *An Account of the Life and Writings of James Beattie*, 1:139.

64. Beattie, *An Essay on the Nature and Immutability of Truth*, 80.

65. Reid, *Essays on the Intellectual Powers of Man*, 1:415.

66. See Beattie, *An Essay on the Nature and Immutability of Truth*, 32; and Reid, *Essays on the Intellectual Powers of Man*, 1:439–440.

67. AUL, David Skene Papers, MS 475, no. 38. On the significance of the *consensus gentium* as a form of proof, especially of God, in early modern culture, see Alan Charles Kors, *Atheism in France, 1650–1729*, vol. 1, *The Orthodox Sources of Disbelief* (Princeton, NJ, 1990), esp. 135–262. As Kors points out (138), the roots of this argument go back to Cicero's claim in his *Tusculan Disputations* that "In every inquiry the unanimity of the [peoples] of the world must be regarded as a law of nature."

68. Reid, *Essays on the Intellectual Powers of Man*, 1:440.

69. Ibid., 1:438.

70. Berkeley, *Philosophical Commentaries*, 405, cited in G. S. Pappas, "Common Sense in Berkeley and Reid," *Revue Internationale de philosophie* (special issue: *Sens Commun/Common Sense*), no. 158 (1986): 298. On Berkeley's attachment to common sense in relation to that of Reid, see, too, Laurent Jaffro, "Le Recours philosophique au sens commun dans les Lumières britaniques," in *Le Sens commun*, ed. Guenancia and Sylvestre, 19–45.

71. See, for example, Norton, "From Moral Sense to Common Sense," 101, on this trope as used by Hutcheson.

72. See AUL, James Beattie Papers, MS 30/16, in which Beattie's "Journal of Sessions" (1761–1798) shows how his teachings combined psychology with practical ethics, jurisprudence, natural theology, economics, politics, logic, rhetoric, aesthetics, and universal grammar—as well as all the days he called in sick.

73. The topics of Beattie's discourses are listed in table A-4, in Ulman, ed., *Minutes*.

74. Beattie mentions "An Essay on the Fundamental Principles of Evidence" in Beattie to Forbes, June 23, 1766, NLS, Fettercairn Papers, box 91; "An Essay on Reason and Common Sense" in Beattie to Robert Arbuthnot, March 2, 1767, in Forbes, *An Account of the Life and Writings of James Beattie*, 1:100; and "An Essay on the Immutability of Truth, Intellectual, Moral, and Critical" in Beattie to Dr. Blacklocke, December 26, 1767, in *The Correspondence of James Beattie*, ed. Roger J. Robinson (Bristol, UK, 2004), 2:57.

75. See Ernest Campbell Mossner, "Beattie's 'The Castle of Scepticism': An Unpublished Allegory against Hume, Voltaire and Hobbes," *Studies in English* 27 (1948): 108–145; and King, *James Beattie*, chap. 5.

76. "Undeceiving" is a trope that repeats in several letters; see Beattie to Forbes, January 17, 1768, in Forbes, *An Account of the Life and Writings of James Beattie,* 1:111; and Beattie to Blacklocke, May 27, 1770, in ibid., 1:170. On the "standard of truth," see Beattie to Dr. Blacklocke, December 26, 1767, in *The Correspondence of James Beattie,* 2:57.

77. On Beattie's life, see Forbes, *An Account of the Life and Writings of James Beattie;* Margaret Forbes, *Beattie and His Friends* (London, 1904); and Ralph Spence Walker, ed., *James Beattie's Day Book, 1773–1798* (Aberdeen, 1948).

78. Beattie to Dr. Blacklocke, December 26, 1767, in *The Correspondence of James Beattie,* 2:57.

79. See Beattie to Robert Arbuthnot, August 8, 1769, NLS, Fettercairn Collection, box 91, on Beattie's desire for Scottish and English versions simultaneously. Other letters focus on the need for translations; see, for example, Beattie to William Laing, November 5, 1771, NLS, Fettercairn Collection, box 91, in which Beattie reports with satisfaction that he hears that translations in French, Dutch, and German are all underway in Utrecht. However, the only eighteenth-century translation that ever saw the light of day was *James Beattie's Versuch über die Natur und Unveränderlichkeit der Wahrheit im Gegensatze der Klügeley und der Zweifelsucht* (Copenhagen and Leipzig, 1772).

80. Beattie to William Forbes, June 19, 1770, in *The Correspondence of James Beattie,* 2:113.

81. *James Beattie's London Diary, 1773,* ed. Ralph Spense Walker (Aberdeen, 1946), details Beattie's quest for an annual pension on his third visit to London. Previous trips occurred in the summer of 1763, when he was still unknown outside of his home country, and in the summer of 1771, by which point he was already enjoying meetings with Johnson, Reynolds, Garrick, Mrs. Montagu, and Mrs. Thrale, based on the success of his *Essay.*

82. See ibid., 25, on the publishing history of Beattie's *Essay.* This history is put in context in Sher, *The Enlightenment and the Book,* 226–227 and 255.

83. On this portrait, see Erna Mandowsky, "Reynolds' Conceptions of Truth," *Burlington Magazine* 77 (December 1940): 195–201; P. Murray, "The Sources of Reynolds' Triumph of Truth," and Ralph Spense Walker, "The Beattie Portrait," in *Aberdeen University Review* 30 (1994): 227–229 and 224–226, respectively; and David Mannings, *Sir Joshua Reynolds: A Complete Catalogue of His Paintings* (New Haven, CT, 2000), 79–80.

84. Beattie to William Forbes, November 20, 1770, in NLS, Fettercairn Collection, box 94. Beattie's constant money worries are also apparent from his "Daybooks" (AUL, James Beattie Papers, MS 30/14 and 15), which cover several decades of household and personal expenditures and constitute a kind of autobiography focused on wealth production and consumption for a precariously middle-class eighteenth-century Scottish family, including all money spent (on spoons, rhubarb, sealing wax, the education of a nephew, taxes, house insurance, debts, coal, a trunk from London, wigs, barbers, library accounts, postage, and maps, among other items) and all monies received.

85. See, e.g., Beattie to James Williamson, September 8, 1771, in Forbes, *An Account of the Life and Writings of James Beattie,* 1:212; and Beattie to Elizabeth Montagu, March 1, 1772, in *The Correspondence of James Beattie,* 2:161.

86. See Beattie to Elizabeth Montagu, March 3, 1772, in *The Correspondence of James Beattie,* 2:166–167, on his reasons for declining a position in Edinburgh.

87. See the anonymous review of Beattie's *Essay,* later identified as the work of the Scottish writer William Rose, in *Monthly Review* 42 (June 1770): 450–457, in *Early Responses to Reid, Oswald, Beattie, and Stewart,* ed. James Fieser (Bristol, UK, 2000), 1:82.

88. On Mrs. Beattie's declining health and Beattie's recounting of her growing ever more "perverse and absurd" at the time of the appearance of his *Essay,* see Roger Robinson, "The Madness of Mrs. Beattie's Family: The Strange Case of the 'Assassin' of John Wilkes," *British Journal for Eighteenth-Century Studies* 19 (1996): 183–197. The situation is ironic only insofar as Beattie and his colleagues repeatedly set madness and lunacy in diametric opposition to common sense.

89. See Diamond, *Common Sense and Improvement,* 34–35.

90. The institutional foundations of Scottish Enlightenment culture, and particularly the focus on higher education as the necessary precondition for participation, meant that women were excluded to a greater degree than in England or France, as Sher points out in *The Enlightenment and the Book.* However, aristocratic female patrons, especially in London, played a vital role in paving the way for men like Beattie, in part by keeping them from having to sully their hands over money matters.

91. Wood, *The Aberdeen Enlightenment,* 128.

92. On Beattie's antislavery positions, see Conrad, *Citizenship and Common Sense,* 392–397; and King, *James Beattie,* 31. See, too, Iain Whyte, *Scotland and the Abolition of Black Slavery, 1756–1838* (Edinburgh, 2006), which places Beattie's Christian opposition in context.

93. Kant, *Prolegomena to Any Future Metaphysics,* trans. Beck, 7.

94. Joseph Priestley, *An Examination of Dr. Reid's Inquiry into the Human Mind on the Principles of Common Sense; Dr. Beattie's Essay on the Nature and Immutability of Truth; and Dr. Oswald's Appeal to Common Sense in Behalf of Religion* (London, 1774), reprinted in *Early Responses to Reid, Oswald, Beattie, and Stewart,* 330.

95. Ibid., 331.

96. On the European impact of Scottish Common Sense philosophy into the nineteenth century, see Manfred Kuehn, *Scottish Common Sense in Germany, 1768–1800: A Contribution to the History of Critical Philosophy* (Montreal and Kingston, 1987); *Victor Cousin, les Idéologues et les écossais: colloque international* (Paris, 1985); James W. Manns, *Reid and His French Disciples* (Leiden, 1994); and Brian Copenhaver and Rebecca Copenhaver, "The Strange Italian Voyage of Thomas Reid: 1800–1860," *British Journal for the History of Philosophy* 14, no. 4 (2006): 601–626. On the American impact, see Chapter 4.

3. THE RADICAL USES OF *BON SENS*

1. See Anon., *La Bibliothèque du bon sens portatif, ou Recueil d'ouvrages sur differentes matières importantes au salut* (London, 1773).

2. See Laurent Bay, "Notes sur la genèse des dictionnaires portatifs français. L'Exemple du Dictionnaire portatif de la langue françoise, extrait du grand dictionnaire de Pierre Richelet, 1756," in *La Lexicographie française du XVIIIe au XXe siècle,* ed. Barbara von Gemmingen and Manfred Höfler (Paris, 1988), 95–112.

3. René Descartes, *Discourse on Method,* trans. Donald A. Cress (Indianapolis, 1993 [1637]), 1.

4. Pierre Richelet, *Dictionnaire François, contenant les mots et les choses* (Geneva, 1680), 2:361: "Car le sens commun n'est pas une qualité si commune qu'on pense. Plusieurs en pensent bien avoir qui n'en ont point."

5. As the neo-Scholastic definition of *le sens commun* (as a faculty of the soul that judges objects perceived by the exterior senses) fell by the wayside, French dictionaries increasingly defined *le sens commun* as synonymous with *le bon sens.* Richelet (ibid.) defines the two identically as "the insight and reasonable intelligence with which any number of people are born." Jean-Francois Féraud, a hundred years later, still lists *le bon sens* et *le sens-commun* as synonyms in his *Dictionnaire critique, de la langue française* (Marseilles, 1787–1789), 3:548. Translators, too, seem to have used the two terms interchangeably; Hoadly's *Preservative against the Principles and Practices of the Non-Jurors* was, for example, translated in 1716 once as *Preservatif contre les principles et les pratiques des Non-Jureurs . . . ou appel à la conscience et au bon sens des Cretiens* [sic] *laiques* and once as *Preservatif contre les principles et les pratiques des non-Jureurs . . . ou appel à la conscience et au sens commun des Chretiens* [sic] *laiques.*

6. Charles de Secondat, Baron de Montesquieu, *Mes Pensées,* in *Oeuvres complètes,* ed. Roger Caillois (Paris, 1949), 1:1417.

7. *Le Dictionnaire de l'Académie française,* 1st ed. (Paris, 1694), 459. The notion of the "homme de bon sens naturel" already figures in Jean Nicot's *Thresor de la langue françoise* (Paris, 1606), 589.

8. Ferdinando Galiani, *Dialogues sur le commerce des bleds* (London [Paris], 1770), 22.

9. Jean-Jacques Rousseau, *Emile, ou De l'éducation* [1762], in *Oeuvres complètes* (Paris, 1969), 4:708. The question of women's capacity for good sense complicates the growing opposition, sketched out in Lieselotte Steinbrügge, *The Moral Sex: Women's Nature in the French Enlightenment,* trans. Pamela E. Selwyn (New York, 1995), between masculine rationality and female emotional sensitivity.

10. Bernard de Fontenelle, "Discours sur la Nature de l'Eglogue" [1688], in *Poesies pastorales* (Paris, 1968), 180.

11. [Denis Diderot], "Bon sens (Métaphysique)," in *Encyclopédie, ou Dictionnaire raisonné des sciences, des arts et des métiers* (Paris, 1751–1765), 2:328–329.

12. Denis Diderot, *Salon de 1767,* ed. J. Seznec and J. Adhemar (Oxford, 1963), 308; in this instance, Diderot uses the term *le sens commun,* which became more popular

after Voltaire's article on the subject in the second edition of his *Dictionnaire philosophique* (see note 86 on p. 289).

13. Abbé de Condillac, *Essai sur l'origine des connoissances humaines* [1746], in *Oeuvres philosophiques,* ed. Georges Le Roy (Paris, 1947–1951), 1:34.

14. Rousseau, *Emile,* in *Oeuvres complètes,* 4:512.

15. This proverb can be found in the first *Dictionnaire de l'Académie française* (1694), 459, and subsequent eighteenth-century editions.

16. The contents of these volumes, whose order varies in each existing set, include: 1. Saint-Évremond [César Chesneau Du Marsais], *Examen de la religion dont on cherche l'élaircissement de bonne foy;* 2. *La Nouvelle liberté de penser;* 3. [Voltaire], *Le Testament de Jean Meslier; Le Catéchisme de l'honnet* [sic] *homme;* and *Le Sermon de* [sic] *cinquante;* 4. [Voltaire], *Les Lettres sur les miracles;* 5/6. Nicolas-Antoine Boulanger [d'Holbach], *Le Christianisme dévoilé,* with the small treatises *La Moïsade;* [Voltaire?], *Le Voyageur Catéchumène;* and Boulanger, *La Dissertation sur Saint-Pierre;* 7. Abbé Bernier [d'Holbach], *La Théologie portative;* 8. T. L. Lau, *Méditations philosophiques sur Dieu, le Monde et l'Homme.*

17. The first edition of d'Holbach's *Le Bon-sens, ou Idées naturelles opposées aux idées surnaturelles* (London, 1772) has been definitively attributed to Rey. Most of the texts in the *Bibliothèque du bon sens* stemmed from Rey's shop as well (despite the title page listing London and individual volumes purporting to be published in Trévoux, London, Geneva, and Königsberg), and this collection shares the first three volumes with *L'Evangile de la raison* (1764, 1765, 1768), which was also published by Rey, as was the similar heterodox collection *Recueil philosophique, ou Mélange de pièces sur la religion et la morale, par différents auteurs* (1770), edited (anonymously) by d'Holbach's aide, Jacques-André Naigeon. However, in "The *Examen de la religion:* A Biographical Note," *Studies on Voltaire and the Eighteenth Century (SVEC),* no. 249 (1987): 132–135, B. E. Schwarzbach and A. W. Fairbairn argue that the *Bibliothèque du bon sens* was likely a pirated edition, built out of many of Rey's previously published seditious texts, by one of his Dutch competitors.

18. On *coutume* in French legal theory, see Donald R. Kelley, *The Human Measure: Social Thought in the Western Legal Tradition* (Cambridge, MA, 1990), esp. 89–90, 100–107, 199–207, and 221–227.

19. Claude Favre de Vaugelas, "Préface," *Remarques sur la langue françoise* (Geneva, 1970 [1647]).

20. See the preface to the 2nd edition (1718) in Bernard Quemada, ed., *Les Préfaces du Dictionnaire de l'Académie française, 1694–1992* (Paris, 1997), 133–134.

21. On the growing importance of experts to early modern governance, see Eric H. Ash, "Introduction: Expertise and the Early Modern State," *Osiris* 25 (2010): 1–24, as well as the articles that follow in the same issue.

22. Vaugelas, "Préface," *Remarques.*

23. Pierre-Antoine Leboux de La Mésangère, in his *Dictionnaire des proverbes français,* 3rd ed. (Paris, 1823), defines proverbs as "maxims full of salt and good sense" (iv), noting that each contains "a naïve truth, built on observation" (1). Despite Enlightenment

disdain for proverbs, many such dictionaries of French sayings were composed throughout the eighteenth century and into the nineteenth. For these historical examples, see [Jean-Yves] Dournon, *Le Dictionnaire des proverbes et dictons de France* (Paris, 1986).

24. Richelet, *Dictionnaire François*, 2:361; the original reads "Pour peu qu'un homme ait du bon sens il faut qu'il avoue qu'il y a un Dieu."

25. Speakers using proverbs, like conveyers of common sense, still frequently change their voice to indicate the existence of an abstract community speaking through them; see Alexandre Greimas, "Idiotismes, proverbs, dictons," *Cahiers de lexicologie* 2 (1969): 56, cited in James Obelkevich, "Proverbs and Social History," in *The Social History of Language,* ed. Peter Burke and Roy Porter (Cambridge, 1987), 44.

26. Duke of Rochefoucault [*sic*], *Moral Maxims and Reflections. In IV Parts,* 2nd ed. (London, 1706), 150 (maxim no. 24). For the original, see La Rochefoucauld, *Maximes, suivie des Réflexions diverses,* ed. Jacques Truchet, 5th ed. (Paris, 1967 [1678]), 83 (maxim no. 347).

27. Descartes, *Discourse on Method,* 6.

28. Pierre Charron, *De la Sagesse* (Geneva, 1968 [1601]), bk. II, chap. 1, 11.

29. See Charles Sorel, "Du Sens commun et du bon Sens," in *De la prudence, ou des bonnes reigles de la vie: pour l'acquisition, la conservation et l'usage légitime des biens du corps et de la fortune, et des biens de l'âme* (Paris, 1673), 263–269. On attitudes toward "opinion" in the seventeenth century, see J. A. W. Gunn, *Queen of the World: Opinion in the Public Life of France from the Renaissance to the Revolution* (Oxford, 1995), esp. 96–97.

30. François de La Mothe le Vayer, *Petit traité sceptique sur cette commune façon de parler "n'avoir pas le sens-commun,"* ed. Lionel Leforestier (Paris, 2003 [1646]), 23. See, too, Sylvia Giocanti, "La perte du sens commun dans l'oeuvre de La Mothe Le Vayer," in *Libertinage et philosophie au XVIIe siècle,* ed. Antony McKenna and Pierre-François Moreau (Saint-Etienne, 1996), 27–51.

31. La Mothe le Vayer, *Petit traité,* 28.

32. See, e.g., Claude Ameline [?], *L'Art de vivre heureux, formé sur les idées les plus claires de la raison, et du bon sens; et sur de très-belles maximes de Monsieur Descartes* (Paris, 1692); Antoine Arnauld, *Règles du bon sens pour bien juger des écrits polémiques dans des matières de science, appliquées à une dispute entre deux Théologiens . . .* (Paris, written 1693, pub. posthum. 1715); and Nicolas Petit-Pied, *Regles de l'équité naturelle et du bon sens pour l'examen de la constitution du 8 septembre 1713* (n.p., 1714).

33. Roland Mortier, "Paradoxe," in *Dictionnaire européen des Lumières,* ed. Michel Delon (Paris, 1997), 819–821, notes that the term initially signified simply a proposition contrary to received opinion. But by the time of the *Encyclopédie* article on "paradoxe," it had come to mean a position that seems absurd because it is contrary to common opinion but that is nevertheless fundamentally true.

34. *Galimatias,* or pompous nonsense, is the opponent of clarity and good sense in Antoine Furetière's *Nouvelle Allégorique, ou histoire des derniers troubles arrivés au*

royaume d'éloquence (Paris, 1658). The term was widely used in the eighteenth century by writers such as DuLaurens, d'Holbach, and Voltaire, whose 1757 *Galimatias dramatique* features Chinese characters who reject, on the basis of common sense, the mysterious language games of the representatives of all the world's main religions.

35. Françoise Charles-Daubert, *Les libertines érudits en France au XVIIe siècle* (Paris, 1998), 59.

36. La Mothe le Vayer, "De la philosophie sceptique," in *Dialogues faits à l'imitation des anciens* (Paris, 1988 [1630–1631]), esp. 49.

37. See, e.g., the complaints of Henri-Joseph DuLaurens in Stéphan Pascau, *Henri-Joseph Dulaurens (1791–1793): rehabilitation d'une oeuvre* (Paris, 2006).

38. Jean-Baptiste de Boyer, Marquis d'Argens, *Mémoires de M. le Marquis d'Argens,* 2nd ed. (London [The Hague], 1737), 308.

39. [D'Argens], *Lettres juives, ou correspondance philosophique, historique, et critique, entre un Juif voyageur à Paris et ses correspondans en divers endroits* (The Hague, 1736–1737), 3:214, 279. On toleration in the Dutch Republic, see Jonathan Israel, *The Dutch Republic: Its Rise, Greatness and Fall, 1477–1806* (Oxford, 1995). On the book trade, see C. Berkvens-Stevelinck and H. Boots, eds., *Le Magasin de l'Univers. The Dutch Republic as the Centre of the European Book Trade* (Leiden, 1992). On press freedom and its limits, see John Christian Laursen, "Imposters and Liars: Clandestine Manuscripts and the Limits of Freedom of the Press in the Huguenot Netherlands," in *New Essays on the Political Thought of the Huguenots of the Refuge,* ed. J. Laursen (Leiden, 1995), 73–108.

40. Shaftesbury, *Essai sur l'usage de la raillerie et de l'enjouement dans les conversations qui roulent sur les matières les plus importantes,* trans. Juste van Effen (The Hague, 1710); *Le Censeur, ou Caractères des moeurs de la Haye* (The Hague, 1715), possibly edited by Jean Rousset de Missy, possibly by Nicolas Gueudeville.

41. On the radical movement in Dutch culture, see Margaret C. Jacob, *The Radical Enlightenment: Pantheists, Freemasons, and Republicans* (London, 1981); Margaret Jacob and Wijnand W. Mijnhardt, eds., *The Dutch Republic in the Eighteenth Century: Decline, Enlightenment, and Revolution* (Ithaca, NY, 1992); and, most recently, Jonathan Israel's *Radical Enlightenment: Philosophy and the Making of Modernity, 1650–1750* (Oxford, 2001) and *Enlightenment Contested: Philosophy, Modernity, and the Emancipation of Man, 1670–1752* (Oxford, 2006).

42. Pierre Bayle, *Commentaire philosophique sur ces paroles de Jesus-Christ, Contrain-les d'entrer* [1686], in *Oeuvres diverses* (The Hague, 1727), 2:371.

43. There is enormous division of opinion over whether Bayle's fideism was a cover for his radicalism and a stealth means to further his support for toleration or whether it is evidence of the limits of his skepticism. For diverse readings, see Elisabeth Labrousse, *Pierre Bayle: héterodoxie et rigorisme* (Paris, 1964); Sean O'Cathesaigh, "Bayle, Commentaire philosophique, 1686," *SVEC* 260 (1989): 159–182; Gianluci Mori, *Bayle philosophe* (Paris, 1999); and Antony McKenna and Gianni Paganini, *Pierre Bayle dans la république des lettres: philosophie, religion, critique* (Paris, 2004),

as well as Israel's *Radical Enlightenment* and *Enlightenment Contested*. On the connection to La Mothe le Vayer, see Ruth Whelan, "The Wisdom of Simonides: Bayle
and La Mothe Le Vayer," in *Scepticism and Irreligion in the Seventeenth and Eighteenth Centuries,* ed. Richard H. Popkin and Arjo Vanderjagt (Leiden, 1993),
230–253.

44. Israel profiles these figures in *Radical Enlightenment* ("French Refugee Deists in
Exile"), 575–590.

45. On the shift in "dialogues of ideas" to a new satirical, ludic mode, in which the purpose was to divide reason and revelation by showing the contradictions between
them, see Roland Mortier, "Variations on the Dialogue in the French Enlightenment," *Studies in Eighteenth-Century Culture* 16 (1986): 225–240; and Stéphane
Pujol, *Le Dialogue d'idées au XVIIIe siècle* (Oxford, 2005).

46. The best source on Lahontan's life and writings is the introduction to his *Oeuvres
complètes,* ed. Réal Ouellet (Montreal, 1990). See, too, C. J. Betts, *Early Deism in
France: From the So-Called "Déistes" of Lyon (1564) to Voltaire's "Lettres philosophiques" (1734)* (The Hague, 1984), 131–136; and Jean-Marie Apostolidès,
"L'Altération du récit: les *Dialogues* de La Hontan," *Etudes françaises* 22, no. 2 (Fall
1986): 73–86.

47. [Louis-Armand de Lom d'Arce, Baron de Lahontan], *Dialogues curieux entre
l'auteur et un sauvage de bon sens qui a voyagé* in *Suplément* [sic] *aux voyages du
baron de Lahontan* (The Hague, 1703), reproduced in *Oeuvres complètes,* 2:791–885.

48. Ibid., 2:802.

49. Jules Michelet, *Histoire de France au dix-huitième siècle. La Régence,* cited in Ouellet's introduction to ibid., 1:191.

50. On the scholar taking on the position once played by the fool, exposing the con-
cealed artificialities of the modern world in the hopes of enhancing the space for
public conversation or politics, see William Connolly, *The Terms of Political Discourse,* 2nd ed. (Princeton, NJ, 1983), 266.

51. *L'Esprit des cours de l'Europe* (June 1699), 29, cited in Aubrey Rosenberg, *Nicolas
Gueudeville and His Work (1652–172?)* (The Hague, 1982), 8.

52. [Nicolas Gueudeville], *Les Motifs de la conversion,* cited in ibid., 3.

53. The third dialogue, written by Gueudeville, is reproduced in full in Lahontan, *Dialogues curieux entre l'auteur et un Sauvage de bon sens qui a voyagé et Mémoires de
l'Amérique Septentrionale,* ed. Gilbert Chinard (Baltimore, 1931), 235–259; see 241.

54. On d'Argens' life, see in addition to his memoirs: Elsie Johnson, *Le Marquis
d'Argens, sa vie et ses oeuvres* (Geneva, 1971 [1928]); Newell Richard Bush, *The Marquis d'Argens and His Philosophical Correspondence* (New York, 1953); Raymond
Trousson, "Voltaire et le Marquis d'Argens," *Studi Francesi* 29 (1966): 226–229;
Jean-Louis Vissière, ed., *Le Marquis d'Argens: colloque international de 1988, Centre aixois d'études et recherches sur le XVIIIe siècle: actes* (Aix, 1990); and Hans-
Ulrich Seifert and Jean-Loup Seban, *Der Marquis d'Argens* (Wiesbaden, 2004).

55. D'Argens, *Mémoires de Monsieur le Marquis d'Argens,* ed. Yves Coirault (Paris,
1993), 88–89 and 158 note.

56. Ibid., 117.

57. In addition to d'Argens' *Lettres juives*, see his *Lettres cabalistiques, ou Correspondance philosophique, historique et critique, entre deux cabalistes, divers esprits élémentaires, et le Seigneur Astaroth* (The Hague, 1737–1738) and *Lettres chinoises, ou Correspondance philosophique, historique et critique entre un Chinois voyageur à Paris et ses correspondans à la Chine, en Moscovie, en Perse, et au Japon* (The Hague, 1739–1740). D'Argens gave these letters, issued biweekly in periodical form, the collective title *Correspondance philosophique*.

58. D'Argens, *La Philosophie du bon sens*, ed. Guillaume Piegeard de Gurbert (Paris, 2002), originally published anonymously as *La Philosophie du bon sens, ou Réflexions philosophiques sur l'incertitude des connaissances humaines, à l'usage des cavaliers et du beau sexe* (London [The Hague], 1737). The first English edition was *The Impartial Philosopher: or, The Philosophy of Common Sense* (London, 1749), and the first German edition appeared as *Die Philosophie der gesunden Vernunft* (Breslau, 1756). See, too, Piegeard de Gurbert, "La philosophie du bon sens de Boyer d'Argens," in *La Philosophie clandestine à l'age classique*, ed. Antony McKenna and Alain Mothu (Oxford, 1997), 367–374; and "Le Marquis d'Argens, ou le matérialisme au style indirect," in *Materia actuosa. Antiquité, Age classique, Lumières, Mélanges en l'honneur d'Olivier Bloch*, ed. Miguel Benítez, Antony McKenna, et al. (Paris, 2000), 437–485.

59. D'Argens, *La Philosophie du bon sens*, preface, 56.

60. Ibid., 77.

61. [François de Salignac de La Mothe] Fénelon, *Traité de l'existence de Dieu*, ed. Jean-Louis Dumas (Paris, 1990 [1713]), 114.

62. On the varied meanings and uses of laughter in the eighteenth century, see Antoine de Baecque, *Les Eclats du rire: la culture des rieurs au XVIIIe siècle* (Paris, 2000); and P. Debailly, J. J. Robrieux, and J. Van den Heuvel, *Le Rire de Voltaire* (Paris, 1994). Humor can be generated by violations of our collective common sense and thus work to reinforce the status quo. Alternately, humor, especially of the satirical variety, can function to bring to light what is incoherent, false, or absurd in what are otherwise the unquestioned assumptions of the day.

63. Israel, *Radical Enlightenment*, 7.

64. [Frederick II and d'Argens], "Avant-Propos," in *Extrait du Dictionnaire historique et critique de Bayle* (Berlin, 1767), iii.

65. Alain Sandrier, *Le Style philosophique du Baron d'Holbach. Conditions et contraintes du prosélytisme athée en France dans la seconde moitié du XVIIIe siècle* (Paris, 2004), 341–345. For example, a chapter called "Ennemis de la Raison" in manuscript is translated as "Ennemis jurés de bon sens" in d'Holbach's version, published by Rey, in 1768.

66. Compare [Baruch Spinoza], *Réflexions curieuses d'un Esprit des-Interressé sur les matières les plus Importantes au Salut, tant Public que Particulier* (Cologne [Amsterdam], 1678), and Anon., *Bibliothèque du bon sens portatif, ou Recueil d'ouvrages sur differentes matières importantes au salut* (London [Amsterdam], 1773).

67. See Geert Mak, *Amsterdam,* trans. Philipp Blom (Cambridge, MA, 2000), esp. 166–188, on the city's eighteenth-century decline.

68. Voltaire, *Les Mensonges imprimés* [1749], cited in Jeroom Vercruysse, "Voltaire et MM Rey," *SVEC* 58 (1967): 1707.

69. See the Rey Correspondence in the Bibliotheek van de Koninklijke Vereeniging ter Bevordering van de Belangen des Boekhandels (Library of the Royal Dutch Association for the Book Trade) in the University Library of Amsterdam, which includes correspondence to Dutch colonial outposts

70. On Rey, see the many articles of Jeroom Vercruysse, including "Marc-Michel Rey, imprimeur philosophe ou philosophique?" *Werkgroep 18e eeuw. Documentatieblad,* nos. 34–35 (1977): 93–121; "Marc-Michel Rey et le livre philosophique," in *Literaturgeschichte als geschichtlicher Auftrag: In Memoriam Werner Krauss* (Berlin, 1978), 149–156; and "Typologie de Marc-Michel Rey," in *Buch und Buchhandel in Europa im achtzehnten Jahrhundert / The Book and Book Trade in Eighteenth-Century Europe. Fünftes Wolfenbütteler Symposium,* ed. Giles Barber and Bernhard Fabian (Hamburg, 1981), 167–184. See, too, the important additions in Max Fajn, "Marc-Michel Rey: Boekhandelaar op de Bloemmark [*sic*] (Amsterdam)," *Proceedings of the American Philosophical Society* 118, no. 3 (June 1974): 260–268; and Raymond Birn, "Michel Rey's Enlightenment," in *Le Magasin de l'Univers,* 23–31.

71. DuLaurens may well have put together for Rey the compendium *L'Evangile de la raison* (see note 17) out of materials pirated from elsewhere.

72. The best source on DuLaurens' life and work is Pascau, *Henri-Joseph Dulaurens (1791–1793),* but see, too, Kurt Schnelle, *Aufklärung und klerikale Reaktion: Der Prozess gegen den Abbé Henri-Joseph Laurens: ein Beitrag zur deutschen und französischen Aufklärung* (Berlin, 1963).

73. [Henri-Joseph DuLaurens], *L'Arrétin; ou, La Débauche de l'esprit en fait de bon sens* (Rome [Amsterdam], 1763), 84. See, too, *Le Compère Mathieu, ou les Bigarrures de l'esprit humain* (London [most likely Amsterdam], 1766), which continues the theme of *le bon sens* as the only legitimate judge.

74. Robert Darnton, "Publishing D'Holbach's Système de la Nature," *SVEC* 265 (1989): 1706–1709.

75. Dumarsais [D'Holbach], *Essai sur les préjugés, ou De l'influence des opinions sur les moeurs et sur le bonheur des Hommes,* ed. Herbert E. Brekle (Münster, 1990 [1770]), 50.

76. [D'Holbach], *Le Bon sens,* ed. Jean Deprun (Paris, 1971), section 195.

77. On attitudes toward *le peuple* among French *philosophes,* including d'Holbach, see *Images du Peuple. Colloque d'Aix-en-Provence* (Paris, 1973); Harry Payne, *The Philosophes and the People* (Cambridge, MA, 1976); Durand Echeverria, *The Maupeou Revolution: A Study in the History of Libertarianism, France, 1770–1774* (Baton Rouge, 1985), 281–295; and de Baecque and Mélonio, "Le Discours sur le peuple," in their *Histoire culturelle de la France,* 74–81.

78. On the relationship between d'Holbach's epistemology and his atheism, see Alan Charles Kors, "The Atheism of D'Holbach and Naigeon," in *Atheism from the Reformation to the Enlightenment,* ed. Michael Hunter and David Wootton (Ox-

ford, 1992), 273–300; Pierre Naville, *D'Holbach et la philosophie scientifique au XVIIIe siècle*, new ed. (Paris, 1967); and Sandrier, *Le Style philosophique du Baron d'Holbach*.

79. The best source on d'Holbach's salon remains Alan Charles Kors, *D'Holbach's Coterie: An Enlightenment in Paris* (Princeton, NJ, 1976), but see, too, Daniel Roche, "Salons, Lumières, engagement politique: la coterie d'Holbach dévoilée," in *Les Républicains des lettres: gens de culture et Lumières au XVIIIe siècle* (Paris, 1988), 242–253; and Antoine Lilti, *Le Monde des salons: sociabilité et mondanité à Paris au XVIIIe siècle* (Paris, 2005).

80. Introduction to d'Holbach, *Ecce homo!* ed. Andrew Hunwick (Berlin, 1995), 17–18.

81. On the argument for God's existence from linguistic proof, see Kors, *Atheism in France*, vol. 1, *The Orthodox Sources of Disbelief*, 175; atheists like d'Holbach used linguistic proof to make the opposite point.

82. D'Argens, La *Philosophie du bon sens*, 59, 153–155, respectively.

83. D'Argens, *Lettres cabalistiques*, letter 76, quoted in Bush, *Marquis d'Argens*, 89.

84. Rosenfeld, *A Revolution in Language*, esp. chap. 1.

85. Abbé Bernier [d'Holbach], *Théologie portative, ou Dictionnaire abrégé de la religion chrétienne* (London [Amsterdam], 1768), 32, 182.

86. Voltaire's definition of "common sense" first appeared in the 2nd edition of his *Dictionnaire philosophique portatif* (Berlin [Troyes], 1765). On this text, which was clearly d'Holbach's model, see especially Sylvain Menant, *Littérature par alphabet: le Dictionnaire philosophique portatif de Voltaire* (Paris, 1994), 72–76; and Christiane Mervaud, *Le Dictionnaire philosophique de Voltaire* (Paris/Oxford, 1994).

87. On this play and Helvétius's interpretation, see Chapter 1.

88. [D'Holbach], *Le Bon sens*, preface.

89. [D'Holbach], *La Politique naturelle, ou Discours sur les vrais principes du gouvernement* (London [Amsterdam], 1774), 1:v.

90. [D'Holbach], *Essai sur les préjugés*, 48.

91. [D'Holbach], *La Politique naturelle*, 1:63; and *Système Social, ou Principes naturels de la morale et de la politique* (London [Amsterdam], 1773), 2:52.

92. Rousseau, *Le Discours sur les Sciences et les Arts* [1750], in *Oeuvres complètes*, 3:6.

93. [Charles-Louis Richard], *L'Anti-Bon-Sens; ou L'Auteur de l'ouvrage intitulé Le Bon-Sens; convaincu d'outrager le bon-sens et la saine raison, à toutes les pages* (Liège, 1779), xxxiv.

94. [Louis Petit de Bachaumont], *Mémoires secrets pour servir à l'histoire de la république des lettres en France, depuis MDCCLXII jusqu'à nos jours* (London, 1783–1788), 6:218 (November 3, 1772).

95. Friedrich Melchior Grimm, *Correspondance littéraire*, ed. Maurice Tourneaux (Paris, 1877–1882), 10:174–76 (January 1773).

96. Jefferson's annotated copy of *Le Bon Sens* is in Houghton Library, Harvard University, AC7.Un33P.Zz3h.

97. See the responses in Annie Becq, ed., *Aspects du discours matérialiste en France autour de 1770* (Caen, 1981).

98. *Arrests de la Cour de Parlement, portant condamnation de plusieurs livres et autres ouvrages imprimés, extrait des Registres de Parlement, du 23 janvier 1759* (Paris, 1759), 2–3.

99. On the tactical opportunities offered by public condemnations of impious books, see Barbara Negroni, *Lectures interdites. Le Travail des censeurs au XVIIIe siècle, 1723–1774* (Paris, 1995), 25.

100. *Arrest de la Cour de Parlement, qui condamne deux libelles intitulés, l'un: Le bon sens; l'autre: De l'homme, de ses facultés intellectuelles et de son éducation; à être lacérés et brulés par l'Exécuteur de la Haute-Justice, extrait des Registres du Parlement, du dix janvier mille sept cent soixante-quatorze* (Paris, 1774), 2.

101. *Procès-verbal de l'assemblée-générale du clergé de France* (1786), cited in Darrin McMahon, *Enemies of the Enlightenment: The French Counter-Enlightenment and the Making of Modernity* (New York, 2001), 21. On the rhetoric of contagion and crisis, see, too, Amos Hofman, "The Origins of the Theory of the *Philosophe* Conspiracy," *French History* 2, no. 2 (1988): 152–172.

102. J. M. De Bujanda, *Index librorum prohibitorum: 1600–1966* (Geneva, 2002), 37; and Johann Goldfriedrich, *Geschichte des Deutschen Buchhandels* (Leipzig, 1909), 66.

103. See L.[ouis] Dutens, *Appel au bon sens* (London, 1777 [1769]).

104. See Stanislas I, *L'Incrédulité combattue par le simple bon sens* [Nancy, 1760], in *Oeuvres du philosophe bienfaisant* (Paris, 1763), vol. 4.

105. Abbé Gabriel Gauchet, *Lettres critiques, ou Analyse et réfutation de divers écrits modernes contre la religion*, vol. 8, *Sur la (Fausse) Philosophie du Bon Sens; et sur la Vraie Philosophie, exprimée dans l'Ami des Hommes, et opposée à nos Philosophes modernes* (Paris, 1757).

106. See William R. Everdell, *Christian Apologetics in France, 1730–1790* (Lewiston, NY, 1987), 45 and 21–22, on the geography of the patronage and production of apologetics and attacks on Parisian *philosophie*. Publishing centers included: Metz and Nancy (where Stanislas had influence over the academies); Besançon, Lyon, and other diocesan cities in the Rhône-Saône valley; Trévoux (site of the publication of the Jesuits' main journal); and Avignon (the papal city where the Jesuits went into exile after 1762).

107. Abbé C. F. Nonnotte, *Dictionnaire philosophique de la Religion, où l'on établit tous les Points de la Religion, attaqués par les Incrédules, et où l'on répond à toutes leurs objections,* new ed. (Besançon, 1774), 1:170–171. Earlier editions appeared in Avignon (1772) and in Lyon, Liège, and Brussels (1773).

108. Aimé-Henri Paulian, *Le Véritable système de la nature, Ouvrage où l'on expose les Loix du Monde Physique et celles du Monde Moral d'une manière conforme à la Raison, et à la Révélation* (Nîmes, 1788).

109. [Richard], *L'Anti-Bon-Sens.* See, too, Anton Maria Gardini, *L'Anima umana e sue proprietà dedotte da' soli principi di ragione contro i materialisti e specialmente contro l'opera intitolata Le Bon Sens* (Padua, 1781 [1778]), written in response to d'Holbach. Earlier redefinitions of *le bon sens* can be found in Gauchet, *Sur la (Fausse) Philosophie;* and in Anon., *Nouvelle philosophie du bon sens, ou l'on oppose les vrais princi-*

pes de la philosophie et de la théologie naturelle à la doctrine monstreuse de l'athéisme, du materialisme, du deisme, de la nouvelle philosophie de nos jours (Vienna, 1771), both responses to the work of d'Argens.

110. Abbé Barruel, *Les Helviennes, ou Lettres provinciales philosophiques,* 7th ed. (Paris, 1830 [1781–1788]), 2:13–14.

111. Ibid., 1:194.

112. Nonnotte, *Dictionnaire philosophique,* xiv, ix.

113. Dutens, *Appel au bon sens,* 15–16.

114. Barruel, *Les Helviennes,* 2:15. This theme in antiphilosophical literature goes back to Charles Palissot de Montenoy's *Le Cerle, ou les Originaux* (1755), where *le philosophe,* when told that philosophy is supposed to be consonant with common sense, declares, "What advantage is there to thinking like everyone else?"

115. See John Lough, "Chaudon's *Dictionnaire anti-philosophique,*" in *Voltaire and His World: Studies Presented to W. H. Barber,* ed. R. J. Howells, A. Mason, et al. (Oxford, 1985), 317. See, too, Hans Ulrich Gumbrecht and Rolf Reichardt, "Philosophe, Philosophie," in *Handbuch politisch-sozialer Grundbegriffe in Frankreich 1680–1820,* vol. 3, ed. R. Reichard and Eberhard Schmitt (Munich, 1985), 7–88.

116. On Bergier's double role, see Didier Masseau, *Les Ennemis des philosophes: l'antiphilosophie au temps des Lumières* (Paris, 2000), 163–169.

117. See Anon., *Tableaux de Louvre, ou il n'y a pas le sens commun, histoire véritable* (Paris, 1777), a conversation about variety in judgment.

118. See Anon., "Les Récréations de Pierre Bouline . . . de l'Académie du sens commun. A St. Malo, 1782" (Franç. 5210, Bibliothèque municipale de Morlaix); and Anon., *Cours de Sens Commun* (808996, printed brochure, n.d., Bibliothèque municipale de Lyon).

4. BUILDING A COMMON SENSE REPUBLIC

1. Classic accounts include Bernard Bailyn, *The Ideological Origins of the American Revolution* (Cambridge, MA, 1967); Eric Foner, *Tom Paine and Revolutionary America* (Oxford, 1976; 2nd ed., 2005); Jack Greene, "Paine, America, and the Modernization of Political Consciousness," *Political Science Quarterly* 93 (Spring 1978): 73–92; Isaac Kramnick, "Introduction," in *Common Sense* (London, 1976), 7–59; and John Keane, *Tom Paine: A Political Life* (New York, 1995), 83–137.

2. For Paine's own claims about sales, see Paine to Henry Laurens (January 14, 1779), in *The Complete Writings of Thomas Paine,* ed. Philip S. Foner (New York, 1945), 2:1163. Trish Loughran argues in *The Republic in Print: Print Culture in the Age of U.S. Nation Building* (New York, 2007), chap. 2, that it is more likely that a maximum of 75,000 copies were printed and distributed, most of them in Philadelphia and other cities to the north. On the multiple editions, see Richard Gimble, *Thomas Paine: A Bibliographical Checklist of "Common Sense" with an Account of Its Publication* (New Haven, CT, 1956).

3. Cited in Pauline Maier, *American Scripture: Making the Declaration of Independence* (New York, 1997), 33.

4. John Adams to James Warren, April 20, 1776, in *Letters of Delegates to Congress, 1974–1789,* ed. Paul H. Smith, et al. (Washington, DC, 1976–1979), 3:558. A similar ambiguity—does the author mean common sense the faculty? a particular set of assumptions? or the pamphlet of that name?—can be found in many written responses of the moment.

5. Samuel Adams to Samuel Cooper, April 30, 1776, in *The Writings of Samuel Adams,* ed. Harry Alonzo Cushing (New York, 1904–1908), 3:282.

6. On the naming of *Common Sense,* see Benjamin Rush to James Cheethan, July 17, 1809, in *Letters of Benjamin Rush,* ed. L. H. Butterfield (Princeton, NJ, 1951), 2:1007–1009. See, too, the similar, though not identical, account in *The Autobiography of Benjamin Rush,* ed. George W. Corner (Princeton, NJ, 1948), 113–115.

7. *The True Merits of a Late Treatise, printed in America, Intitled, Common Sense, Clearly pointed out. Addressed to the Inhabitants of America. By a late Member of the Continental Congress, a Native of a Republican State* (London, 1776), 2. This pamphlet has been attributed variously to South Carolinians Henry Middleton and John Rutledge.

8. Susan E. Klepp, "Demography in Early Philadelphia, 1690–1860," *Proceedings of the American Philosophical Society* 133, no. 2 (June 1989): 85–111, puts the population at 32,000 in 1775. The most commonly given number for 1776 is 33,000.

9. This biographical fact has not stopped a long battle over which books Paine might have read prior to the publication of *Common Sense;* see, e.g., Caroline Robbins, "The Lifelong Education of Thomas Paine (1737–1809). Some Reflections upon His Acquaintance among Books," *Proceedings of the American Philosophical Society* 127 (June 1983): 135–142. Scholarship stressing the impact of Locke on Paine's politics includes Alfred Owen Aldridge, *Thomas Paine's American Ideology* (Newark, DE, 1984), esp. 107–136; and more recently Edward Larkin, *Thomas Paine and the Literature of Revolution* (New York, 2005). On Paine's debts to various republican thinkers, see, in addition to the work of Bailyn and Foner cited earlier, Gregory Claeys, *Thomas Paine: The Social and Political Thought* (Boston, 1989); and David Wootton, "Introduction: The Republican Tradition: From Commonwealth to Common Sense," in *Republicanism, Liberty, and Commercial Society, 1649–1776,* ed. D. Wootton (Stanford, CA, 1994), esp. 26–41. There is also a large body of scholarship on the possible sources of Paine's religious notions.

10. As Paine stated in a note in *Rights of Man, Part Second,* "I saw an opportunity, in which I thought I could do some good, and I followed what my heart dictated. I neither read books, nor studied other people's opinions" (in *The Complete Writings of Thomas Paine,* ed. P. Foner, 1:406, n. 29).

11. [John Dickinson], *A Declaration by the Representatives of the United Colonies of North-America, now met in General Congress at Philadelphia, Setting forth the Causes and Necessity of their taking up Arms* (Philadelphia, July 1775), 2.

12. For efforts to link Paine to Scottish moral sense and/or common sense philosophy, see, e.g., Jay Fliegelman, *Prodigals and Pilgrims: The American Revolution against*

Patriarchal Authority, 1750–1800 (Cambridge, 1982), 103, 289 n. 4; and Jack Frucht-man Jr., *Thomas Paine and the Religion of Nature* (Baltimore, 1993), 20–22. On the impact of Scottish thought in Philadelphia in the 1760s and 1770s, see Richard B. Sher and Jeffrey R. Smitten, eds., *Scotland and America in the Age of Enlightenment* (Princeton, NJ, 1990).

13. Matthew Phelps, "John Witherspoon and the Transmission of Common Sense Phi-losophy from Scotland to America" (D.Phil. thesis, Oxford University, 2002); and Douglas Sloan, *The Scottish Enlightenment and the American College Ideal* (New York, 1971).

14. Benjamin Rush, "Thoughts on Common Sense" (April 1791), in *Essays Literary, Moral and Philosophical,* ed. Michael Meranze (Schenectady, NY, 1988 [1798]), 146–150; and "Of Genius, Intuition, and Common Sense," in *Lectures on the Mind* [1791–1810], ed. Eric T. Carlson, Jeffrey L. Wollock, and Patricia S. Noel (Philadel-phia, 1981), 519–520. On Rush's publisher, William Young, and his efforts to pro-mote Scottish Common Sense philosophy in Philadelphia in the 1790s, including putting out new, cheaper editions of the main works in this tradition, see Sher, *The Enlightenment and the Book,* 562–567. On Rush's intellectual background, see Donald J. D'Elia, *Benjamin Rush: Philosopher of the American Revolution,* in *Trans-actions of the American Philosophical Society* 64, pt. 5 (Philadelphia, 1974), esp. 9–57; and David Freeman Hawke, *Benjamin Rush: Revolutionary Gadfly* (Indiana-polis, 1971).

15. Paine, *Common Sense* (New York, 1995), 21, which follows [Paine], *Common Sense; Addressed to the Inhabitants of America,* 2nd ed. (Philadelphia, February 1776).

16. On Paine's distinctive logical and rhetorical style, see Evelyn J. Hinz, "The Rea-sonable Style of Tom Paine," *Queen's Quarterly* 79 (Summer 1972): 231–241; Bruce Woodcock, "Writing the Revolution: Aspects of Thomas Paine's Prose," *Prose Studies* 15 (August 1992): 171–186; Robert A. Ferguson, "The Commonali-ties of *Common Sense,*" *William and Mary Quarterly,* 3rd ser., 57, no. 3 (July 2000): 465–504; and Larkin, *Thomas Paine and the Literature of Revolution,* esp. 60–67, where Paine's style is contrasted with that of Franklin. David A. Wil-son, in *Paine and Cobbett, The Transatlantic Connection* (Kingston and Mon-treal, 1988), 20–29, also discusses the relevance of the "plain style" tradition for Paine.

17. Paine, *Common Sense,* 8, 16, 14, 4.

18. Ibid., 51, 4, 7, 31, 34, 30.

19. Beattie, *An Essay on the Nature and Immutability of Truth,* 24.

20. Paine, *Common Sense,* 21.

21. This term is borrowed from Edmund S. Morgan, *Inventing the People,* esp. 15.

22. Reid, *An Inquiry into the Human Mind,* 51.

23. Ibid., 39.

24. As evidence of Paine's early populist bent, see Vox Populi [Paine], "Reflections on Titles," *Pennsylvania Magazine* (May 1775): "When I reflect on the pompous titles bestowed on unworthy men, I feel an indignity that instructs me to despise the ab-surdity. The *Honourable* plunderer of his country . . . This sacrifice of common

sense is the certain badge which distinguishes slavery from freedom" (in *The Complete Writings of Thomas Paine*, ed. P. Foner, 1:33).

25. Paine, *Common Sense*, 50.

26. Author of Regulus, *A Defence of the Resolutions and Address of the American Congress, in reply to Taxation no Tyranny . . . To which are added, General Remarks on the Leading Principles of that work . . . and A Short Chain of Deductions from One Clear Position of Common Sense and Experience* (London, 1775), 8, 10.

27. Jonas Hanway, *Common Sense: In Nine Conferences, between A British Merchant and A Candid Merchant of America, in their private capacity as friends; tracing the several causes of the present contests between the mother country and her American subjects* (London, 1775), 71.

28. Ferguson, "The Commonalities of *Common Sense*," 472.

29. Paine, *Common Sense*, [xxvii], 48, 21, 23.

30. Ibid., 24, 23. On Paine's use of the Bible, see Thomas P. Slaughter, ed., *Common Sense and Related Writings* (Boston, 2001), 35.

31. Paine, *Common Sense*, 56, 21, 34, 65. For an exposition of Paine's use of the language of commonality to disguise the fact that he has positioned himself as epistemologically outside the community he constructs, see Edward H. Davidson and William J. Scheick, "Authority in Paine's *Common Sense* and *Crisis Papers*," *Studies in the Humanities* 18 (1991): 124–134. On Paine's approach to time, see Bernard Vincent, *The Transatlantic Republican: Thomas Paine and the Age of Revolutions* (Amsterdam, 2005). On Paine and shock, see Wilson, *Paine and Cobbett*, 55.

32. Rush, "Thoughts on Common Sense," in *Essays Literary, Moral and Philosophical*, 150, 147.

33. Bayle figures among the library's holdings in *Laws of the Library Company of Philadelphia. Made, in Pursuance of their Charter, at a General Meeting, held in the Library, on the Third Day of May, 1742* (Philadelphia, 1746). In *A Catalogue of the Books, Belonging to the Library Company of Philadelphia* (Philadelphia, 1789), works by Bayle are listed alongside those of all of the Scottish figures mentioned earlier. The Presbyterian minister Gilbert Tennent, whose Philadelphia church Rush attended in his youth, also encouraged congregation members to read Bayle; see, for example, Tennent's 1752 sermon "The Divine Government Over All Considered" (cited in Nina Reid-Maroney, *Philadelphia's Enlightenment, 1740–1800: Kingdom of Christ, Empire of Reason* [Westport, CT, 2001], 88).

34. See Benjamin Franklin, "Poor Richard's Almanack, 1733–1758," in *Benjamin Franklin: Writings*, ed. Leo Lemay (New York, 1987), 1181–1304. Poor Richard (like Franklin) evoked the common man and his aphoristic language, on the one hand, and a commitment to "plain truth" (the title of one of Franklin's other pre-revolutionary publications and of Paine's first draft of *Common Sense*), on the other.

35. Ferguson, in "The Commonalities of *Common Sense*," emphasizes the "conflict of alternatives" (468) and the "manic-depressive quality" (467) of Paine's claims. In contrast, I want to highlight the dualist structure of argumentation undergirding the whole as a result of Paine's dependency on the notion of common sense.

36. Cited in Kramnick, "Introduction," in *Common Sense*, 29.

37. George Washington to Joseph Reed, April 1, 1776, in *The Papers of George Washington, Revolutionary Series*, ed. W. W. Abbot, et al. (Charlottesville, VA, 1991), 4:11.

38. In the *Pennsylvania Evening Post* (February 6, 1776), a writer from Maryland claimed that Paine had "worked miracles" with *Common Sense* (cited in Moses Coit Tyler, *The Literary History of the American Revolution, 1763–1783* [New York, 1966], 1:472).

39. "To the Author of the Pamphlet Entitled Common Sense," *Connecticut Gazette* [New London] (March 22, 1776): [1].

40. David Ramsay, *The History of the American Revolution* (Dublin, 1793), 228, 300, 301. Compare with Rush's own account in his *Autobiography*, 114–115.

41. Jefferson to Henry Lee, May 8, 1825, in *Writings of Thomas Jefferson*, ed. Andrew Lipscomb and Albert Ellery Bergh (Washington, 1903), 16:118. On the related issue of the "self-evidence" of the Declaration's principles, see the conflicting interpretations of Morton White, *The Philosophy of the American Revolution* (New York, 1978), esp. 72–78; Garry Wills, *Inventing America: Jefferson's Declaration of Independence* (Garden City, NY, 1979); Michael Zuckert, "Self-Evident Truth and the Declaration of Independence," *Review of Politics* 49, no. 3 (1987): 319–339; and Jay Fliegelman, *Declaring Independence: Jefferson, Natural Language, and the Culture of Performance* (Stanford, CA, 1993), 45, 51–52, 229 n. 32.

42. See, e.g., Noah Webster, *The Prompter; or, A Commentary on Common Sayings and Subjects, which are full of Common Sense, the best Sense in the World: published according to an act of Congress* (Hartford, CT, 1791); and David Everett, *Common Sense in Dishabille; or, The Farmer's Monitor. Containing A Variety of Familiar Essays on Subjects Moral and Economical* (Worcester, MA, 1799).

43. On common sense as a form of proof in early advertising, see James Delbourgo, *A Most Amazing Scene of Wonders: Electricity and Enlightenment in Early America* (Cambridge, MA, 2006), 239–277.

44. Cited in Wilson, *Paine and Cobbett*, 59.

45. See Thomas Bull, *Resolutions of Common Sense about Common Rights* (London, c. 1776); and Common Sense [John Cartwright], *The Memorial of Common-Sense, upon the Present Crisis between Great-Britain and America* (London, 1778). Others replied in the name of, and with appeals to, related concepts; see, e.g., Anon., *Reason. In Answer to a pamphlet entitled Common Sense* (Dublin, 1776); and Candidus [James Chalmers], *Plain Truth; Addressed to the Inhabitants of America, Containing, Remarks on a Late Pamphlet, entitled Common sense* (Philadelphia, 1776). On the pamphlet's reception, see Aldridge, *Thomas Paine's American Ideology*, 158–215.

46. An American [Charles Inglis], *The True Interest of America Impartially Stated, in Certain Strictures on a Pamphlet intitled Common Sense* (Philadelphia, [February] 1776), v–vii.

47. Rationalis, *Another reply to Common sense*, appended to Candidus, *Plain Truth*, 68.

48. Cato [William Smith], "To the People of Pennsylvania. Letter IV," *Pennsylvania Ledger,* no. 62 (March 30, 1776): supplement, [1].

49. Cato, "To the People of Pennsylvania. Letter VII," *Pennsylvania Ledger,* no. 65 (April 20, 1776): [2].

50. Cato, *Extract from the Second Letter to the People of Pennsylvania; being that part of it which relates to Independency,* also appended to Candidus, *Plain Truth,* 80; originally published as "To the People of Pennsylvania. Letter II," *Pennsylvania Ledger,* no. 60 (March 16, 1776): [1].

51. Inglis, *The True Interest of America,* 27, vi.

52. Anon., "To the Worthy Inhabitants of the Province of Pennsylvania," *Pennsylvania Packet* (May 20, 1776): 3.

53. Gordon Wood, *The Creation of the American Republic, 1776–1787* (Chapel Hill, NC, 1969), 83–84.

54. This argument is now associated with an older literature linking the origins of Philadelphia's internal revolution, as well as independence movement, to an ongoing social struggle; see Foner, *Tom Paine;* and Gary Nash, *The Urban Crucible: Social Change, Political Consciousness, and the Origins of the American Revolution* (Cambridge, MA, 1979). For reassessments of the economic situation and political sentiments of "the lower sort" in late colonial Philadelphia, see Steven Rosswurm, *Arms, Country, and Class: The Philadelphia Militia and "Lower Sort" during the American Revolution, 1775–1783* (New Brunswick, NJ, 1987); Billy G. Smith, *The "Lower Sort": Philadelphia's Laboring People, 1750–1800* (Ithaca, NY, 1990); and Ronald Schultz, *The Republic of Labor: Philadelphia Artisans and the Politics of Class, 1720–1830* (Oxford, 1993).

55. "Diary of James Allen, Esq. of Philadelphia, Counsellor-at-Large, 1770–1778," *Pennsylvania Magazine of History and Biography* 9 (1885), 186.

56. See Worthington Chauncey Ford, et al., eds., *Journals of the Continental Congress, 1774–1789* (Washington, DC, 1904–1937), 4:342, 357–358.

57. Anon., *The Alarm: or, An Address to the People of Pennsylvania on the Late Resolve of Congress* (Philadelphia, [May 19,] 1776), reproduced in *American Political Writing during the Founding Era, 1760–1805,* ed. Charles S. Hyneman and Donald S. Lutz (Indianapolis, 1983), 1:322, 324, 326.

58. Specifically on the origins, framing, and content of the 1776 Pennsylvania Constitution, see J. Paul Selsam, *The Pennsylvania Constitution of 1776: A Study in Revolutionary Democracy* (Philadelphia, 1936); David Hawke, *In the Midst of a Revolution* (Philadelphia, 1961); and Richard Alan Ryerson, *Revolution Is Now Begun: The Radical Committees of Philadelphia, 1765–1776* (Philadelphia, 1978).

59. On the history of the idea of popular sovereignty in eighteenth-century America, see Paul K. Conklin, *Self-Evident Truths* (Bloomington, IN, 1974); as well as Michael Kammen, *Sovereignty and Liberty: Constitutional Discourse in American Culture* (Madison, WI, 1988). According to Morgan, in *Inventing the People,* the idea of the people as a source of authority goes back to the English Civil War, if not before. However, in America as in England, it took the removal of a king's authority

for the relationship of this principle to the idea of representation to be explicitly questioned.

60. *Extracts from the Diary of Christopher Marshall,* ed. William Duane (Albany, 1877; repr. 1967), May 18, 1776, 72. On the meeting itself, see the broadside *Philadelphia, May 20. At a meeting, at the Statehouse, of a very large number of the inhabitants of the city in which it was resolved to replace the Assembly,* as well as the proceedings published in *American Archives,* ed. Peter Force, 4th ser. (Washington, 1837–1846), 6:517–519.

61. On the era of state constitution writing, see Willi Paul Adams, *The First American Constitutions: Republican Ideology and the Making of the State Constitutions in the Revolutionary Era,* trans. Rita Kimber and Robert Kimber (Chapel Hill, NC, 1980); Donald S. Lutz, *Popular Consent and Popular Control: Whig Political Theory in the Early State Constitutions* (Baton Rouge, LA, 1980); and Marc W. Kruman, *Between Authority and Liberty: State Constitution Making in Revolutionary America* (Chapel Hill, NC, 1997). Robert F. Williams, in "The State Constitutions of the Founding Decade: Pennsylvania's Radical 1776 Constitution and Its Influences on American Constitutionalism," *Temple Law Review* 62 (1989): 541–585, notes that controversy swirled in most cases less around questions of individual rights than around questions of rulership, that is, who should determine policy and how.

62. Foner, *Tom Paine* (1976 ed.), xvi.

63. On evolving understandings of suffrage in America, see Chilton Williamson, *American Suffrage: From Property to Democracy, 1760–1860* (Princeton, NJ, 1960), esp. 3–19, 92–116; Kruman, *Between Authority and Liberty,* 87–108; and Alexander Keyssar, *The Right to Vote: The Contested History of Democracy in the United States* (New York, 2000), esp. 8–10, who points out that one of the standard arguments for a limited franchise depended on the contradictory claims that the poor should not vote (1) because they did not have a will of their own and (2) because they would threaten the interests of property—that is, they had too much will of their own.

64. John Adams to James Sullivan, May 26, 1776, in *Papers of John Adams,* ed. Robert J. Taylor (Cambridge, MA, 1977), 4:210.

65. See the "Petition from the Committee of Privates of the Military Association of the City and Liberties of Philadelphia," directed to the General Assembly, February 12, 1776, in *American Archives,* 4th ser., 5:662–664.

66. Demophilus [George Bryan?], *The Genuine Principles of the Ancient Saxon, or English Constitution* (Philadelphia, 1776), in *American Political Writing,* ed. Hyneman and Lutz, 1:349. On this mythology, see the classic essay by Christopher Hill, "The Norman Yoke," in *Puritanism and Revolution: Studies in Interpretation of the English Revolution of the Seventeenth Century* (London, 1958), 50–122.

67. On the issue of the expansion of the franchise, as well as limitations regarding political and religious allegiances, see "Proceedings of the Provincial Conference on Committees of the Province of Pennsylvania, held at Carpenter's Hall, at Philadelphia,

begun June 18, and confirmed by adjournments to June 25, 1776," in *American Archives,* 4th ser., 6:951–967.

68. Paine's ideas about the franchise were actually not as radical as those of Cannon and the associators. But his faith in "first principles" and his anti-aristocratic bias are both evident in the fourth of The Forester's Letters, published in *The Pennsylvania Journal* (May 8, 1776); see *The Complete Writings of Thomas Paine,* ed. P. Foner, 2:83.

69. [James Cannon], *To the Several Battalions of Military Associators in the Province of Pennsylvania* (June 26, 1776). Cannon argued later that the circular was the result of the Committee of Privates' deliberation and represented the views of that body (see Rosswurm, *Arms, Country, and Class,* 102), but it has been widely accepted that Cannon is the primary author.

70. A Watchman, "To the Common People of Pennsylvania," *Pennsylvania Packet* (June 10, 1776).

71. [Cannon], *To the Several Battalions.*

72. Pierre-André Taguieff, in *L'Illusion populiste,* makes the important point that one of the hallmarks of populism is a constant tension between demagoguery, or preying on the people's fears and prejudices, and demophilia, or genuine love for the people.

73. Two exceptions are George McKenna, ed., *American Populism* (New York, 1974); and, recently, Ronald P. Formisano, *For the People: American Populist Movements from the Revolution to the 1850s* (Chapel Hill, NC, 2008).

74. Anon., *The Alarm,* 325.

75. A Watchman, "To the Common People of Pennsylvania," *Pennsylvania Packet* (June 10, 1776).

76. See Anon., *An Essay of a Declaration of Rights* (Philadelphia, 1776); and Demophilus, *The Genuine Principles of the Ancient Saxon, or English Constitution,* respectively.

77. On the reign of consensus as the goal of populism, see Laclau, *On Populist Reason.*

78. On membership in the convention, see William H. Egle, "The Constitutional Convention of 1776: Biographical Sketches of Its Members," *Pennsylvania Magazine of History and Biography* 111 (1879). On the convention itself, see the *Minutes of the Proceedings of the Convention of the State of Pennsylvania* (Philadelphia, 1776), reproduced in *American Archives,* 5th ser. (1848–1853), 2:1–62.

79. Morgan, *Inventing the People,* 169.

80. Benjamin Rush identifies the principle architects as Cannon, Matlack, and Young, with Reed, Bryan, and Parson Ewing among the most important defenders; see Benjamin Rush to John Adam, February 24, 1790, in *Letters of Benjamin Rush,* 1:532. There is still no consensus, however, regarding authorship.

81. Bryan, "Letter I. To Ludlow"(May 24, 1777), cited in Joseph Foster, *In Pursuit of Equal Liberty: George Bryan and the Revolution in Pennsylvania* (University Park, PA, 1994), 82.

82. On the arguments for bicameralism and, more unusually, unicameralism in the writing of the first state constitutions, see Jackson T. Main, *The Upper House in Revolutionary America, 1763–1788* (Madison, WI, 1967); and Kruman, *Between Authority and Liberty,* esp. 131–136.

83. "One of the People," *Pennsylvania Evening Post* (November 23, 1776): 585.

84. "The Proposed Plan or Frame of Government for the Commonwealth or State of Pennsylvania" was offered to the public on September 5, 1776. The final, revised version, printed as *The Constitution Of The Common-wealth Of Pennsylvania, As Established By The General Convention Elected For That Purpose,* was adopted on September 28, 1776. The various sections are described in detail in Selsam, *The Pennsylvania Constitution of 1776.* The quote is from section 5 of the Declaration of Rights.

85. On the various oaths adopted for officeholders and voters by the constitutional convention and then the General Assembly, see the *Pennsylvania Archives,* 3rd ser., ed. W. H. Egle (Philadelphia, 1894–1899), 10:766–767; and the *Statutes at Large of Pennsylvania from 1682 to 1801,* ed. James T. Mitchell and Henry Flanders (Philadelphia, 1903), 9:110–114.

86. Robert Williams takes a similar position in "The State Constitutions of the Founding Decade," when he calls the Pennsylvania Constitution "a popular theoretical foundation for a simple, broad-based communitarian republic" (580). In contrast, Eric Foner, in *Tom Paine,* emphasizes the limits of this vision, including the continued exclusion of the unfree and the poor.

87. On opposition to the Pennsylvania Constitution and the conservative backlash, see Robert Brunhouse, *The Counter-Revolution in Pennsylvania, 1776–1790* (Harrisonburg, PA, 1942); and Douglas M. Arnold, *Republican Revolution: Ideology and Politics in Pennsylvania, 1776–1790* (New York, 1989).

88. See, respectively, the broadside *At a Meeting, Held at the Philosophical Society Hall, on Tuesday evening, October 17, 1776* (Philadelphia, 1776); and Thomas Smith to Arthur St. Clair, August 3, 1776, in *The St. Clair Papers. The Life and Public Services of Arthur St. Clair,* ed. William Henry Smith (Cincinnati, 1883), 1:371.

89. Thomas Smith to Arthur St. Clair, August 3, 1776, in *The St. Clair Papers,* 1:371.

90. For a satire of the idea that the constitution was a product of "simplemen" whose principle commitment was to "this damn simplicity of theirs," see "Orator Puff to John his friend, over a bottle of Madeira," *Pennsylvania Evening Post* (October 19, 1776), cited in Selsam, *The Pennsylvania Constitution,* 206.

91. Thomas Smith to Arthur St. Clair, August 22, 1776, in *The St. Clair Papers,* 1:373–374.

92. Cato, "To the People of Pennsylvania," *Pennsylvania Packet* (March 25, 1776).

93. Demophilus, "[Letter to] Messr. Bradford," *Pennsylvania Journal* (September 25, 1776).

94. See the instructions to the representatives of the city of Philadelphia in *At a Meeting of a Number of the Citizens of Philadelphia, in the Philosophical Society-Hall, the 8th*

of November, 1776 (Philadelphia, 1776); and K., "Remarks on the Constitution of Pennsylvania," *Pennsylvania Packet* (September 24, 1776): 2, respectively. Both betray the influence of John Adams's *Thoughts on Government: Applicable to the Present State of the American Colonies* (Philadelphia, 1776), regarding the epistemological necessity of an upper house.

95. Foner, *Tom Paine*, 135.

96. C. A. Bayly, *The Birth of the Modern World, 1780–1914: Global Connections and Comparisons* (Malden, MA, 2004), suggests that the two great innovations of the age of revolutions were, first, the idea that rights were "self-evident" and could be nullified by no authority and, second, the idea of "the people," the possessors of rights, as a potentially creative political force. My argument is that common sense binds them together.

97. The original articles, published in May–June 1777 in the *Pennsylvania Journal*, were reprinted that same year as *Observations upon the Present Government of Pennsylvania in Four Letters;* see *The Selected Writings of Benjamin Rush*, ed. Dagobert D. Runes (New York, 1947), 54–84.

98. Hawke, *Revolutionary Gadfly*, 183.

99. See Rush to Charles Nisbet (August 27, 1784), 1:336, on Cannon; Rush to Anthony Wayne (April 22, 1777), 1:136, on the new constitution as full of "newfangled experiments, absurd in their nature"; Rush to Anthony Wayne (May 19, 1777), 1:148, on the new constitution as a recipe for "mob government"; and Rush to Charles Lee (October 24, 1779), 1:244, where he insists that the "single legislature is big with tyranny" and "all our laws breathe the spirit of town meetings and porter shops"; all citations refer to *The Letters of Benjamin Rush*.

100. Rush, *Observations upon the Present Government of Pennsylvania*, 71, 63, 78.

101. Rush, *Lectures on the Mind*, 520.

102. Wilson discusses common sense extensively in his *Lectures on Law* (1790–1791); see the *Collected Works of James Wilson,* ed. Kermit L. Hall and Mark David Hall (Indianapolis, 2007), 1:599.

103. Addison [James Wilson], "For the Pennsylvania Journal," *Pennsylvania Journal* (May 14, 1777): 2.

104. On Wilson's investment in common sense, see Stephen A. Conrad, "Polite Foundation: Citizenship and Common Sense in James Wilson's Republican Theory," *Supreme Court Review* (1984): 359–388; Shannon C. Stimson, "'A Jury of the Country': Common Sense Philosophy and the Jurisprudence of James Wilson," in *Scotland and America in the Age of Enlightenment,* 193–208; and Robert Green McCloskey, introduction to his edition of *The Works of James Wilson* (Cambridge, MA, 1967), 1:14–17.

105. Wilson anonymously laid out his defense of bicameralism, which no longer depended upon a social distinction between the two houses, in the *Pennsylvania Journal* (July 7, 1784): 2, and (July 10, 1784): 1–2.

106. A recent example is Terry Bouton, *Taming Democracy: "The People," the Founders, and the Troubled Ending of the American Revolution* (New York, 2009).

107. Mark Noll, *America's God: From Jonathan Edwards to Abraham Lincoln* (New York, 2002), 233, points out that common sense was one of the few authorities to survive the American Revolution intact.

108. Herbert J. Strong, *The Complete Anti-Federalist* (Chicago, 1981), 1:54.

109. Philirenaeus, *To the Free and Independent Electors of the City of Philadelphia* (Philadelphia, 1776).

110. J. Paul Selsam, "Brissot de Warville on the Pennsylvania Constitution of 1776," *Pennsylvania Magazine of History and Biography* 72 (January 1948): 25–43; J. Paul Selsam and Joseph G. Rayback, "French Comment on the Pennsylvania Constitution of 1776," *Pennsylvania Magazine of History and Biography* 76 (1952): 311–325; and Horst Dippel, "Aux origines du radicalisme bourgeois: de la constitution de Pennsylvanie de 1776 à la constitution jacobine de 1793," *Francia* 16, no. 2 (1989): 61–73. Dozens of editions of the Pennsylvania Constitution were published in French between late 1776 and 1793, many with versions of *Poor Richard's Almanack* attached; see Durand Echeverria, "French Publications of the Declaration of Independence and the American Constitutions, 1776–1783," *Papers of the Biographical Society of America* 47 (1953): esp. 331.

111. On nineteenth-century Latin American appropriations of Paine, see A. O. Aldridge, "Tom Paine in Latin America," *Early American Literature* 3, no. 3 (Winter 1968–1969): 139–147; as well as the first, anonymous Spanish translation of Paine's tract, *Reflecciones politicas escritas baxo el titulo de instincto commun* (London, 1811; Lima, 1821). To my knowledge, no equivalent article exists for Europe, but see the anonymous pamphlet *Second cri du Sens commun, ou considérations sur la révolution française et sur les moyens de la conduire à sa véritable fin* (Paris, 1848), in which the author seeks to continue the project that began with "a first cry of Common sense" in 1776; and see [Johann Greis], *Republik oder Monarchie? Beantwortet durch Thomas Paine's "gesunder Menschenverstand" und "Menschenrechte"* (Hamburg, 1848).

5. MAKING WAR ON REVOLUTIONARY REASON

1. Here I follow Roger Dupuy, *La Politique du peuple, XVIIIe–XXe siècles: racines, permanences et ambiguïtés du populisme* (Paris, 2002), in seeing populism in France as a product of the French Revolution (of sansculottism but also of popular resistance to the Revolution), rather than as a solely nineteenth-century phenomenon.

2. On "the people" as a political myth that is in tension in all democratic movements with a sociologically diverse people, see (for France) Pierre Rosanvallon, *Le Peuple introuvable: histoire de la représentation démocratique en France* (Paris, 1998).

3. On the Genevan pamphlet war of the late 1770s among the so-called *negatifs,* the *représentants,* and the *natifs,* see Anon., *Lettre d'un citoyen à un de ses amis, sur l'étonnement où il est de voir paroître un aussi grand nombre de brochures* ([Geneva],

January 19, 1777); and [Francis d'Ivernois], *Tableau historique et politique des deux dernieres révolutions de Genève* (London [Geneva?], 1789).

4. [Etienne-Salomon Reybaz], *Lettre à l'auteur de la Réponse aux deuxième, troisième et quatrième Lettres à un négatif modéré. Contenant une courte description de la fête du 15e du courant* (Geneva, December 1780), 7.

5. Letter to M. le Comte de Finkenstein, Minister of the King of Prussia, 1781, in Papers of Reybaz, Bibliothèque publique universitaire de Genève, ms. 923, 10–15ff.

6. See [Etienne-Salomon Reybaz], *Appel au sens commun, ou lettre à l'auteur des Reflexions impartiales, sur un projet de conciliation* ([Geneva], 1777), esp. 9. This tract then occasioned an *Eloge de l'Appel au sens commun, par un ancient natif, dévenu nouveau citoyen. Enrichi de notes politiques et morales d'un étranger qui habite depuis deux siècles parmi nous* ([Geneva], 1777), which in turn generated a *Lettre du neveu natif, à l'auteur de l'Eloge de l'Appel au sens commun* ([Geneva], 1777), both at odds with Reybaz's position.

7. [Etienne-Salomon Reybaz], *Défense apologétique des citoyens et bourgeois représentans, de la Ville et République de Genève. Précédée d'une adresse aux Seigneurs Syndics, remise par les citoyens et bourgeois représentans le 10 novembre 1779* (Geneva, 1779), 34.

8. *Lettre d'un quaker de Philadelphie, capitale de Pensilvanie à un citoyen de Genève. Philadelphie le 1 juin 1771* (1772), in favor of the admission of all *natifs* to the bourgeoisie; [Jacques-Antoine Du Roveray], *Préservatif contre les mensonges politiques adressé à l'auteur des Observations sur les dangers de la Patrie et precédé d'un avertissement* (A Philadelphie, de l'imprimerie des Etats-Unis, 1777), another defense of the *représentant* cause; the *Gazette américaine* (1780) and *Le Postillon de la liberté, ou le courier américain* (1780), both satires of the *négatif* position, the latter featuring "Monsieur Bonsens, Philosophe Cosmopolite"; and *Lettre d'un Bostonois, écrite de Genève à son ami, à Philadelphie* (1781), all published in Geneva.

9. See [Antoine François Lemaire], *Le Sens commun du bon homme Richard sur l'affaire de Nancy* (Philadelphie [Paris], [early September 1790]). See, too, *La Voix du peuple, ou les anecdotes politiques du bon-homme Richard, sur les affaires du temps* (Paris, September–October 1789); *Le Bonhomme Richard aux bonnes gens* (Paris, May–June 1790); *La Puce à l'oreille du bon-homme Richard, capitaine de la garde non soldée, à Paris* (Paris, 1791); and [Jean-Baptiste Jumelin], *Lettre écrite au bonhomme Richard, concernant les assignats* (Paris, [c. 1791]). See, too, James Leith, "La culte de Franklin avant et pendant la Révolution française," *Annales historiques de la Révolution française* (1976): 543–571.

10. See Serviteur Régnier, ed., *Recueil des lois constitutive des colonies angloises* (Philadelphia and Paris, 1778), cited in Echeverria, *Mirage in the West*, 72.

11. [Alexandre Achard de Germane], *Le Sens commun. No. 1er. Idée générale de l'état de la France* (n.p., [early 1790]), 2, 1.

12. The first French edition of Paine's *Common Sense* appeared in Rotterdam in 1776. Long sections of *Common Sense* were also published in French by the pro-American newspaper *Affaires de l'Angleterre et de l'Amérique* (see vol. 1, 33–103) that Franklin

helped launch in 1776; and in 1777, a substantial extract was published either within France or the Low Countries as *Les Principes de la Révolution justifié dans un sermon prêché devant l'Université de Cambridge, le mercredi 29 mai 1776 par Richard Watson . . . suivi d'un extrait du pamphlet américain, intitulé Le commonsense.* Full French translations (in which the author promised to provide in the following pages "que de simple faits, des raisonnemens naturels et du bon sens") then appeared from the publisher Gueffier in Paris in 1791 (*Le Sens commun. Ouvrage adressé aux Américains, et dans lequel on traite de l'origine et de l'objet du gouvernement, de la constitution angloise, de la monarchie héréditaire, et de la situation de l'Amérique Septentrionale,* trans. Antoine-Gilbert Griffet de la Baume); from Buisson in Paris in 1793 (*Le Sens commun, adressé aux habitans de l'Amérique);* and again in a new edition chez Gueffier and Regnier in Paris in 1793 with the 1791 title. When the Imprimerie du Cercle Social published Paine's *Théorie et pratique des droits de l'homme* [*Rights of Man, Part II*] in 1792, in a translation by his close associate François Lanthenas, Paine was described in the introduction as "cet homme libre, qui semble né pour prêché, avec le même succès qu'en Amérique, le SENS COMMUN, à toute la terre" (2). That same year, the Cercle Social published a *placard* entitled *Invocation au Sens-Commun* beginning "O! Sens Commun! . . . chose trop rare! . . . viens éclairer, pour leur honneur et pour leur avantage, tous les Sots et tous les Méchans." And when Lanthenas translated the first edition of Paine's soon-to-be notorious denunciation of organized religion in March 1793, he did so with the onetime title *Le Siècle de la raison; ou, Le sens commun des droits de l'homme.*

13. [Achard de Germane], *Le Sens commun, No. 1er,* 6.
14. On the emergence of a democratic public sphere in Paris and the explosion of speech within, see Jacques Guilhaumou, *L'Avènement des porte-parole de la république (1789–1792). Essai de synthèse sur les langages de la révolution française* (Villeneuve-d'Ascq, 1998); and Raymonde Monnier, *L'Espace public démocratique. Essai sur l'opinion à Paris de la Révolution au Directoire* (Paris, 1994).
15. Quentin Skinner, *Liberty before Liberalism* (Cambridge, 1998), 105.
16. Donald MacRae, "Populism as Ideology," in *Populism: Its Meanings and Natural Characteristics,* 156–158.
17. Anon., *Le Gros bon sens, adressé à l'Assemblée nationale* (Paris, October 1789), 21.
18. [C. D. Lacoste-Mezières], *Lettre d'un vieillard de bon sens aux bonnes gens de Marseille* (Marseille, [c. 1790]). In 1795, the same man edited a journal called *Le Décadaire marseillais, ou les loisirs d'un vieillard de bon sens,* making suspect his earlier claim of illiteracy.
19. Andrea Frisch, *The Invention of the Eyewitness: Witnessing and Testimony in Early Modern France* (Chapel Hill, NC, 2004), recounts the epistemological prestige of seeing, itself rooted in first-person, naked experience, in early modern French law and science. My claim is that this same social epistemology became attached to an increasingly impersonal, mass form of politics during the Revolution.
20. [Lacoste-Mezières], *Lettre d'un vieillard de bon sens,* 2.

21. Alphonse de Serres de La Tour, *Appel au bon sens, dans lequel M. de La Tour soumet à ce juge infaillible les détails de sa conduite, relativement à une affaire qui fait quelque bruit dans le monde* (London, 1788).

22. Anon., *Le Gros bon sens*, 5.

23. On the antirhetorical posture of much revolutionary writing, see Brigitte Schlieben-Lange, "Le Style laconique," *Langages de la Révolution (1770–1815), actes du 4e colloque de lexicologie politique* (Paris, 1996); and Jacques Guilhaumou, "Rhétorique et anti-rhétorique à l'époque de la Révolution française," in *La Légende de la Révolution, actes du colloque international de Clermont-Ferrand*, ed. Christian Croisille and Jean Ehrard (Clermont-Ferrand, 1988), 149–159.

24. Anon., *Adresse intéressante à tous les bons patriots français par un vieillar* [sic] *de bon sens* (Paris, [c. 1790]), 5.

25. On women's speech during the Revolution, see "La Prise de parole publique des femmes," ed. Christine Fauré, a special issue of *Annales historiques de la Révolution française*, no. 344 (April–June 2006). On the debate about women and reason and its political implications, see Geneviève Fraisse, *Muse de la raison, la démocratie exclusive et la différence des sexes* (Paris, 1989).

26. "Cahier de doléances des blanchisseuses et lavandières de Marseille," in *Cahiers de doléances des femmes et autres texts*, ed. Paule-Marie Duhet (Paris, 1981).

27. Etta Palm d'Aelders, *Discours sur l'injustice des Loix en faveur des Hommes, au dépend des Femmes, lu à l'Assemblée Fédérative des Amis de la Vérité, le 30 décembre 1790*, reprinted in *Appel au Françoises sur la régénération des moeurs et nécessité de l'influence des femmes dans un government libre* (Paris, [May 1791]).

28. Anon., *La Femme patriote, ou le gros bon-sens* (n.p., [c. 1792]), 1–2.

29. On the significance that Gramsci attributed to common sense in the revolutionary process, see *The Antonio Gramsci Reader*, ed. David Forgacs (New York, 1988), esp. 323.

30. Olympe de Gouges, *Le Bon sens françois, ou l'Apologie des vrais nobles dédiée aux Jacobins* [April 1792], reprinted in *Olympe de Gouges: Ecrits politiques, 1792–1793*, ed. Olivier Blanc (Paris, 1993), 74–109, quote on 75. Her other invocations of "good sense" include her *Dialogue entre mon Esprit, le Bon Sens et la Raison; ou Critique de mes Oeuvres*, in *Oeuvres de madame de Gouges* (Paris, 1786), vol. 2; her *Le Cri du Sage par une femme*, in which she announced "It is time to raise our voices; good sense and wisdom no longer know how to keep silent" ([Paris], May/June 1789); and her *Le Bon sens du Français, par une Citoyenne* ([Paris], February 1792), which is reprinted as well in *Olympe de Gouges: Ecrits politiques, 1792–1793*.

31. De Gouges, *Le Bon sens françois*, 76, 91.

32. On de Gouges and the complexities of establishing a feminine political voice, see Joan Wallach Scott, *Only Paradoxes to Offer: French Feminists and the Rights of Man* (Cambridge, MA, 1996), 19–56; Janie Vanpée, "Taking the Podium: Olympe de Gouges's Revolutionary Discourse," in *Women Writers in Pre-Revolutionary France: Strategies of Emancipation*, ed. Colette H. Winn and Donna Kuizenga (New York, 1997), 299–312; Olivier Blanc, *Marie-Olympe de Gouges, une humaniste à la fin du*

XVIIIe siècle (Belaye, 2003); and Jurgen Siess, "Un discours politique au feminin. Le projet d'Olympe de Gouges," *Mots. Les Langages du politique*, no. 78 (July 2005): 9–21.

33. See Gwennole Le Menn, ed., *L'Alamanch du Père Gérard de J. M. Collot d'Herbois (1791): le texte français et ses deux traductions en breton* (Saint-Brieuc, 2003); as well as Michel Biard, "L'Almanach du Père Gérard, un example de diffusion des idées jacobines," *Annales historiques de la Révolution française* 283, no. 1 (January–March 1991): 19–29.

34. See Anthony Crubaugh, "The 'Bon Sens Villageois': Images of the Peasantry in French Revolutionary Newspapers," *Proceedings of the Western Society for French History: Selected Papers of the 2002 Annual Meeting*, vol. 30, ed. Barry Rothaus (2004): 10–17, quotation on 10. See, too, Paul H. Johnstone, "The Rural Socrates," *Journal of the History of Ideas* 5, no. 2 (April 1944): 151–175, on the physiocratic motif of the virtuous, thrifty peasant whose "philosophy" is built entirely out of common sense and practical experience.

35. *La Feuille villageoise* (December 15, 1791), cited in *L'Alamanch du Père Gérard de J. M. Collot d'Herbois*, 21.

36. A. Clesse, *Adresse au Grand Lama de Rome, ou le bon sens vengé* (Paris, c. 1792), 5; and Anon., *Adresse intéressante à tous les bons patriots français*, 5.

37. M. Marron, "Article relative de la Constitution: Fragmens d'un discours prononcé le 18 juillet 1790 dans l'oratoire des protestans, au musée de la rue Dauphine," *Journal de la Société de 1789* 9 (July 29, 1790): 22–35.

38. Maximillien Robespierre, "Sur la Constitution à donner à la France" [May 1793], in *Discours*, ed. M. Bouloiseau, G. Lefebvre, and A. Soboul (Paris, 1950–1958), 9:506.

39. Robespierre, "Sur la Guerre" [January 1792], in ibid., 8:90.

40. Abbé Sieyès, "Preliminary to the French Constitution" [August 1789], reproduced in *The French Revolution and Human Rights: A Brief Documentary History*, ed. Lynn Hunt (Boston, 1996), 81.

41. See Keith Michael Baker, *Condorcet: From Natural Philosophy to Social Mathematics* (Chicago, 1975), esp. 225.

42. William Sewell draws attention to the structural dislocation of normal life in the summer of 1789 in "Historical Events as Transformations of Structures: Inventing the Revolution at the Bastille," in *Logics of History: Social Theory and Social Transformation* (Chicago, 2005), 225–270. Peter McPhee, in *Living the French Revolution, 1789–99* (Basingstoke, UK, 2006), emphasizes the transformation of rural experience.

43. On the terms and impact of the Civil Constitution, see Timothy Tackett, *Religion, Revolution, and Regional Culture in Eighteenth-Century France: The Ecclesiastical Oath of 1791* (Princeton, NJ, 1986); Claude Langlois, "La Rupture entre l'Eglise catholique et la Révolution," in *The French Revolution and the Creation of Modern Political Culture*, vol. 3, ed. François Furet and Mona Ozouf (Oxford, 1989), 375–390; and Nigel Aston, *Religion and Revolution in France, 1780–1804* (Basingstoke, UK, 2000), esp. 140–162 and 220–243.

44. On rural women's response, see Aston, *Religion and Revolution in France,* 174 and 206–207; Olwen H. Hufton, *Women and the Limits of Citizenship in the French Revolution* (Toronto, 1992), 91–130; and articles by Timothy Tackett and Claude Le Foll in *Pratiques religieuses, mentalités et spiritualités dans l'Europe révolution-naire: 1770–1820: actes du colloque, Chantilly, 27–29 novembre 1986,* ed. Bernard Plongeron (Turnhout, 1988). On the importance of religion to women's growing autonomy in the eighteenth century, see, too, Sarah Knott and Barbara Taylor, eds., *Women, Gender, and Enlightenment* (Basingstoke, UK, 2005).

45. Suzanne Desan, *Reclaiming the Sacred: Lay Religion and Popular Politics in Revolutionary France* (Ithaca, NY, 1990), 81.

46. Hufton, *Women and the Limits of Citizenship,* 105.

47. On the *monarchien* position, see Robert Howell Griffiths, *Le Centre perdu. Malouet et les "monarchiens" dans la Révolution française* (Grenoble, 1988), esp. 94–128.

48. *Le Stationnaire patriote,* no. 1 (July 11, 1791): 27.

49. Among journals, see *Le Crieur de bon sens et patriote* (January 30–February 14, 1791); *Le Bon sens, réflexions libres sur les affaires actuelles* (February or March 1791); and *Le Stationnaire patriote aux frontières, ou l'appel au bon sens* (July 11–November 3, 1791, with the subtitle beginning in August). Among pamphlets, many of them calling for an end to the polarizing polemics surrounding the oath, see *Tirez le rideau. La farce est jouée* ([Paris], October 1791) and *L'Appel au bon sens* ([Paris], August 1791), both extracts from the *Stationnaire patriote,* and *Mon patience est à bout. Un mot de bon sens à MM. les dénonciateurs des prêtres nonjureurs* (n.p., 1791). See, too, Jacques Guilhaumou, "L'Elite modérée et 'la propriété des mots' (1791). Propagation et usage des mots dans l'opinion publique," in *Les Idéologues. Sémiotique, théories et politiques linguistiques pendant la Révolution française,* ed. Winfried Busse and Jürgen Trabant (Amsterdam, 1986), 323–342, which notes in passing the frequent recourse to the idea of *le bon sens* in many of these texts.

50. *Le Greffe patriotique de la Société des amis du bon sens* (Anthropolis [Paris], [c. March 1791]). On the club proposed in the *Spectator* in 1711, see Chapter 1.

51. On the Counter-Revolution as an intellectual movement starting in 1789, see, in addition to the classic work of Jacques Godechot, *The Counter-Revolution: Doctrine and Action, 1789–1804,* trans. Salvator Attanasio (New York, 1971), the following: Jean Tulard, *La Contre-révolution* (Paris, 1990); Jean-Clément Martin, *Contre-Révolution, Révolution, et Nation en France, 1789–1799* (Paris, 1998); and McMahon, *Enemies of the Enlightenment,* esp. chap. 2.

52. On the counter-revolutionary press, see Jeremy D. Popkin, *The Right-Wing Press in France, 1792–1800* (Chapel Hill, NC, 1980); William James Murray, *The Right-Wing Press in the French Revolution: 1789–92* (Woodbridge, Suffolk, UK, 1986); Jean-Paul Bertaud, *Les Amis du roi: journaux et journalistes royalistes en France de 1789 à 1792* (Paris, 1984); and Annie Duprat, "Les Ecrits contre-révolutionnaires et leur diffusion," in *La Contre-Révolution en Europe, XVIIe–XIXe siècles: réalités politiques et socials, resonances culturelles et idéologiques,* ed. Jean-Clément Martin (Rennes, 2001).

53. On this journal, see Marcellin Pellet, *Un journal royaliste en 1789. Les Actes des Apôtres, 1789–1791* (Paris, 1873); Hélène Maspéro-Clerc, *Un journaliste contre-révolutionnaire. Jean-Gabriel Peltier (1760–1825)* (Paris, 1973), 1–62; and de Baecque, *Les Eclats du rire,* 137–148. The *Actes des Apôtres* was one of the first, but over twenty such antirevolutionary papers existed by the summer of 1790.

54. *Actes des Apôtres,* no. 42 (Winter 1790).

55. See, e.g., the "Discours projetté des demoiselles de la nation de Versailles, à l'Assemblée nationale," *Actes des Apôtres,* no. 79 (Spring 1790), which begins with the ambiguous statement "You have allowed us to get to know the rights of man."

56. *Actes des Apôtres,* no. 68 (Spring 1790).

57. *Actes des Apôtres,* no. 8 (Winter 1789–1790), cited in de Baecque, *Les Eclats du rire,* 142.

58. On female readers of these sorts of materials, see Harvey Chisick, *The Production, Distribution, and Readership of a Conservative Journal of the Early French Revolution: The Ami du Roi of the Abbé Royou* (Philadelphia, 1992); and Laurence Coudart, *La Gazette de Paris. Un journal royaliste pendant la Révolution française (1789–1792)* (Paris, 1995).

59. Hugh Gough, *The Newspaper Press in the French Revolution* (New York, 1988), 212–214, emphasizes that while half the copies of most royalist journals went to the provinces, most of the clientele for the *Actes des Apôtres* was in Paris. Martin, *Contre-Révolution,* 78, estimates, based on subscription figures, an urban readership of 20,000 for all counter-revolutionary journals combined in 1790. Of course, many readers may have borrowed a single issue or heard it read aloud; Coudart, in *La Gazette de Paris,* 144–152, calculates as many as ten readers per subscriber to a counter-revolutionary journal and points out that some issues were always given away for free.

60. Information on all three brothers can be found in Abbé Glaire and Joseph-Alexis Walsh, et al., eds., *Encyclopédie catholique* (Paris, 1842), 4:559–560. The same information is repeated in all the main biographical dictionaries. In most library catalogues, including that of the Bibliothèque nationale française, works are attributed incorrectly among them.

61. Among the products of Adrien-Quentin Buée's time in England, where he became a member of the Committee on Mathematics, Mechanics, and Mechanical Inventions of the Royal Society (according to the minutes preserved in the Archives of the Royal Society, London), are *Mémoire sur les quantités imaginaires,* originally printed in the *Transactions of the Royal Society* in 1806; *Parallel of Romé de l'Isle's and the Abbé Hauy's Theories of Crystallography,* first published in *Philosophical Magazine,* nos. 74 and 75 (1804); a 400-page manuscript, "Recherches mathématiques sur la texture intime des corps" (Bath, 1798), in Bibliothèque nationale française (BNF), n.acq. fr. 4537, for which a bilingual prospectus was the only part ever published; and sonatas for the piano forte (London, c. 1798).

62. On Crapart, see Frédéric Barbier et al., *Dictionnaire des imprimeurs, libraires, et gens du livre à Paris, 1701–1789* (Geneva, 2007), 1:572–574.

63. On Barruel as antirevolutionary polemicist, see Sylva Schaeper-Wimmer, *Augustin Barruel, S. J. (1741–1820): Studien zu Biographie und Werk* (Frankfurt, 1985); Christian Lagrave, "Introduction," *Mémoires pour server à l'histoire du jacobinisme par M. l'Abbé Barruel* (Chiré-en-Montreuil, 2005); and Michel Riquet, *Augustin de Barruel, un Jésuite face aux jacobins francs-maçons, 1741–1820* (Paris, 1989). The Abbé Barruel published his erudite *Journal ecclésiastique* with Crapart until July 1792, when the journal was banned, as well as his fourteen-volume *Collection ecclésiastique* (1791–1793) and a variety of other anti-Constitutional Church pamphlets.

64. For example, an anonymous *Requête adressée au roi, par les prêtres détenus dans le château de Brest en vertu d'un arrêté du département du Finistère* (Paris: Imprimerie de Crapart, [1791]) opens with information that the "the profit derived from this edition will be used to support the needs of these prisoners for whom food is in short supply."

65. See the excellent introduction to Malcolm Cook, ed., *Dialogues révolutionnaires* (Exeter, UK, 1994).

66. Anon., *Première conversation de M. Silvain, bourgeois de Paris, et M. Bon-Sens, frère des écoles chrétiennes, à l'occasion du serment sur la constitution civile du Clergé* ([Paris], 1790), 8.

67. Anon., *Le Seul bon sens: M. Franckin, avocat; le sieur Piccard, maître menuisier; Jean Berdaulou, vigneron* (France, 1790 or 1791), 9.

68. This point is made in Coudart, *La Gazette de Paris,* 296, and Murray, *The Right-Wing Press,* 249, who notes it was not unusual to cite Montaigne to the effect that the people were "a beast, all saddled and bridled, that everyone rides in his turn."

69. On these pamphlets, see Bernadette Fort, "Voice of the People: The Carivalization of Salon Art in Prerevolutionary Pamphlets," *Eighteenth-Century Studies* 22 (1989): 368–394.

70. Anon., *Dialogue intéressant et vrai entre le maire, le procureur-syndic d'une province, le curé, un bourgeois, une riche fermière, un grenadier et deux fédérés* (En France: De l'Imprimerie des amis de la vérité, en province; et se trouve à Paris: Aux enseignes du peuple abusé, des lois renversées, du roi trahi, et de la monarchie détruite, l'an deux de l'anarchie [1790]), pt. I, 9.

71. Anon., *Conversation villageoise entre Pierre la Raison et Jacques la Franchise, tous deux gens de bonne foi (par un Catholique-romain)* (Paris, [c. 1791]), 6.

72. Anon., *Le Bon sens du village, visite et conversation familière entre un officier de la milice nationale et une villageoise* (n.p., 1790).

73. On different versions of Père Duchesne, see Frédéric Braesch, ed., *Le Père Duchesne d'Hébert* (Paris, 1938); Jacques Guilhaumou, "Les Mille langues du Père Duchêne: la parade de la culture populaire pendant la Révolution," *Dix-huitième siècle,* no. 18 (1986): 143–154; and Ouzi Elyada, *Presse populaire et feuilles volantes de la Révolution à Paris, 1789–1792. Inventaire méthodique et critique* (Paris, 1991). On Mère Duchesne, the key source is Ouzi Elyada, "La Mère Duchesne. Masques populaires et guerre pamphletaire, 1789–1791," *Annales historiques de la Révolution française* (January–March 1988): 1–16.

74. [Buée], *Grande Conversion du Père Duchesne par sa femme* (n.p., [January 1791]), 32.

75. [Buée], *La Mère Duchesne corrigeant son mari pour avoir dit du mal de Monsieur l'Abbé M . . . son confesseur* (n.p., [November 1790]). A month later an anonymous pamphlet appeared with the title *Lettre de la Mère Duchêne au j . . . f . . . donneur d'avis au Peuple Normand* (n.p., [December 1790]) that could also conceivably be by Buée, though there is little evidence for this attribution. On earlier prototypes, see Pierre Franz, "Travestis poissards," *Revue des Sciences Humaines* 61, no. 190 (April–June 1983): 7–20, but lower-class women characters largely disappeared from pamphlet literature in early 1790 and only returned with Mère Duchesne.

76. The first real series appeared between January and April 1791, all from Crapart, but not always explicitly so. In addition to the *Grande Conversion du Père Duchesne*, see *De par la mère Duchesne. Anathèmes très-énergiques contre les jureurs, ou Dialogue sur le serment et la nouvelle constitution du clergé, entre M. Bridoye, franc parisien, soldat patriote; M. Recto, marchand de livres, ou tout simplement bouquiniste; M. Tournemine, chantre de paroisse; et la mère Duchesne, négociante à Paris, autrement dit, marchande de vieux chapeaux* (n.p., [February 1791]); *Grande colère de la Mère Duchesne, et deuxième dialogue* (n.p., [March 1791]); and *Grand Jugement de la mère Duchesne, et nouveau dialogue* (Paris, [March 1791]). Three others eventually followed: *Etrennes de la Mère Duchesne. Vivent le Roi, la Reine et leur chère famille, la bonne et heureuse année à tous les honnêtes gens non Jacobins, ni monarchiens, nouveau dialogue* (Paris, [January] 1792); *Le Drapeau rouge de la Mère Duchesne, contre tous les factieux et les intriguans. Dialogue* (Paris, [March] 1792); and *Dialogue entre le Père Duchesne et la Mère Duchesne ou le père Duchesne à bout* (n.p., [February 1793, after Buée's emigration]).

77. [Buée], *Grande Conversion*, 12; and [Buée], *Anathèmes*, 7, 22.

78. [Buée], *Grande colère*, 13.

79. [Buée], *Grande Conversion*, 7.

80. See, e.g., J. A. R., royaliste, *Les Entretiens de la Mère Gérard: ouvrage qui n'a pas remporté de prix aux Jacobins, mais l'auteur en propose un de cent mille francs à celui qui exterminera la gente Jacobite* (En France: aux dépens de toutes les sociétés fraternelles, 1792), 22–23.

81. [Buée], *Anathèmes*, 15.

82. Elyada points out in "La Mère Duchesne" that these pamphlets stress issues (marriage, food, one's relationship to the local priest) that affected women in particular. Further evidence comes from the fact that when the left began producing its own Mère Duchesne pamphlets several months later, they were explicitly aimed at working-class urban women—likely in response to the perceived female readership and focus of the right-wing version.

83. Claude Langlois, in *La Caricature contre-révolutionnaire* (Paris, 1988), takes the six months from November 1791 to April 1792 to be the key moment for the production of all kinds of counter-revolutionary ephemera.

84. See, e.g., references to "un galimathias d'chien" in [Buée], *Anathèmes*, 6, and "quel foutu galimathias" in [Buée], *Grande colère*, 17.

85. [Buée], *Le Drapeau rouge de la Mère Duchesne*, 13–14. This text is often attributed to Pierre-Louis, but it seems much more likely that it, too, was written by Adrien-Quentin. Mère Duchesne's speech reads in French: "Oh ben! Si ça est, foutre, c'est donc le diable qui tient la chandelle . . . c'est clair ça; car, enfin, avec toutes leux lumières' on n'voit toujours que d'la calamité partout, et j'dis qu c'n'est pas l'bon Dieu qui la fait. Je n'sommes qu'une pauvre femme, j'n'ons pas d'esprit, j'n'avons jamais lu dans les gros livres; mais ma raison m'dit qu'tout ça est un embrouillamini d'gueux ou gna que l'diable et des matins-là qui faisont leur compte."

86. Braesch, *Le Père Duchesne*, 65–72 and 136–137.

87. See the "Dialogue entre le Père Duchêne, la Mère Duchêne, et l'abbé Duchêne, leur fils," *Actes des Apôtres* 9–10, no. 254 (1791): 3–16, in which Mère Duchêne has a son who is a priest opposed to the Civil Constitution of the Clergy and thus takes the position of "tous les gens sensés et raisonables."

88. J. A. R., *Les Entretiens de la Mère Gèrard*, 21. Other counter-revolutionary appropriations of Pere Gèrard include the satire "Le bon sens des Bretons [i.e., Jacobins] quelquefois m'épouvante," *Actes des Apôtres* 14–15 (late 1791); and the *Almanach de l'abbé Maury ou réfutation de l'Almanach du père Gèrard* (Koblenz, 1792).

89. [Adrien-Quentin Buée], *Nouveau Dictionnaire, pour servir à l'intelligence des termes mis en vogue par la Révolution, dédié aux amis de la religion, du roi et du sens commun* (Paris, January 1792). On counter-revolutionary dictionaries of revolutionary terms, see, too, Rosenfeld, *A Revolution in Language*, esp. 136–137.

90. [Buée], *Nouveau Dictionnaire*, 6.

91. Ibid., 48.

92. A constant in this literature was the theme that the Civil Constitution of the Clergy constituted a "bouleversement" of all that the church had ever preached; see, e.g., the anonymous pamphlets *Le Peuple enfin éclairé, ou Réponses courtes et claires aux objections communes des partisans de la Religion constitutionelle* (Paris, 1791) and *L'Ange tutélaire de la France, visitant ce royaume et instruisant les catholiques fidèles* (Paris, 1792), in which a visitor to the world devastated by the Revolution realizes that regeneration actually means "le bouleversement."

93. [Pierre-Louis Buée], *Obstacles à ma conversion constitutionnelle, exposés confidemment aux parisiens, pour qu'ils daignent m'aider à les franchir*, 2nd ed. (Paris, January 1792). Note that that same winter saw Pierre-Louis Buée produce a wide variety of other, more strictly religious pamphlets, also for Crapart.

94. Ibid.

95. Adrien-Quentin Buée, "Recherches mathématiques sur la texture intime des corps" (Bath, 1798), BNF, n.acq. fr. 4537.

96. On the breakup of the royalist press and the imposition of new censorship restrictions after August 10, 1792, see Murray, *The Right-Wing Press*, 192–201.

97. John Gifford, *A Plain Address to the Common Sense of the People of England* (London, 1792).

98. On the Association for the Preservation of Liberty and Property against Republicans and Levellers and the popular Loyalist conservatism that it sponsored, see

Robert Hole, "British Counter-Revolutionary Popular Propaganda in the 1790s," in *Britain and Revolutionary France: Conflict, Subversion and Propaganda*, ed. Colin Jones (Exeter, UK, 1983), 53–69; Harry Dickinson, "Popular Loyalism in Britain in the 1790s," in *The Transformation of Political Culture: England and Germany in the Late Eighteenth Century*, ed. Eckhart Hellmuth (Oxford, 1990), 503–533; Mark Philp, "Vulgar Conservatism, 1792–3," *English Historical Review* 110 (1995): 42–69; and Chris Evans, *Debating the Revolution: Britain in the 1790s* (London, 2006).

99. Robert R. Dozier, *For King, Constitution, and Country: English Loyalists and the French Revolution* (Lexington, KY, 1983), 93.

100. [Hannah More], *Village Politics. Addressed to all the mechanics, journeymen and day labourers in Great Britain. By Will Chip, a country carpenter* (London, December 1792).

101. See Mona Scheuermann, *In Praise of Poverty: Hannah More Counters Thomas Paine and the Radical Threat* (Lexington, KY, 2002), 121–124, on the role of More's well-placed female friends in the distribution process.

102. [John Reeves], *Thoughts on the English Government. Addressed to the Quiet Good Sense of the People of England. In a series of Letters* (London, 1795). For other examples of the theme of common sense in the propaganda of Loyalists in Reeves's circle, see "Common Sense, or an Antidote against Paine," in *The Antigallican Songster. No. 2* (London, 1793); "Liberty and Property, Courage, and Common-Sense," in *Liberty and Property. Preserved against Republicans and Levellers. A Collection of Tracts, recommended to perusal at the present crisis* (London, 1793); and William Combes, *Plain Thoughts of a Plain Man, addressed to the Common Sense of the People of Great Britain* (London, 1797).

103. Edmund Burke, *Reflections on the Revolution in France*, ed. Frank M. Turner (New Haven, CT, 2003 [1790]), 49, 68.

104. On sales of More's *Village Politics* and then *Cheap Repository Tracts* (1795–1798), in comparison to sales of works by Paine or other radicals, see H. T. Dickinson, *British Radicalism and the French Revolution, 1789–1815* (Oxford, 1985), 30.

105. Fischer Ames, "Falkland. No II. To New England Men" [February 1801], in *Works of Fisher Ames*, ed. Seth Ames (Boston, 1854), 2:313–336, cited in part in Richard Hofstadter, *Anti-Intellectualism in American Life* (New York, 1963), 149. On the polarizing rhetoric of this moment, see Andrew W. Robertson, *The Language of Democracy: Political Rhetoric in the United States and Britian, 1790–1900* (Ithaca, NY, 1995). On Federalist invective in particular, including that directed against Jefferson, see Linda Kerber, *Federalists in Dissent: Imagery and Ideology in Jeffersonian America* (Ithaca, NY, 1970); and John Ferling, *Adams vs. Jefferson: The Tumultuous Election of 1800* (New York, 2004), 134–161.

106. John Quincy Adams, "Letters of Publicola" [June–July 1791], in *Writings of John Quincy Adams*, ed. Worthington Chauncy Ford (New York, 1913), 1:107. These essays were originally written in response to the American publication of Paine's *Rights of Man* with a letter at the head in which Jefferson noted with approval, "I have no doubt that our citizens will *rally* a second time around the standard of *Common*

Sense," and seemed to cast aspersions on local "political heresies" (i.e., Vice President John Adams's essays criticizing the French) in contrast.

107. *Address of the Republican General Committee of Young Men of the City and Country of New York Friendly to the Election of General Andrew Jackson* (New York, 1838), 38, cited in John William Ward, *Andrew Jackson: Symbol for an Age* (New York, 1955), 52.

108. Sean Wilentz, *The Rise of American Democracy: From Jefferson to Lincoln* (New York, 2005), 309.

109. [Delouit], *Lettre d'un ami du sens commun à un Hollandois . . . au sujet de l'éloge de Benedictus de Spinosa, proposé par la Société Hollandoise des Beaux Arts et des Sciences de Leyde . . . pour le prix d'éloquence de 1809* (Utrecht, 1809).

110. R. R. Palmer, "Notes on the Use of the Word 'Democracy,' 1789–1799," *Political Science Quarterly* 68, no. 2 (June 1953): 233.

111. On Napoleon's undemocratic use of plebiscites, see Isser Wolloch, *The New Regime: Transformations of the French Civic Order, 1789–1820s* (New York, 1994), 109–111. On Tocqueville's reading of Bonapartism, see Melvin Richter, "Tocqueville and French Nineteenth-Century Conceptualizations of the Two Bonapartes and Their Empires," in *Diplomacy in History and Theory: Bonapartism, Caesarism, and Totalitarianism,* ed. Peter Baehr and Melvin Richter (Cambridge, 2004), 83–102.

6. KÖNIGSBERG TO NEW YORK

1. As Manfed Kuehn demonstrates in *Scottish Common Sense in Germany,* the works of Reid, Beattie, and Oswald, not to mention Priestley's attack on all three, were reviewed in detail in German periodicals in the late 1760s and 1770s, and in some cases translated into German, where they had an impact on a variety of thinkers. Kuehn's larger thesis—that Kant was not as hostile to Scottish Common Sense philosophy as it first appears—is, however, more controversial; see John P. Wright, "Critical Notice of Kuehn," *Reid Studies* 2, no. 1 (1998): 49–55.

2. Kant, *Prolegomena to Any Future Metaphysics,* trans. Beck, 119. On the connection to Beattie, see Robert P. Wolff, "Kant's Debt to Hume via Beattie," *Journal of the History of Ideas* 21 (1960): 117–123. As Benjamin W. Redekop points out in "Reid's Influence in Britain, Germany, France, and America," in *The Cambridge Companion to Thomas Reid,* 321, Kant uses four different terms for common sense, none of them rigorously, in an effort to translate a Reidean category: *gemeinen Menschenverstand, gesunden Verstand, geraden* or *schlichten Menschenverstand,* and *gemeinen Verstand.* On occasion, he also employed *Gemeinsinn* as a literal translation of the Latin term *sensus communis.*

3. Kant, *Critique of Judgment,* trans. James Meredith (Oxford, 1952), sec. 40, 151.

4. On the conflict in the late eighteenth century between the so-called *Popularphilosophen,* who argued that philosophy should be both useful in purpose and compre-

hensible in form, and Kant, who insisted repeatedly upon the autonomy of philosophy, see Chad Wellmon, "Kant on the Plague of Literature and the Discipline of Philosophy," forthcoming; and Frederick Beiser, *The Fate of Reason: German Philosophy from Kant to Fichte* (Cambridge, MA, 1996), esp. 165–171.

5. On Abbt and Mendelssohn's interest in Shaftesbury's *Sensus Communis,* see Benjamin Redekop, *Enlightenment and Community: Lessing, Abbt, Herder, and the Quest for a German Public* (Montreal and Kingston, 2000). Shaftesbury was also vital to the philosophy of Friedrich Christoph Oetinger, whose *Die Wahrheit des sensus communis oder des allgemeinen Sinnes* (Tübingen, 1753), included a German translation of Shaftesbury's *Sensus Communis*. On the differences between Shaftesbury and Kant in terms of the meaning given to the *sensus communis,* see Dabney Townsend, "From Shaftesbury to Kant: The Development of the Concept of Aesthetic Experience," *Journal of the History of Ideas* (1987): 287–305. On Shaftesbury's impact more generally on the German Enlightenment, see Christian Weiser, *Shaftesbury und das deutsche Geistesleben* (Leipzig and Berlin, 1916).

6. Kant, *Critique of Judgment,* sec. 21, 84, and sec. 40, 151. On Kant's notion of *sensus communis,* see Paul Guyer, *Kant and the Claims of Taste* (Cambridge, MA, 1979), 279–307; Guyer, "Pleasure and Society in Kant's Theory of Taste," in *Essays in Kant's Aesthetics,* ed. Ted Cohen and Paul Guyer (Chicago, 1982), 21–54; Henry E. Allison, *Kant's Theory of Taste: A Reading of the Critique of Aesthetic Judgment* (Cambridge, 2001), esp. 144–159; David Summers, "Why Did Kant Call Taste a 'Common Sense'?" in *Eighteenth-Century Aesthetics and the Reconstruction of Art,* ed. Paul Mattick Jr. (Cambridge, 1993), 120–151; Luc Ferry, *Homo Aestheticus: The Invention of Taste in the Democratic Age,* trans. Robert de Loaiza (Chicago, 1993); and Robert Nehring, *Kritik des Common Sense: Gesunder Menschenverstand, reflektierende Urteilskraft und Gemeinsinn—der Sensus communis bei Kant* (Berlin, 2010).

7. Kant, *Critique of Judgment,* sec. 21, 84.

8. [Johann Heinrich Metzger], *Äusserungen über Kant, seinen Charakter und seine Meinungen* (Königsberg, 1804), 14f., cited in Manfred Kuehn, *Kant: A Biography* (Cambridge, 2001), 342.

9. See Frederick Beiser, *Enlightenment, Revolution, and Romanticism: The Genesis of Modern German Political Thought, 1790–1800* (Cambridge, MA, 1992), 27–56, on Kant's politics in the 1790s. On the politicization of the German public sphere, see Hans Erich Bödeker, "Prozesse und Strukturen politischer Bewusstseinsbildung der deutschen Aufklärung," in *Aufklärung als Politisierung-Politisierung der Aufklärung,* ed. H. E. Bödeker and Ulrich Herrmann (Hamburg, 1987), 10–31.

10. On the political dimension of Schiller's aesthetic theory, see especially Josef Chytry, *The Aesthetic State: A Quest in Modern German Thought* (Los Angeles and Berkeley, 1989); Karin Schutjer, *Narrating Community after Kant: Schiller, Goethe, and Hölderlin* (Detroit, 2001); and Frederick Beiser, *Schiller as Philosopher: A Re-Examination* (Oxford, 2005).

11. Friedrich Schiller, *On the Aesthetic Education of Man in a Series of Letters,* ed. and trans. Elizabeth M. Wilkinson and L. A. Willoughby (Oxford, 1967 [1795]), 27th letter, 217–218. The translators note that *Gemeinsinn* has two meanings, just like the English cognate *common sense:* the faculty of primary truths and the sense that is common to all mankind based on centuries of experience. It is the latter meaning that they attribute to this passage. But the pairing with taste in the aesthetic state also suggests a direct debt to Kant's conception of *sensus communis.* That the meaning of the term was still subject to debate in the 1790s is evidenced by an article entitled "Ueber den Gemeinsinn," in the *Deutsche Monatsschrift* of 1790 (i, 51–66)), where *Gemeinsinn* is given as synonymous with *gesunder Menschenverstand,* the most common eighteenth-century cognate for "common sense." Similarly, Paine's *Common Sense* appeared first in German as *Gesunde Vernunft* (Philadelphia, 1776) and then as *Gesunder Menschenverstand* (Copenhagen, 1794).

12. Patrick Joyce makes the claim that populist language and values (in contradistinction to class-based arguments, which emphasize conflict and social exclusivity) insinuated themselves after 1848 into multiple strands of English popular politics, including radicalism, liberalism, and Toryism; see his *Visions of the People: Industrial England and the Question of Class, 1848–1914* (Cambridge, 1991). On a more theoretical level, Ernesto Laclau in *On Populist Reason* argues that populism belongs in the modern era to no particular ideology or social group but, rather, that it structures political life more generally. My argument is not for the continuity of any one philosophical tradition; it is for the continuity of a specific vocabulary and set of conceptions across standard political divisions.

13. Alfred Austin, "The Revival of Common Sense," *National Review* (June 1886): 564–565, cited in Fulvio Cammarano, *"Save England from Decline": The National Party of Common Sense: British Conservatism and the Challenge of Democracy, 1885–1892* (Lanham, MD, 2001), 32.

14. Margaret Lavinia Anderson, *Practicing Democracy: Elections and Political Culture in Imperial Germany* (Princeton, NJ, 2000), 4. See, too, Michael Levin, *The Spectre of Democracy: The Rise of Modern Democracy as Seen by Its Opponents* (New York, 1992), on the many forms that arguments against democracy took in the aftermath of the French Revolution.

15. Alexis de Tocqueville, "My Instincts, My Opinions" [c. 1841], in *The Tocqueville Reader: A Life in Letters and Politics,* ed. Olivier Zunz and Alan S. Kahan (Oxford, 2002), 219–220.

16. Jonathan Sperber, *The European Revolutions, 1848–1851,* 2nd ed. (Cambridge, 2005), 5.

17. On citizens reduced to consumers, see Pierre Bourdieu, "Political Representation: Elements for a Theory of the Political Field" [1981], in *Language and Symbolic Power,* ed. John B. Thompson (Cambridge, MA, 1991).

18. Forteau aîné, *Le Bon Sens du Peuple, ou nécessité de larges économies et de l'allégement des impôts* (Condom, [1849]), 7, not to be confused with the absolutely politically opposed *Au Bon Sens du peuple* of L. Correnson (Perpignan, 1849) or *Le Bon sens du*

peuple, journal quotidien, ed. Paul Féval (Paris, March 29–April 15, 1848), or *Le Peuple constituant la république du bon sens,* ed. Alexandre Pierre (Paris, August 1848).

19. Adolphe Baudon, *Le Socialisme devant le bon sens populaire ou simples questions à MM. les socialistes, par n'importe qui* (Paris, 1849).

20. Louis-Bernard Bonjean, *Socialisme et sens commun* (Paris, April 1849), 4.

21. On the invention of the common man as the hero of democracy, see Joyce, *Democratic Subjects,* 136.

22. Léopold de Gaillard, avocat, *Bon Sens. Situation—Les Socialistes—Les Montagnards—La Terreur—Conseils aux Modérés* (Avignon, 1849), 12.

23. G. Braccini, *Un grain de bon sens. Réflexions électorales, par un paysan* (Paris, 1849), 6.

24. Emile de Girardin, *Bon Sens, Bon Foi: 1848, 24 février–3 avril* (Paris, 1848), v.

25. Eugène Boquet-Liancourt, *Le Discours du Roi Bon-Sens, prononcé en faveur du Peuple Français* (Paris, 1850).

26. The philosophical shattering of the idea of universal man or universal human nature that began in the nineteenth century did not render related political tropes instantly obsolete. On the contrary, they have lived on often without deep philosophical justification; see Dunn, *A Politics of the Ordinary.*

27. Thomas Jefferson famously insisted that blacks were intellectually inferior to whites but that the two races were equally in possession of a moral sense that allowed them to determine right from wrong; see his *Notes on the State of Virginia,* which was published in 1785 in Paris, 1787 in London, and 1788 in Philadelphia.

28. Michael A. Morrison and James Brewer Stewart, *Race and the Early Republic: Racial Consciousness and Nation Building in the Early Republic* (Lanham, MD, 2002).

29. See, e.g., the following works by early black abolitionists: Ebenezer Baldwin, *Observations on the Physical, Intellectual and Moral Qualities of Our Colored Population* (New Haven, CT, 1834); and Hosea Easton, *A Treatise on the Intellectual Character, and the Civil and Political Condition of the Colored People of the United States and the Prejudice Exercised towards Them* (Boston, 1837).

30. Beattie, *Elements of Moral Science* (1793), 26, cited in Robert P. Forbes, "Slavery and the Evangelical Enlightenment," in *Religion and the Antebellum Debate over Slavery,* ed. John R. McKivigan and Mitchell Snay (Athens, GA, 1998), 73. On Common Sense philosophy and the slavery question, see Chapter 2.

31. James W. C. Pennington's talk at the 1843 World's Anti-Slavery Convention in London is described in an anonymous column in *The NonConformist,* ed. Edward Miall (1843), n.p.

32. John G. Fee, a minister of the Gospel, *An Anti-Slavery Manual, Being an Examination, in Light of the Bible, of the Facts, into the Moral and Social Wrongs of American Slavery, with a Remedy for the Evil* (Maysville, KY, 1848), v. The citation is from John Millar, *Observations Concerning the Distinction of Ranks in Society* (London, 1771).

33. William Lloyd Garrison, "The Declaration of American Independence," *Liberator* (September 5, 1835). See, too, "Commencement of the Liberator" (1831) on the link to the Declaration of Independence and "The Great Apostate" (1851) on "self-evident truths," both in *Selections from the Writings and Speeches of William Lloyd Garrison* (New York, 1968 [1852]), 62–63 and 211, respectively. Ronald G. Walters, in *The Antislavery Appeal: American Abolitionism after 1830* (Baltimore, 1976), 60–62, 68–69, 86, makes the case for the relationship between Garrison's insistence on slavery as a self-evident wrong and Scottish Common Sense philosophy, but he insists that common sense became moral sense, a clear preference for the heart over head, in its American incarnation, which I do not follow. For Garrison's other strategy—exposing the absurdity and logical inconsistency of what passed as conventional thinking on the other side, most often by means of irony—see Garrison, "Truisms" (1831), in *Against Slavery: An Abolitionist Reader,* ed. Mason Lowance (New York, 2000), 105–108.

34. On the critique of pro-slavery language games and the insistence on plain speech by abolitionists, see the remarks of Daniel J. McInerney, *The Fortunate Heirs of Freedom: Abolition and Republican Thought* (Lincoln, NE, 1994), 133–138.

35. Peter G. Camden, *A Common-Sense, Matter-of-Fact Examination and Discussion of Negro Slavery in the United States of America: In Connection with the Questions of Emancipation and Abolition* (St. Louis, 1855), 7. Among midcentury pro-slavery defenses that rely on the notion of common sense, see, too, Louis Schade, *A Book for the "Impending Crisis"! Appeal to the Common Sense and Patriotism of the United States: "Helperism" Annihilated! The "Irrepressible Conflict" and Its Consequences!* (Washington, DC, 1860); John Anderson, *Common Sense* (New Orleans, c. 1859); and "Common Sense" (editorial), *Mercury* (Charleston, SC, September 18, 1860).

36. Thomas Wentworth Higginson, *Common Sense about Women* (New York, 1894).

37. Mary Putnam Jacobi, *"Common Sense" Applied to Woman Suffrage; a statement of the reasons which justify the demand to extend the suffrage to women, with consideration of the arguments against such enfranchisement, and with special reference to the issues presented to the New York state convention of 1894* (New York, 1894), 9. Jacobi claims her book was written, like Paine's *Common Sense,* to "form public opinion."

38. See the introduction by Frances Maule Björkman to the posthumous second edition of Jacobi's *"Common Sense"* (New York, 1915), iv.

39. See Henry Martyn Dexter, *Common Sense as to Women Suffrage* (Boston, 1885), especially the passages on the insufficiency of women's intellectual capacity, 22–23; the ten essays originally appeared in slightly different form in the *Congregationalist* (February 5–April 9, 1885). For an example of a female writer appealing to the common sense of male and female readers to grasp the unsuitability of women to voting, see [Caroline Fairfield Corbin], *An Appeal to the Common Sense and the Educated Thought of Men and Women against the Proposed Extension of Suffrage to Women* (c. 1895), reprinted by the Illinois Association Opposed to Extension of Suffrage to

Women and in a collection called *Why Women Do Not Want the Ballot* issued by the Massachusetts State Association Opposed to the Further Extension of Suffrage to Women.

40. Ignatius L. Donnelly, "Omaha Platform," published in the *Omaha Morning World-Herald* (July 5, 1892) and reprinted in *A Populist Rader: Selections from the Works of American Populist Leaders,* ed. George Brown Tindall (New York, 1966), 90–96, quoatation on 92.

41. On this tension, see Dominique Schnapper, *Community of Citizens: On the Modern Idea of Nationality,* trans. Séverine Rosée (Edison, NJ, 1998 [1994]).

42. See Chapter 1 on English examples and Chapter 4 on American examples. As for a German example, in a review essay on Thomas Abbt's work, the early nationalist thinker Johann Gottfried von Herder lauds Abbt for distinguishing "plain good sense" (in English) as the national character of the German people; see *Das Bild Thomas Abbts* in Herder's *Sammtliche Werke* 2: 268–273, cited in Redekop, *Enlightenment and Community,* 166.

43. See Laclau, *On Populist Reason,* 83, on the Manichean dimension of populism.

44. Peter Fritzsche, *Germans into Nazis* (Cambridge, MA, 1998), 3.

45. See Michael Billig, *Banal Nationalism* (London, 1995), esp. 10, on the mundane means by which national belonging is constantly enforced; and Bourdieu, *Pascalian Meditations,* 98, on the way common sense, including basic linguistic distinctions, grows more nationally specific under these conditions.

46. Hugo Ball, *Flight out of Time: A Dada Diary,* ed. John Elderfield (1974), 67 (June 16, 1916), cited in *Dada: Zurich, Berlin, Hanover, Cologne, New York, Paris,* ed. Leah Dickerman (Washington, DC, 2005), 22. On Zurich Dada, see, too, Brigitte Pinchon and Karl Riha, eds., *Dada Zurich: A Clown's Game from Nothing* (New York, 1996).

47. Max Ernst, cited in Rudolf Kuenzli, *Dada* (London, 2006), 31.

48. On this point, see Anna Katharina Schaffner, "Assaulting the Order of Signs," in *Dada Culture: Critical Texts of the Avant-Garde,* ed. Dafydd Jones (Amsterdam, 2006), 117–133.

49. Tristan Tzara, "Dada Manifesto 1918," originally published in *Dada 3* (Zurich, December 1918), in *The Dada Reader: A Critical Anthology,* ed. Dawn Ades (Chicago, 2006), 36–42, quotation on 36.

50. Richard Huelsenbeck, "Collective Dada Manifesto" [1918], originally published in *Dada Almanach* (Berlin, 1920), reproduced in translation in Kuenzli, *Dada,* 220–221. On Dada in Berlin, see, too, Hanne Bergius, *Dada Triumphs!: Dada Berlin, 1917–1923. Artistry of Polarities,* trans. Brigitte Pinchon (New York, 2003); and Bruce Altschuler, "DADA ist politisch: The First International Dada Fair, Berlin, June 30–August 25, 1920," in *The Avant-Garde in Exhibition: New Art in the Twentieth Century* (New York, 1994), 98–115.

51. Kuenzli, *Dada,* 27.

52. See Jeffrey T. Schnapp, *Revolutionary Tides: The Art of the Political Poster, 1914–1989* (Milan, 2005).

53. Kazin, *Populist Persuasion: An American History*, 271.

54. Victoria de Grazia, *America's Advance through Twentieth-Century Europe* (Cambridge, MA, 2005), esp. 264–265, on the "capitalist populism" of American ad copy in the first half of the twentieth century and Europe's gradual absorption of this style and message.

55. Joel C. Weinsheimer, *Gadamer's Hermeneutics: A Reading of Truth and Method* (New Haven, CT, 1985), 79.

56. Hans-Georg Gadamer, *Truth and Method,* trans. Joel Weinsheimer and Donald G. Marshall, 2nd ed. (New York, 1995 [1960]), xii.

57. See ibid., 19–34, on the idea of the *sensus communis.* On Gadamer's conception of this term, see, in addition to Weinsheimer, *Gadamer's Hermeneutics*, 77–82, the following: Jean Grondin, *The Philosophy of Gadamer,* trans. Kathryn Plant (Montreal and Kingston, 2003 [1999]), 26–32; Schaeffer, *Sensus Communis: Vico, Rhetoric, and the Limits of Relativism*, 100–126; and Donald Verene, "Gadamer and Vico on Sensus Communis and the Tradition of Human Knowledge," in *The Philosophy of Hans-Georg Gadamer,* ed. Lewis Edwin Hahn (Chicago, 1997), 137–153.

58. Gadamer, *Truth and Method*, 21, 22–23.

59. Ibid., 24.

60. Ibid., 25.

61. Ibid., 26. See Bergson's essay, "Good Sense and Classical Studies" (1895), in *Henri Bergson: Key Writings,* ed. Keith Ansell-Pearson, et al. (New York, 2002).

62. Gadamer, *Truth and Method*, 26–27. On Oetinger, see ibid., 27–30, and note 5 of this chapter.

63. There is not much commentary that considers Arendt and Gadamer together; see, however, Lawrence Biskowski, "Reason in Politics: Arendt and Gadamer on the Role of the Eide," *Polity* 31 (1998): 217–244; and Richard Bernstein, *Beyond Objectivism and Relativism: Science, Hermeneutics, and Praxis* (Philadelphia, 1983), 201–220.

64. Hannah Arendt, *On Revolution* (New York, 1963), 250.

65. Arendt, *The Origins of Totalitarianism* [1951], new ed. (New York, 1973), esp. 468–476.

66. Arendt, "Understanding and Politics" [1954], in *Essays in Understanding, 1930–1954: Formation, Exile, and Totalitarianism,* ed. Jerome Kohn (New York, 1994), 317.

67. Arendt, *The Human Condition* [1958], 2nd ed., ed. Margaret Canovan (Chicago, 1998), 52–53.

68. On this claim, see Sandra K. Hinchman, "Common Sense and Political Barbarism in the Theory of Hannah Arendt," *Polity* 17, no. 2 (1984): 317–339, esp. 319.

69. On Arendt's attraction to the idea of common sense, see, too, Anne-Marie Roviello, *Sens commun et modernité chez Hannah Arendt* (Brussels, 1987); Michael G. Gottsegen, *The Political Thought of Hannah Arendt* (Albany, 1994), 144–184; Andrew J. Norris, "Arendt, Kant, and the Politics of Common Sense," *Polity* 29, no. 2 (Winter 1996): 165–191; Valerie Burks, "The Political Faculty: Arendt's 'Ariadne Thread' of

Common Sense," *Theory and Event* 6, no. 1 (2002); and many of the contributions to Craig Calhoun and John McGowan, eds., *Hannah Arendt and the Meaning of Politics* (Minneapolis, 1997).

70. Norris, "Arendt, Kant, and the Politics of Common Sense," 174.
71. Arendt, "Understanding and Politics," 311.
72. Arendt, *The Life of the Mind,* ed. Mary McCarthy, 2 vols. (New York, 1978), 50.
73. Arendt, *The Human Condition,* 208–209.
74. Arendt, "Understanding and Politics," 316–317.
75. Ibid., 314.
76. Arendt, *Lectures on Kant's Political Philosophy,* ed. Ronald Beiner (Chicago, 1982), 72.
77. Arendt, *The Human Condition,* 208; and "Understanding and Politics," 318, respectively.
78. Arendt, *The Human Condition,* 283. She describes this process in terms of the transformation from *Gemeinsinn* to *gesunder Menschenverstand*—an expression that she ultimately rejects in favor of the English "common sense" and the Latin *sensus communis.*
79. Arendt to Karl Jaspers, August 29, 1957, in *Hannah Arendt/Karl Jaspers Correspondence, 1926–1969,* ed. Lotte Kohler and Hans Saner, trans. Robert and Rita Kimber (New York, 1992).
80. Arendt, *Lectures on Kant's Political Philosophy,* 19.
81. Ibid., 72, 73. On this point, see also Philip Hansen, *Hannah Arendt: Politics, History and Citizenship* (Cambridge, 1993), 211–212.
82. Arendt is not often analyzed within the framework of populism; one exception is Margaret Canovan, "The People, the Masses, and the Mobilization of Power: The Paradox of Hannah Arendt's 'Populism,'" *Social Research* 69, no. 2 (Summer 2002): 403–422, which draws attention to the very different responses of Arendt to what she terms "the people" versus "the masses." On Arendt's related attraction in her political philosophy both to egalitarianism and to elitism, see Hauke Brunkhorst, "Equality and Elitism in Arendt," in *The Cambridge Companion to Hannah Arendt,* ed. Dana Villa (Cambridge, 2000), 178–198.
83. Ronald Reagan, "Farewell Speech" (January 11, 1989), available at http://reagan2020 .us/speeches (accessed June 28, 2010).
84. Ronald Reagan, "Let Them Go Their Way" (2nd Annual CPAC Convention Speech, March 1, 1975) and "Farewell Speech," both available at http://reagan2020 .us/speeches. Compare, too, his "Speech to America" (March 31, 1976): "I believe what we did in California can be done in Washington if government will have faith in the people and let them bring their common sense to bear on the problems bureaucracy hasn't solved. I believe in the people."
85. Arendt, *Lectures on Kant's Political Philosophy,* 73.
86. Holton, "Bourdieu and Common Sense," in *Pierre Bourdieu: Fieldwork in Culture*; and Loïc Wacquant, "Pointers on Pierre Bourdieu and Democratic Politics," *Constellations* 11, no. 1 (2001): 3–15, esp. 11, on the necessity of fracturing the *doxic* acceptance of the status quo.

Acknowledgments

I am lucky to have had much assistance at every stage of this project.

Two invaluable grants got me started. I remain deeply grateful to the Mellon Foundation (and especially to Harriet Zuckerman and Joseph Meisel) for a New Directions Fellowship and to the American Council on Learned Societies for a Frederick Burkhardt Fellowship. The University of Virginia School of Law subsequently provided a marvelous environment in which to do much of the writing; my sincere thanks to (former) Dean John Jeffries, Dean Paul Mahoney, and most especially Vice Dean Liz Magill, as well as the extraordinary library staff and the many faculty members who made me feel welcome personally and intellectually. I am grateful, too, to the College of Arts and Sciences at the University of Virginia for many forms of research support over the years and especially to Dean Meredith Woo, Associate Dean Bruce Holsinger, and the office of the Vice President for Research and Graduate Studies.

It is a testament to the culture of my home institution that I have so many colleagues in so many different departments to thank individually as well—for suggestions, conversations, the reading of drafts and chapters. In the History Department, I have at different points benefitted from the insights of Joe Kett, Paul Halliday, Lenny Berlanstein, Alon

Confino, my former colleague Patrick Griffin, Chuck McCurdy, Allan Megill, Erik Midelfort, Cori Field, Brian Owensby, and Peter Onuf. Then there are all the people in other fields who sent me reading and thinking in new directions: Richard Handler, Stephen White, Jennifer Tsien, Jeff Olick, Krishan Kumar, Paul Hunter, David Summers, my former colleague Josh Dienstag, Chad Wellmon, and especially Rita Felski. Outside the University of Virginia, David Bell, who seems always to put his finger on the critical questions, generously read and commented on the whole manuscript. So did two extraordinarily insightful readers for Harvard University Press: Lynn Hunt and Christopher Grasso. David Armitage could not have been more helpful at numerous junctures. And at Harvard University Press, it has been a great privilege to work with Joyce Seltzer. I am very lucky to have had her guidance, as well as that of Jeannette Estruth and the copyediting help of Julie Palmer-Hoffman and Edward Wade. Thank you to all.

Versions of Chapter 1 and the first half of Chapter 4 appeared previously as "Before Democracy: The Production and Uses of Common Sense," *Journal of Modern History* 80, no. 1 (March 2008) and "Tom Paine's Common Sense and Ours," *William and Mary Quarterly,* 3rd ser., 65, no. 4 (October 2008). Thank you to their respective editors and astute reviewers alike. I am also grateful to a good number of institutions and societies for allowing me the chance to discuss various parts of this project in public: the Remarque Institute at New York University, the History Department of the University of Delaware, the History Department of the University of Maryland, the Humanities Center at Stanford University, the History Department at UC Berkeley, the Fondazione Firpo in Turin, the City University of Hong Kong, San Diego State University, the Eighteenth-Century Workshop at Indiana University, the Seminar on Political and Moral Thought at Johns Hopkins University, the Society for French Historical Studies, the New York Intellectual and Cultural History Seminar, the British Society for Early American History and the Rothmere American Institute at Oxford University, and especially the Ecole des Hautes Etudes en Sciences Sociales, where I was lucky to benefit from the hospitality and wisdom of Roger Chartier and André Burgière, among others.

Like many authors, though, my greatest luck has been to have a supportive family. Otherwise it would have been impossible to get started, much less finish. Few mothers are—I suspect—as devoted readers of drafts (or as effective with a red pen) as mine. Few fathers can be counted on to read quite as carefully afterward. It is also hard to imagine more helpful and engaged in-laws when it comes to matters of universities and books, or sisters and a brother-in-law who know more about writing punchy, effective prose. I am equally fortunate to have an uncle who was willing to digest the entire manuscript at the very end of the process and then offer his wise counsel. Even my children weighed in with assistance (among other things). How else would I have discovered that Albert Einstein, as cited in a recent children's best seller, had something intriguing to say about common sense? Thank you to all: Lucy and Peter Rosenfeld, Mirella and Charles Affron, Marina Rosenfeld, Lucinda Rosenfeld, John Cassidy, Jerry Seigel, Si Affron, and Zoë Affron. And because there is no form of thanks that is remotely adequate when it comes to Matthew Affron, I dedicate this book to him.

Index

Aberdeen, common sense philosophy of, 60–63; Beattie and, 56–57, 74–78, 82–88; Shaftesbury and, 57–59; character and institutions of, 63–65; universities, 65, 70, 74; Philosophical Society of Aberdeen (Wise Club), 65–71; Reid and, 71–74; social and political attitudes in, 78–82, 88–89; Philadelphia connection to, 141–142, 293n14. *See also* Common Sense School

Abolition movement, 233–235

Absurdities: Common Sense School and, 57, 72; radical Enlightenment and, 96; skepticism and, 101; *galimatias* and, 102, 122, 210; religious beliefs and, 105, 125, 134; humor and, 114; Paine and, 144–145, 156; Pennsylvania Constitution and, 172, 175; counter-revolutionary publications and, 212–213; Dada and, 240–241, 242–244

"Abuse of words," 49–50, 123, 156, 212–213

Académie Française, 91, 97–98

Acts of the Apostles (journal), 200–202, 206, 211

Adams, John, 155, 160–161, 162, 164, 175

Adams, John Quincy, 218–219

Adams, Samuel, 137

Addison, Joseph, 14, 27–28, 31–33, 59

Aesthetic taste, 23, 33, 134, 221–225, 245–246

Age of Revolutions, 4, 260n7

Aitken, Robert, 141

Alarm, The (anonymous), 161, 162, 168

Almanac of Père Gérard, 191–192, 205

American Revolution: democracy and, 11; Reid and, 87; *Common Sense* (Paine) and, 136–158; Pennsylvania Constitution and, 158–180; European reaction to, 182–186; myth of common sense and, 219; women's rights and, 236; Arendt and, 248–249

American society: value of common sense and, 154; political discourse and, 178–179; social innovations and, 194–195; slavery and, 233–235; women's rights and, 236

Ames, Fischer, 218

Amsterdam, as intellectual center: *Portable Library of Good Sense* and, 90–91, 93–96; *bon sens* (good sense) and, 91–93; publishing industry and, 95, 116; Old Regime France and, 96–103; émigré literary scene and, 103–115; Rey and, 116–118; d'Holbach and, 118–128; Avignon as Jesuit counterpart to, 131

Anatomy, human, 19–21

Anglo-Saxon England, 165

Année littéraire (journal), 202, 204

Anti-Federalists, 178

Anti-Good-Sense (Richard), 132

Anti-intellectualism, 88, 173–174

Anti-Slavery Manual, The (Fee), 234–235

Appeal to Common Sense (Reybaz), 184

Appeal to Common Sense in Behalf of Religion, An (Oswald), 77

Aquinas, Thomas, 19, 251

Arendt, Hannah, 3, 16, 224, 248–254, 256

Aristotle, 18, 19, 113

Armhurst, Nicholas, 30

Arp, Hans, 240

Art, 225–226, 239–244, 267n51. *See also* Aesthetic taste

Association for the Preservation of Liberty and Property against Republicans and Levellers, 216

Atheism: *Portable Library of Good Sense* and, 95; skepticism and, 102; Rey and, 118; d'Holbach and, 119–120, 121, 128; language and, 126; Catholic refutations of, 130–135

Atlantic intellectual world, 10, 262n22

Authority: of common sense, 18, 61–62; Philosophical Society of Aberdeen (Wise Club) and, 81, 87–88; custom and, 97; "the people" and, 111

Authority, challenging: common sense and, 4–5, 13, 15; men of letters and, 11–12; Bangorian controversy and, 37; *Common Sense* (journal), 41, 42–43; *Portable Library of Good Sense* and, 95–96; custom and, 99–100; skepticism and, 102–103; Dutch Republic and, 104–105, 106–107; Lahontan and, 108–110; Gueudeville and, 110–111; DuLaurens and, 117–118; Catholic response to, 129–135; Dada and, 241–242

Authorship and anonymity: *of Portable Library of Good Sense,* 94–95; Baron d'Holbach and, 122; of French revolutionary writings, 191, 192

Avicenna, 19

Baader, Johannes, 242, 243

Bangorian controversy, 36–38

Barruel, Abbé, 131, 132–133, 204, 207, 209

Bayle, Pierre: Shaftesbury and, 58; religious beliefs and, 105; Gueudeville and, 110;

d'Argens and, 112, 113; Rush and, 150–151, 294n33; populism and, 220

Beattie, James: men of letters and, 11; *An Essay on the Nature and Immutability of Truth* (Beattie), 56–57; skepticism and, 60, 77, 78, 93; evidence and proof of common sense and, 73, 74–76; "the people" and, 80, 82; political discourse and, 82–87; contrast with radicals, 111; Paine and, 142, 144; Kant and, 222; slavery and, 234; truth and, 277–278n42; publications of, 280n79; finances of, 280n81, 280n84

Beck, Glenn, 255

Begriffsgeschichte (history of concepts), 8

Bergier, Abbé, 131, 134

Berkeley, George, 5, 21, 30, 73, 81

Bolingbroke, Lord, 41, 45

Bon sens (good sense): *Portable Library of Good Sense,* and 90–92; skepticism and, 102–103; d'Holbach and, 122–128; disputed meaning of, 129–135; Paine and, 151; French Revolution and, 188; Gadamer and, 247; Arendt and, 251–252

Boulanger, Nicolas-Antoine, 121

Bourdieu, Pierre, 14, 256–257

Brissot de Warville, Jacques Pierre, 179

Bryan, George, 170

Buée, Adrien-Quentin, 307n61; counter-revolutionary views and, 203–204, 214; dialogues and, 206, 208–211; dictionaries and, 212–213

Buée, Pierre-Louis, 203, 213, 214

Bull, Thomas, 156

Burke, Edmund, 213, 215, 217, 251, 273n115

Cabaret Voltaire, 241

Campbell, George, 71

Candide (Voltaire), 239, 240

Cannon, James, 160, 161, 164, 166–167, 175

"Castle of Skepticism, The" (Beattie), 83

Cato (William Smith), 157

Censorship: common sense and, 12–14, 20; self-censorship, 13–14, 198–199;

structural censorship, 33; Walpole and, 47; censorship of the market, 52; Dutch Republic and, 104; Roman Catholic Church and, 128–130; Pennsylvania Constitution and, 170; French Revolution and, 185, 198, 214–215; informal censorship, 198–199, 256

Champion, The (journal), 44

Charron, Pierre, 100–101, 105

Chaudon, Louis-Mayeul, 133–134

Chesterfield, Lord (Philip Stanhope), 40–41, 42–43

Cicero, 22, 59

Citizenship, 228, 229

City of Truth (Del Bene), 20

Civil Constitution of the Clergy (France), 195–197, 202–203, 204–205, 213, 310n92

Club Dada, 242–243

"Collective Dada Manifesto" (Huelsenbeck), 242

Collective wisdom: suffrage requirements and, 167; Pennsylvania Constitution and, 174; European political development and, 183; French Revolution and, 192–193; aesthetic taste and, 223–224

Collot d'Herbois, Jean-Marie, 191

Common law, 34, 42, 97–98

Common Sense: In Nine Conferences (Hanway), 146

Common Sense: Its Nature and Use (anonymous), 52–53

Common Sense about Women (Higginson), 236

"Common Sense" Applied to Woman Suffrage (Jacobi), 236

"Common Sense as a Cultural System" (Geertz), 2

Common sense: defined, 1, 4, 18, 22–23; Aristotle and, 18–19, 21; allegorized, 20; as foundation for a club, 27, 66–68, 198, 242–243; eighteenth-century London and, 36, 53, 264n13; as tribunal, 42, 43, 105, 270n77; Beattie and, 56–57, 74–75; Vico and, 59; Reid and, 72; French terms for, 91–93, 95–96, 282n5;

d'Holbach and, 122; Paine and, 138, 142; counter-revolutionary views and, 213–214, 216; Kant and German terms for, 221, 222–223, 312n2; Schiller and, 225–226, 314n11; nineteenth century and, 227–239; Dada and, 239–244; Arendt and, 251–252. See also *Sensus communis; Bon sens*

Common Sense (journal), 40–47, 47–54, 69, 271n94

Common Sense (Le Sens commun) (journal), 185

Common Sense (Paine): democracy and, 2–3; publication of, 136–139; Paine's understanding of "common sense" and, 139–152; political discourse and, 152–158; impact of, 179, 185; translations of, 301n111, 302–303n12

Common Sense School: *An Inquiry into the Human Mind* (Reid) and, 71–73; Philosophical Society of Aberdeen (Wise Club) and, 81–82, 87–88; Priestley and, 88–89; Kant and, 88, 222, 312n1; Paine and, 141–147, 149; slavery and, 234; Gadamer and, 247; Hume and, 276–277n29; Scottish Enlightenment and, 276n28; Garrison and, 316n33. See also Aberdeen, common sense philosophy of; Beattie; Reid

Condillac, Abbé de, 93, 123

Condorcet, Marquis de, 194

Consensus gentium (universal consent), 81, 97

Conservatism, 78, 82, 147, 181–182, 203–215

Constitutionalism, 5, 6, 7, 158–177, 183

Constitutional monarchists, 197–199

Consumerism, 244

Continental Congress, 140, 141, 160–161

Conventional wisdom: common sense and, 1–2, 23; *bon sens* (good sense) and, 91; Charron on, 100–101; value of common sense and, 154; political discourse and, 256–257. See also Custom

Cooper, Anthony Ashley. See Shaftesbury, Third Earl of

Corruption, eighteenth-century London and, 38, 39–40

Counter-Enlightenment, common sense and, 128–135, 199–200

Counter-revolutionary views: common sense and, 7, 181–182; rural women and, 196–197; constitutional monarchists and, 197–200; dissemination in France of, 200–215; dissemination in England of, 215–217; readership and, 307n59; Civil Constitution of the Clergy (France) and, 310n92

Country Opposition, 38–54, 55

Craftsman, The (journal), 39, 41

Crapart, Jean-Baptiste Nicolas, 204–205, 208–209, 214, 309n76

Critique of Judgment (Kant), 221–224, 253

Crooke, Helkiah, 19–20

Curious Dialogues between the Author and a Savage of Good Sense Who Has Traveled (Lahontan), 108–109, 110–111

Custom, 96, 97–99, 151, 176; Descartes on, 100; *Common Sense* (Paine) and, 147–149; slavery and, 233. *See also* Conventional wisdom

Dada, 239–244

"Dada Manifesto" (Tzara), 241

D'Aelders, Etta Palm, 189

Daily Gazetteer (journal), 51–52

D'Argens, Marquis, 11, 103, 104, 112–115, 122–123, 129, 130, 131

Da Vinci, Leonardo, 19

De Anima (Aristotle), 18, 19

Declaration of Independence, 137, 154, 234, 235

Declaration of the Rights of Woman (de Gouges), 190

Defense of the Resolutions and Address of the American Congress, A (anonymous), 146

Del Bene, Bartolommeo, 20, 83

Demagoguery, 51, 88–89, 155, 228–229, 298n72

Democracy, 2–3, 7, 61–62; political discourse and, 11, 89; populism and, 15, 232–233, 256–257; "the people" and, 55; Philosophical Society of Aberdeen (Wise Club) and, 86–87; d'Holbach and, 127; *Common Sense* (Paine) and, 139, 147, 152, 157–158; Pennsylvania Constitution and, 158, 176–177; European political development and, 182–183; Napoleon Bonaparte and, 220; suffrage requirements and, 228–229; Arendt and, 253–254. *See also* Popular sovereignty

Descartes, René, 21, 22, 91, 92, 100, 102, 247

D'Holbach, Baron, 93, 94, 95–96, 115, 118–128, 129, 130, 132, 201

Dialogues, literary form of, 107–111, 205–212, 216–217, 286n45

Dictionaries, 131–132, 212–213

Diderot, Denis, 92–93, 121

Discourse on Method (Descartes), 91, 100

Doxa (orthodoxy), 9, 97, 102, 106, 110, 129, 135, 257

DuLaurens, Henri-Joseph, 117–118, 130

Du Marsais, César Chesneau, 94

Dutch Republic, 103–104. *See also* Amsterdam, as intellectual center

Dutens, Louis, 130, 133

Egalitarianism: Common Sense School and, 79, 80, 88; Pennsylvania Constitution and, 163; U.S. political discourse and, 178–179

Elections, 170–172, 228–232

Elements of Moral Science (Beattie), 234

Elites and specialists: populism and, 6–7, 237; common sense and, 15, 62–63, 135; eighteenth-century London and, 30, 32–33, 51; Philosophical Society of Aberdeen (Wise Club) and, 78–79; philosophers and, 80–81; role in defining French language and customs, 98, 99–100; skepticism and, 101; Catholic association of *philosophes* with, 133; Paine and, 143, 145, 146, 256; suffrage requirements and, 166; Pennsylvania Constitution and, 173, 174,

175–176; French Revolution and, 186,
190, 192; counter-revolutionary
publications and, 206, 209; politicians
and, 231–232
Empiricism, 68, 71
Encyclopédie (Diderot and D'Alembert),
92, 120, 129
English Civil War, 25
Enthusiasm, 28
Episcopalianism, 28–29, 34, 64
Essay on Human Understanding
(Locke), 49
*Essay on the Nature and Immutability of
Truth, An* (Beattie), 56–57, 74, 82,
83–85
Essays on the Intellectual Powers of Men
(Reid), 80
*Ethnocracy, or Government Founded on
Morality* (d'Holbach), 126
Evidence and proof, nature of, 67, 72–73,
142, 143–145
Experts. *See* Elites and specialists

Factionalism, 25–28, 36. *See also* Opposi-
tion; Political parties
Faith, common sense and, 75, 124–125
Federalists, 217–218
Fee, John, 234–235
Fénelon, François de Salignac de La
Mothe, 114
Fielding, Henry, 17, 39–40, 44, 269n68
First principles: popular sovereignty in
America and, 169–170; French Revolu-
tion and, 193–194
Folk culture, 32, 33, 189–190, 207–208
Fontenelle, Bernard de, 92
Franklin, Benjamin, 151, 161, 179, 184, 185,
294n34
Frederick the Great, 115
Freedom of expression: common sense
and, 12–14; lapsing of the Licensing Act
(England) and, 25–27; eighteenth-
century Britain and, 47, 60–61;
Shaftesbury and, 58; eighteenth-
century Dutch Republic and, 60–61;
Philadelphia and, 139; Pennsylvania

Constitution and, 171–172; French
Revolution and, 185; counter-
revolutionary views and, 198–199; Kant
and, 224; Arendt and, 252; Beattie and,
278n57
Freedom of the press, 47, 170, 200, 212
Free Thinker, The (journal), 33
French émigrés, Dutch Republic and, 104,
106–107, 117
French Good Sense (de Gouges), 190
French Revolution, 11; Beattie and Reid
and, 86; opposition to, 181–182, 195–215;
American democracy and, 184–185;
rhetoric of, 184–195; English reaction
to, 215–217; American reaction to,
217–220; Kant and, 224; Arendt and,
248, 249
*Friend of the King, of the French, of Order
and especially of the Truth* (journal),
204

Gadamer, Hans Georg, 245–248, 251–252
Gall, Franz Josef, 21
Garrison, William Lloyd, 235, 316n33
Gauchet, Gabriel, 131
Gay, John, 39
Gazette de Paris (journal), 206
Geertz, Clifford, 2, 260n4
Gender roles, populism and, 209–211. *See
also* Women
Geneva, political culture of, 183–184
Genlis, Madame de, 131
Gentleman's Magazine (journal), 48
*Genuine Principles of the Ancient Saxons,
The* (anonymous), 165
Gerard, Alexander, 71, 73
Germany, 238–239, 241–243, 245, 247
Girardin, Emile de, 232
God, existence of, 99, 114, 132, 171, 172
Good Sense (d'Holbach), 93, 96, 126,
129–130
Good Sense of the People, The (Forteau),
231
Good Sense of the Village, The (anony-
mous), 208
Gouges, Olympe de, 11, 190, 304n30

Government, forms of: common sense and, 2–3, 5–6; eighteenth-century London and, 24, 46–47; d'Holbach and, 119; *Common Sense* (Paine) and, 139, 152, 157–158; Benjamin Rush and, 150; Pennsylvania Constitution and, 158–177; Arendt and, 249, 250–251
Gramsci, Antonio, 189–190
Gregory, John, 76–77
Gueudeville, Nicolas, 110–111

Hanway, Jonas, 146
Harris, Mike, 255
Hausmann, Raoul, 242, 243
Helvétius, Claude Adrien, 39, 125–126, 129
Helviens, The (Barruel), 132–133
Hennings, Emmy, 240
Hervey, Lord, 49–50
Higginson, Thomas Wentworth, 236
Historical epistemology, 9, 261n17
Hoadly, Benjamin, 36–38
Hobbes, Thomas, 28, 121
Horace, 22–23
Huckabee, Mike, 255
Huelsenbeck, Richard, 240, 242
Huguenots, 104–106
Human Condition, The (Arendt), 250–251
Hume, David, 63; Philosophical Society of Aberdeen (Wise Club) and, 68; Reid and, 70, 71; evidence and proof of common sense and, 73; Beattie and, 76, 83, 85, 86; Gadamer and, 247; Common Sense School and, 276–277n29
Humor: satire, 43–44, 199–200, 211–212, 241–242, 299n90; skepticism and, 102, 103; common sense and, 114–115, 287n62; *Acts of the Apostles* (journal) and, 201–202
Hutcheson, Francis, 59, 70, 74, 247

Ideas, social history of, 8
Incredulity Combated by Simple Good Sense (Stanislas Leszczynski), 130
Independence, of American colonies, 145–146, 148, 154, 157–158, 159
Individualism, 5–6, 37, 82, 133, 223

Inglis, Charles, 156, 157
Inquiry into the Human Mind, An (Reid), 71–73, 77
Inverted inegalitarianism, concept of, 186

Jackson, Andrew, 218–219
Jacobi, Mary Putnam, 236
Janco, Marcel, 240
Jefferson, Thomas, 154, 218, 311–312n106, 315n27
Johnson, Samuel, 32, 146

Kames, Lord, 59, 70
Kant, Immanuel, 4, 221–224; Common Sense School and, 88–89, 312n1; Gadamer and, 245–246; Arendt and, 248, 252, 253, 256; common sense and, 312n2
Knowledge, social history of, 8

Lahontan, Baron de, 107–110, 122
La Mothe le Vayer, François de, 101–102, 103, 105, 113
Language: politics of, in eighteenth-century London, 49–50; Philosophical Society of Aberdeen (Wise Club) and, 67; custom and, 97–98; d'Holbach and, 122–123; religious terminology and, 124–125; atheism and, 126; Catholic refutations of atheism and impiety and, 131–132; Paine and, 142–143, 145, 150, 156; anti-intellectualism and, 187–188; French Revolution and, 188–190, 195; dialogues and, 205; counter-revolutionary publications and, 208; Dada and, 240–241
La Rochefoucault, François de, 99
Latin America, 179
Latitudinarian Anglicans, 28–29, 34, 64
Lau, Théodore Louis, 94
Laurens, André du, 19
Law, William, 37
Laws and legal systems: common law and, 34, 42, 97–98; French civil law, 97–98;

French Revolution and, 192–193; counter-revolutionary views and, 213, 214

Le Pen, Jean-Marie, 255

Letter on Enthusiasm (Shaftesbury), 44

Letters from a Persian in England to His Friend at Ispahan (Lyttelton), 41

Letter to the Author of Common-Sense (Hervey), 49–50

Liberator, The (newspaper), 235

Life and Adventures of Common Sense, The (anonymous), 35

Life of the Mind, The (Arendt), 251, 253

Loci communes (commonly held beliefs), 23, 38

Locke, John, 21, 22, 49, 68, 123

London: political discourse and, 24–30; periodical press and, 30–35; Bangorian controversy and, 36–38; Country Opposition and, 38–54, 55; Beattie and, 84; Reeves and, 216

London Magazine (journal), 48

Loyalty oaths. *See* Oaths of allegiance

Lyttelton, George, 40–42

Majority rule. *See* popular sovereignty

Materialism, philosophy of, 118–128, 129–135

Matlack, Timothy, 160, 161, 164

Mehring, Walter, 243

Memorial of Common-Sense (anonymous), 156

Men of letters, 10–12; and the eighteenth-century Republic of Letters, 57, 59–60, 85–86, 120–121; as revolutionary spokesmen, 183–193. See also *Philosophes*

Mère Duchesne (character), 208–211, 309n76, 309n82

Mère Gérard (character), 211

Mère Saumon (character), 211

Michelet, Jules, 109

Militias, 160, 164

Moderates, counter-revolutionary views and, 197–199

Modesty, and common sense, 85–86

Montagu, Lady Mary Wortley, 50–51, 52

Montagu, Mrs. Elizabeth, 84–85, 217

Montenoy, Palissot de, 291n114

Montesquieu, Baron, 41, 91, 113, 251

Morality: *Common Sense* (journal), 41; eighteenth-century Aberdeen and, 59–60, 67–68; skepticism and, 76–77; science and, 77–78; slavery and, 234–235; Gadamer and, 247

Moral sense theory, 59, 70, 273–274n5, 316n33

More, Hannah, 11, 216–217

Motives for Conversion (Gueudeville), 110

Naigeon, Jacques-André, 120, 121

Napoleon Bonaparte, 220

Nationalism, 237–239

National traits: England and, 33–34, 35; United States and, 154; populism and, 238; Germany and, 239, 317n42

Native Americans, 107, 108–109

Natural light *(lumière naturelle)*, 105, 113, 122, 132

Natural Politics (d'Holbach), 126

Newcomb, Thomas, 51

New Science (Vico), 58–59

Newton, Sir Isaac, 65, 67, 71, 104, 203

Noble savage, concept of, 107, 108–109, 165, 186

Nonnotte, Abbé, 131–132, 133

Nonsense. *See* Absurdities

Nonsense of Common Sense, The (journal), 48, 50

Notes on the State of Virginia (Jefferson), 233

Oaths of allegiance, 171–172, 195–197

Oetinger, Friedrich Christoph, 247

Of Man (Helvétius), 125–126, 129

Of the Mind (Helvétius), 129

Of Wisdom (Charron), 100–101

Ogilvie, William, 87

Only Good Sense, The (anonymous), 206

On Revolution (Arendt), 249

On the Aesthetic Education of Man in a Series of Letters (Schiller), 225–226

On the Origins of Totalitarianism
    (Arendt), 249–250
Opposition: to radical use of *bon sens*
    (good sense), 129–135; to *Common Sense*
    (Paine), 138, 155–158; Pennsylvania
    Constitution and, 172–177; French
    Revolution and, 193. *See also* Counter-
    revolutionary views; Country Opposi-
    tion; Factionalism; Political parties
*Opuscule or Small Skeptical Treatise on the
    Common Expression "To not have any
    Common Sense"* (La Mothe le Vayer),
    101–102
Oswald, James, 77, 278n55
"Others" or outsiders: popular sovereignty
    and, 168; Pennsylvania Constitution
    and, 171–172; counter-revolutionary
    publications and, 209; populism and,
    237, 238; Dada and, 241
Overton, Richard, 46

Paine, Thomas: democracy and, 2–3;
    Atlantic intellectual milieu and, 10, 11;
    publication of *Common Sense* and,
    136–139; attacks on, 155–158; Pennsylva-
    nia Constitution and, 158, 160, 163, 166,
    172; Benjamin Rush and, 174; transatlan-
    tic influence of, 179–180; French
    Revolution and, 184, 185; English
    reaction to, 215; women's rights and,
    236; right-wing politics and, 255, 256;
    education of, 292n9; suffrage require-
    ments and, 298n68. See also *Common
    Sense* (Paine); *Rights of Man* (Paine)
Palin, Sarah, 238, 255
Paradox, 9, 102, 110, 284n33
Paris: Enlightenment and, 115, 120–121;
    pre-revolutionary, 182, 184–193; French
    Revolution and, 193–215; counter-
    revolutionary views and, 197–215
Pasquin (Fielding), 17, 39–40, 47, 125,
    269n68
Passions of the Soul (Descartes), 21
Patriotic Woman or Solid Good Sense, The
    (anonymous), 189
Paulian, Aimé-Henri, 132

Peale, Charles Willson, 142, 160
Peltier, Jean-Gabriel, 201
Penn, John, 137
Pennington, J. W. C., 234
Pennsylvania Constitution (1776): forms of
    government and, 158–177; political
    discourse and, 177–180; revolutionary
    politics and, 179–180; influence in
    France, 185, 201; satire and, 299n90
"People, the": political participation and, 3;
    shared ideas and, 4; populism and, 6–7,
    261n13; men of letters and, 11, 12;
    Spectator newspaper and, 31–32; *Common
    Sense* (journal) and, 46; democracy and,
    55; authority and, 61–63, 111; Beattie and,
    74, 75; elites and specialists in relation to,
    79, 80–81; political appeals to, 82;
    Common Sense School and, 88; *bon sens*
    (good sense) and, 93, 97, 119, 135; Bayle
    and, 105; noble savages and, 107; writers
    as identifying with, 110; *Philosophy of
    Good Sense* (d'Argens) and, 113; govern-
    ment and, 127; Paine and, 138–139,
    145–146; American independence and,
    154; *Common Sense* (Paine) and, 157;
    Pennsylvania Constitution and, 161;
    suffrage requirements and, 167–168;
    political power and, 182–183; French
    Revolution and, 186–193; authenticity of,
    191, 192; political judgment of, 194, 217,
    227–228, 230, 249; Père Gérard (charac-
    ter), 195, 205, 211; counter-revolutionary
    publications and, 206–207, 207–212; Père
    Duchesne (character), 208, 211; Napoleon
    Bonaparte and, 220; self-evidence and,
    300n96. *See also* Popular sovereignty;
    Representative government
Periodical press: London and, 30–34;
    Common Sense (journal), 40–47; Whig
    Party and, 47–54; Scotland and,
    69–70; Catholic refutations of atheism
    and impiety and, 131; Paine and, 136;
    Rush and, 175; Geneva and, 183–184;
    counter-revolutionary Paris and, 198,
    200–215, 307n59
Philadelphia: compared with Aberdeen,
    63–64; intellectual environment of,

139–140, 151–152; political radicalism and, 158–159; pre-revolutionary Europe and, 184; populism and, 215

Phillips, Edward, 264n13

Philosophes: Old Regime France and, 96–103; émigré literary scene and, 103–115; Rey and, 116–118; d'Holbach and, 118–128; anti-*philosophes* and, 128–135; Federalist attitudes toward, 217–218. *See also* Men of letters

Philosophical Commentary on These Words of Jesus Christ (Bayle), 105

Philosophical history, 16, 263n28

Philosophical societies, 65–66

Philosophical Society of Aberdeen (Wise Club), 65–71; publications and, 71–78; political conflict and, 78–89; democracy and, 86–87; "the people" and, 135; Philadelphia intellectual environment and, 141

Philosophy: common sense and, 5, 291n114; eighteenth-century London and, 30, 33; eighteenth-century Aberdeen and, 59–60; Common Sense School and, 71–73, 81–83, 88; elites and specialists and, 80–81; Catholic refutations of atheism and impiety and, 129–135; *Critique of Judgment* (Kant), 221–224. *See also* Berkeley; d'Argens; Descartes; Hume; Locke; Reid; Scholastic philosophy

Philosophy of Good Sense (d'Argens), 112–115, 122, 129, 131

Pietism, 247

Plays and theater, 39–40, 44, 47, 70

Politeness, 26

Political cartoons and prints, 44, 215

Political judgment: in English Opposition thought, 46; Whig understanding of suffrage and, 163–164, 166–167; Pennsylvania Constitution and, 173–174, 175–176; French Revolution and, 194; "the people" and, 207–212, 227–228, 230, 249; Arendt and, 253

Political parties, 27, 38–54, 249. *See also* Factionalism; Opposition

Politicians, 6, 231–232, 242–243

Poor Richard's Almanac (Franklin), 151, 185, 192, 294n34

Pope, Alexander, 40, 59

Popular sovereignty: common sense and, 4, 5–6, 7; "the people" and, 55, 164; Reid and, 81; Pennsylvania Constitution and, 162–167, 169–170; Anti-Federalists and, 178; Napoleon Bonaparte and, 220; electoral politics and, 229–230. *See also* Democracy

Populism: common sense and, 6–7, 9, 62; *Common Sense* (journal) and, 46; "protesting" populism, 46, 271n91; Beattie and, 82, 84, 85; political discourse and, 89, 314n12; *bon sens* (good sense) and, 96, 135; French émigré writers and, 111; *Common Sense* (Paine) and, 152; Philadelphia and, 159–160; Pennsylvania Constitution and, 167–168; popular sovereignty and, 169–170; French Revolution and, 192, 193; counter-revolutionary views and, 203–215; as reaction to French Revolution, 218–220; nineteenth century and, 227–230; women's rights and, 236; nationalism and, 237–239; in post–World War II era, 244; Arendt and, 253–254, 319n82; right-wing politics and, 254–256; "the people" and, 261n13; demagoguery and, 298n72

Populist Party, 237

Portable Library of Good Sense, 90–91, 92, 93–95, 96, 116, 124

Portable Philosophical Dictionary (Voltaire), 90, 125, 129

Portable Theology or Abridged Dictionary of the Christian Religion (d'Holbach), 124–125, 130

Post–World War II era, 244–257

Presbyterianism, 64, 71, 160

Preservative against the Principles and Practices of the Nonjurors Both in Church and State, A (Hoadly), 37

Priestley, Joseph, 86, 88–89

Prolegomena to Any Future Metaphysics (Kant), 222

Proof. *See* evidence and proof, nature of
Protestantism, 11, 24, 28–29, 36–38, 54, 62, 65, 160, 184
Proverbs, 98–99, 283–284n13, 284n25
Public opinion: 11; *Common Sense* (journal) and, 52; *Good Sense* (d'Holbach) and, 128–129; *Common Sense* (Paine) and, 137, 153–154; Paine and, 138–139; French Revolution and, 186
Publishing industry: London and, 30–34; Common Sense School and, 70, 84; Amsterdam and, 95, 103–104; Philadelphia and, 114, 293n14; Rey and, 116–118; d'Holbach and clandestinity, 121–128; Crapart and, 204–205, 214. *See also* Periodical press
Pyle, Thomas, 37

Quakers, 151–152, 159, 172, 184
Quintillian, 23

Racism, 209, 233–234, 315n27
Radicalism: publishing and, 116–118, 121–128; *Common Sense* (Paine) and, 147–152; common sense and, 150–151; Philadelphia and, 158–159; Pennsylvania Constitution and, 160–177; Dada and, 239–244. *See also* Revolutionary politics
Ramsay, David, 153–154
Randolph, Edmund, 153
Rawls, John, 3, 260n5
Readers: *Spectator* and, 31–33; French émigré writers and, 111; d'Holbach and, 118–119, 128; Catholic refutations of atheism and impiety and, 131; *Common Sense* (Paine) and, 137; counter-revolutionary views and, 202, 204–205, 307n59
Reagan, Ronald, 255–256, 319n84
Reason: democracy and, 5; Beattie and, 74; *bon sens* (good sense) and, 92; Descartes on, 100; Bayle and, 105; language and, 125, 126; French Revolution and, 194; Arendt and, 252
Reasonableness, 29–30, 265n33

Red Flag of Mother Duchesne (Buée), 210–211
Reeves, John, 216, 217
Reid, Thomas: authority of common sense and, 61; Philosophical Society of Aberdeen (Wise Club) and, 70; *An Inquiry into the Human Mind*, 71–73; professional career of, 73–74; skepticism and, 77, 93; "the people" and, 79–80; Beattie and, 83; democracy and, 86–87; political discourse and, 89; Paine and, 145; Wilson and, 177; Gadamer and, 247
Religious beliefs: common sense and, 11; factionalism and, 28–29; Protestantism and, 28–29, 36–38, 62; Aberdeen and, 65; Beattie and, 77; custom and, 99; Dutch Republic and, 103–104, 104–105, 106–107; Lahontan and, 108, 109–110; Gueudeville and, 110–111; d'Holbach and, 119–120, 122–128; Pennsylvania Constitution and, 171, 172. *See also* Protestantism; Roman Catholic Church
Religious toleration, 25–26, 60–61, 64, 103–104, 158–159
Remonstrance of Many Citizens, A (Overton), 46
Representative government, 32, 46–47, 160–177, 244
Resolutions of Common Sense About Common Rights (Bull), 156
Revolutionary politics: common sense and, 127–128; *Common Sense* (Paine) and, 149–150; Pennsylvania Constitution and, 179–180; pre-revolutionary Europe and, 182–193; French Revolution and, 193–215; English reaction to, 215–217; American reaction to, 217–220; Revolutions of 1848, 230–233; Arendt and, 248–249
Revolution of 1688 (England), 24, 25, 34, 35
Revolutions of 1848, 230–233, 301n111
Rey, Marc-Michel, 95, 116–118, 121, 283n17
Reybaz, Etienne-Salomon, 184
Reynolds, Sir Joshua, 85

Richelet, Pierre, 91, 114

Right reason *(droit raison)*, 105

Rights of Man, Part II (Paine), 215, 218, 311–312n106

Right-wing politics, contemporary, 254–256

Rittenhouse, David, 160, 161, 164

Rivarol, Antoine, 201

Robespierre, Maximilien, 193–194

Roman Catholic Church: English opposition to, 28; Lahontan and, 108, 109–110; Gueudeville and, 110; censorship and, 128–130; refutations of atheism and impiety and, 130–135; French Revolution and, 185, 195–197; counter-revolutionary views and, 200

Rousseau, Jean-Jacques, 92, 93, 118, 120, 127, 184

Royalists, 200–215. *See also* Counter-revolutionary views

Ruralism: Country Party (England) and, 44; French Revolution and, 195–197; counter-revolutionary views and, 197, 200, 202, 203, 207–212; Populist Party (U.S.) and, 237

Rush, Benjamin, 138, 141–142, 150–151, 160, 174–176

Rymer, Thomas, 267n51

Satire: *Common Sense* (journal), 43–44; counter-revolutionary views and, 199–200, 211–212; *Acts of the Apostles* (journal) and, 201–202; Dada and, 241–242; Pennsylvania Constitution and, 299n90. *See also* Humor

Schiller, Friedrich, 225–226, 243

Scholastic philosophy, as opposed to common sense: 19, 30, 67, 92, 113, 122

Science, 9, 19–21, 65, 77–78, 246

Scottish Enlightenment, 63, 275n14, 281n90. *See also* Aberdeen, common sense philosophy of; Common Sense School

Self-censorship, 13–14, 198–199

Self-evidence: as basis for law, 35; Reid and, 72; Beattie and, 75; popular

sovereignty and, 139, 169; Paine and, 143, 145, 149–150; Declaration of Independence and, 154; French Revolution and, 187–188; counter-revolutionary views and, 214; suffrage requirements and, 230; slavery and, 234; "the people" and, 300n96

Self-rule. *See* Popular sovereignty

Sensus Communis: An Essay on the Freedom of Wit and Humour (Shaftesbury), 23, 44, 59, 104

Sensus communis (communal sense): defined, 19–20; Descartes and, 21; Roman notion of, 22–23; Shaftesbury and, 23, 27, 44, 57, 61, 66, 104; Vico and, 58–59, 298; Kant and, 221, 222–223, 223–224, 227; Schiller and, 225; Dada and, 239–240; Gadamer and, 245, 246, 247; Arendt and, 248, 252

Sensus Communis: An Essay on the Freedom of Wit and Humour (Shaftesbury), 23, 44, 59, 104

Serner, Walter, 241–242

Shadwell, Thomas, 34–35

Shaftesbury, Third Earl of: *sensus communis* (communal sense) and, 23, 27, 61, 66, 104; toleration and, 26; religious sectarianism and, 28; literary style of, 31; elites and, 32, 62; satire and, 44–45; travels of, 57–59; moral philosophy and, 62; Reid and, 70, 71; Beattie and, 76; translation of work of, 104; Kant and, 222–223; Gadamer and, 246, 247

Sieyès, Abbé, 194

Skene, David, 68, 79, 81

Skepticism: common sense opposed to, 28; Aberdeen and the reaction against, 59–60, 67, 68, 71–7276–77, 83; as a seventeenth-century French intellectual trend, 101–103; *Philosophy of Good Sense* (d'Argens) and, 114; d'Holbach and, 126; Roman Catholic Church and the reaction against, 129–135

Slaves and slavery, 87, 140, 172, 233–235

Smith, Adam, 74

Smith, Thomas, 173

Smith, William (Cato), 157

Social classes: men of letters and, 10–11, 11–12; London and, 50–51, 54; Philosophical Society of Aberdeen (Wise Club) and, 79, 87; Paine and, 145; American colonies and, 146; Philadelphia and, 159; Pennsylvania Constitution and, 163, 173–174, 175–176; suffrage requirements and, 163–164, 297n63; French Revolution and, 187; Revolutions of 1848 and, 230–231; populism and, 237; *Common Sense* (journal) and, 271n94; Scottish Enlightenment and, 275n14

Social cohesion: as a function of common sense, 6, 14; London and, 26–27, 27–28, 54; Vico and, 59; skepticism as threat to, 60–61, 76–78; individualism as threat to, 82; Common Sense School and, 88; custom and, 99; *Common Sense* (Paine) and, 147; Dada and, 240, 241; Gadamer and, 246; totalitarianism and, 249–250; Arendt and, 250–251, 252

Social hierarchies: custom and, 97; d'Holbach and, 118–119; French Revolution and, 195; counterrevolutionary views and, 206–207, 209, 214

Socialism and Common Sense (Bonjean), 231

Socialism in Confrontation with Popular Good Sense (Baudon), 231

Social System, The (d'Holbach), 126

Solid Good Sense Addressed to the National Assembly (anonymous), 187

Sorel, Charles, 101

Spain, British war with, 52–53, 273n115

Specialists. *See* Elites and specialists

Spectator, The (journal), 31–33, 66, 69

Spinozism, 28, 104, 115–116, 220

Stanhope, Philip. *See* Chesterfield, Lord (Philip Stanhope)

Stanislas Leszczynski (Stanislas I), 130

Steele, Richard, 14, 31–33, 59

Stewart, Dugald, 76

Stillingfleet, Edward, 28, 29

Stoic philosophy, 22–23, 59

Suffrage requirements: "the people" and, 12; Pennsylvania Constitution and,

162–163, 164–165, 166–167, 171–172; social classes and, 163–164, 297n63; women and, 190, 236; nineteenth century and, 228–229; Revolutions of 1848 and, 230–231; Paine and, 298n68

Superstitions and prejudices: eighteenth-century London and, 30, 32; Beattie on, 75; Descartes on, 100; radical Enlightenment and, 123–124; Paine and, 148–149, 151; French Revolution and, 188, 191, 194; Gadamer and, 247

The System of Nature (d'Holbach), 118, 128, 129

Tea Party movement, 255

Test Act of 1777 (Philadelphia), 171

Theatrical Licensing Act of 1737 (England), 47

Theology. *See* religious beliefs

Thiry, Paul Henri. *See* d'Holbach, Baron

"Thoughts on Common Sense" (Rush), 142, 150

Thoughts on English Government (Reeves), 217

Tillotson, John, 28, 29

Tocqueville, Alexis de, 220, 228–229

Toland, John, 121

Totalitarianism, 248, 249–250

Town governments (American), 249, 250–251

Tractatus-Theologico-Politicus (Spinoza), 116

"Treaty of the Three Imposters, The," 115–116

True Interest of America Impartially Stated, The (Inglis), 156

True Merits of a Late Treatise, The (anonymous), 138

Truth, as a function of common sense: satire and, 44–45; Whig Party and, 48–49; Reid and, 72; Descartes and, 100; skepticism and, 102; intersubjectivity and, 114–115; language and, 123; simplicity and, 143; French revolutionary rhetoric and, 186; Kant and, 224; Beattie and, 277–278n42

Truth and Method (Gadamer), 245–248
Turnbull, George, 59, 65, 70
Tzara, Tristan, 240, 241–242, 257

"Understanding and Politics" (Arendt),
249–250, 251
Universal Morality (d'Holbach), 126
U.S. Constitution (1787), 177, 178

Valéry, Paul, 251–252
Valletta, Giuseppe, 58
Vaugelas, Claude Favre de, 97, 98
Vico, Giambattista, 58–59, 97, 238, 246
Village Newssheet, The (journal),
191–192
Village Politics (More), 216–217
Vision and optics, 187, 218
"Vision of the Golden Rump" *(Common Sense)*, 43, 44
Voltaire, 125, 126, 239; Beattie and, 85;
Portable Library of Good Sense and, 94;
Philosophy of Good Sense (d'Argens) and,
113; publishing industry and, 116, 118;
d'Holbach and, 120, 128; attacks on,
129; literary style of, 131, 201, 212;
Dada and, 240
Voting rights. *See* Suffrage requirements

Walpole, Sir Robert, 38, 43–44, 47, 48, 49, 52
Washington, George, 153
Whichcote, Benjamin, 28
Whigs (American), 162, 163–164, 166, 174
Whigs (English), 26, 30–31, 34–35, 47–54
Whit of Good Sense, A (Braccini), 232
Willis, Thomas, 19
Wilson, James, 176–177
Wise Club. *See* Philosophical Society of
Aberdeen (Wise Club)
Witherspoon, John, 141
Women: common sense and, 11; *Spectator*
newspaper and, 31, 32; risks of
publishing of, 49; *bon sens* (good sense)
and, 92; *Philosophy of Good Sense*
(d'Argens) and, 113; exclusion from
suffrage in Pennsylvania Constitution,
172; French Revolution and, 188–190,
196–197; counter-revolutionary
publications and, 197, 208–212, 216–217;
suffrage rights and, 229, 236; eighteenth-
century London and, 267n52; *Common
Sense* (journal) and, 271n94; Scottish
Enlightenment and, 281n90; Mère
Duchesne (character) and, 309n82
World War I, 238–239

Young, Thomas, 160